The Other Tongue

Published in conjunction with the

OFFICE OF INTERNATIONAL
PROGRAMS AND STUDIES

THE OTHER TONGUE

English across Cultures

Edited by
BRAJ B. KACHRU

UNIVERSITY OF ILLINOIS PRESS

Urbana   Chicago   London

Publication of this work has been made possible
in part by a grant from the Andrew W. Mellon Foundation.

Library of Congress Cataloging in Publication Data

Main entry under title:

The Other tongue.

    Bibliography: p.
    Includes index.
    1. English language—Study and teaching —
Foreign students—Addresses, essays, lectures.
2. English language—Variation—Addresses, essays,
lectures. 3. Biculturalism—Addresses, essays,
lectures.   I. Kachru, Braj B.
PE1128.A2086   428.2′4′07   81-14798
ISBN 0-252-00896-0   AACR2

Contents

Foreword

The papers collected in this volume are important for the world of language scholarship — and the "real world" that lies outside it — in at least three ways. They deal with one of the most significant linguistic phenomena of our time, the incredible spread of English as a global language. They deal directly with one of the most debated current foci of linguistic research, the nature and extent of variation in natural languages. And they deal with an important topic long neglected by linguists, the structure and use of non-native varieties. Let me say a few words about each of these, in reverse order.

Non-Native Varieties of Language

Linguists, perhaps especially American linguists, have long given a special place to the "native speaker" as the only truly valid and reliable source of language data, whether those data are the elicited texts of the descriptivist or the intuitions the theorist works with. Yet much of the world's verbal communication takes place by means of languages which are not the users' "mother tongue," but their second, third, or nth language, acquired one way or another and used when appropriate. Some languages, for example, spread widely as lingua francas between speakers of different languages or serve as languages of special functions in communities of non-native speakers; this kind of language use merits the attention of linguists as much as do the more traditional objects of their research. In fact, the whole mystique of native speaker and mother tongue should probably be quietly dropped from the linguists' set of professional myths about language.

First, it is often hard to draw the boundary. Of what linguistic significance is X's native-speaking competence in language A if he has not used it since childhood and is much more at home in his later-acquired language B? Why is there something special about Y's knowledge of the local language if her parents have chosen to speak with her largely in another language so she can "get ahead"? Or what of child bilingualism, or a talented writer's use of his national language instead of his mother tongue?

Second, universal explanatory principles or a general theory of language should account for all linguistic behavior. Variation in structure as between L_1 and L_2 seems just as interesting a subject as dialect or register variation in a completely monolingual community. The phenomena of language acquisition, language convergence over time, and language shift are at the very heart of linguistics, offering valuable evidence on the learnability of natural languages by humans and the nature of linguistic change.

In describing a particular language or language variety, it it necessary to identify its users and to locate its place in the verbal repertoires of the speech communities in which it is used. Without this identification many aspects of the grammar will be mysterious, and those mysteries may range from details of phonology to features of discourse. Most of the papers in this volume make serious efforts at the necessary identifications. They are highly suggestive of possible directions for more sophisticated and linguistically significant social and individual identifications of repertoire and use.

Linguistic Variation

Recognizing that linguistics has made its greatest advances, both in theory and in the practice of writing grammars, when it takes cases of relatively homogeneous or normalized or idealized languages as its objects of description, modern linguists are increasingly tackling heterogeneous bodies of data and the variation in language structure and use which is one of the prime characteristics of human language. They are doing so in part because of inadequacies in existing theories and grammars, but probably more so because of fascination with the phenomena, the linguistically significant generalizations they find, and the new understandings they may reach of the processes of dialect differentiation and language change and the more general social and cognitive aspects of human behavior.

Variation-oriented research in linguistics, however, has been limited to a very few types. Social dialect variation, creole continua, and bilingual code-switching account for the bulk of the current research. The two kinds of variation most prominent in the worldwide development of giant speech "communities" are hardly touched. I refer, in the first place, to the standardization process by which divergent regional dialects are gradually overwhelmed by supra-dialectal norms, and the resulting standards develop regionally colored variation re-

lated in complex ways to the earlier dialect variation. In the second
place, I refer to the spread of languages as lingua francas, or as added
components within existing repertoires, or as complete replacements
for other languages; in all these cases the spreading language shows
variation related in complex ways to the earlier language competences
of the new users.

It is one of the outstanding merits of this book that these two
phenomena are acknowledged and that these kinds of variation are
described and discussed. At this stage of research, the papers cannot
go very far toward constructing theories or models of variation, but
they certainly suggest possible lines of theory development. A sociolinguistic theory accounting for the phenomena of standardization
and language spread would make a tremendous contribution toward
human self-understanding and thoughts about possible futures for
the inhabitants of the planet.

Spread of English

The spread of one language in relation to others is a phenomenon which presumably goes as far back in human history as the existence of a multiplicity of languages. Certainly it is documented as
far back as written records go; e.g., in the second millennium B.C.,
Akkadian replaced Sumerian but the speech community retained the
latter in certain learned uses. Also, it is a familiar phenomenon for
one language to serve as a lingua franca or language of special functions (religious, commercial) over a large area of many languages:
Sanskrit, Greek, Latin, Arabic, and French are examples at various
periods and in different parts of the world. But there has never before been a single language which spread for such purposes over *most*
of the world, as English has done in this century. The importance of
this fact is often overlooked in discussions of the characteristic features of this age. The spread of English is as significant in its way as
is the modern use of computers. When the amount of information
needing to be processed came to exceed human capabilities, the computer appeared on the scene, transforming the processes of planning
and calculation. When the need for global communication came to
exceed the limits set by language barriers, the spread of English accelerated, transforming existing patterns of international communication.

We cannot know what the future will bring. At some point the
spread of English may be halted, and some other language may spread
to take its place. Or newly emerging patterns of communication may

eliminate the need for such a single global language. But for the present the spread of English continues, with no sign of diminishing (although its use may contract in certain areas), and two trends are gaining strength. English is less and less regarded as a European language, and its development is less and less determined by the usage of its native speakers.

For some time after its transplantation by settlement and colonial administration, English was still centered on England. However, by the end of the nineteenth century North American English assumed an importance challenging the dominance of the original center. In the second half of the twentieth century England is only one of many centers of innovation and norm creation, and some authors are claiming English as an African language and as an Asian language. The predominant view, that English is a European language, is steadily being eroded and seems likely to disappear.

In some sense, the native speakers of a language may be said to "own" it or to "control" it; i.e., to determine its future structure and use by their own usage and their beliefs about the language. There are, however, cases where the control of the future passes to non-native speakers. This has most often been discussed in terms of a standard variety that is based on one region or sector of the population and then begins to take on a life of its own, diverging from its source dialect. The same phenomenon can happen with the language as a whole. In Eastern Africa there are native speakers of Swahili, descendants of native speakers of Swahili, who resent the standard variety taught in schools that is increasingly spoken by others as a second language and by new native speakers not descended from the original native-speaking community. The linguistic influence mostly works from school standard onto other varieties, though, and some of the traditional native speakers find themselves adopting features of pronunciation, verb morphology, and syntax from the standard. The "control" of the language has passed to other people. This process is just beginning in English. Because there is no single non-native standard, the outcome will be different from the Swahili example, but the passing of control is increasingly evident.

English is widely used on the European continent as an international language. Frequently conferences are conducted in English (and their proceedings published in English) when only a few of the participants are native speakers. At such conferences the English spoken often shows features at variance with the English of England but shared by the other speakers. Continental meanings of *eventual* and *actual,* continental uses of tenses, calques on French formulas of conference procedure, various details of pronunciation, and dozens of other features mark the English as an emerging continental norm. Native speakers of English attending the conference may find themselves using some of these features as the verbal interaction takes place. It is this adaptation which I cite as an example of the trend.

For now, this trend is very limited. Native speakers in many situations around the world may have confidence that they "know" the language better than others, but the differences among native speakers from different areas and the growing importance of non-native norms will increasingly affect this confidence. Whatever the outcome, *The Other Tongue* will contribute to our understanding of these processes and will deepen our appreciation of the different kinds of Englishes in the world and the rich variety of communication and self-expression that takes place in them.

Braj B. Kachru deserves our admiration for the way he has stayed for two decades with these important questions of the spread of English, its linguistic variation, and its non-native varieties. He and his fellow contributors deserve our gratitude for this new volume of studies which pushes the field of English across cultures far ahead and should stimulate the thinking of linguists, specialists in English language and literature, developmental planners, and futurists.

Stanford University, 1981 — Charles A. Ferguson

Preface

This collection of articles, like every book, has its own genesis. It is both the culmination of a collective effort in shared research interests, and a step toward my long-standing personal goal of understanding English across cultures. *The Other Tongue: English across Cultures* is, in essence, the outcome of a cross-cultural and cross-linguistic conference held at the University of Illinois at Urbana-Champaign in 1978. It was just a coincidence that during that year the status of English as an international and intranational language was explicitly dealt with in two conferences held only three months apart. The East-West Learning Institute of the East-West Center, Honolulu, Hawaii, organized a conference in April (1-15). A selection of papers presented at that conference has been edited by its organizer, Larry E. Smith, under the title *English for Cross-Cultural Communication* (London: Macmillan, 1981). I organized the second conference, "English in Non-Native Contexts" (June 30-July 2), in conjunction with the Linguistic Institute of the Linguistic Society of America; it was hosted by the University of Illinois at Urbana-Champaign. At that conference twenty-five invited presentations dealt with English in over a dozen countries, including Ghana, India, Kenya, the Philippines, Sri Lanka, Taiwan, the United States, the United Kingdom, the West Indies, and Zaire.

A number of papers included here (to be exact, 60 percent) are substantially revised versions of papers presented at the Urbana-Champaign conference. The rest were specifically commissioned from scholars who were not present at that conference. This volume, then, is not the proceedings of the conference in a literal sense; rather, the conference provided a theme and a focus for *The Other Tongue.* In more than one sense, the conference broke the traditional pattern of such deliberations: no inconvenient question was swept under the rug. The professionals, both linguists and literary scholars, and native and non-native users of English, had frank and stimulating discussions. The issues related to English were discussed in divergent linguistic and cultural contexts, and useful generalizations were made using ample empirical data. The English-using community in various continents was for the first time viewed in its totality. A number of cross-cultural perspectives were brought to bear upon our understanding of English in a global context, of language variation, of language acquisition, and of the bilinguals' — or a multilinguals' — use of English. The implications of such research on language studies in general and with particular reference to English has been lucidly discussed by Charles A. Ferguson in his foreword to this volume. In this sense, then, *The Other Tongue* is issue oriented, and not merely an anthology of case studies of English as a world language. It is true that such an anthology is overdue, but that is not the primary goal of this volume.

It was not just an accident that this conference was hosted by the University of Illinois at Urbana-Champaign. During the last two decades the University of Illinois has taken a leadership role in the study and research on English in non-native contexts through faculty research, in graduate courses, and at various conferences. The Division of Applied Linguistics of the University considers non-native English to be one of its major research areas.

I hope this volume reflects the importance of the theme, the freshness of approach, and the pragmatic view of English in the world context which were hallmarks of the conference. A new perspective on English across cultures understandably entails differences in emphasis and variations in approach to the topic. That such a perspective is needed was amply demonstrated in the presentations, and in the congenial and frank interactions in the cross-cultural setting of the conference. What transpired in discussion periods and in various social events was equally important. All that could not be captured in this volume.

This volume should serve as the first step toward our understanding of the complex issues involved in the formal and functional characteristics of the Englishes around the world. One thing is certain: there are no simple answers, no easy solutions, and no methodological remedies which apply to all users of English across cultures. No one group can carry this linguistic burden; it must be shared by the users of this international language, whether they are its native or non-native speakers.

The conference and this volume are the result of the enthusiasm, cooperation, support, and patience of many agencies, organizations, and individuals. My gratitude is particularly due to the Ford Foundation, New York, for their initial grant for the conference and to Foundation Program officers Elinor G. Barber and Melvin J. Fox for their counsel and interest. (Fox has since retired from the Foundation after making a substantial contribution to language-related research internationally, and specifically in Africa.) George K. Brinegar, Director, Office of International Programs and Studies, University of Illinois, and Carl W. Deal, Chairperson, Publications Committee of the same office, deserve thanks for including this volume in the series. The Research Board of the Graduate College of the University of Illinois supported various projects which directly or indirectly contributed toward our understanding of English across cultures. I am indebted to Charles A. Ferguson for his foreword to the volume; to James E. Alatis, Henry Kahane, Peter Strevens, Rudolph C. Troike, G. Richard Tucker, and Ladislav Zgusta for their advice and support in planning the conference; to Josephine Wilcock for her assistance in organizational matters and beyond; to Farida Cassimjee and Tamara M. Valentine for helping in library research and in preparing the final version of the manuscript; and to Ann Lowry Weir, senior editor at the University of Illinois Press, for her technical skill, expert editorial advice, and cooperation above and beyond the call of duty.

University of Illinois, 1981   — Braj B. Kachru

Introduction: The Other Side of English

BRAJ B. KACHRU

The other side of English is concerned with English as the "other tongue," or as a second language. "Other tongue" is not an innocent term; actually it is a multi-faceted concept with a long history and different manifestations in various regions of the world. The vision of an other tongue evokes memories of language being used as a powerful — sometimes ruthless — instrument for religious and cultural subjugation and for colonization. There are elevated (standard) varieties, and not-so-elevated (pidgin) varieties for local commerce, international trade, and even political maneuvering. In the past the other tongues (as second or foreign languages) have been associated with majestic empires (e.g., Arabic, Chinese, Greek, Latin, Persian, Sanskrit). In our time Dutch, English, French, Japanese, Spanish, and Portuguese have been used, in varying degrees, as the tongues of colonizers. A language has often been used as a tool for unifying a nation, for establishing political boundaries, and for creating dissent. How a language may be used (for non-communicative ends) in a particular national context is difficult to predict. But the powerful ruler, the wily colonizer, the commercial exploiter, and the religious zealot are not the only ones who envision their language being recognized — or imposed on people — as the other tongue.

The association of worldly power or religious sanctity with the spread of other tongues across cultures tells only part of the story. There have always been linguistic romanticists, representing various disciplines, who have seen the limitations of a culture-bound natural language as a universal language. In their view — and rightly so — a natural language always has cultural and linguistic affinities. Those who use it as their first language thus have advantages over those for whom it is a second language.

Why not have an artificial or constructed language as an international language? It would function as an extra linguistic tool, ideally speaking, with no cultural or linguistic connotations. Consequently, no ethnocentrism would arise. As yet, no such perfect proposal has come forward, for most constructed languages show the cultural or linguistic influences of one or more natural languages.[1] The proposals for such constructed languages have come from concerned universalists of various orientations — for example, Esperanto (1887), from a Polish physician named Ludwig Zamenhof; Volapük (1880), from a German bishop named Johann Martin Schleyer; Ido (1907), from the French logician Louis de Beaufront; Interlingua (Latino sine Flexione, 1903), from an Italian mathematician named Giuseppe Peano; and Novial (1928), from the Danish linguist Otto Jespersen. This is only a partial list, since such attempts still continue, one of the latest being Lincos, "a language for cosmic intercourse" (Freudenthal 1960). Most of these attempts have met with no success. The partial acceptance of Esperanto was also short lived, though the enthusiasm of its adherents has not yet abated. Most such attempts are now considered linguistic esoterica, mere symbols of the desire of universalist thinkers for a code of communication which would cut across cultures.

There was, however, one visionary, John Adams (1735-1826), the second president of the United States. Although he was not a linguistic romanticist, he made a prediction about the universal role of English which eventually came true. Languages, like human beings, seem to have their destinies; some human beings can see that destiny, and even work toward realizing it for a particular language. Adams — perhaps to the amazement of his contemporaries — foresaw the destiny of English when he said, "English will be the most respectable language in the world and the most universally read and spoken in the next century, if not before the close of this one" (*Life and Works IX;* see Mathews 1931). This prophecy was made two hundred years ago, on September 23, 1780.

The Other Tongue is concerned with the unfolding of this vision across the world, and with the spread of a language which, in John Adams's words, was "destined to be in the next and succeeding centuries more generally the language of the world than Latin was in the last or French is in the present age" (quoted in Mathews 1931: 42).

The spread of English across cultures has two sides. First, a significant segment of the world's population uses it as their *other* tongue (as a *second* or *foreign* language). Such use varies from broken English to almost native (or ambilingual) competence. It is this side of English which has actually elevated it to the status of an international (or universal) language. But we still know very little about the form and function of the varieties which have developed as the

other tongues. The discussion on such varieties is still restricted to
the realms of pedagogy, or to methods for teaching English as second
language.[2] These are only two restricted aspects; other, more interesting aspects seem to be left out.[3] The other side of English is therefore not viewed in its proper sociological, linguistic, and literary manifestations. The global consequences (good and bad) of English as the
other tongue have hardly been presented, and certainly the perspective of those who use it as the other tongue has been largely ignored.
The side of the *native* speaker has been concentrated upon, to a point
where it has acquired a questionable status in terms of *norm, description,* and *prescription* (see Ferguson's foreword to this volume).

How realistic and appropriate is such an attitude for our understanding of English in a world context? The demographic distribution of the two sides of English tells its own story. In Chapter 3 we
get some idea about such distribution (see also Fishman et al. 1977,
esp. Chs. 1, 2, and 3, and Kachru 1981b). One might hazard a linguistic guess here. If the spread of English continues at the current
pace, by the year 2000 its non-native speakers will outnumber its
native speakers (see Chapter 1). This will, of course, be the day when
the visionaries' wish for a "universal language" comes true.

But others are alarmed even with the present international profile of English.[4] The spread of English has been viewed both as a
unique phenomenon of our times and as an unprecedented form of
linguistic and cultural colonization. I shall not dwell upon that aspect — and controversy — of glottopolitics here.

Our knowledge about the motivations and attitudes favoring
the spread of English is still very restricted. Fragmentary case studies
have focused only on selected aspects, and very few of them have
insightful historical and contemporary dimensions. It is, however,
certain that the colonist's arm has not always been instrumental in
the spread of English. Let us therefore look at some other reasons
for the language's spread.

English is often learned because of its heritage, because of the
status it may confer on the reader or speaker, because of the doors
which it opens in technology, science, trade, and diplomacy. On
the one hand, for example, we have the well-known case of an institutionalized variety, Indian English. In India, less than fifty years
after John Adams's prophecy, Raja Rammohun Roy (1772-1833)
wrote a historic plea to Lord Amherst. Trying to overcome his si-
lence he "humbly" says:

"The present Rulers of India, coming from a distance of

many thousand miles to govern a people whose language,
literature, manners, customs, and ideas are almost entirely
new and strange to them, cannot easily become so inti-
mately acquainted with their real circumstances as the
natives of the country are themselves. We should therefore be guilty of ourselves, and afford our Rulers just
ground of complaint at our apathy, did we omit on occasions of importance like the present to supply them
with such accurate information as might enable them to
devise and adopt measures calculated to be beneficial to
the country, and thus second by our local knowledge
and experience, their declared benevolent intentions
for its improvement.
. . . When this Seminary of learning (Sanskrit School in
Calcutta) was proposed, we understand that the Government in England had ordered a considerable sum of
money to be annually devoted to the instruction of its
Indian subjects. We were filled with sanguine hopes that
this sum would be laid out in employing European gentlemen of talents and education to instruct the natives
of India in mathematics, natural philosophy, chemistry,
anatomy, and other useful sciences, which the natives
of Europe have carried to a degree of perfection that
has raised them above the inhabitants of other parts of
the world. . . .
We now find that the Government are establishing a
Sanskrit school under Hindoo Pundits to impart such
knowledge as is clearly current in India. . . ."
Roy then gives some arguments against spending
money on Sanskrit studies and continues: "If it had
been intended to keep the British nation in ignorance
of real knowledge the Baconian philosophy would not
have been allowed to displace the system of the school-
men, which was the best calculated to keep the country
in darkness, if such had been the policy of the British
legislature" (see Sharp 1920-22: I, 99-101).

But less well known are the cases of linguistically insulated
areas. In Japan, even though English continues to be a performance
variety, it has penetrated deep into the Japanese language and culture. In its Japanized form, English has acquired a stable status in
the communicative strategies of Japanese people (see Chapter 11).
Japan also provides a historical footnote for the spread of English
which is important for our understanding of English in a world context. Almost a century ago, there was a proposal to abandon Japa-

nese and "adopt instead some better, richer, stronger language, such as English or French" (Miller 1977: 41). (Note here the attitudinally significant modifiers *better, richer,* and *stronger.*) The first such proposal came from Mori Arinori (1847-99), and a later one came from Shiga Naoya (1883-1972). In his proposal Mori says:

> Without the aid of Chinese, our language has never been taught or used for any purpose of communication. This shows its poverty. The march of civilization in Japan has already reached the heart of the nation — the English language following it suppresses the use of both Chinese and Japanese. The commercial power of the English-speaking race which now rules the world drives our people into some knowledge of their commercial ways and habits. The absolute necessity of mastering the English language is thus forced upon us. It is a requisite of our independence in the community of nations. Under the circumstances, our meagre language, which can never be of any use outside of our islands, is doomed to yield to the domination of the English tongue, especially when the power of steam and electricity shall have pervaded the land. Our intelligent race, eager in the pursuit of knowledge, cannot depend upon a weak and uncertain medium of communication in its endeavor to grasp the principal truths from the precious treasury of Western science and art and religion. The laws of state can never be preserved in the language of Japan. All reasons suggest its disuse. [Mori 1873: I, vi; quoted in Hall 1973: 189]

These thoughts come from a country which was not under the influence of an English-speaking power, as was, for example, India.

In Rammohun Roy and Mori we find the prediction of John Adams being realized. Adams's time schedule was a little off the mark, but he was correct in claiming that English would become the language of the world, "because increasing population in America, and their universal connection and correspondence with all nations will . . . force their language into general use" (Mathews 1931: 42).

The impetus and support for such diffusion no doubt came from the extended period of colonization.[5] After all, the sun never set on the British Empire, and the English language was naturally basking in that global sunshine. Once English was adopted in a region, whether for science, technology, literature, prestige, elitism or "modernization," it went through a reincarnation which was partly linguistic and partly cultural. It was essentially caused by the new bilingual (or multilingual) setting, and by the new context in which English had to function. Such reincarnations of English are well established in the regions where it has been used as an intranational language, in addition to serving international purposes (see Kachru and Quirk 1981). These non-native *uses* of English raise many issues in, for example, the teaching of English, curriculum design, or methodology, all of which have in the past been viewed mainly from the native speaker's perspective. The linguistic, literary, sociolinguistic, and educational issues are interrelated; if each is seen in isolation, the totality is lost (see Chapter 3).

The Other Tongue is the first attempt to integrate and address provocative issues relevant to a deeper understanding of the forms and functions of English. The questions one might ask about this bilingual (or multilingual) English speech community are not necessarily the same questions one might ask about those users whose first or only language is English. For example, what were the historical reasons for initiating bilingualism in English in various parts of Asia or Africa? What factors motivated the retention of English after the end of the colonial period? What is the sociolinguistic profile for each variety, and how does it contribute to the development of subvarieties? What linguistic and contextual parameters resulted in the *nativization* of English on the one hand, and in the *Englishization* of the native languages on the other? What new English-based codes of communication have resulted from communicative strategies such as code-mixing and code-switching? What type of interaction is there between non-native and native users in a particular setting, and what determines the choice of an endo-normative or exo-normative "standard" for each? What are the stylistic and other characteristics of the new English literatures, and in what senses are these localized? What differentiates a bilingual's use of English from a monolingual's view of language use? What is the typology of non-native varieties of English at various levels?

The following chapters seek to provide answers to such questions. The situation, however, is complex. There is no one procrustean bed into which all the non-native varieties can be forced. There are institutionalized and performance varieties, and within each variety there is further variation (Kachru 1981a; Kachru and Quirk 1981; Smith 1981). Non-native varieties are marked by their linguistic and cultural nativization. It is the processes of nativization, and their results, to which both native and some non-native speakers have reacted. (For detailed discussions, see Part II; see also Kachru in press [a]).

Let me now turn to the five parts of *The Other Tongue* in order to show their relevance to some of the questions raised above.

English in Non-Native Contexts: Directions and Issues (Part I) pro-

vides an overview of four vital issues about English in its global context.
Chapter 1 views the sociology of English as an additional language, bringing out the factors favoring the "stable and widespread image of English."
Two realities concerning English are worthy of note: the fostering of the
spread of English by its non-mother-tongue users, and the contribution
to its functional expansion and regulation by local political authorities
(e.g., in India, Sri Lanka, Nigeria, and Kenya). Chapters 2, 3, and 4 concentrate on three vital issues for understanding the pragmatics of English as the other tongue: the functional roles of localized varieties, the
relationship between the context of situation and the choice of an endo-
normative or exo-normative standard for the institutionalized varieties,
and the approaches to research on intelligibility and its limitations and
challenges. In a sense, these four chapters provide a backdrop for the
four subsequent parts of the book.

In *Nativization: Formal and Functional* (Part II) we turn to another
aspect. Contributors illustrate and consider motivations for nativization
in the localized varieties of English, and they relate various types of formal processes of nativization to the functions of English. This theme appears, in one form or another, throughout *The Other Tongue.*

What types of nativization and acculturation has English under-
gone in various contextually distinct world settings? This question is
addressed by several contributors. The usefulness of the distinction between institutionalized and performance varieties becomes clearer in
these chapters; this distinction also provides a framework for determining the status, functions, and relationships of the nativized innovations.
One must pause before using terms which are like double-edged swords —
for example, "error" or "mistake" (see especially Chapter 20).

Two extensively studied components of nativization are phonology
and lexis. A number of studies have been devoted to these under the
guise of contrastive analysis, or under another incarnation, error
analysis. But nativization goes beyond such labels, in using productive
processes for collocational innovation, in syntactic simplification or
overgeneralization, and in the use of native rhetorical and stylistic devices. In short, nativization creates a new ecology for a non-native language. Who is to judge the appropriateness (or acceptance) of formations such as *swadeshi cloth, military hotel* (non-vegetarian hotel), or
lathi charge in the Indian context; *dunno drums, bodim bead, chewing-
sponge,* or *knocking-fee* in the African context; and *minor-wife* in the
Thai context? This question is, of course, directly related to intelligibility and language use.

The nativization of three types of English is presented. First are
the institutionalized varieties, Nigerian (Chapter 6), Kenyan (Chapter

7), and Singapore English (Chapter 10). Second come the performance varieties, Chinese (Chapter 8) and Japanese (Chapter 11). Finally, we look at a first-language variety used in the Caribbean (Chapters 12 and 13). In these chapters it is clearly shown that the nightmare about the *divisiveness* of the varieties of English is, after all, not as real as the linguistic alarmist would have us believe. The productive formal variations and the underlying motivations for such innovations are, by and large, shared (see also Kachru, in press [a]). Such innovations are primarily the result of the new contexts into which English has been transplanted, and are consequently a manifestation of language pragmatics.

In Chapter 9 we have a microanalysis: a profile of English in an Indian city. Although Indian English in its linguistic and literary aspects has formed part of several studies (see Aggarwal 1981, Kachru in press [a]), we still have very few empirical regional profiles of this variety.

The nativization of the "other tongue" Englishes is the result of language contact and change. The processes involved are not unique to these varieties of English; they are also shared by the transplanted varieties such as American, Australian, or West Indian (see e.g., Kachru 1981a, b).

What is Standard English, and what is the model for it? This question invariably results in a controversy with its own history, even with respect to the native varieties. *Contact and Change: Question of a Standard* (Part III) presents a comparative perspective which leads to an understanding of the issues. Chapters 14 and 15 discuss the considerations which led to the rise of American English from a "colonial substandard" to a "prestige language." The British attitude toward American English was essentially based on the changes which American English underwent due to the contact with different varieties and dialects and with the influence of other ethnic languages. (For further discussion of these differences, see also Heath 1976, 1977; Kachru 1981b; Markwardt and Quirk 1964; Strevens 1972.) Chapters 16 and 17 provide other perspectives on contact. One discusses the specific case of English in Puerto Rico, and the other, the life cycle of a non-native variety.

There is another way in which English excels as a world language. English literatures have developed as non-native literatures across several cultures and languages.[6] This facet of English is introduced in *New English Literatures: Themes and Styles* (Part IV). In many respects this use of English is unprecedented; among other things, it reveals the writer's emotional attachment to a second language for creative purposes, his or her identity with it, and its roots across cultures. True, these literatures have become controversial. Their recognition has been slow in coming, and native speakers are cynical about them. But that is a question of attitude unrelated to my point.

The creative processes displayed in non-native literatures have generally been ignored in linguistic studies, to the detriment of studies on stylistics, contrastive discourse, and language acculturation. This neglect reflects the dichotomy of theories and methodologies which has traditionally existed between linguists and literary critics. Chapters 18 and 19 introduce the reader to the context of such literatures (primarily in Africa and South Asia), to the specific stylistic experimentation of two Indian English writers, Mulk Raj Anand and R.K. Narayan, and to the geographically hard-to-place V.S. Naipaul. Chapter 18 also discusses the attitudes toward such literatures, and their relevance to English studies and to programs on English as a second (or foreign) language. Such programs have generally adopted an ostrich-like attitude to this vast body of literature, and to the exciting issues which it raises on language use and the study of literature itself.

There is another dimension to such literatures: they use English as a window onto other Western and non-Western cultures. The medium is familiar, but it is used in entirely different semiotic and cultural systems. *Contextualization: Text in Context* (Part V) shows how what is "deviation" for one user of English provides "meaning" for another user. English is used in other cultures for creativity (as discussed in Chapters 18 and 19) and for maintaining local patterns of life. Chapter 20 attempts to develop an ethnography of English as the other tongue; it brings to its finale the theme which recurs throughout the volume. The examples in the last chapter show, I believe, that when English is adapted to another culture — to non-English contexts — it is *decontextualized from its Englishness* (or *Americanness*). In the interactional networks of its new users, it provides an additional, redefined communicative strategy. What is a *deviation* for one beholder is a *communicative act* for another language user. We see this clearly in code-mixing, in code-switching, or in typical uses of language in, for example, obituaries, letters, matrimonial advertisements, and in the non-native English literatures. While the typical communication may be shared by all the members of the English speech community, the strategies to organize language to fulfill these purposes are not necessarily shared, since such communicative acts are organized in localized (culture-bound) stylistic conventions for various text types. English, then, acquires a new identity, a local habitat, and a name. This phenomenon is not unprecedented, but the extent and degree of the spread of English, and its manifestations in various cultures, is unequaled. In the distant past, the same thing happened to Sanskrit in South India, or to Persian in India. In the not-so-distant past we again witnessed this phenomenon — for example, with French in francophone areas of the world, and with Spanish in the New World.

The Other Tongue provides both a new perspective and a challenge. On the one hand, the acquisition of English across cultures has broader promise and is not restricted to a language specialist. It is a symbol of an urge to extend oneself and one's roles beyond the confines of one's culture and language. English has been accepted in this spreading role across cultures and language groups, even since and despite the depressing colonial experience. English thus is used as the medium of interchange between cultures. The medium has no claims to intrinsic superiority; rather, its preeminent role developed due to extralinguistic factors. The importance is in what the medium conveys about technology, science, law, and (in the case of English) literature. English has now, as a consequence of its status, been associated with universalism, liberalism, and internationalism. In this sense it is a symbol of the concept which Indians have aptly expressed as *vasudhaiva kuṭumbakaṃ* (the whole Universe is a family).

The present spread of English, and its adoption across cultures, should be reassuring for societies which believe that bilingualism (multilingualism) is an aberration. Acquiring and maintaining another language has historically been a *normal* human activity, and monolingualism is not such an ideal state. It is through other tongues that other cultures can be appreciated and perhaps understood. The Indian pragmatist Mohandas K. Gandhi (1869-1948) said it so well: "I do not want my house to be walled in on all sides and my windows to be stuffed. I want cultures of all lands to be blown about my house as freely as possible. But I refuse to be blown off my feet anyway" (cited in John, n.d.: epigraph).

I hope that *The Other Tongue* has raised some meaningful questions and has also provided some answers. Asking significant questions is not easy; providing insightful answers is — as we know — extremely difficult, even more so if the topic cuts across world cultures and languages. If this volume has even partially accomplished its goal, that is a significant step in the right direction. Through such steps challenging and provocative questions will continue to be asked. Through such probing we shall grow to understand the role of the other tongue in general, and of English across cultures in particular. But the other side of English is significant in other ways, too: it offers a laboratory for the study of data, a testing ground for theories, and an ample field — in Asia, Africa, and the West — for interdisciplinary research. It is therefore a challenging field for theoretical linguistics and various branches of applied linguistics. The need, then, is to ask right questions in the right spirit.

NOTES

1. For a detailed history and description of such proposals see, e.g., Guerard 1922 and Jacob 1947.

2. Note that even in books of "readings" meant for such consumers very little, if anything, is said about the formal and functional characteristics of the institutionalized varieties. A typical study is Croft 1980, which is meant "to enlarge teacher's perspectives — to give them a broader view of the field they work in" (xiii). No effort has been made to present the non-native user's perspective. Another book, Michaels and Ricks 1980, assesses "the state of the language" and is the result of a project initiated by the English-Speaking Union, San Francisco. The "other tongue" aspect of English is completely overlooked in this volume.

3. The attitude exhibited in such approaches is generally as shown in Prator 1968. See a response to it in Kachru 1976; see also Preston 1981.

4. The acceptance of English as the other tongue in the post-colonial period is not, of course, unqualified and universal. Vocal groups in each English-using country resist the continued use and dominance of English. See, e.g., for South Asia, Kachru (in press [b]).

5. For a detailed discussion and case studies see, e.g., Brosnahan 1963; Calvet 1974; Fishman et al. 1977; Spencer 1971.

6. For selected reference on African writing in English, see Chapter 18; for India, Chapters 19 and 20. See also Aggarwal 1981, Kachru in press (a), and Narasimhaiah 1976. For Malaysia, Singapore, and Sri Lanka, see, e.g., Fernando 1972, Thumboo 1976, and Kandiah 1981. In their anthologies Fernando and Thumboo provide excellent introductions with specimens of writing. See also Jones 1965; King 1974, 1980.

REFERENCES

Aggarwal, Narindar K. 1981. *English in South Asia: a bibliographical survey of resources.* Gurgaon and New Delhi: Indian Documentation Service.

Brosnahan, L. F. 1963. Some historical cases of language imposition. In J. F. Spencer, ed., *Languages in Africa.* Cambridge: Cambridge University Press.

Calvet, Louis-Jean. 1974. *Linguistique et colonialisme: petit traité de glottophagie.* Série Bibliothèque Scientifique. Paris: Payot.

Croft, Kenneth, ed. 1980. *Readings on English as a second language.* 2nd ed. Cambridge: Winthrop.

Fernando, Lloyd, ed. 1972. *New drama one.* Kuala Lumpur: Oxford University Press.

Fishman, Joshua A.; Cooper, R. L.; and Conrad, A. W. 1977. *The spread of English: the sociology of English as an additional language.* Rowley, Mass.: Newbury House.

Freudenthal, Hans. 1960. *Lincos: design of a language for cosmic intercourse.* Amsterdam: North-Holland.

Guerard, Albert L. 1922. *A short history of international language movement.* London: T. Fisher Unwin.

Hall, Ivan Parker. 1973. *Mori Arinori.* Cambridge: Harvard University Press.

Heath, Shirley Brice. 1976. A national language academy? Debate in the new nation. *International Journal of the Sociology of Language* 11: 9-43.

————. 1977. Language and politics in the United States. In M. Saville-Troike, ed., *Georgetown University Round Table on language and linguistics.* Washington: Georgetown University Press.

Jacob, Henry. 1947. *A planned auxiliary language.* London: Dennis Dobson.

John, K. K. n.d. *The only solution to India's language problem.* Madras: Published by the author.

Jones, Joseph. 1965. *Terranglia: the case for English as world literature.* New York: Twayne.

Kachru, Braj B. 1976. Models of English for the Third World: white man's linguistic burden or language pragmatics? *TESOL Quarterly* 10: 221-39.

———. 1981a. The pragmatics of non-native varieties of English. In L. Smith, ed., 1981.

———. 1981b. American English and other Englishes. In Charles A. Ferguson and Shirley B. Heath, eds., *Language in the U.S.A.* New York and Cambridge: Cambridge University Press.

———. In press (a). *The Indianization of English: the English language in India.* New Delhi: Oxford University Press.

———. In press (b). South Asian English. In Richard W. Bailey and M. Görlach, eds., *English as a world language.* Ann Arbor: University of Michigan Press.

———, and Randolph Quirk. 1981. Introduction. In L. Smith, ed., 1981.

Kandiah, Thiru. 1981. Lankan English schizoglossia. *English worldwide: a journal of varieties of English* 2(1): 63-81.

King, Bruce. 1974. *Literatures of the world in English.* London: Routledge and Kegan Paul.

———. 1980. *The new English literatures: cultural nationalism in changing world.* New York: St. Martin's Press.

Markwardt, Albert H., and Quirk, R. 1964. *A common language: British and American English.* London: British Broadcasting Corporation.

Mathews, M. M. 1931. *The beginnings of American English: essays and comments.* Chicago: University of Chicago Press.

Michaels, Leonard, and Ricks, C. 1980. *The state of the language.* Berkeley: University of California Press.

Miller, Roy A. 1977. *The Japanese language in contemporary Japan.* Washington: American Enterprise Institute for Public Policy Research.

Mori, Arinori. 1873. *Education in Japan: a series of letters addressed by prominent Americans to Arinori Mori.* New York: Appleton.

Narasimhaiah, C. D., ed. 1976. *Commonwealth literature: a handbook of select reading lists.* New Delhi: Oxford University Press.

Prator, Clifford H. 1968. The British heresy in TESL. In Joshua A. Fishman, C. A. Ferguson, and J. Das Gupta, eds., *Language problems of developing nations.* New York: John Wiley and Sons.

Preston, Dennis R. 1981. The ethnography of TESOL. *TESOL Quarterly* 15(2): 105-16.

Sharp, Sir Henry, ed. 1920-22. *Selections from educational records.* Calcutta: Bureau of Education, Government of India.

Smith, Larry E., ed. 1981. *English for cross-cultural communication.* London: Macmillan.

Spencer, John. 1971. Colonial language policies and their legacies. In T. A. Sebeok, ed., *Current trends in linguistics.* Vol. VII: Linguistics in Sub-Saharan Africa. The Hague: Mouton.

Strevens, Peter, 1972. *British and American English.* London: Collier-Macmillan.

Thumboo, Edwin. 1976. *The second tongue: an anthology of poetry from Malaysia and Singapore.* Singapore: Heinemann Educational Books.

PART I

English in Non-Native Contexts:
Directions and Issues

1

Sociology of English as an Additional Language

JOSHUA A. FISHMAN

The ongoing nativization of non-native Englishes in various parts of the world proceeds within the penumbra of a rather stable and widespread image of English. This image is itself both influenced by and, in turn, contributory to an international sociolinguistic balance of power that characterizes the latter part of the twentieth century. This balance of power rests solidly on three realities: 1) not only is English increasingly associated with technological modernity and power, but this association is now being fostered by non-English mother-tongue interests; 2) English is both functionally fostered and regulated by local political authorities; and 3) indigenous "preferred languages" are complementarily fostered and regulated by these same authorities.

Not only is English still spreading, but it is even being spread by non-English mother-tongue interests.

The world has previously witnessed the spread of languages of empire, the diffusion of lingua francas, and the growth of international languages. In most respects, therefore, the continued spread of English for international and intranational purposes is not novel in the annals of world history — or, if it is novel, it is so primarily in a quantitative sense, in terms of scale, rate, and degree, rather than in any qualitative sense or in terms of kind. If there is something qualitatively new under the sun in conjunction with the spread of English in the non-English mother-tongue world, it is merely that the spread has reached such an order of magnitude that it is now significantly fostered by the *non*-English mother-tongue world, rather than being predominantly dependent on resources, efforts, or personnel of the English mother-tongue world (Conrad and Fishman 1977). Whether we monitor the veritable army of English-speaking econo-technical specialists, advisors, and representatives, or whether we examine the diffusion of English publications, films, radio and television programs, literacy programs and educational

opportunities, it is becoming increasingly clear that non-English
mother-tongue countries are significantly active in each of these
connections. Nor is their involvement merely that of Third World
recipients of Western largesse. True, Third World nations *are* themselves fostering massive efforts via and on behalf of English. On the
other hand, however, equally massive programs via English are being
conducted by the Soviet Union, the Arab world, and mainland
China — world powers that have their own well-developed standard
languages and that normally oppose various political, philosophical,
and economic goals of the English mother-tongue world.

Whereas the international and intranational roles of French
also continue to be fostered (as do, to a lesser degree, such roles for
Spanish, Russian, German, Portuguese, etc.) such efforts are conducted exclusively by current francophone (hispanoparlante, etc.)
nations or by countries under French (Spanish, etc.) cultural, political, or economic domination (Gordon 1978). Similarly, English is
massively employed, particularly in higher-level governmental, technological, and educational pursuits, by countries under former (or
current) Anglo-American domination (Fishman, Cooper, and Rosenbaum 1977). However, English today has surpassed the charmed
circle of Anglo-American econo-political control, and is being fostered both by its opponents and by "third parties." English has become a major medium of indigenous elites ("native foreigners"),
of tourism ("foreign foreigners"), of popular media, of technical
publications, of the metaphor of mastery, of teenage slang, and even
of language-planning models and anti-models all over the world.
While the omnipresence of English also adds to the opposition to
English, it obviously fosters the growth of indigenous non-native
varieties (Smith 1981; Kachru and Quirk 1981). Finally, never before has any one language been so simultaneously sought after and
regulated, so that it would "grow" yet "stay in its place" (i.e., be
used only in functions for which it was authoritatively desired).
Thus, if the *continued spread and growth of English* is one aspect of
the current international sociolinguistic balance of power, another
such aspect is the recurring need to control, regulate, or tame that
spread.

English is being regulated via both status and corpus planning.

The growth of English-speaking "false foreigners" in various
parts of the non-English mother-tongue world (e.g., West Africa,
East Africa, India, Puerto Rico) is an indication that a non-native
variety of English may succeed not only in stabilizing itself cross-

generationally (i.e., in nativizing itself), but also in becoming a mother tongue in certain speech networks. The latter phenomenon is much more worrisome than the former to local authorities, but taken together and added to the continued growth of English in many parts of the world (growth in listening to English, in understanding English, in speaking English, in reading English, and even in writing English) it is no surprise that these authorities have frequently decided to do something about it. A common *status-planning* goal has recently been implemented by the Philippines: English as a medium of education has been restricted to mathematics and natural sciences (the "ethnically less encumbered" subjects), whereas the bulk of the curriculum (particularly history, civics, and vocational education; i.e., the "ethnically more encumbered subjects") has been reserved for Pilipino as a medium of instruction (Fishman 1977a). This policy is in line with the relinguification and re-ethnification (Pilipinization and Philippinization) goals of the local authorities, who recognize, at the same time, that English reigns supreme in the econo-technical area. "A little bit of English for almost everyone" is considered a good thing, as is a lot of English for a select few, provided the language can be confined to its alotted domains (Cooper, Fishman, Lown, Schaier and Seckbach 1977). Similar steps to make sure that English does not intrude upon the domains of local ideology, literature, history, and citizenship have multiplied in Tanzania, Taiwan, India, France, and Puerto Rico, and can be expected, quietly but increasingly, elsewhere as well.

Thus, in addition to the distinction of having spread further and having been indigenized more frequently than any previous lingua franca, English also has the distinction of being more frequently subjected to language-planning efforts (Fishman 1977b). Even in the corpus-planning field, "academies" and other agencies responsible for attaining language modernization plus safeguarding language authenticity ("purity," "distinctiveness," "originality," etc.) constantly point to English as the most common source of unwelcome interferences/influences (Allony-Fainberg 1977). Whether in France or in French Canada, whether in Hebrew or in Yiddish, whether in Spain or in Spanish America, whether in Hindi, Indonesian, or Swahili — in every area and language the impact of English must be watched and regulated. At times this influence is disguised as "internationalisms," "Europeanisms," or "Westernisms," but in actuality it is more likely to be Englishisms than anything else (Ronen, Seckbach, and Cooper 1977). The academies are fre-

quently successful in combatting Englishisms in the standard written
language, but in the informal spoken language they often confront
well-entrenched Englishisms that have become part and parcel of
popular culture and that are essentially impossible to extirpate, even
among loyalists and purists (Allony-Fainberg 1974). Nevertheless,
the epic struggles of officially and centrally conducted language-
planning authorities since the end of World War II have all had to
face up to English, and by and large they have succeeded with respect to the written language, insofar as political circumstances have
permitted. Regardless of what may have happened to the British Empire, the sun never sets on the English language; yet, little languages
have learned to stand their ground with respect to English, and to
carve out domains into which English has little or no entree (Rubin,
Hernudd, Das Gupta, Fishman, and Ferguson 1977).

More and more local languages are being accorded special protection.

Writing in the early 1940's, Karl Deutsch reviewed the slow
growth in the number of standard/literary languages in Europe:
from sixteen in 1800, to thirty in 1900, to fifty-three in 1940
(Deutsch 1942). However, the growth of standard/literary languages
has not stopped at the boundaries of Europe; indeed, since the end
of World War II this growth has accelerated at a rate more rapid than
anyone would have predicted. The number of literary languages today
is easily in the neighborhood of two hundred and is still growing. On
the one hand, this explosion of literary languages is due to the fact
that there are more polities in the world today than at any previous
time since the universalization of literacy (Fishman 1972). On the
other hand, the forces of intranational cultural democracy are also
receiving more recognition (or more permissive treatment) from
central authorities than before (Fishman 1976). Bilingual education
and even the sociolinguistic enterprise itself have contributed to
(and benefited from) both of these processes, and the end is not yet
in sight. There are potentially hundreds of additional ethnolinguistic
collectivities seeking some recognized, protected, and elevated (i.e.,
literacy/power related) status for one or another of their vernacular
tongues.

Thus, the Philippines, mentioned above as a prime example of
a nation "regulating" English in the pursuit of a new (Pilipino/Philip-
pine) integrative identity, has permitted local languages to become
media of instruction during the earlier elementary grades, as well as
subjects of instruction in all subsequent grades. A three-language
policy is thus envisaged, much as it is in India. Such policies promise

to become increasingly common for minority nationalities/regional ethnicities in various parts of the globe: the "national language," an even wider language of communication (very often English), and a preferred "narrower" language all find protected niches for themselves in the local educational/cultural/commercial/vocational economy.

Obviously, multilingualism is not a new phenomenon. What *is* at least somewhat new is the fact that more and more of the world's multilingualism is being governmentally recognized, sponsored, planned, and protected. This is indeed an unusual situation insofar as the spread of English is concerned, and it constitutes the third force in the international sociolinguistic balance of power. English is spreading, but its spread is being controlled and counterbalanced by the sponsored, protected spread of national and subnational languages. As a result, more and more of those who learn English do so in the context of other languages that have their own perquisites and potentials. This necessarily influences the image of English in many parts of the non-English mother-tongue world, as well as in the English mother-tongue world itself.

The Image of English: Mirror, Mirror on the Wall

Throughout the non-English mother-tongue world, English is recurringly associated with practical and powerful pursuits (Cooper and Seckbach 1977). This becomes evident when the image of English is compared, on the one hand, with the image of French and, on the other hand, with that of local integrative languages which have been fairly recently standardized. Relative to the latter, English is viewed as *less* suitable for military operations (local soldiers do not know that much English yet), for lying, joking, cursing, or bargaining (spontaneous emotion and animation are not yet expressed via English), and for unmediated prayer. On the other hand, English is recurringly viewed as *more* suitable than local integrative languages for science, international diplomacy, industry/commerce, high oratory, and pop songs (Cooper and Fishman 1977).

The image of English vis-à-vis French is even more revealing, in that the former has risen and the latter has fallen in the international balance of power. In the Third World (excluding former anglophone and francophone colonies) French is considered *more suitable* than English for only one function: opera. It is considered *the equal of English* for reading good novels or poetry and for personal prayer (the local integrative language being widely viewed as superior to both English and French in this connection). But outside the realm of aesthetics, the Ugly Duckling reigns supreme. French is widely viewed as more beautiful, musical, pleasant, rhythmic, refined, intimate, pure, soothing, graceful, tender, and lovely, but English is viewed as richer, more precise, more logical, more sophisticated, and more competence related. English is less loved but more used; French is more loved but less used. Nature abhors a vacuum: as the functional load of a formerly prestigious variety declines, affect rushes in to take up the slack. The non-francophone world has "nothing but love" for French, and in the cruel real world that is a sign of a weakness. The displacement of Irish is suffused with love. The replacement of Yiddish is accompanied by panegyrics as to its intimacy and authenticity. English gets along without love, without sighs, without tears, and almost without affect of any kind (Fishman 1977c). In a world where econo-technical superiority is what really counts, the heightened aesthetic-affective image of French smacks of weakness, innocence, and triviality.

The local integrative languages are recurringly viewed as more useful than French, although less useful "in the highest circles" than English. On the other hand, these languages, recipients of planned public protection, are recurringly viewed as less beautiful than French but more beautiful than English. There was a time not so long ago — indeed, less than a century has elapsed since then — when languages were viewed as having "made the grade" when they could boast of great poetry. Nowadays the market for poetry is down, and the absence or availability of computer programming manuals tells us whether or not a language will be "taken seriously" by its own and nearby speech communities. Given such sociolinguistic values and goals, is it any wonder that local integrative languages are viewed as Prince Charmings in overalls? They combine a modicum of affect with a modicum of practicality. But the real "powerhouse" is still English. It doesn't have to worry about being loved because, loved or not, it works. It makes the world go round, and few indeed can afford to "knock it."

Nor is the non-English mother-tongue world unique in its nononsense view of English. Much of the English mother-tongue world is itself quite unemotional about English, viewing it as a medium pure and simple rather than as either a symbol or a message. Most English mother-tongue countries are recent centers of mass immigration. High proportions of their populations (even among their academicians) reveal no more than a single generation of association with English. This shallowness of association with "Mother English" is, in turn, related to Anglophonie's permissiveness toward non-native Englishes all over the world, each of which likewise has little affect associated with it. The constellation sketched above seems stable enough at the moment, but the lesson of History is quite clear, even if its pace is not predictable. If a powerful shift in *Zeitgeist* has eroded the image and functions of French (and it did so, to some extent, even within the very borders of Francophonie), then what would a massive shift in the balance of econo-technical power do to the preeminence of English? Third-party inertia would continue to reinforce English for decades or longer, but ultimately a shift would take place. If and when such a shift occurs, there may be few who will shed a tear. The world has no tears left. At any rate, crying takes time and, as all the world has learned from American English, "time is money."

REFERENCES

Allony-Fainberg, Yaffa. 1974. Official Hebrew terms for parts of the car: a study of knowledge, usage and attitudes. Pp. 493-518 in J. A. Fishman, ed. (1974).
——— . 1977. The influence of English on formal terminology in Hebrew. Pp. 223-28 in J. A. Fishman, R. L. Cooper, A. W. Conrad et al. (1977).
Conrad, Andrew W., and Fishman, Joshua A. 1977. English as a world language: the evidence. Pp. 3-76 in J. A. Fishman, R. L. Cooper, A. W. Conrad et al. (1977).
Cooper, Robert L., and Fishman, Joshua A. 1977. A study of language attitudes. Pp. 239-76 in J. A. Fishman, R. L. Cooper, A. W. Conrad et al. (1977).
——— and Seckbach, Fern. 1977. Economic incentives for learning a language of wider communication. Pp. 212-22 in J. A. Fishman, R. L. Cooper, A. W. Conrad et al. (1977).
——— ; Fishman, Joshua A.; Lown, Linda; Schaier, Barbara; and Seckbach, Fern. 1977. Pp. 197-211 in J. A. Fishman, R. L. Cooper, A. W. Conrad et al. (1977).
Deutsch, Karl W. 1942. The trend of European nationalism: the language aspect. *American Political Science Review* 36: 533-41.
Fishman, Joshua A. 1972. *Language and nationalism.* Rowley, Mass.: Newbury House.
——— . 1976. *Bilingual education: an international sociological perspective.* Rowley, Mass.: Newbury House.
——— . 1977a. English in the context of international societal bilingualism. Pp. 329-36 in J. A. Fishman, R. L. Cooper, A. W. Conrad et al. (1977).
——— . 1977b. The spread of English as a new perspective for the study of "language maintenance and language shift." Pp. 108-35 in J. A. Fishman, R. L. Cooper, A. W. Conrad et al. (1977).
——— . 1977c. Knowing, using, and liking English as an additional language. Pp. 302-27 in J. A. Fishman, R. L. Cooper, A. W. Conrad et al. (1977).
——— , et al. 1968. *Readings in the sociology of language.* The Hague: Mouton.
——— , ed. 1974. *Advances in language planning.* The Hague: Mouton.
——— ; Cooper, R. L.; Conrad, A. W.; et al. 1977. *The spread of English.* Rowley, Mass.: Newbury House.

———— ; Cooper, Robert L.; and Rosenbaum, Yehudi. 1977. English around the world. Pp. 77-107 in J. A. Fishman, R. L. Cooper, A. W. Conrad et al. (1977).

Gordon, David C. 1978. *The French language and national identity.* The Hague: Mouton.

Kachru, Braj B., and Quirk, Randolph. 1981. "Introduction." In Smith (1981).

Ronen, Miriam; Seckbach, Fern; and Cooper, Robert L. 1977. Foreign loanwords in Hebrew newspapers. Pp. 229-38 in J. A. Fishman, R. L. Cooper, A. W. Conrad et al. (1977).

Rubin, Joan; Jernudd, B.; Das Gupta, J.; Fishman, J. A.; and Ferguson, C. A., eds. 1977. *Language planning process.* The Hague: Mouton.

Smith, Larry. 1981. *English for cross-cultural communication.* London: Macmillan.

2

The Localized Forms of English

PETER STREVENS

A central problem of linguistic study is how to reconcile a convenient and necessary fiction with a great mass of inconvenient facts. The fiction is the notion of "a language" — English, Chinese, Navajo, Kashmiri. The facts reside in the mass of diversity exhibited in the actual performance of individuals when they use a given language.

In the case of the language called English, the sheer numbers of those whose individual performances (and competences) are encompassed within the fiction, their worldwide geographical distribution, the great range of social needs and purposes they serve, and the resulting myriad of identifiably different versions of English all combine to produce a paradox: as English becomes ever more widely used, so it becomes ever more difficult to characterize in ways that support the fiction of a simple, single language.

We must assume that there *is* a link between the diverse manifestations of English: in the writings of Chinua Achebe or William Faulkner; in the speech of a taxidriver at a Calcutta railway station or a Nigerian professor of economics; in the discourse rules of British diplomatic negotiation or bar conversation in Nairobi. The link is not fortuitous, but obviously it is highly complex. Being so complex, it admits of many alternative modes of analysis. Here I propose to view the fiction of "English" as being manifested in two distinct ways, each having its own separate determining influences. The first manifestation of English is social: English-using communities develop *localized forms of English* (LFEs) which display numerous variable features. The second manifestation is at the level of the individual user, whose command and use of the English language is a mixture both of conformity to one or more LFEs and at the same time the consequence of specific features in his personal identity.

Localized Forms of English

For over a century, and increasingly in recent times, it has been commonplace to use labels such as "Indian English," "Hong Kong English," "Australian English," "West African English," etc. At various times the identity of such notions has been felt to reside in idiosyncrasies of lexis, syntax, or style; or else it has been ascribed solely to the dimension of accent and dialect; or it has been subsumed within sociolinguistic studies, or to lectal choice, between *acrolect, mesolect,* and *basilect.* Sometimes it has been analyzed in terms of "common errors," that is, institutionalized inventories of deviations from a presumed norm. Many of these studies have been of great value in illuminating and describing further layers of the onionskins of language. Most of them have been carried out from a nativist standpoint; that is, they incorporate an unstated assumption that whatever diversity may occur in the English usage of those for whom English is not the mother tongue, there exists in the usage of the native speaker both a unity and a hierarchical superiority.

It would be naive to treat this as simple chauvinism and to make the contrary assumption that all Englishes are "equal" (whatever that means) in every possible sense, including public belief and social prejudice. For the purposes of this chapter it is necessary to remove value judgments from consideration, to accept that English manifests itself in a large number of forms, and that among the differing characteristics of such forms one must include the native/non-native dimension.

The first step, then, in moving from the global fiction of "the language" toward the unitary fiction of "the idiolect" is to regard a language as being realized in many forms, these forms reflecting various communities of users. Discussion of these forms and communities inevitably has a geographical and socio-cultural aspect; furthermore, the word *form,* standing alone, is already preempted elsewhere within linguistics. Hence the choice of the expression *localized forms of English* (LFE). As a working definition, we may say that *an LFE is an identifiable version of English associated with a given community of English users.* Its identifiable characteristics may lie in any combination of lexical, syntactic, phonological, discoursal, or semantic features.[1]

Variables That Determine LFEs

The analysis and description of LFEs entails two distinct considerations: (a) the needs and purposes of the community which the LFE serves; (b) the defining and differentiating characteristics of each LFE.

Needs and purposes served by an LFE

Recent discussions (at a conference held at the East-West Center, Hawaii; Smith [1981]) have drawn attention to a distinction between *international* and *intra-national* needs and purposes for English. Some English-using communities require the use of the language (largely by individuals and in limited numbers) for contact with the external world, for communication with other individuals and communities, for access to science and the other international uses for which English is the vehicle; these *international* needs constitute the major requirement for English in certain countries (e.g., Japan, Turkey, Brazil). Other English-using communities require the language for these purposes, but in addition they need English for *intra-national* purposes: for use by large populations within the community.[2] This applies to countries where English is the native language of the majority of the inhabitants, obviously. What is less obvious, and is the rather recent result of profound sociolinguistic changes, is that other countries — notably India and Singapore, arguably Malaysia, in the future doubtless others — also have major intra-national needs for English, even though English is never, in these countries, an indigenous language.

Countries with international needs only for English, and countries with that plus intra-national needs, will be referred to as INTER and INTRA types respectively. Thus, those countries in which significant use is made of English although it is an L_2 (secondary, not primary language) for the great majority of the population, are of two kinds: some are INTRA, but others are INTER (i.e., their needs are international only.)[3]

In addition, the LFE of INTER type countries is always *dependent:* it values itself and is valued by others against closeness to an L_1 model (i.e., speakers of English in an INTER country seek to approximate a native-speaker model). INTRA type LFEs, by contrast, while they often express some affinities toward one or another L_1 type (e.g., Puerto Rican English has affinities toward American models; West African English has more affinities with British models) are generally *independent*. They do not value themselves directly on closeness to an L_1 type — although

the educational system may still adhere to former ideas, left over
from an era when such sociolinguistic and educational independence was not yet acceptable, either in British or American eyes,
or in the country concerned.

It follows from these somewhat complex relationships that
the precise values of the second set of considerations in determining the analysis and description of LFEs — namely, their defining and differentiating characteristics — will be strongly influenced by whether a given LFE is *dependent* upon a native (L_1)
model, or *independent* of it.

Defining and Differentiating Features of an LFE

Accent and dialect. The combination of these two linguistic
features (phonological and grammatical/lexical, respectively) carries
indexical information about geographical provenance and social/
educational background.

(1) *Lectal range.* Each LFE has its own characteristic range between *acrolect, mesolect,* and *basilect,* and its own social interpretations of when each is appropriate, and by people of what role in
society.

(2) *Variety range.* Allied to lectal range, yet distinct from it,
is the range of varieties — registers, familiarity/unfamiliarity and
formality/informality scales, the availability of sets of items of
slang, abuse, swearing, etc., and the rules about when these are
acceptable for use by different groups of people. These two ranges,
of *lects* and of *varieties,* are of considerable extent and subtlety;
they permit large and easily identifiable differences between localized forms of English.

Discoursal rules. LFEs differ as to the procedures for achieving
a particular illocutionary force, rules for joining and opting out of
conversation, techniques for persuasion, and mechanisms for regulating social discourse. These differences reflect, to varying degrees,
the equivalent usages in the society concerned, as when an Indian
interacts in English with a person he regards as a guru, or a Japanese works out how he uses English when he is joined, during a conversation with foreigners, by other Japanese of a social status clearly
different from his own.

"Standard" dialect. A peculiarity of English is that one dialect
is non-localized, is not essentially paired with a particular accent,
and is accepted by the public, worldwide, as a suitable educational
model. This dialect (i.e., set of grammatical and lexical features) is
usually known as Standard English. In LFEs having a wide lectal

range, the acrolect typically consists of Standard English with a local accent, together with an admixture of some local expressions.[4] The importance of Standard English as an item in this catalogue of features is simply that it plays a greater or a lesser part in one LFE compared with another: the extent of use and acceptance of Standard English is part of the defining characteristics of an LFE.

Status, attitudes, and affinities. LFEs vary greatly in the status they enjoy within the community. (Compare the status of the LFE of Francophone Canadians in Quebec with that of the LFE of Francophone Africans in Cameroun.) Also varying are the attitudes toward them on the part of local intellectual and educational communities. These attitudes are frequently backward-looking and hostile to change; but they must be considered, because they form an inescapable part of the sociolinguistic framework of any LFE.

The LFE as a vehicle for education, administration, science and technology, literature, the media, entertainment, and publicity. In some countries English is the medium of instruction in particular areas of education, and of administration and the law; in other countries it is not. In some countries it is the vehicle (perhaps the only vehicle) for discussing or teaching science. In others English is a vehicle for literature, i.e., for literature written in English by writers for whom it is not the mother tongue. In some, English is one of the vehicles for the press, for international entertainment, for publicity and advertising. The precise nature of the LFE in a given country is influenced by the particular uses of English as a vehicle.

To sum up this section of the argument, whether an LFE is of an INTER or INTRA type, its identity will include the precise profile of values of each of the six parameters outlined above. These features define the LFE, which is in one sense as much of a fiction as is "English." No individual speaker/writer of English actually produces all or only the LFE of his community. The nature of the LFE is a gross generalization perceived behind and through the idiolectal performance of individuals. They, in turn, are subject to other influences; it is essential to take these into account, because their performance makes up the LFE.

Variables Reflected in Individual Performance

A question now arises: How should we view the English actually used by an individual? He or she will have been subject to a degree of social pressure, which varies depending on community and personal history, to conform to a localized form of English — or not to do so:

perhaps to conform to some other model. This might be called the variable of *personal history*. It applies to both native and non-native speakers, though to differing extents.

In addition, the actual performance of the individual may be subject to *shortfall variations,* "shortfall" here in the sense of "not achieving mastery of the acrolect." Such variations are due to at least three causes.

Incomplete learning. Particularly for the non-native speaker, it will make a difference how early he got off the English-learning escalator. The difference between the performance of the Calcutta taxi driver and the Delhi professor of zoology is partly a consequence of the latter having spent more time under pressure to conform.[5]

Ineffective learning. Sometimes the effectiveness of learning, rather than its total duration, has the greatest influence in producing shortfall variations. Ineffectiveness may have its origins in poor teaching, poor learning, or both.

Tacit fossilization. It is very commonly observed that individuals cease to learn or to acquire a foreign language long before they have reached the presumed limits of their ability to do so. The phenomenon referred to by Selinker, Corder and others as *fossilization* is often of this kind: the individual decides he can manage his communication needs without further learning, so learning ceases. Or a learner, as part of his growing emotional and social maturity, identifies further language learning with unwelcome social, cultural, or political attitudes; he turns off his learning, temporarily or permanently. When communication needs change and increase, learning resumes. Most people learn as much or as little of a foreign language as they need — *not* as much as they are taught. In the case of the localized forms of English, the limited performance of individuals can frequently be ascribed to tacit fossilization, i.e., to an unspoken decision that what he has is sufficient for his needs.

The individual, then, will exhibit his personal set of features, probably within the overall description of the LFE, but certainly not identical to the whole of it. The nature of his idiolectal performance will be determined by (1) his *personal history,* and (2) his own personal set of *shortfall variations.*

Conclusion

Between the general envelope of "English" on the one hand, and the actual performance of the individual user of English on the other hand, we have considered two major concepts. The first is the notion of localized forms of English; these fall into two types, according to the needs and purposes of the community, and their description is the sum of a number of sociolinguistic variables. The second concept is that of two main types of variables that influence the individual's actual performance; they relate both to his degree of conformity to a localized form of English, and to his idiosyncrasy as a member of his English-using community.[6]

NOTES

1. The conventional terms *accent, dialect,* and *register* are of course useful in many ways. But they are insufficiently differentiated or delicate to accommodate all the distinctions required for the characterization of LFEs; nor do they allow all the necessary distinctions between individual speakers.

2. An obvious example of the latter category is India. The great railway system and the nation's posts, telephones, and telegraphic communications are run largely in English, but by Indians for whom English is not the native language.

3. This distinction is well known in the field of teaching English as a foreign or second language. L_2 INTER countries are those where the language is taught and learned as a *foreign* language; L_2 INTRA countries are those where English is taught as a *second* language. The reason for using a separate term is that *foreign* and *second* are terms from the profession of language teaching and are insufficiently subtle for the more precise descriptive task we are here engaged upon.

4. Standard English, it should be noted, is not imposed by any authority; there are no inherent moral reasons for valuing it more highly than other dialects; it is not the dialect used by the majority. Nevertheless, it is accorded high prestige in the educational world.

5. The same kind of difference, and the problem of how it should be regarded, lies at the center of Bernstein's (1967) sociolinguistic observations in the native-speaker situation.

6. The theoretical and methodological points discussed here are elaborated in the references listed below.

REFERENCES

Bernstein, B. 1967. Elaborated and restricted codes. In Lieberson (1967).

Bickerton, D. 1975. *Dynamics of a creole system.* London: Cambridge University Press.

Candlin, C. N. 1976. Communicative language teaching and the debt to pragmatics. In Rameh (1976).

Crewe, W. 1978. *The English language in Singapore.* Singapore: Eastern Universities Press.

Halliday, M. A. K. 1978. *Language as social semiotic.* London: Arnold.

———, and Hasan, R. 1976. *Cohesion in English.* London: Arnold.

Kachru, Braj B. 1965. The *Indianness* of Indian English. *Word* (21): 391-410.

———. 1976. Models of English for the Third World: white man's linguistic burden, or language pragmatics? *TESOL Quarterly* 10(2): 221-39.

————. 1981. The pragmatics of non-native varieties of English. In Smith, ed. (1981).

Lieberson, S., ed. 1967. *Explorations in sociolinguistics.* Publication 44, Indiana University Research Center in Anthropology, Folklore, and Linguistics. Bloomington, Indiana.

Quirk, R.; Greenbaum, S.; Leech, G.; and Svartvik, J. 1972. *A grammar of contemporary English.* (See especially introduction.) London: Longman.

Rameh, C., ed. 1976. *27th Round table monograph on languages and linguistics.* Washington, D.C.: Georgetown University Press.

Richards, Jack C. 1978a. *Understanding second and foreign language learning: a survey of issues and approaches.* Rowley, Mass.: Newbury House.

————. 1978b. Variation in Singapore English. In Crewe (1978).

Smith, Larry E., ed. 1981. *English for cross-cultural communication.* London: Macmillan.

Spencer, John. 1963. *Language in Africa.* London: Cambridge University Press.

Strevens, Peter. 1972. *British and American English.* London: Collier-Macmillan.

————. 1977. *New orientations in the teaching of English.* London: Oxford University Press.

————. 1978a. English as an international language: when is a local form of English a suitable target for teaching purposes? In *English as an international language.* London: British Council

————. 1978b. Forms of English: an analysis of the variables. In Smith, ed. (1981).

————. 1978c. The nature of language teaching. In Richards (1978a).

Tongue, R. K. 1974. *The English of Singapore and Malaysia.* Singapore: Eastern Universities Press.

3

Models for Non-Native Englishes

BRAJ B. KACHRU

In discussing the concept "model," a distinction has to be made between the use of this term in theory construction — for example, a *model* for linguistic description (see, e.g., Revzin 1966)—and its use in pedagogical literature, where *model* is sometimes interrelated with *method* (see, e.g., Brooks 1960; Christophersen 1973; Cochran 1954; Finnocchiaro 1964; Gauntlett 1957; Halliday et al. 1964; Lado 1964; and Stevick 1957).[1] In pedagogical literature the term "model" is used in two senses: first, in the sense of acceptability, generally by the native speakers of a language; second, in the sense of fulfilling codified prerequisites according to a given "standard" or "norm" at various linguistic levels. In this sense, then, we may say that a model provides a *proficiency scale*. This *scale* may be used to ascertain if a learner has attained proficiency according to a given norm. The term "norm" is again used in two senses: in one sense it entails prescriptivism, and in another it entails conformity with the usage of the majority of native speakers, defined statistically. (For a detailed discussion, see Lara 1976.)

Motivations for a Model

The question of a model for English has acquired immense pedagogical importance, mainly for two reasons. First, non-native varieties of English have emerged in areas such as South Asia (Kachru 1969 and later), Southeast Asia (Crewe 1977; Richards and Tay 1981), Africa (Spencer 1971a), the Philippines (Llamzon 1969), and the West Indies (Craig 1982; Haynes 1982). Second, in those areas where English is a native language, as in North America and Scotland, this question of model has often been raised with reference to bidialectism.

The identification of specific "non-standard" dialects leads to questions: Which dialect should be taught for what function? And what should be the role of bidialectism in the school system? These and related questions are being debated in educational and linguistic circles (see, e.g., Bailey 1970; Bernstein 1964; Burling 1970; Ellis 1967; Labov 1966, 1969; Riley 1978; Shuy 1971; Sledd 1969; Stewart 1970; and Wolfram 1970). Educators and linguists are also concerned about maintaining national and international intelligibility in various varieties of English (see, e.g., Christophersen 1960; Kachru 1976a; and Prator 1968).

We may discuss "model" either as a general concept, or as a language-specific concept. In language-specific terms, for example, as in the case of English, one has to discuss it in the context of sociocultural, educational, and political motivations for the spread of English. The term "spread" is used here to refer to "an increase, over time, in the proportion of a communications network that adopts a given language variety for given communicative function" (Cooper 1979: 23).

The question of a "model" is then also related to the question of language spread. In the case of the spread of English, one might ask, Does English have an organized agency which undertakes the job of providing direction toward a *standardized* model, and toward controlling *language change*—as is the case, for example, with French? Such attempts to control innovations or deviations from a "standard" in English through an Academy were not taken very seriously in Britain or in North America. The first such proposals by Jonathan Swift in Britain (around 1712) and by John Adams (in 1821; see Heath 1977) in America were not received with enthusiasm. One must then ask: In spite of the non-existence of an organized Academy, what factors have determined linguistic "etiquette" in English, and what models of acquisition have been suggested?

The documented models of English have no authority of codification from a government or a body of scholars as is the case, for example, with Spanish (see Bolinger 1975: 569) or French. The sanctity of models of English stems more from social and attitudinal factors than from reasons of authority. These models, more widely violated than followed, stand more for elitism than for authority—and in that sense they have a disadvantage. The native models of English were documented partly for pragmatic and pedagogical reasons. There was a demand from the non-native learners of English for materials on learning and teaching pronunciation, for standards of usage and correctness, and for linguistic "table manners" for identifying with native speakers.

Some native speakers also wanted "authoritative" or normative codes for "proper" linguistic behavior. Of course, there have always been linguistic entrepreneurs who have catered to such demands from consumers. In 1589 Puttenham recommended that the model should be the "usual speech of the court, and that of London and the shires lying about London within 60 miles and not much above." Cooper (1687) went a step further and provided such a book for "gentlemen, ladies, merchants, tradesmen, schools and strangers," with the enticing title *The English Teacher, or The Discovery of the Art of Teaching and Learning the English Tongue.*

This non-authoritarian elitist prescriptivism is also found in several manuals and books on usage. A typical title, following this tradition, is *The Grammarian; or The Writer and Speaker's Assistant; comprising shall and will made easy to foreigners, with instances of their misuse on the part of the natives of England.* This book by J. Beattie appeared in 1838. The often-quoted work on *Modern English Usage* by Fowler (1926) also belongs to this tradition. (See also, e.g., Alford 1869; Baker 1770; also relevant to this discussion are Hill 1954; Leonard 1929; Whitten and Whitaker 1939.)

In English when one talks of a model, the reference is usually to two well-documented models, namely Received Pronunciation (RP) and General American (GA). Non-native speakers of English often aim at a close approximation of these models, even at the risk of sounding affected. The works of Daniel Jones and John S. Kenyon encouraged such attempts. What Jones's *Outline of English Phonetics* (1918) or *English Pronouncing Dictionary* (1956) did for RP, Kenyon's *American Pronunciation* (1924) did for GA in a restricted sense.

What type of "standard" do these pronunciation norms provide? RP as a model is about a hundred years old, and is closely associated with the English public schools. Abercrombie, in his excellent paper, considers it unique "because the public schools are themselves unique" (1951: 12). Because it is acquired unconsciously, says Abercrombie, "there is no question of deliberately teaching it." The status of RP is based on social judgement and has no official authority. The advent of broadcasting played an important role in making RP widely known; it was therefore identified with the British Broadcasting Corporation (BBC) and also termed "BBC English" (see Gimson 1970: 83; Ward 1929: chs. 1, 2). In the changed British context, Abercrombie makes three points. First, the concept of a standard pronunciation such as RP is "a bad rather than a good thing. It is an anachronism in present-day democratic society" (1951: 14). Second, it provides an "accent-bar" which does not reflect the social reality of England. "The accent-bar is a little like colour-bar—to many people, on the right side of the bar, it appears eminently reasonable"

(1951: 15). Finally, RP does not necessarily represent "educated English," for while "those who talk RP can justly consider themselves educated, they are outnumbered these days by the undoubtedly educated people who do not talk RP" (1951: 15).

The term "General American" refers to the variety of English spoken by about 90 million people in the central and western United States and in most of Canada. (See Krapp 1919; Kenyon 1924: vii, 14.) In describing GA, Kenyon was not presenting a model in the same sense in which Jones had earlier presented his. Rather, Kenyon suggests linguistic tolerance toward various American varieties of English. He is conscious of the harm done by the elitist, prescriptivist manuals for pronunciation and therefore is concerned that "we accept rules of pronunciation as authoritative without inquiry into either the validity of the rules or the fitness of their authors to promulgate them" (1924: 3). The cause for such easy "judgment" or quick "advice" on matters connected with pronunciation is that people are "influenced by certain types of teaching in the schools, by the undiscriminating use of textbooks on grammar and rhetoric, by unintelligent use of the dictionary, by manuals of 'correct English,' each with its favorite (and different) shibboleth" (1924: 3).

Kenyon's distaste for linguistic homogeneity is clear when he says, "Probably no intelligent person actually expects cultivated people in the South, the East, and the West to pronounce alike. Yet much criticism, or politely silent contempt, of the pronunciations of cultivated people in other localities than our own is common" (1924: 5). In his view the remedy for this intolerance is the study of phonetics. A student of phonetics "soon learns not only to refrain from criticizing pronunciations that differ from his own, but to expect them and listen for them with respectful, intelligent interest."

Now, despite the arbitrariness of the above two models, one usually is asked the questions: What is a standard (or model) for English?[2] And what model should be accepted? The first question is easy, and Ward (1929: 1) has given the answer in crisp words: "No one can adequately define it, because such a thing does not exist." And, in the case of English, as Strevens (1981) says, "'standard' here does *not* imply 'imposed,' nor yet 'of the majority.' One interesting aspect of Standard English is that in every English-using community those who habitually use *only* standard English are in a minority."

Model and the Norm

It has generally been claimed (see, e.g., Bloomfield 1933: 56) that being bilingual entails having "native-like" proficiency in a language. A rigid application of this rather elusive yardstick is evident in the fast-increasing literature and growing number of texts for the teaching of English as L_2. It is more evident in the structural method which followed the tenets of structural linguistics in America. Consider for example the following, which is typical of such an attitude (see Lado 1964: 89):

> Authentic models: Teachers can now provide authentic pronunciation models easily for their students by means of a tape recorder or a phonograph. Visitors and professional speakers can be recorded for the benefit of students, thus bringing to the class a variety of good native speakers even when the teacher does not happen to be a native speaker of the target language.

In purely pedagogical methods, with no underlying serious theoretical framework, such as the structural method developed at the Institute of Education, London,[3] the same ideal goal for pronunciation was propounded.

One cannot disagree that the criterion of "native-like" control is appropriate for *most* language-learning situations. But then, one must pause and reconsider whether such a goal for performance can be applied to the case of English in *all* situations. The case of English is unique because of its global *spread* in various linguistically and culturally pluralistic societies; its differing *roles* in language planning in each English-using country; and the special historical factors involved in the introduction and diffusion of English in each English-speaking country. Therefore it is rather difficult to define the "norm" for various speakers of Englishes.

Origin of Non-Native Models

The origin of non-native models therefore must be related to what is termed "the context of situation"—the historical context, and the educational setting. Furthermore, it should be emphasized that the question of a "model" for English did not originally arise with reference to a model for "non-native" users of English. This issue has a rather interesting history, essentially with reference to the transplanted *native* varieties of English. The attitude of American English users provides a fascinating and illuminating controversy on this topic, which eventually turned into a national debate (see Heath 1977; Kahane and Kahane 1977).[4] This national debate provides a good case study of the relationship of political emancipation to language, and identification of language with nationalism. The controversy of the *American* identity of the English language has received more attention and therefore is better known, for which credit must be given to Mencken (1919). But in Britain itself there is the case of Scottish identity, and on a far-off continent, Australia, murmurs for such identity have been heard in an occasional publication.

In the case of *non-native* varieties, the situation is much different. There has never been a Mencken, or a Webster. The local identity for English was never related to political emancipation or national pride. On the contrary, the general idea was that, with the end of the Raj, the English language would be replaced by a native language or languages. The demand was not for an identity with English, but for abolition of English; not for nativization of English, but for its replacement. In recent years, however, the concept has been primarily discussed with reference to non-native Englishes. What do we understand by that term? The distinction between *native* and *non-native* varieties of English (Kachru 1981; Kachru and Quirk 1981) is crucial for understanding the formal and functional characteristics of English.

In the international context, it is more realistic to consider a spectrum of Englishes which vary widely, ranging from standard native varieties to standard non-native varieties (see Kachru 1976a, 1981, in press a; Quirk et al. 1972: 13-32). The situation of English is historically and linguistically interesting and complex for several reasons. First, the number of non-native speakers of English is significant; if the current trend continues, there will soon be more non-native than native speakers of English. At present there are 266 million native speakers and 115 million non-native speakers. That is, 33.1% of English speakers are non-native users. This figure, which includes only those who are enrolled in schools, therefore does not provide the total picture. Consider the following statement of distribution:[5]

Native Varieties (in millions)

British	American	Australian	Canadian	New Zealand
55	182	13	13	3

Non-Native Varieties (in millions)				
Asia (excl. USSR)	Africa	West and Central Europe	USSR	Western Hemisphere
60	20	15	10	10

The spread of English is unique in another respect. Because the language is used in geographically, linguistically, and culturally diverse areas, its use cuts across political boundaries (Fishman et al. 1977; Smith 1981). The large range of varieties of English cannot be discussed from any one point of view. There are several, mutually *non*-exclusive ways to discuss their form and function. One might, for example, consider them in *acquisitional* terms, in *socio-cultural* terms, in *motivational* terms, and in *functional* terms. These may further be divided as follows:

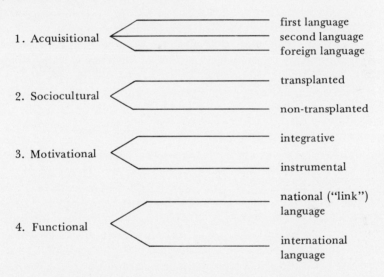

1. Acquisitional — first language / second language / foreign language

2. Sociocultural — transplanted / non-transplanted

3. Motivational — integrative / instrumental

4. Functional — national ("link") language / international language

A further distinction is necessary between English as a second language and English as a *foreign* language. (See Christophersen 1973: 30-31; Quirk et al. 1972: 3-4.) The second language varieties of English are essentially institutionalized varieties, as in, for example, South Asia and West Africa. The foreign language varieties are primarily performance varieties, as in Iran, Japan, etc. This distinction is also important with reference to the role and functions of English in the educational, administrative, and sociocultural context of a country in which English is used as a non-native language. The distinction between a transplanted variety (e.g., American English, Indian English) and a

non-transplanted variety is important for the understanding of the
acculturation and "nativization" of the transplanted varieties. (For
specific case studies see, e.g., Abdulaziz 1978; Bokamba 1982; Craig
1982; Haynes 1982; Kachru 1981 and in press a; Kandiah 1978;
Richards and Tay 1981; Wong 1981; and Zuengler 1982.)

In the literature, two types of motivations have been suggested
for second language acquisition: integrative and instrumental. The
distinction is essentially based on what function the L_2 learner en-
visions for the acquired language. If the learner's motivation is integrative, then the desire is "to identify with the members of the other
linguistic cultural group and be willing to take on very subtle aspects
of their language *or even their style of speech*" (Prator 1968: 474;
his italics). On the other hand, the instrumental approach has been
defined as basically "utilitarian"; a language is acquired as a linguistic tool, not as an instrument for cultural integration. Terms such as
library language, *auxiliary* language, *link* language, or language for
special purposes (LSP) are essentially utilitarian concepts, in which
language is seen as a "restricted" code for a specific goal. In such
contexts, acquiring a second culture is not the main motivation for
learning the language. (See also Christophersen 1973.)

If we look at the global spectrum of English as a *non-native*
language, we can clearly divide, as stated earlier, the non-native uses
of English into two broad categories, namely, the performance varieties and the institutionalized varieties. This distinction is extremely
useful and is directly related to the question of a model.

The Performance Varieties

Performance varieties include essentially those varieties which
are used as *foreign* languages. Identificational modifiers, such as
Japanese English or *Iranian* English, are indicative of geographical
or national performance characteristics. These do not indicate an
institutionalized status. The performance varieties of English have
a highly restricted functional range in specific contexts; for example,
those of tourism, commerce, and other international transactions.

Institutionalized Varieties

It is the institutionalized varieties which have some ontological
status. The main characteristics of such varieties are that (a) they
have an extended range of uses in the sociolinguistic context of a
nation; (b) they have an extended register and style range; (c) a process of *nativization* of the registers and styles has taken place, both
in formal and in contextual terms; and (d) a body of nativized En-

glish literature has developed which has formal and contextual characteristics which mark it *localized.* On the other hand, such a body of writing is considered a part of the larger body of writing labeled English literature.

An institutionalized variety always starts as a performance variety, with various characteristics slowly giving it a different status. The main characteristics of an institutionalized variety seem to be (a) the length of time in use; (b) the extension of use; (c) the emotional attachment of L_2 users with the variety; (d) functional importance; and (e) sociolinguistic status. In the development of non-native models two processes seem to work simultaneously: the *attitudinal* process, and the *linguistic* process.

A non-native model may be treated as a competitive model for teaching English as L_2 if it fulfills certain conditions. In attitudinal terms, a majority of L_2 speakers should identify themselves with the modifying label which marks the non-nativeness of a model: for example, *Indian* English speakers, *Lankan* English speakers, *Ghanaian* English speakers. A person may be a user of *Indian* English in his linguistic behavior but may not consider it the "norm" for his linguistic performance. There is thus a confusion between linguistic norm and linguistic behavior.

In linguistic terms, a viable model should describe the formal characteristics of a *generally acceptable* variety. If English is used in a culturally and linguistically pluralistic context, the norm for the model should cut across linguistic and cultural boundaries. It is natural that in such a variety a part of the lexicon will have been nativized in two ways. On the one hand, native items will be used in localized registers and styles to contextualize the language. On the other hand, English lexical items may have acquired extended or restricted semantic markers. This process then extends to other levels of language, as has been shown in several studies. (See, e.g., Kachru 1981 and in press a.)

Development of Non-Native Models

The term "development" is used here not in the Darwinian sense, but in an essentially historical sense. I shall attempt to discuss it with reference to changing attitudes toward a model, in terms of a scale of acceptance. A variety may exist, but unless it is *recognized* and *accepted* as a model it does not acquire a status. A large majority of the non-native speakers of institutionalized varieties of English use a local variety of English, but when told so, they are hesitant to accept the fact.

The non-native institutionalized varieties of English seem to pass through several phases which are not mutually exclusive. At the initial stage there is a *non-recognition* of the local variety, and conscious identification with the native speakers. In South Asian terms, it may be called the *brown sahib* attitude. A "brown sahib" is more English than the Englishman; he identifies with the "white sahib" in manners, speech, and attitude, and feels that his brown or black color is a burden. At this stage an "imitation model" is elitist, powerful, and perhaps politically advantageous, since it identifies a person with the rulers. This is also the stage when English is associated with the colonizer, and therefore may be a symbol of anti-nationalism.

The second stage is related to extensive diffusion of bilingualism in English, which slowly leads to the development of varieties *within* a variety. The tendency then is to claim that the *other* person is using the *Indianized, Ghanaianized,* or *Lankanized* English. The local model is still low on the attitudinal scale, though it may be widely used in various functions. South Asia provides an excellent example of this attitude. In India, for example, the norm for English was unrealistic and (worse) unavailable — the British variety. In actual performance, typical *Indian* English was used. But to have one's English labeled *Indian* was an ego-cracking linguistic insult.

The third stage starts when the non-native variety is slowly accepted as the norm, and the division between the linguistic norm and behavior is reduced. The final stage seems to be that of *recognition.* This recognition may manifest itself in two ways; first in attitudinal terms, when one does not necessarily show a division between linguistic norm and linguistic behavior. This indicates linguistic realism and attitudinal identification with the variety. Only during the last twenty years or so do we find this attitude developing among the users of non-native varieties of English. Second, the teaching materials are *contextualized* in the native sociocultural milieu. One then begins to recognize the national uses (and importance) of English, and to consider its international uses only marginal.

The literature provides enough evidence that the institutionalized varieties of English have passed through one or more of these stages in Africa, South Asia, Southeast Asia, or the Philippines. I shall not elaborate on this point here.

Functional Uses of Non-Native Englishes

I have earlier used the term "context of situation" without explaining it in the context of the English L_2 situation. There is a relationship between the *context of situation,* the sociolinguistic profile, and the pedagogical model. Before claiming universality for a model, one must understand that what is linguistic medicine for one geographical area may prove linguistic poison for another area.

A sociolinguistic profile should consider the type of information suggested in Catford (1959: 141-42), and in Ferguson (1966: 309-15). The linguistically relevant information is as important as are the political, geographical, and economic factors. In addition, the attitudinal reactions toward an *external* or an *internal* model cannot be neglected. I shall return to that point in the two following sections.

The sociolinguistic context might show a cline (a graded series) both in terms of *proficiency* in English and in its *functional* uses. The English-using community must be seen in a new framework, in which a linguistic activity is under analysis within a specific sociocultural context. Within the framework of *user* and *uses* one has to take into consideration cline of participants, cline of roles, and cline of intelligibility.

Without the perspective of this relationship it is difficult for native speakers of English to understand the uses of non-native Englishes. This type of approach has been used and recommended in several studies. (See especially Candlin 1981; Kachru 1965, 1966, 1981, in press a and b; Richards and Tay 1981.)

The institutionalized varieties of non-native English may be arranged along a lectal continuum. This continuum is not necessarily *developmental* but may be functional. All subvarieties within a variety (for example, basilects, mesolects and acrolects) have functional values, and may stand as clues to code diversity as well as to code development. These are, however, not mutually exclusive.

Let me now briefly elaborate on the functional aspects of a cline. One can claim that, for example, in South Asia, English is used in four functions: the *instrumental,* the *regulative,* the *interpersonal,* and the *imaginative/innovative.*[6] In each function we have a cline in performance which varies from what may be termed an "educated" or "standard" variety to a pidginized or "broken" variety. The varieties *within* a variety also seem to perform their functions, as they do in any native variety of English. (For details see Brook 1973; Kachru 1981, esp. subsection on "The Cline of Varieties"; and Quirk et al. 1972: 13-32.)

A discussion on the non-native uses of English in "un-English" contexts will entail presenting several sociolinguistic profiles relevant to a number of institutionalized varieties of English. Since I have not set that as my goal here, I will merely provide a general view of the possible functional range of non-native varieties of English.

In the case of some varieties, the English language is used in all four functions mentioned earlier. The *instrumental function* is performed by English as a medium of learning at various stages in the educational system of the country. The *regulative function* entails use of English in those contexts in which language is used to regulate conduct; for example, the legal system and administration. The *interpersonal function* is performed in two senses: first, as a *link* language between speakers of various (often mutually unintelligible) languages and dialects in linguistically and culturally pluralistic societies; and second, by providing a code which symbolizes modernization and elitism (see Sridhar 1982). The *imaginative/innovative function* refers to the use of English in various literary *genres*. In this function, the non-native users of English have shown great creativity in using the English language in "unEnglish" contexts. This aspect of non-native Englishes has unfortunately not attracted much attention from linguists, but has now been taken seriously by literary scholars.[7] (See Kachru in press b.)

The Range and Depth of Functional Uses

The functional uses of the non-native varieties extend in two senses. The term "range" means the extension of English into various cultural, social, educational, and commercial contexts. The wider the range, the greater the variety of uses. By "depth" we mean the penetration of English-knowing bilingualism to various societal levels. One has to consider, for example, whether bilingualism in English is restricted to the urban upper and middle classes, or whether it has penetrated to other societal levels, too. What are the implications of these functions, and their range and depth, for a model?

The degrees of *nativization* of a variety of English are related to two factors: the range and depth of the functions of English in a non-native context, and the period for which the society has been exposed to bilingualism in English. The greater the number of functions and the longer the period, the more nativized is the variety. The nativization has two manifestations, cultural and linguistic, with "cultural" here referring to the acculturation of English. The result is that, both culturally and formally, the English language comes closer to the socio-cultural context of what may be termed the *adopted* "context of situation." This new, changed "context of situation" contributes to the deviations from what originally might have been a linguistic "norm" or "model."

Attitude of Native and Non-Native Users
toward Non-Native Varieties

In view of the unique developments and functions of the institutionalized non-native varieties of English, one might ask: What has been the attitude of native speakers and native users of English toward such non-native Englishes? The native speakers' attitude toward the development and the nativization of institutionalized varieties has traditionally not been one of acceptance or ontological recognition. Because of the linguistic manifestation of the nativization, these varieties have been considered *deficient* models of language acquisition. This attitude has not been restricted to speech performance, but extends to lexical and collocational items which are determined by the *new* sociocultural context in which the English language is used in Africa or Asia. It seems that the contextual *dislocation* (or transplantation) of English has not been recognized as a valid reason for "deviations" and innovations. Thus, the parameters for making judgments on the formal and functional uses of English continue to be culturally and linguistically ethnocentric, though the pragmatic context for such Englishes is "un-English" and "non-native" (see Kachru 1981, in press a). A decade ago, I mentioned with some elation (Kachru 1969) that with World War II a new attitude of "linguistic tolerance" had developed, which was reflected in proclamations such as "hands off pidgins" (Hall 1955) and "status for colonial Englishes." Now, a decade later, this statement warrants a postscript with reference to colonial Englishes. One has to qualify the earlier statement and say that this attitude was restricted to two circles. First, a body of literary scholars slowly started to recognize and accept the commonwealth literature in English written by non-native users of the language as a noteworthy linguistic and literary activity. Britain was somewhat earlier in this recognition. Second, a few British linguists, notably Firth (1957: 97), Halliday et al. (1964), Strevens (1977: 140), and Quirk et al. (1972: 26), accept the linguistic and functional distinctiveness of the institutionalized non-native varieties. It seems that even in America the linguistic fringe has been rather slow in providing such recognition and looking at these varieties in a pragmatic perspective. (For a detailed discussion, see Kachru 1976a, 1981, in press a and b.)

The non-native speakers themselves have not yet been able to accept what may be termed the "ecological validity" of their *nativized* or *local* Englishes. One would have expected such acceptance, given the acculturation and linguistic nativization of the new varieties. On the other hand, the *non*-native models of English (such as

RP or GA) are not accepted without reservations. There is thus a case of linguistic schizophrenia, the underlying causes of which have yet to be studied. Consider, for example, the following tables. (For details, see Kachru 1976a.)

Table 1. Indian Graduate Students' Attitude toward Various Models of English and Ranking of Models According to Preference

Model	Preference		
	I	II	III
American English	5.17	13.19	21.08
British English	67.60	9.65	1.08
Indian English	22.72	17.82	10.74
I don't care		5.03	
"Good" English		1.08	

Table 2. Faculty Preference for Models of English for Instruction

Model	Preference		
	I	II	III
American English	3.07	14.35	25.64
British English	66.66	13.33	1.53
Indian English	26.66	25.64	11.79
I don't know		5.12	

Table 3. Graduate Students' Self-Labeling of the Variety of Their English

Identity marker	%
American English	2.58
British English	29.11
Indian English	55.64
"Mixture" of all three	2.99
I don't know	8.97
"Good" English	.27

What does such an attitude imply? In Ghana, for example, *educated* Ghanaian English is acceptable; but as Sey (1973: 1) warns us, it does not entail competence in speaking RP since in Ghana "the type that strives too obviously to approximate to RP is frowned upon as distasteful and pedantic." In Nigeria the situation is not different from Ghana or India (see Kachru 1976a). Bamgboṣe (1971: 41) emphasizes that "the aim is not to produce speakers of British Received Pronunciation (even if this were feasible!) . . . Many Nigerians will consider as affected or even snobbish any Nigerians who speak like a native speaker of English." In another English-using country, the Philippines, the model for "Standard Filipino English" is *the type of English which educated Filipinos speak and which is acceptable in educated Filipino circles"* (Llamzon 1969: 15). There seems to be some agreement that an *external* model does not suit the linguistic and sociolinguistic ecology of Africa, the Philippines, or South Asia.

Deviation, Mistake, and the Norm

I have used the term "deviation" in this study and earlier (Kachru 1965: 396-98) with reference to the linguistic and contextual *nativeness* in the non-native varieties of English. This term needs further elucidation since it is crucial to our understanding of the question of the model. The inevitable questions concerning the linguistic and contextual deviation are: What is the distinction between a "deviation" and a "mistake"? And, how much deviation from the norm is acceptable pedagogically, linguistically, and (above all) with reference to intelligibility?

We shall make a distinction between the terms "mistake" and "deviation" on linguistic and contextual levels. A "mistake" may be unacceptable by a native speaker since it does not belong to the linguistic "norm" of the English language; it cannot be justified with reference to the sociocultural context of a non-native variety; and it is not the result of the productive processes used in an institutionalized non-native variety of English. On the other hand, a "deviation" has the following characteristics: it is different from the norm in the sense that it is the result of the new "un-English" linguistic and cultural setting in which the English language is used; it is the result of a productive process which marks the typical variety-specific features; and it is systemic within a variety, and not idiosyncratic. There is thus an explanation for each deviation within the context of situation. It can be shown that a large number of deviations "deviate" only with reference to an idealized norm. A number of "deviations" labeled as "mistakes" are present in native varieties of English but are not accepted when used by a non-native speaker.

In earlier studies on the non-native Englishes by educators, specialists in the teaching of English, and native speakers in general, the deviations in such varieties of English have been treated essentially as "deficiencies" in foreign language learning (e.g., Goffin 1934, Passé 1947, and Smith-Pearse 1934 for South Asian English; Hocking 1974 for African English). It seems to me that a crucial distinction is warranted between a deficient variety and a different variety. Deficiency refers to acquisitional and/or performance deficiency within the context in which English functions as L_2. On the other hand, a different model refers to the *identificational* features which mark an educated variety of language distinct from another educated variety. The exponents of "difference" may be at one or more linguistic levels. The following examples from South Asian English illustrate identificational features.

1. *Phonetics/Phonology*
   (a) *Series substitution* involves substitution of the retroflex consonant series for the English alveolar series.
   (b) *Systemic membership substitution* involves the substitution of members in a system with members of another class; for example, the use of stops in place of fricative θ and ð, or substitution of "clear l" for "dark l."
   (c) *Rhythmic interference* entails the use of syllable-timed rhythm in place of the stress-timed rhythm of English (see Nelson 1982).

2. *Grammar*
   I shall list some characteristics discussed earlier in Kachru (1965, 1969, 1976b). A discussion on African varieties of English is available in Bokamba (1982), Bamgboṣe (1982), Sey (1973), and Zuengler (1982).
   (a) There is tendency to use complex sentences.
   (b) Selection restrictions are "violated" in *be + ing* constructions (e.g., use of *hear* and *see* in *I am hearing, I am seeing*).
   (c) A "deviant" pattern appears in the use of articles.
   (d) Reduplication is common (e.g., *small small things, hot hot tea*).
   (e) Interrogatives are formed without changing the position of subject and auxiliary items (e.g., *What you would like to eat?*)

3. *Lexis*

The productive processes used in lexis have been discussed, for example, in Sey (1973), Kachru (1965, 1975, 1981) and Llamzon (1969). The term "lexis" includes here what may be termed non-native collocations (Kachru 1965: 403-5). Consider, for example, *turmeric ceremony, dung-wash, caste mark, police wala,* and *lathi charge* from Indian English, *chewing-sponge, cover-shoulder, knocking fee, dunno drums,* and *bodom head* from Ghanaian English.

4. *Cohesiveness*

Discussion of phonology, grammar, and lexis presents only one part of the total picture of the difference between "deficient" and "different" in a non-native variety. It is equally important to account for the following:

(a) the cohesive characteristics of the text which mark it distinct, for example, in terms of its Nigerianness, Kenyanness, Indianness, or Caribbeanness;

(b) the lexical and grammatical features which mark the register type and the style type;

(c) the features which separate the literary genres of one non-native variety from another non-native variety.

The focus is then on setting up a relationship between the communication domains or contexts and their formal manifestations.

A non-native variety is "deviant" not only in having specific phonetic, lexical, or grammatical characteristics, but it is also "deviant" as a communicative unit, if we compare it with other native or non-native communicative units. It is therefore necessary to establish what Firth terms a "renewal of connection" (see Firth 1956: 99 and 1957: 175) between the "interpretive context" ("the context of situation"), which gives the text a meaning, and its formal characteristics. The "differences" in each institutionalized non-native variety may thus be viewed in a larger context, which incorporates the "context of situation," and not purely from the view of language deficiency. (See figure.)

If one adopts a functional view of the institutionalized varieties, it might help to abandon earlier views about two very important questions concerning intelligibility and the applicability of a monomodel approach to all the non-native varieties of English. I shall now discuss these briefly.

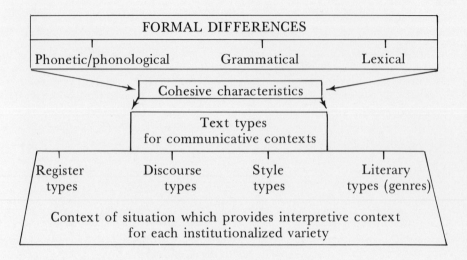

Model vs. Intelligibility

In the prescriptive literature on second language acquisition,
the concepts "norm" or "model" seem to play a pivotal role, primarily with regard to the non-native speaker's being "intelligible"
to native speakers of English. The concept of "intelligibility" is the
least researched and least understood in linguistic or pedagogical
literature (see Kachru 1981; Nelson 1982). The difficulty is that intelligibility seems to have a number of variables, and when used
with reference to English it becomes more elusive. Therefore we
must use the term in a specific sense. The questions one has to ask
are: What is meant by intelligibility with reference to each linguistic
level? Who is the judge for determining intelligibility in various varieties of English — the users of the varieties themselves, or the idealized native speakers? What parameters should be used to distinguish
intelligibility between those varieties of English which are essentially
regional or national (e.g., Indian English), and those varieties within
a variety which have exclusively *international* functions? What role
does a native speaker of English (and what type of native speaker)
play concerning the judgment about the non-native varieties? What
is the relationship between intelligibility of formal (linguistic) exponents and the contextual exponents?

"Intelligibility" has been interpreted in a rather narrow sense
in earlier studies. Such studies have focused primarily on decoding
a phonetic/phonological signal at the lexical level. Earlier studies,

especially those of Catford (1950) and Voegelin and Harris (1951), mentioned the importance of "situation" and "effectiveness" in intelligibility. Nelson (1982) attempts to provide the parameters of intelligibility for non-native Englishes.

The intelligibility of the institutionalized non-native varieties of English forms a cline. Some speakers are more intelligible than are others, the variables being education, role, region, etc. The situation in the non-native varieties is not different from that in Britain or the U.S.A. The situation in Britain has been succinctly presented by Ward:

> It is obvious that in a country the size of the British Isles, any one speaker should be capable of understanding any other when he is talking English. At the present moment, such is not the case: a Cockney speaker would not be understood by a dialect speaker of Edinburgh or Leeds or Truro, and dialect speakers of much nearer districts than these would have difficulty in understanding each other.

In a well-known cone-shaped diagram (see Ward 1929: 5) Daniel Jones has graphically represented the situation: "as we near the apex, the divergencies which still exist have become so small as to be noticed only by a finely trained ear" (Ward 1929: 6). Ward also rightly presents the argument of "convenience or expediency" (1929: 7), observing that "the regional dialect may suffice for those people who have no need to move from their own districts."

The case seems to be identical to that of non-native varieties of English. Intelligibility then has to be defined in regional, national, and international terms.

Monomodel vs. Polymodel Approach

In view of the special characteristics of the English speech community in various parts of the world, the pragmatic question is: Is it possible to suggest a monomodel approach, as opposed to a polymodel approach (Kachru 1977)? A monomodel approach presupposes that there is a homogeneous English L_2 speech community, and that the functional roles assigned to English in each area are more or less identical. More important, it assumes that the goals for the study of English in various parts of the world are more or less similar. Such a position presupposes that the "context of situation" for the use of English in all the English-speaking areas is identical. It has already been demonstrated that such is not the case (see, e.g., Kachru 1976, 1981; Richards 1972; Strevens 1977).

The assumptions underlying a *polymodel* approach are diametrically opposed to the *monomodel* approach. A polymodel approach is based upon pragmatism and functional realism. It presupposes three types of variability in teaching English for cross-cultural communications; namely, variability related to *acquisition,* variability related to *function,* and variability related to the *context of situation.* We may then have to recognize a *cline* in terms of the formal characteristics of an L$_2$ variety of English; *functional* diversity in each English speaking area; and diversity in *proficiency.*

The concept of "cline of bilingualism" (Kachru 1965: 393-96) may, therefore, be recognized as fundamental for the discussion of a model for English. The cline applies not only to the proficiency at the phonetic/phonological levels; it must also be interpreted in a broader sense, including the overall sociolinguistic context.

Conclusion

And now, in conclusion, let us face reality. The truth is that the non-native Englishes — institutionalized or non-institutionalized — are linguistic orphans in search of their parents. Several native and non-native users of English do not understand that they are adding insult to injury by calling these varieties "deficient Englishes." The development of such varieties is not unique to English; in a lesser degree Hindi, Persian, French, and Spanish have also developed such transplanted varieties.

The problem is that even when the non-native models of English are linguistically identifiable, geographically definable, and functionally valuable, they are still not necessarily attitudinally acceptable. There is an "accent bar" which continues to segregate the non-native users. The acceptance of a model depends on its users: the users must demonstrate a solidarity, identity, and loyalty toward a language variety. In the past, the Americans demonstrated it (though not unanimously), and the result is a vigorous and dynamic *American* English. But then, when it comes to recognizing and accepting the varieties within American English, or accepting other non-native Englishes, Americans have shown reluctance, condescension, or indifference. The users of non-native varieties also seem to pass through linguistic schizophrenia, unable to decide whether to accept a mythical non-native model, or to recognize the local functional model instead.

I must also mention the unique international position of English, which is certainly unparalleled in the history of the world.

For the first time a natural language has attained the status of an international (universal) language, essentially for cross-cultural communication. Whatever the reasons for the earlier spread of English, we should now consider it a positive development in the twentieth-century world context. We should realize that this new role of English puts a burden on those who use it as their *first* language, as well as on those who use it as their *second* language. This responsibility demands what may be termed "attitudinal readjustment." I have elsewhere discussed "the seven attitudinal sins" (Kachru 1976a: 223-29) which the native speakers are committing in their attitude toward the non-native varieties; a classic case is presented in Prator (1968).

The non-native users' attitudinal readjustment toward English entails the following acts, among others. First, non-native users must now dissociate English from the colonial past, and not treat it as a colonizer's linguistic tool.

Second, they must avoid regarding English as an evil influence which necessarily leads to Westernization. In South Asia and Africa the role of English in developing nationalism and mobilizing the intelligentsia at large for struggles toward freedom cannot be overemphasized. Although it is true that such use of English has resulted in a linguistic elitism, that has also been true in the past of Sanskrit and Persian, and recently of Hindi.

Third, non-native users should accept the large body of English literature written by local creative writers as part of the native literary tradition. Indian English literature, West African English literature, and Philippine English literature not only have pannational reading publics, but have also become part of a larger body of world writing in English. These literatures not only interpret the national traditions and aspirations to readers across linguistically and culturally pluralistic areas; in addition, they have an international reading public. (See, e.g., for Indian English literature, Kachru 1976b: 168-73, 1978a, 1978b, and in press b; Lal 1969: i-cliv; for other literatures in English see Bailey and Görlach, in press.)

Fourth, it is important to distinguish between the national and the international uses of English. It is primarily the national uses of the institutionalized varieties which contribute toward the nativization of these varieties.

Fifth, non-native users ought to develop an identity with the local model of English without feeling that it is a "deficient" model. The local (non-native) models of English are functionally as much a part of the linguistic repertoire of people as are the native (non-Western) languages. After all, in Asia or Africa it is not unusual to find that the number of users of English exceeds the number of speakers of several of what the Indian constitution terms "scheduled languages" (or nationally recognized languages). In India, the number of English-using bilinguals is about 3 percent of the total population; the numbers of speakers of six scheduled languages are close to or even much less than this figure, i.e., Assamese (1.63%), Kannada (3.96%), Kashmiri (0.45%), Malayalam (4%), Oriya (3.62%), and Punjabi (3%).

The international profile of the functions of English is encouraging: we may at last have a universal language as an offshoot of the colonial period. In this context, two questions may be asked. First, is there a coordinating agency which has a realistic view of the international and national functions of English? Second, do the non-native users of English feel that any significant theoretical and methodological leadership is being provided by those British or U.S. agencies which are involved in the teaching or diffusion of English? The answers to these questions, while not discussed in this chapter, are closely related to our concern for studying English in the world context.

NOTES

1. I am grateful to several agencies for their support of my research on this and related topics on non-native varieties of English, specifically to the Research Board of the Graduate College and the Center for International Comparative Studies, both of the University of Illinois at Urbana-Champaign. This is a revision of a paper presented at a conference on "Progress in Language Planning," Language Research Center, William Paterson College, April 30-May 1, 1979.

2. I should mention that other models, such as Scottish (English) or Australian, have been suggested in the literature. But the main viable models in the past have been RP and GA.

3. The term "structural" in this method is not related to structural linguistics as understood in North America or in Britain.

4. Also see Jones (1965) for a survey of the "triumph" of English and "a history of ideas concerning the English tongue — its nature, use, and improvement — during the period 1476-1660."

5. See Gage and Ohannessian (1977).

6. My view of these four terms is somewhat different from that of Basil Bernstein, who originally used these terms. The functional model proposed in Halliday (1973) extends the model to nine language functions: *instrumental, regulatory, interactional, personal, heuristic, imaginative, representative* or *informative, ludic,* and *ritual.*

7. This fast-growing body of writing provides impressive evidence for linguistic and contextual nativization of the English language. The result is the development of English literatures with areal modifiers, such as *West African*

English literature, *Indian* English literature, *Caribbean* English literature, and so on. These modifiers convey not only the geographical variation, but also the cultural and sociolinguistic attitudes. These literatures are one manifestation of the national literatures in multilingual and multicultural non-Western English-using nations. In India, for example, one can claim that there are only three languages in which pan-Indian literature is produced with an *all-India* reading public: English, Sanskrit, and Hindi (Kachru 1981). For a detailed bibliography on commonwealth literature in English, specifically in Africa, India, and the West Indies, see Narasimhaiah (1976).

REFERENCES

Abdulaziz, M. 1978. Influence of English on Swahili: a case study of language development. Paper presented at the Conference on English in Non-Native Contexts, University of Illinois, Urbana.

Abercrombie, D. 1951. R.P. and local accent. *The Listener,* 6 September 1951. [Reprinted in Abercrombie, D., *Studies in phonetics and linguistics.* London: Oxford University Press.]

Alatis, J., ed. 1969. *Georgetown monograph on language and linguistics.* Washington D.C.: Georgetown University Press.

――――, ed. 1978. International dimensions of bilingual education. Georgetown University roundtable on languages and linguistics, 1978. Washington D.C.: Georgetown University Press.

――――, and G. R. Tucker, eds. 1979. Language in public life. Georgetown University roundtable on languages and linguistics, 1979. Washington D.C.: Georgetown University Press.

Alford, H. 1869. A plea for the Queen's English. London: Strahan.

Avis, W. S. 1967. A dictionary of Canadianisms on historical principles. Toronto.

Bailey, B. L. 1970. Some arguments against the use of dialect readers in the teaching of initial reading. *Florida FL Reporter* Spring/Fall 3: 47.

Bailey, R. W., and Görlach, M. Forthcoming. English as a world language.

Baker, R. 1770. Reflections on the English language. 2nd edition (1779) entitled 'Remarks on . . .' London: Bell.

Bamgboṣe, A. 1971. The English language in Nigeria. In Spencer (1971a).

――――. MS. Issues in the investigation of a standard Nigerian English.

Bazell, C. E., et al., eds. 1966. *In memory of J. R. Firth.* London: Longmans.

Beattie, J. 1838. The grammarian; or, the writer and speaker's assistant; comprising shall and will made easy to foreigners, with instances of their misuse on the part of the natives of England. London.

Bernstein, B. 1964. Elaborated and restricted codes: their social origins and some consequences. *American Anthropologist* 66: 55-69.

Bloomfield, L. 1933. *Language.* New York: Holt, Rinehart and Winston.

Bokamba, E. MS. The Africanization of English.

Bolinger, D. 1975. *Aspects of language.* New York: Harcourt Brace Jovanovich.

Bright, W., ed. 1966. *Sociolinguistics: proceedings of the UCLA sociolinguistics conferences, 1964.* The Hague: Mouton.

Brook, G. L. 1973. *Varieties of English.* London: Macmillan.

Brooks, N. 1960. *Language and language learning: theory and practice.* New York: Harcourt, Brace and World.

Burling, R. 1970. Colloquial and standard written English: some implications for teaching literacy to non-standard speakers. *Florida FL Reporter* Spring/Fall: 9-15, 47.

Candlin, C. 1981. Discoursal patterning and the equalising of interpretive opportunity. In Smith (1981).

Catford, J. C. 1950. Intelligibility. *English Language Teaching* 1: 7-15.

———. 1959. The teaching of English as a foreign language. In *The teaching of English*, ed. R. Quirk and A. H. Smith. London: Martin, Secker and Warburg. [Reprinted London: Oxford University Press, 1964.]

Christophersen, P. 1960. Toward a standard of international English. *English Language Teaching* 14: 127-38.

———. 1973. *Second-language learning: myth and reality*. Harmondsworth: Penguin.

Cochran, A. 1954. *Modern methods of teaching English as a foreign language: a guide to modern material with particular reference to the Far East*. Washington, D.C.: Educational Services.

Cooper, R. L. 1979. Language planning, language spread, and language change. In *Language in public life*, ed. J. Alatis and G. R. Tucker. Washington: Georgetown University Press.

Craig, D. 1982. Toward a description of Caribbean English. In this volume.

Crewe, W., ed. 1977. *The English language in Singapore*. Singapore: Eastern Universities Press.

Ellis, D. S. 1967. Speech and social status in America. *Social Forces* 45: 431-37.

Ferguson, C. A. 1966. National sociolinguistic profile formulas. In *Sociolinguistics: proceedings of the UCLA sociolinguistic conference, 1964*. The Hague: Mouton.

Finnocchiaro, M. 1964. *English as a second language from theory to practice*. New York: Regents.

Firth, J. R. 1956. Descriptive linguistics and the study of English. In Palmer (1968).

———. 1957. A synopsis of linguistic theory, 1930-55. In Palmer (1968).

Fishman, R., Cooper, R. L., and Conrad, A. W. 1977. *The spread of English*. Rowley, Mass.: Newbury House.

Fowler, H. W. 1926. *A dictionary of modern English usage*. London: Oxford University Press.

Gage, W. W., and Ohannessian, S. 1977. ESOL enrollments throughout the world. *Linguistic Reporter* November. [Reprinted in *English Teaching Forum* July 1977.]

Gauntlett, J. O. 1957. *Teaching English as a foreign language*. London: Macmillan.

Gimson, A. C. 1962. *An introduction to the pronunciation of English*. London: Edward Arnold.

Goffin, R. C. 1934. *Some notes on Indian English*. S.P.E. Tract No. 41. Oxford.

Hall, R. A. 1955. *Hands off pidgin English!* Sydney: Pacific.

Halliday, M. A. K. 1973. *Explorations in the functions of language*. London: Edward Arnold.

———, McIntosh, A.; and Strevens, P. 1964. The linguistic sciences and language teaching. London: Longmans.

Haynes, L. 1982. Caribbean English: form and function. In this volume.

Heath, S. B. 1977. A national language academy? Debate in the nation. *Linguistics: An International Review* 189: 9-43.

Hill, A. A. 1954. Prescriptivism and linguistics in language teaching. *College English* 15 (April): 395-99. [Reprinted in H. Allen, ed., *Readings in applied English linguistics.* New York: Appleton-Century, 1958.]

Hocking, B. D. W. 1974. *All what I was taught and other mistakes: a handbook of common errors in English.* Nairobi: Oxford University Press.

Jones, D. 1918. *An outline of English phonetics.* [Rev. ed., 1956.] Cambridge: Heffer.

———. 1956. *Everyman's English pronouncing dictionary.* London: Dent.

Jones, R. F. 1965. *The triumph of the English language.* Stanford: Stanford University Press.

Kachru, B. B. 1965. The Indianness in Indian English. *Word* 21: 391-410.

———. 1966. Indian English: a study in contextualization. *In memory of J. R. Firth,* ed. C. E. Bazell, J. C. Catford, M. A. K. Halliday, R. H. Robins. London: Longman.

———. 1969. English in South Asia. In *Current trends in linguistics,* V, ed. T. Sebeok. The Hague: Mouton.

———. 1973. Toward a lexicon of Indian English. In *Issues in linguistics: papers in honor of Henry and Renée Kahane,* ed. B. B. Kachru, R. B. Lees, Y. Malkiel, A. Pietrangeli, S. Saporta. Urbana: University of Illinois Press.

———. 1975. Lexical innovations in South Asian English. *International Journal of the Sociology of Language* 4: 55-94.

———. 1976a. Models of English for the third world: white man's linguistic burden or language pragmatics? *TESOL Quarterly* 10(2): 221-39.

———. 1976b. Indian English: a sociolinguistic profile of a transplanted language. In *Dimensions of bilingualism: theory and case studies.* Special issue of *Studies in Language Learning.* Urbana: Unit for Foreign Language Study and Research, University of Illinois.

———. 1977. The new Englishes and old models. *English Language Forum* July 15(3): 29-35.

———. 1978a. Toward structuring code-mixing: an Indian perspective. In *Aspects of sociolinguistics in South Asia,* special issue of *International Journal of the Sociology of Language* 16: 27-46.

———. 1978b. Toward structuring code-mixing: an Indian perspective. In *International dimensions of bilingual education,* ed. J. Alatis. Washington: Georgetown University Press.

———. 1979. The Englishization of Hindi: language rivalry and language change. In *Linguistic method: essays in honor of Herbert Penzl,* ed. I. Rauch and G. Carr. The Hague: Mouton.

———. 1981. The pragmatics of non-native varieties of English. In Smith (1981).

———. in press a. *The Indianization of English: The English language in India.* New Delhi: Oxford University Press.

———. in press b. South Asian English. In Bailey and Görlach (in press).

———, and Quirk, R. 1981. Introduction. In Smith (1981).

Kahane, H., and Kahane, R. 1977. Virtues and vices in the American language: a history of attitudes. *TESOL Quarterly* 11(2): 185-202.

Kandiah, T. 1978. Disinherited Englishes: the case of Lankan English. Paper presented at the Conference on English in Non-native Contexts, University of Illinois, Urbana, June 30-July 2.

Kenyon, J. S. 1924. *American pronunciation.* Ann Arbor: George Wahr.

————— and Knott, T. A. 1953. *A pronouncing dictionary of American English.*
Springfield, Mass.: Merriam.

Krapp, G. P. 1919. *Pronunciation of standard English in America.* New York:
Oxford University Press.

Labov, W. 1966. Some sources of reading problems for Negro speakers of non-
standard English. In *New directions in elementary English,* ed. A. Frazier.
Champaign, Ill.: National Council of Teachers of English.

—————. 1969. Contraction, deletion, and inherent variability of the English
copula. *Language* 45(4): 715-62.

Lado, R. 1964. *Language teaching: a scientific approach.* New York: Mc-Graw-
Hill.

Lara, L. F. 1976. *El concepto de norma en linguistica.* Mexico, D.F.: El Colegio
de Mexico.

Leonard, S. A. 1929. The doctrine of correctness in English usage, 1700-1800.
University of Wisconsin *Studies in Language and Literature* No. 25.

Llamzon, T. A. 1969. *Standard Filipino English.* Manila: Anteneo University
Press.

Mencken, H. L. 1919. *The American language.* New York: Alfred A. Knopf.

Narasimhaiah, C. D. 1976. *Commonwealth literature: a handbook of select
reading lists.* Delhi: Oxford University Press.

Nelson, C. L. 1978. Intelligibility and non-native varieties of English. In this
volume.

Palmer, F. R., ed. 1968. *Selected papers of J. R. Firth, 1952-59.* London:
Longman.

Passé, H. A. 1947. The English language in Ceylon. Ph.D. dissertation, University of London.

Pickering, J. 1816. A vocabulary or collection of words and phrases which
have been supposed to be peculiar to the United States of America. In
The beginnings of American English: essays and comments. Chicago:
University of Chicago Press, 1931.

Platt, J. T. 1975. The Singapore English speech continuum and basilect 'singlish' as a 'creoloid.' *Anthropological Linguistics* 17: 7.

—————. 1976. The sub-varieties of Singapore English: their sociolectal and
functional status. In W. Crewe (1977).

Prator, C. H. 1968. The British heresy in TESL. In *Language problems of
developing nations,* ed. J. A. Fishman, C. A. Ferguson, and J. Das Gupta.
New York: John Wiley and Sons.

Puttenham, G. 1589. *Arte of English poesie.* London.

Quirk, R.; Greenbaum, S.; and Svartvik, J. 1972. *A grammar of contemporary
English.* London: Longman.

Revzin, I. I. 1966. *Models of language.* London: Methuen. [Originally published in Russian, 1962.]

Richards, Jack C. 1972. Social factors, interlanguage and language learning.
Language Learning 22(2): 159-88.

—————, and Tay, M. W. J. 1981. Norm and variability in language use. In
Smith (1981).

Riley, R. D. 1978. Should we teach urban black students standard English?
Lektos: Interdisciplinary Working Papers in Language Sciences 3(1):
93-119.

Sey, K. A. 1973. *Ghanaian English: an exploratory survey.* London: Macmillan.

Shuy, R. W. 1971. Social dialects and second language learning: a case of territorial overlap. *TESOL Newsletter* September-December.

Sledd, J. 1969. Bidialectism: the linguistics of white supremacy. *English Journal* 58: 1307-15, 1329.

Smith, L., ed. 1981. *English for cross-cultural communication.* London: Macmillan.

Smith-Pearse, T. L. N. 1934. *English errors in Indian schools.* Bombay: Oxford University Press.

Spencer, J., ed. 1963. *Language in Africa.* London: Cambridge University Press.

———. 1971a. *The English language in West Africa.* London: Longman.

———. 1971b. Colonial language policies and their legacies. In *Current trends in linguistics,* VII, ed. T. Sebeok. The Hague: Mouton.

Sridhar, K. K. 1978. English in a South Indian urban context. In this volume.

Stevick, E. W. 1957. *Helping people learn English: a manual for teachers of English as a second language.* New York: Abingdon Press.

Stewart, W. 1970. Current issues in the use of Negro dialect in the beginning reading texts. *Florida FL Reporter* 3-6.

Strevens, P. 1977. *New orientations in the teaching of English.* London: Oxford University Press.

———. 1981. Forms of English: an analysis of the variables. In Smith (1981).

Voegelin, C., and Harris, Z. 1951. Determining intelligibility among dialects. *Proceedings* of the American Philological Society 95(3): 322-29.

Ward, I. C. 1929. *The phonetics of English.* Cambridge: Heffer.

Whitten, W., and Whitaker, F. 1939. *Good and bad English.* London: Newnes.

Wolfram, W. 1970. Sociolinguistic implications for educational sequencing. In *Teaching standard English in the inner city,* ed. R. Fasold and R. Shuy. Washington: Center for Applied Linguistics.

Wong, I. F. H. 1979. English in Malaysia. In Smith (1981).

Zuengler, J. E. 1982. Kenyan English. In this volume.

4

Intelligibility and Non-Native Varieties of English

CECIL NELSON

In this study the term "variety" of English is intended to refer to some clearly established form, such as American English, Australian English, or British English. The term "non-native variety" is primarily intended, following Kachru and others (e.g., Kachru 1977, 1981; Halliday et al. 1964), to include the institutionalized varieties established as second languages, as in Africa and India, where English has developed marked African and Indian varieties in terms of its formal and functional characteristics (see, e.g., Kachru 1981). In recent years a wide variety of localized institutional and performance varieties of English have been identified. In this context Quirk (1981) observes that "the divergence between one country's English and another's is seen to be in danger of growing much more seriously wide, with no common educational or communicational policy even theoretically applicable, but rather with nationalism strongly (if haphazardly and even unconsciously) endorsing a linguistic independence to match political and other aspects of independence." Kachru (1977: 30) addresses this question from the point of view of a non-native speaker of English: "The recent concern and controversy about the models of English is primarily addressed to those who have acquired English as their second or foreign language. This concern has further intensified as a reaction to the development of the non-native varieties of English into local varieties, distinct registers, and culture-bound styles."

This question of *variety* vs. *distinct language* is directly analogous to the *dialect* vs. *language* investigations of the sort initiated by Voegelin and Harris, who sought to distinguish empirically between dialect and language by counting "samenesses" between the codes in question (Voegelin and Harris 1951: 323), and by testing intelligibility between speakers of the two codes. Their use of the term "intelligibility" referred not only to the formal *samenesses,* but also to consideration of "differences in the way words are used" (1951: 327). Furthermore, they did not limit their evaluation of intelligibility to previously shared knowledge between speakers of the codes in question. They were primarily interested "in how people of community B understand the speech of community A — when they hear it. When they hear the speech of A they unavoidably get some information — from the parts they understand. If this information helps them understand things in A's speech which they would not have otherwise, that is included in the very situation of hearing and understanding speech, and so can be included in the answer to our question about intelligibility" (1951: 329).

Voegelin and Harris clearly include the Malinowskian and Firthian concept of *context of situation* (see Kachru 1980) in their definition of intelligibility. "Being intelligible" means being understood by an interlocutor at a given time in a given situation. We want to examine whether a speaker of a non-native variety of English is intelligible to a speaker of a native variety, and, if not, why not. If the speech is considered understandable but "marked" (as non-native), again we would like to examine the parameters on which the native speaker's impressions are formed. Halliday et al. (1964) point out various motivations for language labeling; calling the large group of mutually unintelligible languages spoken in mainland China "Chinese" is indicative of political, ethnic, and historical pressures, rather than of synchronic linguistic considerations. Because there are no such unities to justify calling the varieties of English now extant in the world "English," such motivation must stem from these varieties' mutual intelligibility, in their international aspects, with other varieties, including the native ones.

"Being intelligible" also involves the question, "Intelligible to whom?" Intelligibility presumes participants, people who may not be from the same speech community, or even speakers of the same variety. The extent to which they share characteristics of cultural background, as well as the extent to which their languages share phonological and grammatical features, will determine the degree to which they find one another "intelligible." Kachru (1976: 231) presents a tabular summary of test results from Bansal (1969); a portion of this table is reproduced here.

Table 1. The Intelligibility of Indian English

Participants	Highest %	Lowest %	Average
Indian English and Received Pronunciation speakers	73	67	70
Indian English and American English speakers	81	72	74
RP speakers with other RP speakers	100	95	97

A brief discussion of what Bansal apparently meant by his use of "intelligibility" follows. For the moment, however, one sees that the figures indicate a high degree of compatibility between Indian English-speaking participants, and between Indian English and American English-speaking participants, with the very highest average degree (97%) obtaining between speakers of the Received Pronunciation. That is, speakers with shared cultural and linguistic norms obtain higher degrees of intelligibility in their language interactions.

Smith and Rafiqzad (1979: 375) likewise write: "In every country except one (Korea) the listeners were able to fill in the cloze procedure test of their fellow countryman's text with 75% accuracy or above." The following is a portion of their findings (1979: 374):

Table 2. Intelligibility as Measured by the Cloze Procedure Test

Listeners	India	Nepal	Average Accuracy (%)
Speakers			
India	92	55	78
Nepal	92	75	72
Sri Lanka	93	84	79
USA	82	23	55
Average	86	44	—

In both studies from which the above figures are taken, phonological criteria were taken as measures of intelligibility.

Toward a Definition of Intelligibility

The term "degree of intelligibility" refers to the extent to which one is understandable. It will vary according to certain parameters, all subsumed under the context of situation. Catford (1950) asserts that speech is used for eliciting cooperation from those to whom one is speaking; he holds that utterances are "effective" if they produce appropriate and desired results. Trying to communicate only conveys that one is trying to communicate; depending on the context of situation, such an attempt may be effective because of its attention-getting properties. (For example, someone dashes into our seminar room in an obviously agitated state, pointing at the door and shouting a word we don't understand. Wisps of smoke and the smell of something burning waft through the open door. The attempt at communication has had its desired effect.) Catford allows that an unintelligible utterance might be effective by such chance response to extra-linguistic clues. However, tying intelligibility too closely to the notion of effectiveness may be problematic when dealing with some functions of language. For example, if you try but fail to persuade someone to do something, the utterance has not been "effective"; however, the hearer may have understood perfectly well what you were saying. Catford (1950: 9) realizes that "it may occasionally be necessary to refer separately and specifically to intelligibility and effectiveness."

The question of intelligibility based on counts of sameness is also difficult to resolve, when one considers the extent of variation that is evident among native varieties, or within one native variety such as American English, or even within a localized speech community within that variety. In the view of Kachru (1981), "the concept of [e.g.] dog-ness is an abstract concept, and so is the concept speech community. The beholder is only the judge, but he also has preconceived notions which are reflected in his language attitudes. From a native speaker's point of view, perhaps the range and variation in non-native varieties is alarming." Even within native varieties, differences are notable to the layman: a North Carolinian's "accent" is likely to be noticed in Chicago, while he writes to the folks back home that "the people up here sure do talk funny." To account for the fact that the two regional varieties are in fact mutually intelligible, reference must be made to the "shared and transparent features" which the varieties have in common (Kachru 1981). If varieties are similar enough to effect mutual intelligibility, presumably they are close enough to be labeled under the same "English" rubric.

Intelligibility often seems to be viewed as something rather different from "being understandable," or at least to be interpreted in some very narrow sense. For example, Bansal (1969: 55), describing the method followed in his study on this topic, says: "Each sentence was played back separately, and the listener asked to repeat or write the sentence. . . . Each word was played back separately and the listener asked to repeat it or write it down. When a listener's own pronunciation made it somewhat doubtful what word he meant, he was asked to write the words, instead of saying them." It seems to me that this is not "intelligibility" of a very interesting sort. Any trained linguistic fieldworker could "repeat or write the sentence" he had just heard, without knowing what it meant or being able to use it correctly with regard to the context of situation. To consider the intelligibility of an utterance is to deal with what the listener understands the speaker to be saying with respect to the sociolinguistic context, and involves "intelligibility" in a fuller sense of the word. The speaker must correctly select and execute linguistic items, and the hearer accordingly discriminates linguistic input and associates it with "appropriate elements in the situation" (Catford 1950: 10).

Smith and Rafiqzad (1979) deal with intelligibility in a similarly constrained way. Their study involves the administration of a cloze passage test in a number of countries where "educated English" is used as a second language. Their stated purpose is "to compare the degree of intelligibility between native and non-native varieties of educated English" (1979: 371). In a footnote to this statement, they write:

> Our operational definition for intelligibility is capacity for understanding a word or words when spoken/read in the context of a sentence being spoken/read at natural speed. We felt the degree of this capacity for understanding, i.e., the intelligibility, could be checked by constructing a cloze procedure test . . . of the passage spoken/read and asking listeners to attempt to fill in the blanks of this test. The more words the listeners were able to accurately write in, the greater the speaker's intelligibility. This cloze test was not a check on comprehension, since we feel comprehension involves a great deal more than intelligibility; however we realize that the greater the comprehension of the context material, the more likely intelligibility will occur.

The reader notices three terms used in this quotation: "understanding," "intelligibility," and "comprehension." "Intelligibility" and "understanding" are apparently interchangeable; "comprehension," since it "involves a great deal more," may be taken as closer to "intelligibility" as dealt with by Voegelin and Harris, and by Catford. Voegelin and Harris required translation (checked against a third source) of material from language A to language B in an effort to determine whether the informant really understood the material he was dealing with. The use of the cloze passage by Smith and Rafiqzad indicates that their definition of intelligibility resembles Bansal's. Smith and Rafiqzad did not consider spelling, so subjects alert to phonological cues and reasonably familiar with English spelling conventions might be expected to do fairly well on the test.

Smith and Rafiqzad's Listening Comprehension Questionnaire (1979: 375) is, they admit, subjective. The informant is asked to report his own estimates of how easily and how much he was able to "understand." It is not clear to the reader which sort of understanding is referred to — "comprehension," as in the title of the questionnaire, or their technical use of "understanding."

Kachru (1976, 1977) has introduced the concept of "cline of

intelligibility" to indicate reference to the linguistic proficiency of participants and roles in a situation, and the fact that a speaker may switch within his range of verbal repertoires to meet varying communicational needs. In this larger framework a meaningful definition of intelligibility should be sought. Olsson (1978: 5) gives the following definition of intelligibility: "In this study a linguistic message is considered to be intelligible when it is comprehended by a receiver in the sense intended by the speaker. By comprehension I mean here that a receiver can distinguish the message from other possible alternatives. Degree of intelligibility indicates the likelihood that an utterance will be interpreted in its intended sense." In the context of Olsson's study, the definition is problematic. The "sense intended" is in fact in the mind of the researcher, and there might be room for discrepancy between Olsson's apprehension of the provided stimuli and the informant's. The listener was meant to search for the intended sense on the basis of little or no context. However, "intelligibility" in the real world should meaningfully be defined as something like "apprehension of the message in the sense intended by the speaker."

The Parameters of Intelligibility

There are linguistic and non-linguistic parameters of intelligibility. Formally, intelligibility is a function of the linguistic systems involved in the situation. A standard example of pronunciation deviance in Indian English is the replacement of English alveolar stops [t d] by retroflex counterparts. The Hindi stop system is formally richer than the English, where, in addition to voiced vs. voiceless in three articulatory positions [p b, t d, k g], there is the crucial distinction of aspirate vs. non-aspirate in four positions [p ph b bh, t th d dh, ṭ ṭh ḍ ḍh, k kh g gh]. The Indian English speaker typically replaces English [t] with his [ṭ], [d] with [ḍ]. This well-attested substitution is one of the major defining (stereotyping) characteristics of the "Indian accent" in English.

Such comparisons can be made at all linguistic levels. The amount of tolerable deviation from one's own model may vary according to the attitude toward the user, as well as the level of language in which the deviation occurs. For example, the English of a multilingual professor of chemistry who speaks "with an accent" is likely to be tolerated quite well by his students, while a foreign teaching assistant of the course is likely to come under attack in the campus newspaper for not being understandable. Deviation in phonology generally seems to be more readily tolerated than deviation in lexis or grammar.

The introduction of loanwords from a speaker's first language is often both linguistic and non-linguistic in its import. For example, in culture-bound and hybridized items such as Indian English *hair-cutting ceremony* or *aroti-time* (Kachru 1966: 280), an American interlocutor would be drawn into the cultural meanings involved with the items, and all that they imply to the member of the Indian-language culture. All this is to be taken into consideration in the context of situation. In Firth's view (1935: 27),

> The central concept of the whole of semantics . . . is the context of situation. In that context are the human participants, what they say, and what is going on. The phonetician can find his phonetic context and the grammarian and the lexicographer theirs. And if you want to bring in general cultural background, you have the contexts of experience of the participants. Every man carries his culture and much of his social reality about with him wherever he goes.

Firth, and later Halliday (1976), Hymes (1967), Kachru (1966, 1969, 1980, 1981), Labov (1970), and Weinreich (1966) have put forward this important view: that language as a communication system cannot be divorced from its social functioning, which requires heterogeneity for a range of situation types and functions.

Familiarity with cultural and situational context figures prominently in Paulston's (1974) treatment of communicative competence. She asserts that communicative competence "is not simply a term; it is a concept basic to understanding social interaction," and that in teaching a second language one must "go beyond referential meaning to the social meaning of language" (1974: 349). In setting up her "model for language teaching," Paulston says, "Linguistic performance is the actual utterance . . . which often imperfectly reflects the underlying competence (Chomsky 1968). Communicative competence is the social rules of language use, 'the systemic sets of social interactional rules' in Grimshaw's terms" (1974: 350). A meaningful definition of "being intelligible" would have to include both "purely" linguistic and social aspects of competence. In the context of situation, inappropriateness can stem from any of the various levels of the linguistic and participant-background context, to the detriment of effective communication.

One can gain more or less familiarity with cultural differentials. Systematic phonological and grammatical substitutions may be rendered amenable to decoding, even upon limited exposure, by the hearer whose variety of English is different from that of the speaker. Let us now turn our attention to the patterns of rhythm of native as compared with a non-native English, in an investigation of a little-explored parameter of intelligibility.

It is hypothesized that the Indian English speaker unconsciously transfers the rhythm patterns of his first language to his variety of English, causing a subtle detriment of intelligibility across varieties. Kachru (1969: 643) asserts, for example, "All the main South Asian languages are syllable-timed languages, as opposed to English, which is a stress-timed language. This results in a distinct South Asian rhythm in South Asian English. . . . This may be the reason for labeling South Asian English as a sing-song English, and for stating that it hampers intelligibility with the L_1 speakers of English."

The Importance and Description of Rhythm in Speech

William Stannard Allen (1954: xi-xii) claims:

> Speech is essentially movement. However accurately we learn to pronounce the isolated sounds of a language we must still train ourselves to set them in motion in the right manner if we wish to make ourselves easily understood. . . .
>
> Broadly speaking, a reasonably correct speech-flow is more important for intelligibility than correct sounds. It is possible to carry on an intelligible conversation in a series of mumbles and grunts, provided the voice-movement is correct.

And George Allen (1968b: 61) argues that rhythm should be fitted in to the description of language because "there are some simple relationships between the temporal rhythms of speech and certain phonological rules (e.g. stress in English), and these relationships . . . make the whole study of speech timing linguistically interesting."

Because of the common existence of "rhythmizing" in all speakers, and the structuring of hearers' perceptions on the basis of "some highly organized transformations of our sensations" (Allen 1968b: 65), it is to be expected that the rhythmic patterns of a second language would be interpreted by a language user in ways peculiar to his own linguistic system's predispositions. In particular, for the present topic, a native speaker of South Asian languages might apply his native syllable-timing system to his variety of English, as Kachru has suggested.

Regarding the relationship of stress to rhythm, William Sydney

Allen (1973: 100) writes: "Implicitly or explicitly underlying this identity of stress as the basis of rhythm is the conception of rhythm as movement, and of stress, in the production of audible linguistic phenomena, as the motor activity par excellence." George Allen (1968b: 67) has found that the rhythmic focus in utterances is at the onset of the nuclear vowel of stressed syllables. He continues:

> Because some languages (e.g., Japanese) do not differentiate the accent associated with successive syllables to any appreciable degree, while others (e.g., English) do, the former languages are rhythmically structured as simple successions of syllables and the latter are alternations of strong and weak beats. If there were no further qualifications to the rhythms of these languages, the former could be said to be "syllable-timed" (Pike 1945), with equal time distance between successive syllables, while the latter would be "stress-timed" (ibid.) with equal time between stresses.

The necessary qualification is that "many and perhaps all languages" tend to alternate accents. (See also Abercrombie 1967, esp. Ch. 6.)

The average preferred rate for simple motor acts performed by subjects at a natural pace has been found to be within a range of 0.2 to 1.0 seconds per act. Speech might be expected to participate in this pacing. Allen cites three studies showing that most interstress intervals in English fall between .2 and .8 seconds in length (Allen 1968b: 69, 71): "the rate of succession of stressed syllables is comfortably within the range of preferred rates of rhythmic succession in other motor tasks . . . however, the rate of the beats in syllable-timed languages, that is, the rate of succession of syllables, is a little too fast to match the preferred rates well." This evaluation by Allen would account for the sing-song, staccato impression that South Asian English may make on the American hearer. Compare also the following statement by Tay and Gupta (1981: 6) regarding educated Singapore English: "Standard Singapore English is spoken mainly with a syllable-timed rhythm; this means that all syllables recur at equal intervals of time, stressed or unstressed. This 'machine-gun rhythm' is characteristic of all natural speech, even among highly educated Singaporeans." A similar appraisal may be found in Platt and Weber (1980: 57).

Allen asserts that speech rhythm conveys several sorts of information. Most notably, it identifies the particular language being spoken (Allen 1968b: 75). This follows, if languages have their own general (type-associated) and specific rhythms. Stress-timed languages have their stresses associated with the periodic beats of phrases over

a breath group, while syllable-timed languages organize their timing
with respect to short, syllable-length intervals. Adams (1979: 3)
found that "The non-native speaker . . . is almost always painfully
conscious of his failure to realize the rhythmic impulse of the foreign
language but, as often as not, has no idea of the nature of the elusive
system he is trying to cope with; for while all languages are characterized by rhythmicality there is considerable diversity among languages
both in the arrangement of the rhythm units and the means by which
they are marked." Adams's students are reported to have produced
utterances which indicate interference in rhythm patterns caused by
their syllable-timed first languages. (For a summary, see Dubois and
Ram 1980.)

Huggins (1972b) cited his own and others' research to motivate
the assertions that "tip-of-the-tongue" trial items have the same stress
pattern as the target over 70 percent of the time, and that when deaf
speakers are explicitly taught temporal patterns, they are more intelligible than those who have been taught only segmental articulations
(Huggins 1972b: 1282). In another study, subjects listened to recorded stimuli that had been tampered with. The subjects were asked
to classify as "normal," "long," or "short" the lengths of the consonants and vowels in question. Varying the lengths of segments caused
perceived stress to vary for all subjects. Huggins reports, "When subjects based their judgements [regarding segment length] on changes
in perceived stress or rhythm, they were usually able to detect smaller
changes in duration than when they attended to other aspects of the
stimuli. . . . This points to the importance of higher-order organization
in speech" (Huggins 1972a: 1278). Huggins (1972b: 1279) further
wrote, "The results suggest that . . . it is important to maintain the
rhythm of the sentence, as defined by the onsets of vowels (especially
stressed vowels), if the sentence is to sound temporally fluent." These
suggestive findings relate to the importance of rhythm in contributing
to (or detracting from) intelligibility across varieties with different
timing systems.

Furthermore, Huggins (1972b: 1282) states that hearers rely on
prosodic cues when these conflict with segmental cues. His contrasts
with the position held by Berkovits (1980: 271), who writes: "prosodic
features are generally ignored when other cues (e.g., semantic and pragmatic) are available." This statement is qualified in the conclusion of
the paper, however, leaving open the question of the importance of
rhythm as a valid area of investigation: "Disambiguating surface-struc-
ture ambiguities . . . generally involves the acoustic features of junc-
ture and duration. . . . Thus, whereas the present results indicate paral-

lels in native versus non-native perception of these prosodic cues, this
does not preclude differences in the perception of other aspects of intonation" (Berkovits 1980: 279; see also O'Connor 1976).

The nature of stress in Hindi, a "typical" South Asian language
and the first language of many speakers of Indian English, has been
problematic. Ohala (1977) presents a concise discussion of the problems, pointing out that all the work cited has been impressionistic,
without rigorous instrumental studies to determine the actual phonetic correlates of stress in Hindi. (See also Kelkar 1968.)

The most likely candidates for the major phonetic correlate of
stress are duration and pitch. Ohala found that duration failed to correlate directly with predicted stress. Her study suggests that "in general the syllable which was identified . . . as the 'stressed,' i.e. the
prominent syllable, has a rising pitch on it and a falling pitch on the
syllable following it" (Ohala 1977: 322). Certainly pitch is an important (if not the most important) cue for stress in Hindi, as indeed it
is in English. In Ohala's view, Hindi stress is "far weaker than in English, perhaps because unstressed syllables are not detectably reduced,
as they are in English." Also, in contrast with English, stress plays a
very marginal role in Hindi: "no words are differentiated solely by
stress" (1977: 327). The syllable-timed structuring of Hindi seems to
contrast with the stress-timed rhythm of English. In Hindi the beats
come in faster sequence than in English, and they do not distinctively
differentiate lexical items; in English the beats are fairly evenly spaced
temporally, but the amount of phonetic material within each interstress group is variable. If South Asian speakers impose their native
timing system on their variety of English, then some sorts of intelligibility problems can be expected to result. (See also Tiffin 1974 for
Nigerian English.)

From the American speaker's point of view, one of the most
striking features of the Indian English flow of speech is likely to be
the placement of stress on a syllable adjacent to the one where it is
expected; for example, *dévelopment* for *devélopment,* or *charácter*
for *cháracter* (compare Platt and Weber 1980: 56). Sometimes listeners will report the "correct" syllable and an adjacent one as stressed.
This may be a function of intonation contour: note Ohala's characterization of Hindi stress as rising on the accented syllable. If an Indian
English speaker has lexicalized *character,* for example, with the accent on the second syllable, and is rising toward that peak rather than
"hitting" it, stress might well be perceived on two contiguous syllables.
Also, unstressed vowel reduction is not as pervasive in Indian English
as it is in American English (cf. Ohala's remarks on Hindi stress, noted

above). This feature would further contribute to the impression of stress where it does not actually fall.

In his 1968 papers George Allen queried how the time interval between primary stresses separated by one unstressed syllable could be the same as when there is no unstressed syllable intervening. He cited Bolinger (1965), who found that stressed syllables shortened before unstressed syllables, and so proposed a time-borrowing principle to account for the phenomenon. In his study Bolinger (1965: 168) claims:

> what of the peculiar status of monosyllables . . .? Here I believe we have what more than any other one thing has promoted the feeling that accentual groups tend to be of equal length. If a one-syllable word tends to be as long or almost as long as a two-syllable word, and one- and two-syllable words make up a high enough running count of English words, it is not hard to see how an impression of isochronism might be created. This is especially true as the most radical difference in number of syllables — 100% — is between one- and two-syllable words.

This relationship between the timing of interstress intervals containing zero and one unstressed syllable can be taken as one more bit of evidence in favor of the isochronicity principle; i.e., that English speakers *perceive* English as tending to keep interstress time intervals approximately the same, within a narrow range of variation. The borrowing principle certainly does not apply to unstressed syllables after the first: additional unstressed syllables lengthen the interval, although the nature of this lengthening is problematic (cf. Allen 1968a, b).

With regard to the suggestion that the perception set for isochronicity in American English is created largely on the basis of the contrast of interstress intervals having zero and one unstressed syllable, I measured interval lengths on spectrograms of sentence data contrasting these two cases. The findings suggested that, in general, Indian English speakers do not shorten the stressed syllable before an unstressed to the extent that American speakers do. Lehiste (1972: 2018) conducted an experiment in American English, comparing the lengths of words and the segmentally identical syllables in derived forms of the words, and found that "the duration of the base part of the derived word was considerably shortened, so that even with the addition of a fairly long -*y* [on adjectives; e.g., *speedy*] the over-all duration of the derived words was not much longer than the base words."

My measurement of spectrograms from the final parts of the utterances *We warned them that speed kills* and *We talked with Mr.
Speedy Kills* for two speakers of American English and of Indian English produced the following figures: the ratio of the averaged length
of *speed* to that of *speedy* was .97 for the American English speakers,
while it was .82 for the Indian English speakers; *speedy* was thus longer in comparison with *speed* for the Indian English speakers than for
the American English speakers. The ratio of the base *speed-* (from
speedy) to the word *speed* was .72 for the American English speakers
(the base was considerably shortened), and .86 for the Indian English
speakers (not so much shortening of the base: one Indian English
speaker's ratio was .92, indicating that, as might be expected, some
speakers manifest this feature more than others).

Following this pilot study, a similar but somewhat more extensive study has been carried out. Recorded utterances from seven Indian English and five American English speakers have been measured
and compared. Subjects recorded seventeen sentences, reading each
sentence twice. Spectrograms were made of the appropriate parts of
the utterances, and they were measured from point to point within
and across words and phrases. In most cases the lengths of the two
readings showed some degree of consistency. The time lengths from
the two readings of each item were averaged. Then these average
lengths were compared, to yield ratios of compared lengths.

For example, one contrasted pair of sentences contained the
phrases *speed kills* and *speedy kills;* the length of *speed* was divided
by that of *speedy* to yield a fraction. For Indian English speakers,
one expects a result a good deal less than 1.0; since the base *speed-*
in *speedy* is not expected to be reduced, one would, on the basis of
numbers of segments, expect 4:5, or about 80 percent. In order to
avoid variability caused by the indeterminacy of the start of the *s-*
on the spectrograms, however, figures here are from the onset of the
stressed vowel to the end of the word. This comparison yielded the
following figures: for Indian English speakers, the ratio of the length
of *speed* to that of *speedy* was .66; for American English speakers,
the ratio was .90. The figures for *fear/fearful* are more striking: Indian English, .56; American English, .97. In these examples, the
hypothesis appears to be borne out; i.e., the American English speaker reduces the length of time given to the base of the derived word,
thus fitting the derived word into very nearly the same time as the
base word, while the Indian English speaker does not.

For Indian English speakers, one expects that the length of the
base *speed-* divided by the length of the word *speed* will be approxi-

mately 1; the data yield .87. *Fear-/fear* is more convincing with .96. The American English data yield .60 and .52, respectively, indicating the expected shortening of the base.

Finally, the length of time from onset to onset of the stressed vowels in *speed kills* divided by that in *speedy kills* should yield a small figure for Indian English speakers, but about 1 for American English speakers: the figures are .79 and .99, respectively. These data indicate real differences between Indian English and American English in the organization of timing of rhythm units having one or no unstressed syllables following a stressed.

Conclusion

There is ample reason to expect stress and timing phenomena to have a significant effect on intelligibility across varieties of English, and some data do indicate that cross-linguistic influences exist. Intelligibility across varieties is more problematic than within one variety because of the lack of shared cultural-situational features. Definitions of "intelligibility" may vary. A definition at once well defined and broad enough to accord with the concept of context of situation needs to be developed. Given the existence of divergent sorts of functions (intranational vs. international) and different sorts of varieties (institutionalized vs. performance), it might be wise to think of setting up norms of intelligibility that would coincide with the situations and functions at hand. As Hymes (1972: 278) has written, "There are rules of use without which the rules of grammar would be useless." Intelligibility derives its substance from the features of the context of situation as they are interpreted and expressed by the participants in that context, and rhythm is but one parameter crucial to full effectiveness of participants in any sociolinguistic context.

The first step toward understanding the relationship of rhythm to intelligibility, and toward understanding the various rhythms of contemporary varieties of English, is to develop a typology of rhythm patterns across varieties. Functionally, it would be useful to categorize these in terms of institutional and performance varieties. One pedagogical expectation might be that non-native varieties would be drawn closer to native models where that would be in keeping with the function of the variety. At least speakers (and teachers) of native varieties should become aware of the differences in rhythm that may exist across varieties of English.

REFERENCES

Abercrombie, David. 1967. *Elements of general phonetics.* Chicago: Aldine.

Adams, Corrine. 1979. *English speech rhythm and the foreign learner.* Janua Linguarum Series Practica 69. The Hague: Mouton.

Allen, George. 1968a. Experiments on the rhythm of English speech. *UCLA Working Papers in Phonetics* 10: 42-46. Los Angeles: University of California.

————. 1968b. On testing for certain stress-timing effects. *UCLA Working Papers in Phonetics* 10: 60-84. Los Angeles: University of California.

Allen, William Stannard. 1954. *Living English speech.* London: Longmans.

Allen, William Sydney. 1973. *Accent and rhythm.* Cambridge: Cambridge University Press.

Bansal, R. K. 1969. *The intelligibility of Indian English.* Hyderabad: Central Institute of English and Foreign Languages.

Berkovits, Rochele. 1980. Perception of intonation in native and non-native speakers of English. *Language and Speech* 23(3): 271-80.

Bolinger, Dwight. 1965. Pitch accent and sentence rhythm. Pp. 17-56 in *Forms of English: accent, morpheme, order,* ed. Isamu Abe and T. Kanekivo. Cambridge: Harvard University Press.

Catford, John. 1950. Intelligibility. *English Language Teaching* 1: 7-15.

Chomsky, Noam, and Halle, Morris. 1968. *The sound pattern of English.* New York: Harper and Row.

Dubois, Betty Lou, and Ram, Sylvia Candelaria de. 1980. Review of Adams (1979). *TESOL Quarterly* 14(3): 375-78.

Firth, J. R. 1935. The technique of semantics. *Transactions of the Philological Society.* London. Reprinted in *Papers in Linguistics 1934-1951,* pp. 7-33. London: Oxford University Press, 1957.

Halliday, M. A. K. 1976. Language structure and language function. Pp. 140-65 in *New horizons in linguistics,* ed. John Lyons. Harmondsworth: Penguin.

————; MacIntosh, Angus; and Strevens, Peter. 1964. The users and uses of language. In *The linguistic sciences and language teaching.* London: Longmans. Reprinted in *Varieties of present-day English,* ed. Richard Bailey and Jay Robinson. New York: Macmillan, 1973.

Huggins, A. W. F. 1972a. Just noticeable differences for segment duration in natural speech. *Journal of the Acoustical Society of America* 51/4(2): 1270-78.

————. 1972b. On the perception of temporal phenomena in speech. *Journal of the Acoustical Society of America* 51/4(2): 1279-91.

Hymes, Dell. 1967. The anthropology of communication. Pp. 1-39 in *Human communication,* ed. F. E. X. Dance. New York: Holt, Rinehart and Winston.

————. 1972. On communicative competence. Pp. 269-93 in *Sociolinguistics,* ed. John B. Pride and J. Holmes. Hammondsworth: Penguin.

Kachru, Braj B. 1966. Indian English: a study in contextualization. Pp. 265-87 in *In memory of J. R. Firth,* ed. C. E. Bazell et al. London: Longmans.

————. 1969. English in South Asia. Pp. 627-78 in *Current trends in linguistics V,* ed. Thomas Sebeok. The Hague: Mouton.

————. 1976. Models of English for the third world. *TESOL Quarterly* 10(2): 221-39.

————. 1977. The new Englishes and old models. *English Teaching Forum* XV(3): 29-35.

————. 1980. Socially realistic linguistics: the Firthian tradition. *Studies in the Linguistic Sciences* 10(1): 85-111.

————. 1981. The pragmatics of non-native varieties of English. In Smith (1981).

Kelkar, A. 1968. *Studies in Hindi-Urdu I: introduction and word phonology.* Poona: Deccan College Research Institute.

Labov, William. 1970. The study of language in its social context. *Studium Generale* 23: 30-87. Reprinted in *Advances in the sociology of language*, ed. Joshua Fishman. The Hague: Mouton, 1972.

Lehiste, Ilse. 1972. The timing of utterances and linguistic boundaries. *Journal of the Acoustical Society of America* 5/6(2): 2018-24.

O'Connor, J. D. 1976. *Stress, rhythm and intonation.* 5th ed. London: British Broadcasting Corporation.

Ohala, Manjari. 1977. Stress in Hindi. Pp. 327-38 in *Studies in stress and accent: Southern California occasional papers in linguistics, vol. 4*, ed. Larry M. Hyman. Los Angeles: Department of Linguistics, University of Southern California.

Olsson, Margareta. 1978. *Intelligibility: an evaluation of some features of English produced by Swedish 14-year-olds. Gothenburg Studies in English* 40. Goteborg: Acta Universitatis Gothoburgensis.

Paulston, Christina. 1974. Linguistic and communicative competence. *TESOL Quarterly* 8(4): 347-62.

Platt, John, and Weber, Heidi. 1980. *English in Singapore and Malaysia.* Kuala Lumpur: Oxford University Press.

Quirk, Randolph. 1981. International communication and the concept of nuclear English. In Smith (1981).

Smith, Larry E., ed. 1981. *English for cross-cultural communication.* London: Macmillan.

————, and Rafiqzad, Khalilullah. 1979. English for cross-cultural communication: the question of intelligibility. *TESOL Quarterly* 13(3): 371-80.

Tay, Mary W. J., and Gupta, Anthea Fraser. 1981. Toward a description of standard Singapore English. Paper presented at the Sixteenth Regional Seminar, SEAMEO Regional Language Center, Singapore, April 20-24, 1981.

Tiffin, Brian. 1974. The intelligibility of Nigerian English. Ph.D. dissertation, University of London.

Voegelin, Charles, and Harris, Zellig. 1951. Determining intelligibility among dialects. *Proceedings of the American Philological Society* 95/3: 322-29.

Weinreich, Uriel. 1966. *Languages in contact: findings and problems.* The Hague: Mouton.

PART II

Nativization: Formal and
Functional

5

The Africanization of English

EYAMBA G. BOKAMBA

Africa is considered today to be perhaps the most multilingual region in the world, with more languages spoken per capita than anywhere else. It is estimated that 1,000 to 1,140 languages are spoken in Africa today (Voegelin and Voegelin 1964).[1] Except in a very few cases, African nations are multilingual; the typical country lacks both an indigenous nationwide language of communication and a language policy that proposes the development and implementation of such a language.[2] This situation has facilitated the penetration and entrenchment of the former colonial powers' languages (i.e., English, French, and Portuguese) as the official media of communication for administration, education, commerce, and diplomacy in African states.

As is to be expected in such a multilingual contact situation, the interaction of the three European languages with African languages has produced very interesting sociolinguistic phenomena, e.g., code-switching and code-mixing, structural changes in the European and African languages involved, and continued debates on the Africanization of education and the language of instruction.

The phenomena of code-switching and code-mixing in English have been discussed at some length in the literature (Ansre 1971; Scotton 1972; Abdulaziz 1972; Parkin 1974; Agheyisi 1977; Scotton and Ury 1977). A great deal of attention has recently been devoted to the question of language policies in African education, and there is every indication that this will continue (see, e.g., Ansre 1970, 1975; Gbedemah 1971; Foster 1971; Whiteley 1971; Spencer 1971b; Mhina 1975; Bamgboṣe 1976; Bokamba 1976, 1979; and Bokamba and Tlou 1977). Very little attention, however, has been given to the study of the influence of African languages on European languages in general, and on English in particular. The reverse situation, viz., the influence of English, French, and Portuguese on African languages, has remained almost completely neglected.

These are areas of great sociolinguistic interest that might be pursued simultaneously with promising theoretical and practical results. Such a study, however, is beyond the scope of this chapter.

Here I shall focus on the varieties of English referred to collectively as *African English*. In particular, I shall discuss the influence of African languages on English, with special reference to Ghanaian, Nigerian, and the Eastern Bantu languages of Kenya and Tanzania. I shall then examine briefly the sociolinguistic implications of this phenomenon on English, and on African languages in general.

Africanisms in African English

The paucity of studies on what I shall term African English seems to suggest that there is no such distinct variety of English. Yet, when a Nigerian or a Ghanaian speaks English, no matter what his/her level of education, native speakers of English have no difficulty identifying the accent as African. While the contact between African languages and English during the colonial period was much shorter (about eighty-five years) than that between Indian languages and English, where a number of interesting varieties of English have emerged (Spencer 1971b; Kachru 1976a, 1976b), it is still possible to identify nascent varieties that one might call Liberian,[3] Sierra Leonean, Ghanaian, Nigerian, Kenyan, or East African English.

These Englishes share certain properties that can be identified as *Africanisms,* in that they reflect structural characteristics of African languages. Specifically, these properties can be discovered at all linguistic levels: phonological, morphological, semantic, and syntactic. For my present purposes, any English construction that reflects a structural property of an African language will be called an Africanism. My discussion will be restricted to the syntactico-semantic properties of sentences produced by educated[4] Africans, because of the lack of data from other speakers.

Consider in this regard, first, the case of syntactic constructions. Bamgbose (1971: 37) cites a letter from a primary school graduate which contained the following passage:

(1)   With much pleasre [*sic*] and respect I inscribe you
      this few lines and with the hope that *it* will *meet*
      you in good condition of health [emphasis added].

This was the opening sentence of the letter. Bamgbose does not reveal the author's native language, though he may have been a Yoruba speaker. But regardless of the author's mother tongue, the sentence indicates the embedding of the syntactic properties of a West African language in the derivation of an English sentence. These properties are adjectival agreement and subject-verb agreement. Most West African lan-

guages (unlike Bantu) do not require overt agreement markers between a noun and its modifier if the latter is a quantifier or is part of
an expression containing such an element, as in "this few lines,"
above.

Furthermore, there is no overt subject-verb agreement in most
West African languages (again, unlike Bantu). The incorrect choice of
the subject pronoun "it" in the second clause in (1) seems to reflect
this characteristic. Note that the pronoun agrees with the adjectival
phrase "this few" rather than with the noun "lines," as expected. A
general syntactico-semantic property of African languages is reflected
in the expression "meet you in good condition of health." Part of the
problem here is due to the fact that in many African languages the
verbs *find, meet,* and *encounter* are realized by a single verb which is
often the equivalent of *meet* in English. The other problem is cultural: African languages characteristically inquire about or make reference to an addressee's welfare as an initial step in either face-to-face
greetings or letter writing. Such a tradition does not exist in English;
hence the inappropriateness of the expression in the sentence cited
in (1).

The very obvious deviations from Standard (British?) English
exemplified in (1) may suggest that the speaker was translating directly from his mother tongue.[5] Whether or not this was the case is
not at issue here; the point is that the sentence reflects known characteristics of a group of African languages, and that these are easy to
detect. In certain cases, however, the embedding of an African language structure into English is accomplished with such sophistication
that it becomes difficult, if not altogether impossible, to detect it unless one is familiar with the speaker's native language. Consider the
following passage cited by Kirk-Greene (1971: 132) from a published
work in Nigerian English:

(2)　It is now known to my poorself the hows and whys of
politics. As from now I shall call group of politicians –
Peoples [*sic*] of varied wishes that assume one name.
Politics is forced out tears by intense anger. One can not
remember any time both in dream and normal life that
poorself stood among honourable ones, expressing in
opposition terms against a number more than one, of
course, except in concerts. That eyes, so unforseeing
have forced the youths to talk with anger, what they
have tried with all politeness. . . . It is therefore the
idea to exchange ideas. The exchange of ideas in plays
and conversation about down fall or up lift of any part

of earth. This will result to total wipe off of ignorance
and plant eternal freedom of thought with unlimited
progress and wide knowledge.

According to Kirk-Greene, the author of this passage was an Igbo
speaker. While the passage is admittedly deviant in many respects, it
sounds more English than the sentence cited in (1). Furthermore, (2)
might be taken as a philosophical essay by a non-English speaker who
is not necessarily an African. But anyone who is familiar with African
languages will be able to identify many of the lexical expressions and
syntactic constructions as originating from a West African language —
in this case, Igbo. Other examples cited by Kirk-Greene from speakers
of the same language include the following:

> (3)   a. The effect of this attitude was compensating.
>   b. I can wipe off any uncalled for time of assumptions
>   in any person's mind.
>   c. Today will be marked at the boards of your hearts.

These sentences, as Kirk-Greene correctly points out, are difficult to
explain syntactically and semantically. The medium is English, but
the meaning is very obscure unless one knows the language and/or
culture underlying expressions such as "uncalled for time of assumptions" and "boards of hearts."

A number of other typical deviations in syntax have been noted
in Nigerian, Ghanaian, and Kenyan Englishes (Kirk-Greene 1971; Sey
1973; Chinebuah 1976; Angogo and Hancock 1980; Zuengler 1982).
These include: 1) omission of function words; 2) semantic extension
of certain lexical items from African languages to cover various meanings and functions in English; 3) occurrence of certain redundancies,
including the pluralization of mass nouns; 4) retention of anaphoric
pronouns in non-subject relativization; 5) use of affirmative answers
to yes/no questions; 6) unusual word order in adjectival phrases containing demonstrative or possessive pronouns; and 7) omission of the
element "more" in comparative constructions. Each of these deviations is discussed briefly below.

Of these common characteristics, the omission of function
words such as definite and indefinite articles appears most widespread
in African English. Kirk-Greene (1971: 133), for example, has found
sentences such as (4) to be common in the Nigerian English of Hausa,
Igbo, and Yoruba speakers:

> (4)   a. Let strong football team be organized.
>   b. He won by overwhelming majority.
>   c. He gave me tough time.

Similar constructions have been observed by Sey (1973: 29ff.) in what he terms Educated Ghanaian English (EGE). Examples cited by Sey include the following:

(5) a. I am going to cinema.
     b. I am going to post office.
     c. I may continue with the interview or examine few
        more applications.

This deviation is not restricted to the speech and writing of low-level speakers of English (e.g., those having only a secondary education). It has been observed at higher levels as well. The passage cited in (2) is one example; a second example consists of the following sentences found in the introductory page of an official document published by the Ministry of Information of Nigeria (1977: 3).

(6) a. Education in Nigeria is no more a private enter-
        prise, but a huge Government venture that has
        witnessed a progressive evolution of Government's
        complete and dynamic intervention . . . .
     b. It is Government's wish that any existing contra-
        dictions, ambiguities, and lack of uniformity in
        educational practices in the different parts of the
        Federation should be removed . . . .

Admittedly, the omission of the definite article here is sporadic; but the fact that there is any omission at all in a document of this type is sufficient to indicate the spread of the phenomenon. From a comparative point of view, it is noteworthy that the same phenomenon is exhibited in South Asian English (Kachru 1976b).

One major source of errors that lead to the production of deviant sentences like those in (4)-(6) is transference from the speaker's native languages (Kirk-Greene 1971; Sey 1973; Chinebuah 1976; Angogo and Hancock 1980). Most African languages do not have overt articles, so determination is achieved derivatively. Another source is analogy from Standard English itself, particularly from certain idiomatic expressions such as "going to hospital/church/school." It is difficult to determine with any certainty, therefore, the main source of such deviations. My inclination is to believe that interference from African languages plays a critical role.

Somewhat related to the deviation just exemplified is the influence of certain generic lexical items in African languages in conveying meanings and covering functions such as those performed by indefinite articles and/or pronouns, as well as a range of adjectives, in English. In Bantu-speaking Africa, for example, it is not uncommon to hear or read sentences like the following:

(7)   a. The boy saw one person [i.e., someone].
      b. He is a real/whole person [i.e., an adult].

Such constructions appear to be, in part, translation equivalents of lexical items like the Swahili *mtu mmoja* (one person/someone) and *mtu mzima* (an adult/a fine or wholesome person). The Hausa words *wani* and *wata,* which have several meanings including "another," "a certain," and the indefinite article, have, according to Kirk-Greene (1971), a similar influence on English spoken by Hausas. He cites the following examples —

(8)   a. You are a big somebody [i.e., an important person].
      b. You are a sociable somebody [i.e., sociable person].

— and points out that analogous constructions can be found in Igbo and Yoruba English.

Although structures like these have been noted in more than one Anglophone African nation, they do not appear to be as prevalent or as troublesome as the redundant pluralizations of uncountable nouns. Consider, for instance, the sentences in (9) from Nigerian English (Kirk-Greene 1971: 134) and those in (10) from Ghanaian English (Sey 1973: 26-27).

(9)   a. I lost all my *furnitures* and many valuable *properties.*
      b. There were thunderous *noises* of laughter and *chats.*
      c. She walked in such *paces* that combined her college *learnings* of how to behave.

(10) a. The teachers will be given the *respects* they deserve.
      b. But in modern warfare . . . the *damages* caused are great.
      c. I was in charge of all *correspondences.*

Kirk-Greene does not indicate at what level of English proficiency sentences like (9) are produced, but he states that they are drawn from letters and published novelettes. This suggests that we are dealing with advanced speakers of English as a second language (i.e., those with post-primary education). As for the sentences in (10), Sey states that such deviations are commonly observed in the speech and writing of pre-university speakers in Ghana.

The problem illustrated in (9)-(10) is due less to the lack of a distinction between countable and mass nouns in African languages than to the semantic inconsistencies of English itself. As Sey (1973: 27) quite correctly points out,

(11) There appears to be (a) no consistent semantic relationship
between countable and uncountable uses of nouns [in
English], nor (b) any clearly discernible motivation for
using some normally uncountable nouns in countable
functions but not others.

African languages in general do distinguish between mass and countable nouns, but the range of the former does not correspond to that
of English. For example, nouns such as *fish, chicken,* and *lamb,*
which are considered as either countable or uncountable in English,
depending on whether they are taken as food items or as living entities, are classified as countable in most African languages. In other
words, the ambiguous category found in English does not commonly
occur in African languages. It is not surprising, therefore, to find
words like *furniture, property, chat, pace, shade,* and *correspondence*
pluralized in African English. All of these (except perhaps *noise,*
which generally occurs only in the plural) are countable in most African languages.

A related deviation is the interposing of an independent subject
pronoun between a subject noun and its verb. Such a phenomenon is
often observed in the English speech of Bantu language speakers (e.g.,
Kenyans, Tanzanians, Zambians):

(12) a. My daughter *she* is attending the University of
Nairobi.
b. The boys *they* like to play outside even if it is cold.
c. Robert *he* is currently employed by the UNESCO.

The most probable source of this deviation is the redundancy found
in the subject-verb agreement system of Bantu languages, whereby a
subject prefix obligatorily occurs with a finite verb whether or not
the subject noun surfaces. A number of other interesting deviations
from a Bantu-speaking area are discussed in Zuengler (1982).

Another characteristic deviation noted in African English is the
occurrence of resumptive anaphoric pronouns in non-subject relativization.

(13) a. The guests whom I invited *them* have arrived.
b. The book which I bought *it* is lost.
c. Taking a course in a country which *her* language
you did not know is a big problem.
d. You are going to do your course [i.e., studies] in
a country where you have never been *there* before.

Chinebuah (1976: 75-76) asserts that sentences like (13c-d) are widespread in West African English and specific to the Kwa and Gur sub-

families. In fact, these structures are much more widespread than
Chinebuah seems to believe: relative clauses with resumptive pronouns are a typological characteristic of many African languages, including Arabic. One finds them in West African and East African English as well. This deviation can, therefore, be best explained as a
transference error.

Of the various syntactico-semantic deviations found in African
English, none has perhaps caused more confusion in communication
than the use of affirmative answers to negative yes/no questions. For
instance, the typical responses to questions like (14a) and (15a) in
African English would be (14b) and (15b), respectively, or simply *yes:*

> (14)   a. Hasn't the President left for Nairobi yet?
>   b. Yes, the President hasn't left for Nairobi yet.

> (15)   a. Didn't you see anyone at the compound?
>   b. Yes, I didn't see anyone at the compound.

When a full answer such as (14b) or (15b) is given, there is less confusion than when *yes* alone is used. This is evidenced in sentences
like (16b) below, which is the response to comment (16a).

> (16)   a. I hope you won't have any difficulty with your fees
>   next term.
>   b. I hope so [i.e., I hope what you have said will indeed
>   be true].

This phenomenon is not unique to African English: it has also been
observed in South Asian English (Kachru 1976b). Constructions such
as (14)-(16) have parallels in many African languages, and may be
reasonably analyzed as instances of interference. For example, (17c)
would be acceptable as a reply to the Lingala (a Bantu language) question (17a) only if the second part of the sentence is affirmative. Similarly, (17b) would be acceptable only with the parenthesized meaning,
and (17d) is unacceptable.

> (17)   a. Boliyáki'te?   Didn't you (pl.) eat?
>   b. Ee. (Toliyáki'te.)   Yes. (We didn't eat.)
>   c. *Te. (Toliyáki'te.)   No. (We didn't eat.)
>   d. *Ee. (Toliyáki.)   Yes. (We ate.)

Kirk-Greene (1971: 133-34) cites similar examples from Hausa:

> (18)   a. bai zo ba?   Hasn't he come?
>   b. i   Yes [i.e., what you have said is
>   right: he has not come].
>   c. a'a   No [i.e., what you have said is
>   wrong: he has come].

In contrast, the replies corresponding to (14b), (15b), and (16b) in English would involve negation:

(19)   a. No, the President hasn't left for Nairobi yet.
        b. No, I didn't see anyone at the compound.
        c. I hope not.

Generally, an affirmative answer to questions like (14a) and (15a) would be given only if the facts were contrary to what the questions implied. As can be seen from the examples in (14)-(16), the logic of negative yes/no questions in African English deviates from this pattern; however, it is consistent with the pattern found in African languages.

Word order in constructions involving possessive or demonstrative pronouns constitutes another area of difficulty. In Bantu languages, for example, adjectives generally follow the noun they modify. When a possessive and a demonstrative pronoun occur in the same noun phrase, they follow the noun, with the possessive generally preceding the demonstrative. In Hausa (a West African language), the possessive follows the noun and the demonstrative precedes it (Kirk-Greene 1971). These structural characteristics often influence the production of English sentences by primary school learners, as may be seen in the following sentences.

(20)   a. I met the teacher our new.
        b. Your both children want to speak to you.
        c. That your brother, will he come?
        d. Saying Amen to those his prayers . . .

(20a,b) were produced by Bantu-speaking Africans and (20c,d) by Hausa speakers.

Another area in which African English is characteristically deviant involves comparative constructions. In English, comparatives generally require the comparison of two terms, the *standard* (in the main clause) and the *compared* (in the comparative clause), with regard to some shared property. The standard is introduced by a comparative element such as -*er* (suffixed to a class of adjectives), *more, less,* or *worse,* and is followed by the correlative element *than* in the comparative clause:

(21)   a. Kenyatta was older than Nkrumah.
        b. Nkrumah was younger than Kenyatta.
        c. Monkeys are more dexterous than leopards.
        d. Leopards are less dexterous than monkeys.

In many West African and Bantu languages, however, the standard is
generally introduced by a verb such as *exceed* or *surpass,* which already incorporates the notion of superiority. In constructions involving comparison of inequality, as in (21) above, no comparative elements are needed: the comparison is simply conveyed by the verb, as
may be seen from the Lingala and Swahili sentences in (22) and (23).

(22) *Lingala:* (a) Lomekano lu:na *lulekákí* luye na makasi.
                      test   that   *it-exceeded* this in difficulty
                      (That test was harder/more difficult than this one.
                 (b) Ngomba ya Kilimanzaro *eleki* (ngomba) ya Kenya
                      na molai.
                      Mt. of Kilimanjaro *it-exceed* mt. of Kenya in
                      height
                      (Mount Kilimanjaro is higher/taller than Mount
                      Kenya.)

(23) *Swahili:* (a) Mtihani ule ulikuwa mgumu *kuliko* huu.
                      test that it-was hard *exceeding* this
                      (That test was harder/more difficult than this
                      one.)
                 (b) Mlima wa Kilimanjaro ni mrefu *kuliko* (mlima)
                      wa Kenya.
                      Mt. of Kilimanjaro is tall *exceeding* (Mt.) of
                      Kenya
                      (Mount Kilimanjaro is taller/higher than Mount
                      Kenya.)

Similar constructions in many other African languages appear to influence the production of comparatives in English, as suggested by the
following sentences (Chinebuah 1976).

(24) a. It is the youths who are skillful in performing tasks *than*
        the adults.
     b. They would have *more* powder on the hand and in their
        faces.

These sentences indicate that the speakers were aware of the rule for
deriving comparison of inequality constructions, but that they applied it only partially. This is a common deviation found in African
English.

    Let us now turn to semantic deviations. This is perhaps the most
interesting and dynamic area in which African English shows its creativity, particularly with regard to the derivation of new words. Lexical items in African English may be created in four principal ways:
by semantic extension, semantic shift, semantic transfer, and coinage
(Kirk-Greene 1971; Sey 1973).

Semantic extension involves adding a meaning(s) to a Standard English word. Consider, for example, the meanings of the italicized words in the following sentences (Sey 1973: 95-98).

(25) a. He sent me some *amount.*
     b. People have been running (away) with my huge *amounts.*

(26) a. I had no ticket, but I got in by *arrangement.*
     b. By *arrangement* you can go to heaven.

(27) a. I know him very well. He is in fact my *bench.*
     b. He is my *benchman.*

(28) a. He *bluffs* too much.
     b. He replied, putting his hands inside his pockets and *bluffing* arrogantly, boistering eye signals of inviolable romance.
     c. The fellow is too *boisterous* — too much. The store-keeper said.

According to Sey (1973), each italicized item in these sentences maintains its Standard English meaning, but has also acquired additional ones. In particular, the word *amount* in (25) means "money," with which it is used interchangeably, as well as "cash." The word *arrangement* in (26) refers to special arrangement, preferential treatment, or mutual arrangement. This word also occurs adjectivally, usually with *man* and rarely with *woman,* in expressions such as "he is an arrangement man" — that is, a person who habitually gets what he wants, not by normal means, but through his connections (Sey 1973). A similar expression in Nigerian English is "long legs," as in "he has long legs." *Bench* and *benchman* in (27) are synonyms and mean "a crony or intimate friend"; *bluff* in (28a, b) has the reading of either "to give the impression of self-importance in an amusing way" or "to dress ornately/fashionably" (Sey 1973). In (28c), *boisterous* means to "be bad tempered or quarrelsome." The words *bluff* and *arrangement* are not restricted to Ghanaian English; they occur also in Nigerian and East African English.

Closely related to this mode of derivation are semantic shifts. These involve the redefinition of the characteristic patterns of a word within the semantic field so that its central contexts become marginal, and vice versa (Sey 1973). Sometimes archaic and technical terms replace common ones in everyday speech. For example, the italicized words in (29) have as their meanings those given in parentheses, rather than the generally accepted ones:

(29) a. Even watering the Agricultural Survey Officer's garden
was more dignified than what I had to do — *carrying*
[on head] *blocks* [i.e., rectangular blocks of concrete
for building] for the markets that were being built.
b. The most important point however is that already we
are seven and a half million strong and quite a number
of these cannot get jobs to do, so we should cut down
on *bringing forth* [i.e., having babies].

Other examples include the use of *family* for descendants of the same
ancestor, house, or lineage; *machine* for sewing machine; *minerals* for
soft drinks; *play* for dance; *senior service* for upper class; *park* for
football field; *serviceable* for a person (or, occasionally, an animal)
that is always willing to serve.[6]

Another mode of deriving new words involves semantic transfer:
the complete reassignment of the meaning of a word. For example,
the expressions *to see red, steer, cut,* and *town council* in (30) have
readings that are completely different from or inconsistent with those
generally accepted:

(30) a. You'll *see red!* Said the angry carpenter to the frightened boy.
b. To my surprise I found him [the driver] resting on the
steer and fell asleep.
c. As a result, he lost control of the *steer* and the car run
into a nearby bush.
d. I asked her to dance, but she *cut* me.
e. They must pay the *town council* people more because
they are responsible for the health of the people.

Sentence (30d) is from Kenyan English, whereas the rest are from
Ghanaian English. The expression *to see red* in (30a) is a threat to
harm or punish a person, while *steer* in (30b, c) means "steering
wheel." The verb *cut* in a sentence like (30d) has the reading "to refuse"; it appears to be common in the speech of Swahili speakers at
the pre-university level. The same expression is also reported to be
common in South Asian English and might also occur in Black American English. *Town council* in West African English refers to a sani-
tary department, especially to lower-ranking officers (Sey 1973).

The final and most interesting mode of lexical derivation is deliberate coinage. It is in coinage that African English exhibits the rich
derivational morphology that is so characteristic of African languages:
new lexical items can be derived via prefixation, suffixation, combination of both, or by reduplication and compounding. These processes
apply equally to nominal, verbal, adjectival, and adverbial derivations.

Nominalization via prefixation and suffixation is illustrated by sentences (31a-f) and (31g), cited in Kirk-Greene (1971: 139) and Sey (1973: 80), respectively:

(31) a. Both U. and E. had pre-knowledge of one another's *wheretos* of going and *whereabouts*.
b. There's no *rigging* it, I've got to learn French.
c. The girls are facing a lot of *hardcap* [i.e., hardship].
d. The ladies of the town conferred them [titles] on me after a very ripe *deservation*.
e. [It is] his wife to whom he has given nothing *coinable* [i.e., no money].
f. Be you assured that members are *impossibles, impregnables* of the country.
g. The people described the *enstoolment* of X as illegal.

All of these, despite their oddity, are derived analogically according to existing English rules, although they do not occur in Standard English.

In addition to affixational derivations, one commonly finds cases of compounding:

(32) a. You have to be careful with these *been-to* boys. You can't trust them.
b. Where in the world did you get such a *me-and-my-darling* [i.e., a small sofa or love seat]?
c. We stopped at Awutu to buy some *bush-meat* [i.e., game].
d. He doesn't use a *chewing-stick* to clean his teeth.
e. The *gate fee* for the cinema show is four shillings.
f. I saw your *my dear* at the church [i.e., girlfriend/boyfriend].
g. I have been going to the *small room* a lot, sir [i.e., toilet].
h. I was a *tight friend* of your sister [i.e., close/intimate friend].

Examples (32c-h) are cited by Sey (1973) as Ghanaianisms, but they occur elsewhere in West African English, though perhaps less frequently (see, e.g., Bamgbose 1971, 1982). Other examples of compound nominals include *bone-to-flesh dance* (a close dance between a man and a woman), *push baby* (maidservant), *European appointment* (high-level white-collar position), *known faces* (acquaintances), and *white-black-man* (black intellectual who behaves as a white man). Some of these are loan translations from African languages, while others are derived analogically.

Equally interesting are derivations involving verbs, which exploit
the morphology of English and African languages to their fullest extent. Some of the most interesting examples are given in Kirk-Greene
(1971: 140).

(33) a. U. with his dazzling red eyes . . . *shadowed* R. much.
     b. Each and every day one was well informed to *cope up*
        with any eventuality.
     c. My gentleman *naked* himself [i.e., undressed].
     d. I was *coupled* at the dance [i.e., found a dancing
        partner].
     e. Are you *nauseating* for Nigeria yet [i.e., are you
        homesick]?
     f. Any persons who were interested in any of the social
        clubs he had mentioned or *unmentioned* . . .
     g. I opened the door and *visualized* [i.e., saw] a very
        familiar face.
     h. Sorry not to have been *chanced* to write before.

Other common verbs in African English include *destool, enstool,
fabricate, manage with, branch, chase, to be on seat, take in, to be
with,* and *to move with,* as in the examples below (Kirk-Greene 1971;
Bamgbose 1971; Sey 1973).

(34) a. Nana X claimed that since he had been illegally *destooled*
        by the old regime, and the N.L.C. brought him back to
        the stool, he would not give it back . . .
     b. They were *enstooled* in the stool house where they poured
        libation to the ancestors whom they had succeeded.
     c. All my mates there have paid their money, and if I beg
        them to *manage with* them . . .
     d. Do you *fabricate* [i.e., make] chairs and other types of
        furniture at the Carpentery School?
     e. I am going to *chase* that girl [i.e., win her affection].
     f. I am going to *branch* at my uncle's house.
     g. The minister *is not on seat.* Come back later.
     h. My wife *took in* [i.e., became pregnant] last month.
     i. The servant *is with* your knife.
     j. I don't like it when my son *moves with* bush boys.
     k. I *hear* a smell. Is something burning in the kitchen?

Sentences like these are found both in everyday speech and in published works, and are not to be considered simply as slips of the
tongue. Very few of them (e.g., 34a, i, k) can be explained in terms
of L_1 interference; the rest are independent developments based on
English rules.

While one might argue that these verbs and many others like them can be derived both from English and African sources, the formation of adverbs in African English appears to be a uniquely African phenomenon. Most African languages do not have many adverbs or adjectives, for that matter. To compensate, they exploit the process of reduplication, using either nouns or adjectives to derive adverbs:

(35) a. *Hausa:*   sànnu   slow(ly)
     b.   sànnu sànnu   slowly, carefully
     c.   baḳi   black (masc.)
     d.   baḳi baḳi   blackish

(36) a. *Lingala:*   noki   quick
     b.   noki noki   quickly
     c.   malémbe   slow; soft/gentle
     d.   malémbe malémbe   slowly; softly/gently

(37) a. *Swahili:*   pole   meek, mild, gentle
     b.   pole pole   meekly, mildly, gently
     c.   mmoja   an individual
     d.   mmoja mmoja   individually/singly

This process leads to the production of deviant sentences like (38) in African English

(38) a. Don't drag your feet, son! Walk *quick quick!*
     b. Life is a big challenge, you have to take it *small small.*
     c. You are eating too *fastly.* Take your time and eat *slow slow.*

where *quick quick* means "quickly," *small small* means either "slowly" or "bit by bit," and *slow slow* means "slowly." This type of reduplication cannot be interpreted as an expression of intensity, as might otherwise be the case in certain African languages; the reduplicated adjectives in these sentences function as adverbs.

Why do such syntactic and semantic deviations occur in the English varieties spoken in Africa? The discussion thus far has suggested two possible sources for these deviant constructions: L_1 or mother tongue interference, and analogical derivation based on English. It has been suggested, further, that L_1 interference may be more pervasive than analogical derivations (see also Bamgboṣe 1982).

While such an answer might adequately account for the phenomena observed here, it fails to explain why interference and analogical derivations of the type noted here occur at all. Furthermore, such an answer treats African English as an isolated phenomenon, failing to take into account the milieu in and the conditions under

which English is learned and used in Anglophone Africa. The fact of
the matter is that African English is simply an aspect of a more general phenomenon that has been taking place with regard to what Kachru (1976a) calls "transplanted" languages. Many of the syntactic and
semantic deviations presented here have been noted in other varieties
of English (Kachru 1965, 1975, 1976a, 1981; Bailey and Robinson
1973; Strevens 1977). Kachru (1965: 398-99), for example, discusses
many of the modes of lexical derivation identified in this chapter. Kachru (1976a: 156-58) presents five major syntactic deviations characteristic of Indian English. Two of these (reduplication and misuse of articles) are analogous to the ones noted with respect to African English.

The fact that such similarities cut across language and national
boundaries clearly indicates that African English is not a unique phenomenon, but a common development to be expected, given the milieu in which English is taught and spoken as a foreign language in Africa. These similarities suggest, further, that certain shared factors underlie the production of these varieties of English. Such factors have
been referred to in the literature under the generic terms *indigenization, contextualization,* or *nativization* (Kachru 1965, 1981; Bailey
and Robinson 1973; Strevens 1977). That is, English is adapted to
local or regional linguistic conditions, and thereby deviates system-
atically from the Standard dialect.

It should be pointed out here that the situation in which English is learned and spoken in Anglophone Africa (excluding Liberia,
Zimbabwe, and South Africa) is essentially no different from that in
which other European languages are used officially. Africa is traditionally divided into three linguistic zones (Anglophone, Francophone, and Lusophone) in terms of the official language adopted by
each country. However, these divisions reflect more the political
zones of influence of the former colonial powers (Britain, Belgium,
France, and Portugal) than the objective realities of the language situation in the continent. It is estimated, for instance, that no more than
10 percent of the population of any African country speaks the official language (Alexandre 1967), except in the English-settled nations
of Liberia, South Africa, and Zimbabwe. If that is correct (as it seems
to be, on the basis of educational development statistics), we are dealing here with populations that are 90 percent non-conversant in English, French, or Portuguese, and whose only media of communication are African languages. It is therefore inaccurate to refer to African nations as Anglophone, Francophone, and Lusophone.

Admittedly, the number of English speakers in Africa will increase steadily as the use of English as a compulsory school subject

expands. Fishman et al. (1977) have amassed impressive statistics on the spread of English in the world, showing that, among other things, English is becoming one of the most important languages in Africa with regard to mass media, international communication, and education. In education, for example, Fishman et al. (1977: 16) report that 47.1 percent of primary school students and 96.9 percent of those in secondary schools throughout Africa are enrolled in English classes. These are the highest percentages on any continent, according to the authors.

But they do not say anything about the number of speakers. This number, contrary to Mazrui's (1975) claim regarding the growth of what he terms "Afro-Saxons," will remain very small for some time to come, for several reasons. First, except in an infinitesimally small number of interracial families where English is the language of communication at home (Mazrui 1975), African speakers learn English at school and use it for very specific functions: education, official business (including office work, administration, and commerce), international diplomacy, and broadcasting. Broadcasting is also carried out in African linguae francae (e.g., Hausa, Igbo, and Yoruba in Nigeria; Akan, Ga, and Ewe in Ghana; Swahili and Kikuyu in Kenya), as is daily communication. Second and third, the mastery of English is not possible until about the third year in secondary school, and there are very few qualified teachers to effectively implement the use of English as the medium of instruction at all levels of education. Under these conditions, it is not surprising to find so many deviations from Standard English in African English.

An equally important dimension of this Africanization of English in Africa is the deliberate attempt by African writers, especially novelists, to preserve and communicate African culture in their writing. Consider in this regard the following passage from Gabriel Okara's book, *The Voice* (1970: 25).

(39) When Okolo came to know himself, he was lying on a floor, on a cold, cold floor lying. He opened his eyes to see but nothing he saw, nothing he saw, for the darkness was evil darkness and the outside night was black black night. Okolo lay still in the darkness enclosed by darkness, and he/his thoughts picked in his inside. Then his picked thoughts his eyes opened but his vision only met a rock-like darkness. The picked thoughts then drew his legs but his legs did not come. They were as heavy as a canoe full of sand. His thoughts in his inside began to fly in his inside darkness like frightened birds hither, thither, homeless. . . . Then the flying thoughts drew his hands but the

hands did not belong to him, it seemed. So Okolo on the
cold cold floor lay with his body as soft as an over-pounded
foo foo. So Okolo lay with his eyes open wide in the rock-
like darkness staring, staring.

Okara is one of Nigeria's and Africa's finest poets. The above passage
is often said to represent the author's conscious effort to impose the
structure of Ijö (his mother tongue) on English in an attempt to preserve the African thought (Madubuike 1975). Another African writer,
the renown Nigerian novelist Chinua Achebe (1966: 20), has also experimented with the idea of integrating African language structure
and thereby transmitting African thought in English:

(40) a. I want one of my sons to join these people and be my
eyes there. If there is nothing in it you will come back.
But if there is something there you will bring home my
share. The world is like a Mask, dancing. If you want to
see it well you do not stand in one place. My spirit tells
me that those who do not befriend the white man today
will be saying *had we known* tomorrow.
b. I am sending you as my representative among those
people — just to be on the safe side in case the new
religion develops. One has to move with the times or
else one is left behind. I have a hunch that those who
fail to come to terms with the white man may well
regret their lack of foresight.

The first passage reflects not only an Igbo cultural background, but
also a linguistic style that is not uncommon in many African languages.
The second passage, in contrast, lacks these characteristics and gives
the impression that something is missing.

All these factors — interference from mother tongues, adaptations necessitated by the language learning and contact situation in
multilingual African societies, and the deliberate attempts by Africans
to preserve and transmit African cultural thought in English — con-
spire, as it were, to form what I have termed African English. These
factors constitute the sources and *raison d'être* of this variety of
English.

Implications for Language Policies in Education

The occurrence and development of African English raise a number of important questions that bear critically on the issue of language
policies vis-à-vis education in Africa. Various arguments have been advanced to support the retention of English, French, and Portuguese as

the languages of instruction in African education (Alexandre 1967; Foster 1971; Whiteley 1971). Because the fallacy of these arguments has already been demonstrated in Ansre (1975), Bokamba (1976), and Bokamba and Tlou (1977), the subject needs no more discussion here, except to point out a few implications of these data for current policies.

The literature on language acquisition tells us that second-language learning is a task beset from the outset by all sorts of problems (Lenneberg 1967; Dulay and Burt 1974; Jain 1974; Seliger 1978). The situation is further complicated when L_2 is learned in a non-native context. That African English should show consistent deviations from Standard English is not at all surprising; rather, it is consonant with current theories of language acquisition. But what these deviations show, in part, is that learners have not quite mastered the official language; as a result, poor academic performances on the part of the students and low outputs for the academic institutions are unavoidable. There is reason to believe that the high failure rates in African secondary school and university admission examinations is directly related to proficiency in the language of instruction (Gbedemah 1971; Apronti 1974; Bokamba 1976, 1979; Bokamba and Tlou 1977; Bokamba forthcoming; Afolayan 1976). Given that primary education is currently *terminal* for 85 to 90 percent of the children, one wonders about the utility of English and other European languages for such children. It is clear from such statistics (UNESCO 1976) that the use of these languages as media of instruction at this level is both counterproductive and unnecessarily costly; therefore, such use cannot be viewed as efficient or conducive to national progress.

Even if one were to grant that some degree of progress is achieved, to the extent that African schools forge a small intellectual elite at exorbitantly high cost of human and financial resources, these benefits are more than offset by the fact that the entrenchment and expansion of the official languages preclude the development of African languages.[7] If African languages cannot be developed to serve as media of education and wider communication within and across national boundaries, then the emerging intellegentsia become culturally alienated from and useless to their societies. The roles of European and African languages in African education must, therefore, be carefully evaluated so that comprehensive and realistic language policies that are consonant with African developmental goals can be adopted.

NOTES

1. Our knowledge of the actual number of languages (as opposed to dialects) spoken in Africa is very sketchy at this point; thus these estimates must be taken with a great deal of caution.

2. Except for the Northern African nations which have adopted Arabic as their national language, only three Sub-Saharan states have adopted indigenous national languages. These are: Amharic for Ethiopia; Somali for Somalia; and Swahili for Tanzania. Kenya declared Swahili the official language of the government in 1974, but has not yet implemented a language policy. The remaining countries have adopted the languages of their former colonizing powers.

3. I am aware that there is very little agreement on what constitutes, for example, Liberian English or Nigerian English; but to the extent that we can isolate certain features of English as characteristic of African languages, we have a variety of a sort.

4. The term "educated African" will here refer to any African who has at least completed primary school.

5. When Bamgboṣe (1971) was published, a graduate of an elementary school in Nigeria was expected to have received at least three years of training in and use of English. It is unlikely, therefore, that the student in question was consciously translating his letter word-for-word from his mother tongue.

6. Peter Trudgill (in personal communication) has informed me that *minerals* and *park* are used in the same way in British English and should, therefore, be properly called *Britishisms*.

7. One consequence of the French colonial language policy, which forbade the use of African languages in education in the colonies, is that the development and standardization of these languages were delayed by several decades. This policy contrasted with those of Britain and Belgium, whereby African languages were incorporated into the educational system as subjects and media of instruction; as a result, a number of linguae francae developed and flourished to an extent unparalleled in the former French colonies. Current African policies may have a similar effect on the further development of African languages if nothing is done to modify them.

REFERENCES

Abdulaziz, M. 1972. Triglossia and Swahili-English bilingualism in Tanzania. *Sociology of Language* 1: 197-213.

Achebe, C. 1966. The English language and the African writer. *Insight* 20.

Afolayan, A. 1976. The six-year primary project in Nigeria. Pp. 113-34 in Bamgboṣe, ed. (1976).

Agheyisi, R. 1977. Language interlarding in the speech of Nigerians. Pp. 97-110 in Kotey and Der-Houssikian, eds. (1977).

Alexandre, P. 1967. *Langues et langage en Afrique Noire*. Paris: Payot.

Angogo, R., and Hancock, I. 1980. English in Africa: emerging standards or diverging regionalisms? *English World-Wide: A Journal of Varieties of English* 1(1): 67-96.

Ansre, G. 1970. Language policy for the promotion of national unity and understanding in West Africa. Mimeographed. Lagon: Institute of African Studies, University of Ghana.

———. 1971. The influence of English on West African languages. In Spencer, ed. (1971a).

————. 1975. Four rationalisations for maintaining the European languages in education in Africa. Paper read at the International Congress of African Studies on the Use of African Languages in Education, Kinshasa, Zaire, December, 1975.

Apronti, E. O. 1974. Sociolinguistics and the question of national language: the case of Ghana. *Studies in African Linguistics* Supplement 5: 1-20.

Bailey, R. W., and Robinson, J. L. 1973. *Varieties of present-day English.* New York: Macmillan.

Bamgboṣe, A. 1971. The English language in Nigeria. In J. Spencer, ed. (1971a).

————, ed. 1976. *Mother tongue education: the West African experience.* Paris: UNESCO.

————. 1982. Standard Nigerian English. In this volume.

Bokamba, E. G. 1976. Authenticity and the choice of a national language: the case of Zaire. *Présence Africaine* 99/100: 104-42. Also in *Studies in the Linguistic Sciences* 6(2): 23-64.

————. 1979. On the necessity of a bilingual educational policy in Sub-Saharan Africa. Paper read at the Symposium on Language Policies in African Education, University of Illinois, Urbana, July, 1978. (To appear in Bokamba, forthcoming.)

————, ed. Forthcoming. *Language policies in African education.* Washington, D.C.: University Press of America.

————, and Tlou, J.L. 1977. The consequences of the language policies of African states vis-à-vis education. In Kotey and Der-Houssikian, eds. (1977).

Chinebuah, I. K. 1976. Grammatical deviance and first language interference. *West African Journal of Modern Languages* 1: 67-78.

Dulay, H., and Burt, M. K. 1974. A new perspective on the creative construction process in child second language acquisition. *Language Learning* 24: 253-78.

Fishman, J. A.; Cooper, R. L.; and Conrad, A. W., eds. 1977. *The spread of English: the sociology of English as an additional language.* Rowley, Mass.: Newbury House.

Foster, P. 1971. Problems of literacy in Sub-Saharan Africa. In Sebeok, ed. (1971).

Gbedemah, F. K. 1971. Alternative language policies for education in Ghana. Ph.D. dissertation, UCLA.

Herbert, R. K., ed. 1975. *Patterns in language, culture, and society: Sub-Saharan Africa.* Special of Working Papers in Linguistics, no. 19. Columbus: Ohio State University.

Jain, M. P. 1974. Error analysis: source, cause and significance. In Richards, ed. (1974).

Kachru, Braj B. 1965. The Indianness in Indian English. *Word* 21(3): 391-410.

————. 1975. Lexical innovations in South Asian English. *International Journal of the Sociology of Language* 4: 55-74.

————. 1976a. Models of English for the Third World: white man's linguistic burden or language pragmatics? *TESOL Quarterly* 10(2): 221-39.

————. 1976b. Indian English: a sociolinguistic profile of a transplanted language. In Kachru (1976c).

————. 1976c. *Dimensions of bilingualism: theory and case studies.* Special issue of *Studies in Language Learning.* Unit for Foreign Language Study and Research, University of Illinois, Urbana.

————. 1981. The pragmatics of non-native varieties of English. In Smith, ed. (1981).

Kirk-Greene, A. 1971. The influence of West African languages on English. In Spencer, ed. (1971a).

Kotey, P. F., and Der-Houssikian, H., eds. 1977. *Language and linguistic problems in Africa: proceedings of the VIIth Conference on African linguistics.* Columbia, N.C.: Hornbeam Press.

Lenneberg, E. H. 1967. *Biological foundations of language.* New York: John Wiley & Sons.

Madubuike, I. 1975. African literary communications and the European languages: the case of Francophone writers of Senegal. In Herbert, ed. (1975).

Mazrui, A. 1975. *The political sociology of the English language: an African perspective.* The Hague: Mouton.

Mhina, G. A. 1975. The Tanzania experience in the use of Kiswahili in education. Paper read at the International Congress of African Studies on the Use of African Languages in Education, Kinshasa, Zaire, December, 1975.

Ministry of Information, Nigeria. 1977. *Federal Republic of Nigeria national policy on education.* Lagos: Federal Ministry of Information Printing Division.

Okara, G. 1970. *The Voice.* London: Heinemann Educational Books.

Parkin, D. J. 1974. Language switching in Nairobi. In Whiteley, ed. (1974).

Richards, J. C., ed. 1974. *Error analysis: perspectives on second language acquisition.* London: Longman.

Ritchie, W. C., ed. 1978. *Second language acquisition research: issues and implications.* New York: Academic Press.

Scotton, M. C. 1972. *Choosing a lingua franca in an African capital.* Edmonton, Alberta: Linguistic Research, Inc.

————, and Ury, W. 1977. Bilingual strategies: the social functions of code-switching. *Linguistics: An International Review* 193: 5-20.

Sebeok, T., ed. 1971. *Current trends in linguistics, vol. 7: linguistics in Sub-Saharan Africa.* The Hague: Mouton.

Seliger, H. W. 1978. Implications of a multiple critical periods hypothesis for second language learning. In Ritchie, ed. (1978).

Sey, K. A. 1973. *Ghanaian English: an exploratory survey.* London: Macmillan.

Smith, L., ed. 1981. *English for cross-cultural communication.* London: Macmillan.

Spencer, J., ed. 1971a. *The English language in West Africa.* London: Longmans.

————. 1971b. Colonial languages and their legacies. In Sebeok, ed. (1971).

————. 1971c. West Africa and the English language. In Spencer, ed. (1971a).

Strevens, P. 1977. *New orientations in the teaching of English.* London: Oxford University Press.

UNESCO. 1976. *Education in Africa since 1960: a statistical review.* Conference of Ministers of Education of African Member States, Lagos, January 27-February 4, 1976. Paris: UNESCO.

Voegelin, C. F., and Voegelin, F. M. 1964. *Languages of the world: African fascicle one. Anthropological Linguistics* 6(5).

Whiteley, W. H. 1971. Language policies of independent African states. In Sebeok, ed. (1971).

————, ed. 1974. *Language in Kenya.* Nairobi: Oxford University Press.

Zuengler, J. 1982. Kenyan English. In this volume.

6

Standard Nigerian English:
Issues of Identification

AYỌ BAMGBOṢE

The question whether there is a "Nigerian English" should, at this point, have become a non-issue. For one thing, it is generally known that in a language contact situation, particularly a close one where an exoglossic language becomes a second language with an official role in a country, the second language is bound to be influenced by its linguistic and cultural environment.[1] For another, the existence of several different "Englishes" is now generally accepted by linguists.[2] However, many educated Nigerians still believe there is no such thing as Nigerian English, even though their own speech and usage provide ample evidence of its existence.[3] A Nigerian expert in TEFL declared recently: "I do not believe that there is *Nigerian English* now in the linguistic, demographic, and sociological senses in which there is an American English, Australian English and British English."[4]

Some of those who deny that there is a Nigerian English may genuinely believe that the English they speak is no different from one of the native varieties of English; but I have a feeling that those who feel this way must be very few. Most of those who refuse to accept that there is a Nigerian English are genuinely worried about the implication of accepting a Nigerian variety of English as an appropriate model, particularly in language teaching. They fear that, in time, such a variety may degenerate into a different language, like pidgin English. Hence, they insist that "only the best, native-speaker, performance level should be aimed at"[5] in higher education. Closely related to this view is a tendency towards purism. The so-called deviant or non-standard forms found in Nigerian English are regarded by some as "mistakes," rather than as evidence of a distinct type of English in Nigeria.[6]

One noticeable effect of the refusal to accept the existence of a Nigerian English is the perpetuation of the myth that the English taught in Nigerian schools is just the same as, say, British English; a corollary myth is that teachers of English, even at the primary school level, are capable of teaching this model effectively. In our teaching and examinations we concentrate on drilling and testing out of existence forms of speech that even the teachers will use freely when they do not have their textbooks open before them.

Identifying Varieties of Nigerian English

Lack of acceptance of the existence of a Nigerian English has not deterred linguists from observing and describing the varieties of English used in Nigeria. Brosnahan started a trend of ranging the varieties on a scale and linking them with levels of education: "The speakers of English in Nigeria encompass all gradations from the British educated speakers of an approximation to Received Pronunciation of Southern English to the large numbers whose knowledge of English is limited to a few words of a pidgin variety" (1958: 99). Brosnahan then went on to identify four levels of Nigerian English:

Level I: Pidgin; spoken by those without any formal education.

Level II: Spoken by those who have had primary school education. Most speakers belong to this level.

Level III: Spoken by those who have had secondary school education. Marked by increased fluency, wider vocabulary, and conscious avoidance of Level I usage.

Level IV: Close to Standard English but retaining some features of Levels II and III. Spoken by those with university education.

Banjo (1971a: 169-70) took the identification further by indicating the linguistic characteristics of the different varieties and introducing variables of international intelligibility and social acceptability. His own four varieties are as follows:

Variety 1:   Marked by wholesale transfer of phonological, syntactic, and lexical features of Kwa or Niger-Congo to English. Spoken by those whose knowledge of English is very imperfect. Neither socially acceptable in Nigeria nor internationally intelligible.

Variety 2:   Syntax close to that of Standard British English, but with strongly marked phonological and lexical peculiarities. Spoken by up to 75 percent of those who speak English in the country. Socially acceptable, but with rather low international intelligibility.

Variety 3:   Close to Standard British English both in syntax and in semantics; similar in phonology, but different in phonetic features as well as with regard to certain lexi-

cal peculiarities. Socially acceptable and internationally intelligible. Spoken by less than 10 percent of the
population.

Variety 4:   Identical with Standard British English in syntax and
semantics, and having identical phonological and phonetic features of a British regional dialect of English.
Maximally internationally intelligible, but socially unacceptable. Spoken by only a handful of Nigerians
born or brought up in England.

A comparison of the two schemes shows a remarkable similarity,
except at the bottom and top ends of the scale. In Banjọ's scheme,
pidgin (Brosnahan's Level I) is excluded and treated as a separate language from English, while in Brosnahan's scheme Native English (Banjọ's Variety 4) is not treated as a variety of Nigerian English.[7] We are
left with the following correspondences: Level II = Variety 1; Level
III = Variety 2; and Level IV = Variety 3.

Two issues arise from the varieties identified above. The first is
the question of education as a variable in identifying speakers of the
different varieties. The second is the question of which variety is the
best candidate for a standard Nigerian English.

Level of education is an attractive parameter for characterizing
level of usage; it has been used not only for Nigerian English, but also
for Ghanaian English.[8] But it is open to one main objection: there are
speakers who perform below, or above, the expected level of competence based on their level of education. Several writers have drawn
attention to this problem.[9] In fairness to Brosnahan (1958), who
based his varieties of Nigerian English on level of education, it must
be pointed out that he was aware of the need to qualify the criterion:
he adds that "opportunity for its use [i.e., English], innate ability
and intelligence and perseverance with schemes of private study and
correspondence schools all tend to smooth out the differences left
by different opportunities of formal education" (Brosnahan 1958:
100). What this means, in effect, is that education as a variable is to
be used flexibly. One would expect a university graduate to be a
Variety 3 speaker, but if a few such graduates cannot attain that
standard, they should be classified with speakers of the appropriate
lower variety. Similarly, a primary school leaver who has had prolonged exposure to English or who has been able to improve himself
through private study will be classified with speakers of a higher
variety. Used in this way, level of education will be no more than a
statement of probability. The expectation will of course be that *most*
university graduates will be Variety 3 speakers, while most primary

school leavers who have had no additional exposure to English will
be Variety 1 or 2 speakers.

There is remarkable unanimity about the variety of English that
can be called "Educated Nigerian English." It is that variety which is
closest to Native English, being "same" with it in syntax and phonology, "similar" in semantics, but "different" in lexis and phonetics.
Criper (1971) has identified for Ghanaian English a subtype of this
variety which is identical in all respects, except that its phonology
is not "same" but only "similar" to that of Native English. It is quite
possible that there are Nigerian speakers of Variety 3 English who
make all the phonological distinctions found in a native variety of
English; but my guess is that such people must be very few in number. A recent study (Ekong 1978) has shown that a group of perfectly intelligible Variety 3 speakers of Nigerian English produce
consistently only sixteen vowel contrasts out of a possible twenty-
four contrasts (including diphthongs and triphthongs) in Received
Pronunciation as described by Daniel Jones.[10] This situation seems
more typical of the vast majority of Variety 3 speakers. When the
two other variables of acceptability and international intelligibility
are considered, Variety 3 or Educated Nigerian English stands out
as the only plausible candidate for a standard Nigerian English.

Identifying Nigerian Usages in Nigerian English

An inevitable point of departure in describing usage in a second-
language situation is a conscious or unconscious comparison with a
native variety of the language concerned. This is precisely what has
been done in the description of Nigerian English. Labels such as
"same", "different," or "similar" must be justified in terms of observed usage in the varieties to which they are applied. Three approaches may be identified: the interference approach, the deviation
approach, and the creativity approach.

The interference approach attempts to trace Nigerian usages to
the influence of the Nigerian languages. This approach is certainly
most relevant as far as the phonetics of Nigerian English is concerned.[11]
But as I have pointed out elsewhere, even at this level there are "features which are typical of the pronunciation of most Nigerian speakers
of English" (Bamgboṣe 1971: 42) irrespective of their first-language
background. Besides, a typical pronunciation may result from a factor
other than interference. For example, most speakers of English from
the eastern part of Nigeria pronounce the possessive "your" as [jua]
or [ja], even though all the languages in that area have the sound [ɔ].

The prevalence of this pronunciation is no doubt due to its widespread use by teachers and generations of pupils who have passed through the same schools.

The interference approach is even less justifiable in lexis and syntax. Adekunle (1974) attributes all of Standard Nigerian English's Nigerian usages in lexis and syntax to interference from the mother tongue. It is quite easy to show that while some usages can be so attributed, the vast majority, at least in Educated Nigerian English, arise from the normal process of language development involving a narrowing or extension of meaning or the creation of new idioms. And most such usages cut across all first-language backgrounds. For example, when "travel" is used in the sense "to be away," as in *My father has traveled* (= My father is away), it is not a transfer of a first-language expression into English, but a modification of the meaning of the verb "to travel."

One final objection to the interference approach is that not all cases of interference can validly be considered Nigerian usages. Some clearly belong to the level of pidgin English. For instance, the absence of a gender distinction in third-person pronominal reference may result from first-language interference, e.g., *He talk say . . .* (= He/She says that . . .), but it is unlikely that this will be considered a feature of any variety of Nigerian English.[12]

The deviation approach involves a comparison of observed Nigerian usage with Native English, and the labeling of all differences as "deviant."[13] Such deviance may result from interference, or from an imperfect attempt to reproduce the target expressions. For example, *Borrow me your pen* (= Lend me your pen) is clearly a case of interference from a first language which makes no lexical distinction between "lend" and "borrow." On the other hand, the pluralization of "equipment" in *We bought the equipments* indicates a failure to grasp the distinction between countable and mass nouns.

There are two main weaknesses in the deviation approach. First, it tends to suggest that the observed usage is "imperfect" or "nonstandard" English. The fact that some so-called deviations have now achieved the status of identifying markers of a standard Nigerian English tends to be overlooked in a description that lumps all divergences together as deviant usage. Second, the deviation approach ignores the fact that certain characteristic Nigerian usages in English result from the creativity of the users.

The creativity approach tends to focus on the exploitation of the resources of Nigerian languages as well as of English to create new idioms and expressions. According to this approach, a usage which might otherwise have been classified as resulting from interference or deviation is seen as a legitimate second-language creation.[14] Thus, from the expression *She has been to Britain* a new noun, *been-to,* has been created to describe anyone who has traveled overseas, particularly to Britain. (See also Chapter 20.)

The main advantage of the creativity approach is that it recognizes the development of Nigerian English as a type in its own right. But not all cases of usage in Nigerian English can properly be regarded as arising from creativity. Besides, certain usages motivated by creativity are, at best, substandard English. Amos Tutuọla's novel, *My Life in the Bush of Ghosts,* is a good example of this. The incidents in the novel take place "in those days of unknown year" when "slave wars were causing dead luck to both young and old"; and the hero visits "Deads'-town" and sees "born and die babies" as well as "triplet ghosts and ghostesses."[15]

The above discussion shows that while each approach throws some light on the nature of Nigerian English, none is by itself adequate to characterize the whole spectrum of Nigerian English. Besides, not every feature thrown up by each approach necessarily exemplifies Nigerian English. A combination of all approaches is therefore required, and a certain amount of subjective judgment regarding acceptability will be required in determining what falls within or outside the scope of Nigerian English.

One issue which constantly arises in determining a truly Nigerian usage is whether what is being held out as a local variant is not instead "incorrect" English. There are a number of reasons why this continues to be a serious issue. First, as has already been mentioned, it is inherent in a second-language situation for a comparison to be made with a native variety of the language concerned. Differences then have to be classified somehow; often opinions differ as to whether some are "errors" or correct local variants.[16] Perhaps this point is best illustrated by the following opinion: "My contention is that although one finds some differences between certain usages by some Nigerians and, for instance, British usages, most of such differences are due to mistakes of some sort; they should not be regarded as 'typically Nigerian' especially as they have not been proved to be general" (Salami 1968: 105).

Second, arising from the tradition of "error analysis" among practitioners of TESL, which has generally involved taking schoolchildren's or students' essays to bits and carefully noting the "errors" and "deviations," it has become difficult to draw the line between a local variant and an actual error. Some cite extremely numerous examples of usages in such essays as instances of Nigerian English, while others maintain that they are merely "mistakes and solecisms."[17]

Third, the teaching and examining of English in Nigeria tends to ensure that local variants will continue to be labeled "errors." Children are taught that to say "senior brother" is wrong; they should say "elder brother." Yet the former is used by a majority of educated Nigerian speakers of English. I recall a moderation meeting for the English paper of the West African school certificate examination. One of the idioms to be tested was "putting back the clock," which in Nigerian English is putting back *the hands* of the clock. It is interesting that only two of the persons present at this meeting knew the correct version of this idiom. One was a native speaker; the other had consulted a dictionary of English idioms in preparation for the meeting. Quite clearly, this is a case where the latter version has become an authentic Nigerian usage in English.

There can be no solution to the issue of errors until another related issue is considered. This is the question of whose usage is to be accepted as typical or standard. I have already subscribed to the view that majority usage will not necessarily determine the standard; that is why I accept Banjọ's Variety 3 as the only plausible Standard Nigerian English. But Variety 3 itself contains usages which may be regarded as nonstandard.[18] The subjective element again enters: Whose usage is to be accepted? I hasten to suggest that it should not be that of the purist (who does not believe in a Nigerian English anyway), nor that of the foreign-educated elite (whose usage is, on the whole, not very different from a standard variety of English). The natural and spontaneous usage of the locally educated Nigerian user of English is a more reliable guide to the identification of typical Nigerian usage.[19]

Some Typical Features of Standard Nigerian English

In order to illustrate such features as I consider typical, I provide (below) examples based on my general observation of the use of English by Variety 3 speakers. I believe these features cut across different first-language backgrounds, and no amount of drilling or stigmatization is going to lead to their abandonment. The features are identified at the following levels: phonetics and phonology, morphology and syntax, lexis and semantics, and context.[20]

Phonetics and Phonology

Several phonetic features reflect the first language or regional background of the speakers; but there are also general phonetic features, such as the following: 1) A reduced vowel system involves various substitutions, such as [e] for [ei], [o] for [ou], [a] for [ɒ:] and [ə], and a frequent obliteration of the distinction in vowel quality between the vowels of *beat* and *bit, cord* and *cod,* with the former being substituted for the latter. 2) Syllable-timed instead of stress-timed rhythm is employed, with a reduced system of intonation. 3) An epenthetic vowel [u] or [i] may be introduced between a word-final syllabic consonant and the preceding consonant; e.g., in *bottle* and *button,* respectively. 4) Consistent spelling pronunciation occurs in words ending in orthographic *-mb, -ng,* and their derivatives; e.g., *bomb, climb, bomber, plumber, sing, hang, singer, hanger.* 5) Characteristic stress patterns occur, as in the following words: 'success, main'tenance, ˌrecog'nize, ˌinvesti'gate, ˌcongratu'late, ma'dam, 'circumference. 6) Contrastive stress is avoided in sentences. Instead of *"John* did it," we are likely to have "It was John who did it."

Morphology and Syntax

These are generally the same as in Standard English, except for features such as the following: 1) Peculiar word formation may occur with plurals (e.g., *equipments, aircrafts, deadwoods*), antonyms (*indisciplined*), and adverbials (*singlehandedly*). 2) Dropping of "to" from the infinitive after certain verbs; e.g., *enable him do it.* 3) A preposition may be employed where Native English will avoid or will use a different preposition; e.g., *voice out* instead of "voice" (I am going to voice out my opinion), *discuss about* instead of "discuss" (We shall discuss about that later), *congratulate for* instead of "congratulate on" (I congratulate you for your brilliant performance). 4) A focus construction is often used, involving the subject of the sentence as focus and an anaphoric pronoun subject, e.g., *The politicians and their supporters, they don't often listen to advice.*[21] *A person who has no experience, can he be a good leader?*

Lexis and Semantics

As has often been observed, most differences between Nigerian English and other forms of English are to be found in the innovations in lexical items and idioms and their meanings. Following are some of the features concerned. 1) New lexical items may either be coined from existing lexical items or borrowed from the local languages or from pidgin, either directly or in translation. For examples of coinage, consider *barb* (to cut [hair]) from "barber," *invitee* (guest) from "invite," *head-tie* (woman's headdress), and *go-slow* (traffic jam). Loanwords and loan translations are generally drawn from different

aspects of the cultural background, including food, dress, and customs for which there are quite often no exact equivalent lexical items
in English; e.g., *akara balls* (beancakes), *juju music* (a type of dance
music), *bush meat* (game), *tie-dye cloth* (cloth into which patterns
are made by tying up parts of it before dyeing), and *white-cap chiefs*
(senior chiefs in Lagos whose rank is shown by the white caps they
wear). 2) Some lexical items acquire new meanings; e.g., a *corner* becomes a "bend in a road," *globe* is an "electric bulb," *wet* means
"to water (flowers)," and a *launcher* is someone called upon to declare open a fund-raising function. *Locate* means "to assign to a
school or town" and is used when speaking of newly qualified teachers. *Land* is "to finish one's intervention or speech," *environment* is
a "neighborhood," and *bluff* means "to give an air of importance."
3) Other lexical items have retained older meanings no longer current
in Native English. *Dress,* "move at the end of a row so as to create
room for additional persons," is a retention of the earlier meaning
recorded by the *Shorter Oxford English Dictionary:* "to form in proper alignment." *Station,* "the town or city in which a person works,"
is a retention of the earlier meaning recorded by the same source:
"the locality to which an official is appointed for the exercise of his
functions." 4) Certain idioms acquire new forms or meanings. *To eat
one's cake and have it* is an inversion of "to have one's cake and eat
it" (Example: You can't eat your cake and have it). *As at now* replaces "as of now" (Example: As at now, there are only two men
available). 5) Some totally new idioms are developed; e.g., *to take
in* for "to become pregnant" (Example: She has just taken in). *Off-
head,* "from memory," is similar to Standard English *offhand* (Example: I can't tell you the number off-head). *To take the light* means
to make a power cut (Example: Has the National Electrical Power
Authority (N.E.P.A.) taken the light again?). And *social wake-keeping*
refers to feasting, drumming, and dancing after a burial (Example:
There will be social wake-keeping from 10 p.m. till dawn).

Context

Even when lexical items or idioms have roughly the same meanings as in Native English, they may be used in completely different
contexts. Examples which have been given in the literature include
the use of *sorry* as an expression of sympathy, for example, to someone who sneezes or stumbles, or *wonderful* as an exclamation of surprise.[22] To these may be added the use of *please* as an indication of
politeness (for example, in a formal or official letter), *Dear Sir* for
opening a personal letter to someone older than oneself,[23] and *my
dear* for addressing practically anyone, including strangers.

One aspect of context that goes into the making of Nigerian English is the use of certain characteristic expressions in given registers. To take just the example of the language of obituaries, one knows immediately that one is dealing with Nigerian English when one sees such expressions as: "With gratitude to God for a life well spent, we regret to announce the death of our beloved father, grandfather, and great-grandfather, Chief Dr. X," where the opening phrase, together with the multiple reference to the deceased, have become a cliché; or "The wicked have done their worst," which reflects the widespread belief that most deaths result from the wicked action of some known or unknown enemies.

In spite of many educated Nigerians' reluctance to accept the above features as manifestations of Nigerian English, there is some proof that the pressure exerted by their widespread use is beginning to force such people to adopt some of the expressions in order to communicate effectively. Take, for instance, someone trying to describe a *traffic jam* and quickly correcting himself to say a *go-slow*. Recently I caught myself saying, *Let's go and wet the flowers,* even though I know that the appropriate expression is *Let's go and water the flowers*. What all this shows is that standardizing factors already exist which will tend to pull usage in the direction of more characteristically Nigerian forms. This trend will be hastened by the fact that education is now available to many more people, and that some of the best models of Nigerian English are now to be found among university graduates, including secondary school and university teachers.

Conclusion

Discussions of particular types of English necessarily tend to concentrate on the features peculiar to each type, because of the initial preoccupation with establishing an identity for the type in question. It is unfortunate, however, that such discussions have tended to play down the similarities between the type being described and other types. As Quirk (1962: 95-96) has rightly pointed out, "the remarkable thing is the very high degree of unanimity, the small amount of divergence" between the various Englishes of the world. This basic similarity makes it possible for each type to absorb a fair number of distinctive local variants and usages.

Writing about what he calls "the British heresy in TESL," Prator (1968: 464) describes "a second-language variety of English" as "a tongue caught up in a process that tends to transform it swiftly and quite predictably into an utterly dissimilar tongue." Suffice it to say that this prediction has been borne out neither by Nigerian English nor by the other Englishes of West Africa. Mazrui (1975: 16) has also predicted that those who speak English as a native language in Africa — "the Afro-Saxons" — are bound to multiply. Even if this prediction turns out to be untrue (as seems likely), the continued use of English as a second language by a sizable proportion of Nigerians of different generations is bound to ensure the continued development of a Standard Nigerian English.

NOTES

1. Note in this connection the perceptive comment by Christophersen (1960: 131) about the difference between a foreign language and a second language, the former being used for "absorbing the culture of another nation" and the latter "as an alternative way of expressing the culture of one's own."

2. See, e.g., the reference by Quirk (1962: 95) to Standard English as an "ideal" which "cannot be perfectly realized," since we must expect different realization. In this connection, Halliday, McIntosh and Strevens (1964: 294) specifically draw attention to the emergence of an "educated West African English" which is in the process of replacing "British English with RP" as a model.

3. One important personality, while visiting our department of linguistics, was told that the department was interested in research on Nigerian English; he commented that that was a waste of time, as there was no such thing as Nigerian English. A few minutes later he said, on being interrupted, "let me land" — the Nigerian equivalent of "let me finish."

4. This statement, made in a discussion by Professor S. H. O. Tomori, who claims an experience of "fifty years of listening to English and thirty years of teaching it," is reported in the *International Association of the Teachers of English as a Foreign Language Newsletter*, no. 54 (August, 1978): 15.

5. Ibid.

6. See, e.g., Salami 1968: 104-5.

7. Criper (1971), in a classification of Ghanaian English, rules out both pidgin and Native English. This appears to be a more satisfactory solution because pidgin has become a language in its own right, and Native English cannot properly be considered a variety of Ghanaian or Nigerian English.

8. See, e.g., Criper (1971: 7) and Sey (1973: 18).

9. See Salami (1968: 102-3), Bamgbose (1971: 38), Banjo (1971a)

10. In this experiment, consistent production of vowel contrast is based on elicitation from more than half of the informants with respect to each vowel. The lowest score was 51 percent for the vowel [iə] and the highest was 100 percent for [i] and [ɛ]. See Ekong (1978: 82).

11. Dunstan (1969) provides a good illustration of the interference of certain Nigerian languages in the spoken English of speakers of those languages.

12. Note that the absence of concord between the subject and the verb is also a feature of lower varieties of Nigerian English.

13. See, e.g., Adesanoye (1973), who regards as "deviations" all the features marking his different varieties of written English in Nigeria.

14. For an example of such an approach, see Obiechina (1974).

15. See Tutuola (1954: 17,18,62,63). Note "dead luck" (= bad fortune), "Deads' town" (= City of the Dead) and "born and die babies" (= babies who are believed to die and return, usually to the same parents).

16. An example of such disagreement is Walsh (1967: 47), who says that expressions such as "all the equipments" and someone running "for his dear life" are instances of legitimate Nigerian English, while Adesanoye (1973: 45) says that these expressions "are very clearly errors."

17. Compare the attitude of Kirk-Green (1971), who leans toward acceptance of such usages as Nigerian English, with that of Salami (1968), who rejects them.

18. Banjo (1971b: 126) draws attention to the "varying quantities of what could be regarded as substandard features in the formal prose of Nigerian graduates."

19. The level of education will generally be university, although, as stated earlier, others with lower levels of education but prolonged exposure to English will also qualify as Variety 3 users of English.

20. Some features in morphology, lexis, and semantics are similar to those found in Ghanaian English; see, e.g., Sey (1973). This shows that there is a basis for talking about larger varieties such as "West African English."

21. Such sentences appear to be acceptable in Native English only if there is a demonstrative or a contrastive stress on the pronoun subject: e.g., "These politicians and their supporters, *they* are the ones who don't often listen to advice."

22. See Bamgbose (1971: 44) and Kirk-Green (1971: 137).

23. Quirk (1962: 217) has drawn attention to the fact that formulas for opening and closing personal or official letters are fixed: "well-educated people do not mix these formulas and they tend to think poorly of those who do." However, as Bamgbose (1969: 87) has pointed out, in the context of Nigerian English, one has little choice but to mix formulas (i.e., to open with "Dear Sir" and close with "Yours sincerely"), since it will be considered impolite to address an older person by his surname, and positively disrespectful, if not impudent, to use his first name.

REFERENCES

Adekunle, M. A. 1974. The standard Nigerian English. *Journal of the Nigeria English Studies Association* 6(1): 24-37.

Adesanoye, F. 1973. A study of the varieties of written English in Nigeria. Ph.D. thesis, University of Ibadan.

Bamgbose, Ayo. 1969. Registers of English. *Journal of the Nigeria English Studies Association* 4(1): 81-88.

————. 1971. The English language in Nigeria. Pp. 35-48 in Spencer (1971).

Banjo, L. Ayo. 1971a. Towards a definition of "standard Nigerian spoken English." *Actes du 8e Congres de la Societe Linguistique de l'Afrique Occidentale.* Abidjan: Université d'Abidjan. Pp. 165-75.

————. 1971b. Standards of correctness in Nigerian English. *West African Journal of Education* 15(2): 123-27.

Brosnahan, L. F. 1958. English in southern Nigeria. *English Studies* (39): 97-110.

Christophersen, Paul. 1960. Towards a standard of international English. *English Language Teaching* 14(3): 127-38.

Criper, Lindsay. 1971. A classification of types of English in Ghana. *Journal of African Languages* 10(3): 6-17.

Dunstan, Elizabeth, ed. 1969. *Twelve Nigerian languages (a handbook on their sound systems for teachers of English).* London: Longmans.

Ekong, Pamela A. 1978. On describing the vowel systems of a standard variety of Nigerian spoken English. M.A. project, University of Ibadan.

Fishman, J. A.; Ferguson, C. A.; and Das Gupta, J., eds. 1968. *Language problems of developing nations.* New York: John Wiley and Sons.

Halliday, M. A. K.; McIntosh, A.; and Strevens, P. 1964. *The linguistic sciences and language teaching.* London: Longmans, Green.

Kirk-Green, A. 1971. The influence of West African languages on English. Pp. 123-44 in Spencer (1971).

Mazrui, Ali A. 1975. *The political sociology of the English language.* The Hague: Mouton.

Obiechina, E. N. 1974. Varieties differentiation in English usage. *Journal of the Nigeria English Studies Association* 6(1).

Prator, C. H. 1968. The British heresy in TESL. Pp. 459-76 in Fishman, Ferguson, and Das Gupta (1968).

Quirk, Randolph. 1963. *The use of English.* London: Longmans, Green.

Salami, A. 1968. Defining "a Standard Nigerian English." *Journal of the Nigeria English Studies Association* 2(2): 99-106.

Spencer, John, ed. 1971. *The English language in West Africa.* London: Longmans.

Sey, K. A. 1973. *Ghanaian English: an exploratory survey.* London: Macmillan.

Tutuola, Amos. 1954. *My life in the bush of ghosts.* London: Faber and Faber.

Walsh, N. G. 1967. Distinguishing types and varieties of English in Nigeria. *Journal of the Nigeria English Studies Association* no. 2, 47-55.

7

Kenyan English

JANE E. ZUENGLER

What follows is an investigation into the form and functions of English within the non-native context of Kenya. An analysis of some aspects of this variety[1] can only be tentative; very little research has been done on English within the Kenyan context. Whiteley (1974) investigated code-switching, code-mixing, and the use and teaching of English in the schools. Some descriptive data from English speech and use of English by creative writers were discussed by Angogo and Hancock (1980), but only within the larger context of English in Africa. The only collection of aspects of English limited to Kenyan speakers was prepared for prescriptive purposes, described as a list of "common errors" (Hocking 1974). Very little exists, then, on Kenyan English per se — diachronically or synchronically.

It is not known how many varieties of English exist in Kenya. Angogo and Hancock, using wider parameters ("East African and West African English"), suggest four "types."[2] This typology is largely arbitrary; it is not yet established that there is one overriding variety that covers both East and West African contexts, nor has it been established that the three East African countries (Kenya, Uganda, and Tanzania — each having different historical, political, and linguistic characteristics) share an English that could be called "East African English." Furthermore, any assertion that some East Africans speak English as a *second* language (ESL) while others speak English as a *foreign* language (EFL) (Type III versus Type IV) is debatable. Instead of breaking the non-native types into these two categories, a more useful way to assess proficiency variation might be to postulate a "cline of bilingualism" (Kachru 1976: 6), ranging from almost no proficiency to ambilingualism. Therefore, until further evidence is supplied that may prove this proposal sociolinguistically unjustified, the parameters for a discussion of a variety of African English should be narrowed. What follows will limit itself to English in Kenya.

The discussion of English in Kenya is divided into three sections. First is a description of the role of English in Kenyan society.

The second and third sections, which are exploratory and based on
a restricted body of data, discuss some aspects of what might be
called the *Kenyanness* of English,[3] and analyze the use of language
in Kenyan creative writing.

English in Kenyan Society

The linguistic composition of Kenya is discussed extensively in
Whiteley (1974). English, introduced early in Kenya's colonial history, has been largely a "taught" language, conveyed through formal
education. Its penetration in Kenya and assumption, over time, of a
major role in the upper primary grades and beyond are described by
Gorman (1974b) in a historical discussion of Kenyan language policy
development, and in Hemphill's (1974) survey of current primary
school language use.

The Africans perceived the significance of English very early
on; when it became clear that knowledge of English was a means by
which they could obtain paid employment, they began pressing for
more and more English in the schools. In fact, when the 1930's saw
the first organized African response to colonial educational policy in
the establishment of private, African-run primary schools, the most
salient characteristic of these "rebel" schools was the teaching of
English at a stage *earlier* than that proposed by the policy-makers
(Native Affairs Department Annual Report 1936).

In addition to serving an important function in the educational
system, English served a second function which Mazrui (1975: 48)
acknowledges. It played a significant role in the growth of nationalism: "Resistance to foreign rule in Africa does indeed antedate the
coming of the English language, but that resistance did not become
'nationalistic' until its leaders became English-speakers." Learning
English, Mazrui further argues, allowed the Africans an important
"point of entry into the habits of thought of [English-speaking]
people." It was English which helped to make the intellectuals nationalistic; the intellectuals, in turn, led the masses in the same direction (Mazrui 1975: 90). And knowledge of English enabled the
Kenyans to communicate with other Africans and Indians, as well
as with diaspora blacks in the West Indies and the United States.
There is evidence, however, that this role has changed. Although
English has been used by one influential contemporary Kenyan
writer to convey political themes, the language's function as a promoter of nationalism appears to have diminished in present-day
Kenya. I shall return to this point later.

In the economic and legal spheres of the society, as well as the mass media, English continues to dominate, despite the fact that Kiswahili was declared the official language in 1974. Gorman (1974b) provides a detailed discussion of this situation. In my experience in Kenya, communication observed between colleagues in insurance companies, banks, dentists' and doctors' offices, etc., was conducted in English. Only if there was a great status difference and the addressee had little formal education would another language be used.

It is not surprising, considering the pervasiveness of English throughout the upper stratum of Kenyan society, that the research conducted by the Survey of Language Use in Kenya (Whiteley: 1974) revealed English use as an indicator of higher socio-economic status. Parkin's (1974: 196) analysis of marketplace transactions provided some evidence for the use of English to set off status differences; the performer's switch to English could serve to indicate social exclusiveness and high socio-economic rank. Schoolchildren interviewed by Gorman preferred to use English in talking about school in public. Gorman suggests that this might be because English could likewise serve as an index of status in such settings (Gorman 1974a: 369).

There are no institutionalized varieties of English in Kenya comparable to India's *Kitchen English, Babu English, Boxwallah English*, etc. (Kachru 1981), or to West Africa's Pidgin English. Moore (1969: xx-xxi) suggests that no creolized form has appeared in East Africa because of the area's relatively late contact with English. He further states that there is no distinct dialect of English, and that therefore "English [may] not prove to be a major vehicle for initial literary creation in Eastern Africa" (1969: 157). This assertion, however, has already been proven false: most literature in Kenya is indeed in English, and the publications are increasing, from dime-store novels to more sophisticated examples which form part of the African literature syllabus in schools and the university.

Moore may be prematurely dismissing English only because the variety and its registers are possibly incipient; because these have not yet been described, they are difficult to refer to. This feeling that a local form does not yet exist appears in Hocking's (1974: 59-60) writing as well: "It is possible that we may eventually develop a local, East African form of English ourselves, and if we ever do, it may be that some of the mistakes we are dealing with in this book will be part of it. However, that time has hardly come yet." Hocking further claims that if such a form of English does develop, it will most likely be deemed "incorrect" by educated East Africans.

That situation is impossible to predict at this point, although he may be creating a self-fulfilling prophecy. In 1975 and 1976, some secondary schools had begun to use Hocking's book of "common errors." If the list of phrases and lexical items therein is taught, as he suggests, as *mistakes* (rather than as possible legitimate "deviations" [Kachru 1976: 14]), it may well influence the Kenyans' attitude about the English they speak. Angogo and Hancock (1980: 79) consider this possibility: "It is a fact that if one is told something deprecatory about oneself for long enough, one begins to accept it as part of the nature of things."

No research has yet appeared concerning attitudes of Kenyans toward the English spoken in Kenya, or attitudes about the kind of model to be used in the educational system. The model used throughout the colonial period and in present-day Kenya is a British one (RP). Aside from Angogo and Hancock, no objection to this model has appeared pertaining to the Kenyan English situation. An argument for a polymodel concept (Kachru 1977) of English teaching may therefore be premature, pending popular acknowledgment of a Kenyan variety of English.

The Kenyanness of English: Some Formal Aspects

Functioning in Kenya largely as a non-native variety, English has been influenced by Kenyan sociocultural and linguistic contexts, resulting in its *nativization* (Kachru 1981). Consequently, there are certain formal aspects of English which distinguish it from standard, native speaker varieties of English. Nativization occurs as a general process, transferring cultural and linguistic patterns into English across registers and contexts. In addition, registers and speech functions (Kachru 1965: 399) have been nativized. Reference to a restricted body of English in Kenya may help to illustrate these processes. There is evidence of lexical, semantic, and syntactic nativization; because the examples were drawn from written texts, phonological aspects will not be dealt with here.[4]

Nativization as a general process

This process in Kenyan English includes direct lexical transfer, usually of single items, from Kenyan languages. Many items are directly transferred if they have no exact equivalent in English. In the case of items denoting unity and nationalism, the Kiswahili form is retained regardless of existing equivalent forms in English; this reflects the national language status of Kiswahili. Other nativized items, both single and higher rank, can be best explained as translations into English of various semantic and syntactic patterns in Bantu languages.

Direct lexical transfers occur with reference to cooking and drinking, such as *njohi* (homemade beer; Kk, JMG 130), *kuon* (boiled cornmeal; L, PL 13), *ojuri* (type of Luo food; L, PL 102), *irio* (food; Kk, PB 2), *busaa* (homebrewed beer; L, S2.28, S3.13), *sufuria* (wide-bottomed aluminum pot; Ks, S3.7), *ugali* (boiled cornmeal; Ks, S3.7), and *sukumawiki* (lit. "push the week," ref. to spinach-like greens; Ks, S3.7). Other semantic categories refer to farming and the rural environment, including *githemithu, gathano* (names of seasons; Kk, PB 8), *mwariki tree* (castor seed tree; Kk, RB 92), *jembe* (hoe; Ks, RB 77), *rungu* (blunt blade for hitting; Kk, S2.13), *panga* (curved-bladed tool for cutting; Ks, S2.13, S3.7), *kuni* (firewood; Ks, SL 58), and *shamba* (cultivated plot of land; Ks, RB 11, S5.31), as well as societal concepts and relationships: *kihii* (uncircumcised boy; Kk, RB 45), *thingira* (a man's hut; Kk, RB 10), *thahu* (a curse; Kk, RB 144), *baba* (father; Ks, SL 55), *majengo* (ghetto; Ks, S5.31). Expressions of unity and nationalism are retained in Kiswahili, and include *wananchi* (people, citizens; Ks, S5.31, S3.6), *harambee* (lit. "let's pull together," the national motto; Ks, S2.13, S5.31), *uhuru* (freedom, independence; Ks, S2.13, S5.31), and *baraza* (large official meeting; Ks, S3.13).

Semantic shifts occur when first language meanings are transferred, resulting in extended, restricted, or redefined meanings in English. Examples of semantic extension and redefinition include *get* (to give birth to; SL 53),[5] *hear* (listen: TTT 7),[6] *brat* (illegitimate child; S3.13),[7] and kinship terms like *my young husband* (mother addressing son; JMG 42), *second husband* (brother-in-law; EC 5), and *daughter* (husband addressing wife; PL 19,98).

Syntactic shifts result in some items taking on new or different grammatical forms in Kenyan English. *School* (JMG 167) and *tone* (S3.10) function additionally as verbs; *rest* (S3.1) can be a transitive verb, and *sack* (to fire someone; S2.13) is also used as a noun. Particularly in the noun phrase, different syntactic combinations are found: *pure-gold jewels* (S3.9), *a ten cents piece* (S3.11), *thatchroof* (VD 10). The non-occurrence of prenominal possessive forms in Bantu languages accounts for *women groups* (S3.1) and *children welfare* (S3.9). Different distributions of Bantu count and non-count nouns result in *fruits* (S3.16), *ammunitions* (S3.13), *hardwares* (S5.31), and *trouser* (S3.10). Reduplication, possible in Kiswahili and other Bantu languages, occurs as well in Kenyan English, and is used for emphasis: *small small whisky* (VD 28), *long long one* (VD 26).

Nativization of speech functions and registers

Greetings, abuses and threats, forms of address, and riddles and proverbs are speech functions common in many languages. These contextual units function in Kenyan English, but because the language is embedded socioculturally, they differ from their counterparts in native varieties of English. This process is not restricted to speech functions; registers and stylistic devices of Kenyan novelists differ as well from native English varieties.

The following *speech functions* illustrate the influence of Kenyan context on English forms:

1) Greetings: *Is it well with you? It is well* (TTT 1, RB 95, SL 50); *Mother I greet you* (TTT 23).

2) Forms of Address:[8] *Daughter of the Rulers* (husband addressing wife; PL 19); *son of Sipul* (neighbor to neighbor; PL 75); *son of my mother* (brother to brother; PL 37); *Mwalimu* (teacher; Ks, PB 11); *Bwana* (African to non-African male; Ks, DK 12, SL 41); *Memsahib* (orig. Indian, African to non-African female; SL 41).

3) Abuses/Threats: *go away and eat ashes* (JMG 137); *"You will know who I am." "Cow,"* cried Kinuthia with pain. *"Hyena." "Even you,"* Kinuthia hissed back (conversation between two boys; RB 6).

4) Riddles/Proverbs: these involve code-switching and translation, as in *Kagutui ka Mucii gatihakugwo Ageni; the oilskin of the house is not for rubbing into the skin of strangers* (Kk, RB 3); they also contain minimal mixing in *I am Atai castor-oil, the oil that is given to cause diarrhoea to girls who lack a slim waist-line* (PL 106).

Register in Kenyan English can be illustrated by letters to newspaper editors. In native varieties of English, the following expressions would be considered archaic or overly formal; they are, however, quite common in Kenyan English. They include *I have to alight now [from the bus]* (S3.7); *This system should be stopped forthwith* (S3.7); *Allow me space in the paper we trust* (S3.13); and *I should be grateful if you would spare me a small space in your column* (S5.31).

Stylistic devices used by Kenyan authors serve to contextualize their writing. While each author has an individual style, there are nonetheless certain shared characteristics observable in their English. Similes have a noticeable Kenyan quality about them: *We hated each other like a woman and a snake* (JMG 59); *the spotted bush that crouched*

like men (TTT 2); *My heart is full like Guru River in flood* (DK 39).
Metaphorical language is very common: *You were once a she-goat*
(JMG 45); *bent into an Akamba-bow shape* (SL 58); *before he sleeps
with his forefathers* (PL 38); *Waiyaki wanted to dance the magic and
ritual of the moon* (ref. to sexual arousal; RB 88); *light that comes
from wires in dry trees to make day out of night* (ref. to electricity;
PB 6).

Another stylistic characteristic of the Kenyan texts is that
which corresponds to biblical style: *The white man cannot speak the
language of the hills. And knows not the ways of the land* (RB 9);
she is with child (TTT 25). Angogo and Hancock (1980: 78) acknowledge that the Bible has influenced African writing in English, but
Bamgboṣe (1971: 46), referring to the same characteristic in West
African English, raises an interesting point regarding such a "biblical
register." He suggests that it may be a "stylistic echo of tradition,"
instead of a style created by exposure to the Bible. A similar style already existed in oral literature; writing it down made it look biblical,
while it was in fact African: "the language of the Bible was in accord
with certain features of a traditional oral literature; it did not of itself
bring about a declamatory style in West African writing." While
Bamgboṣe's evidence is from West African oral literature, investigation into its East African counterpart might indicate that this, like
the other aspects discussed in this section, is also a result of cultural
and linguistic transfer.

Language in Ngugi and Mugo's "The Trial of Dedan Kimathi"

In 1974 there were more writers, artists, and critics in Nairobi
than any other city in Africa.[9] One of the most prominent Kenyan
writers is Ngugi wa Thiong'o. His writing has become popularized in
Kenya through its inclusion on school syllabuses; most of his work
is distributed overseas as well. Like other African writers, he faces
the challenge of conveying ideas and experiences through a second
language.

The Trial of Dedan Kimathi, a play Ngugi wrote with Micere
Mugo, is particularly insightful in its portrayal of the functional relationships of languages in Kenyan contexts. An example of songs
from the play, as well as examples of dramatic dialogue, will serve
to illustrate how the authors have achieved this.

The play reconstructs the period of the Mau Mau struggle for
independence in the 1950's. Dedan Kimathi was one of the guerrilla
leaders who was captured, put on trial, and then executed by the

colonialists. The ethnic group inhabiting the area in which the major struggle took place is the Gikuyu; most Mau Mau leaders were also members of this group. While the authors emphasize a nationalistic rather than an ethnic theme, the plot is set in an area where a non-national language, Kikuyu, is the mother tongue, and Kiswahili and English are the second languages.

Although the play's medium is English, it is framed by songs in Kiswahili. The lyrics are strongly political, as the excerpt indicates (in the text, no English translation is provided):

Tutanyakua	(We shall seize by force
Mashamba yetu	our shambas [plots of land]
Tupiganie	and fight
Uhuru wetu	for our Uhuru [freedom]
Natukomboe	and liberate
Elimu yetu	our education
Tutanyakua	We shall seize by force
Viwanda vyetu	our industries
Utamaduni	culture
Ni mashamba yetu	They are our shambas
Damu naajasho	and their blood and sweat
Zatiririka	will flow
Tutakomboa	We shall liberate
Udongo wetu! [4]	our soil!)

This same political theme is conveyed in the play's final song. The authors' choice of Kiswahili here reflects its use in expressing concepts of unity and nationhood. To use English would be to use the language of the oppressor to protest oppression; singing in any other Kenyan African language would ethnically mark it.

1) Dialogue between a white police officer and an African soldier:

Waitina:	Askari!
Second Soldier:	Fande!
Waitina:	Line up those Mau Mau villagers two by two.
Second Soldier:	Tayari Bwana!
Waitina:	March them to the screening ground. He . . . can guard the street. And tell him to wake up for Christ's sake! Sikia?
Second Soldier:	Ndio Bwana. [6-7]

The white officer (Waitina) is the superior; he gives the orders, while the African replies in short affirmatives. The code mixing with Kiswahili indicates that this conversation would have taken place not in English but rather in Kiswahili, or more specifically, Pidgin-Swahili. It was more common for whites to speak Pidgin-Swahili with Africans, particularly in situations involving commonly occurring sentence types like commands.

2) Dialogue between the main female character and a white soldier:

Woman: Uuu--u! Nduri ici ni kii giki! [Kikuyu]
Johnnie: Simama kabisa! Good. Passbook.
Woman: Ati passi?
            [is it a passbook]
Johnnie: Ndiyo, passbook. Wapi passbook?
            [yes]   [where is]
Woman: Sina.
            [I don't have]
Johnnie: Sema Afande
            [say "commander"]
Woman: Afande.
Johnnie: Sina, Afande!
            [I don't have, commander]
Woman: Sina Afande. [8-9]

The woman is a local peasant, which is made clear by her use of Kikuyu in the first line. The expression in Kikuyu has two functions: 1) it identifies the woman as coming from that region, and 2) it is the most adequate way of representing someone being taken off-guard (i.e., in such a situation one would automatically use the mother tongue). Johnnie, the white soldier, then appears and orders her to stand. His communication with her is also interspersed with Pidgin-Swahili, which indicates that this communication, too, would in reality be conducted in such. His manner with the woman is similar to that of the white police officer in the previous dialogue. However, because she is questioned as a possibly suspicious character, Johnnie forces her to answer him respectfully. In responding she uses his medium, Pidgin-Swahili.

3) Dialogue between two African soldiers:

First Soldier: Where are the terrorists who were
                    supposed to be all over Nyeri? We've
                    been patrolling all night without as

much as catching sight of a single one
of them. Simply harassing innocent
villagers. The way mzungu makes us
thirst to kill one another!

Second Soldier: The bloodyfuckin' Mau Mau are finished without that bugger Kimathi!

First Soldier: What is the idea of arresting a whole
village then? [12]

There is no status difference between the characters, as each expresses himself without restraint. (Contrast this with the African soldier's replies to the white police officer in the first example.) Except
for the word *mzungu,* which is commonly used in Kenyan English to
mean "a white person," the language is entirely English. There are no
cues that Pidgin-Swahili or Kiswahili is being used; it is not likely that
the medium would really be English, since soldiers usually lack the
formal education which would enable them to express themselves so
fluently in English. English is here used to represent mother-tongue
communication between characters.

4) A conversation occurs between an American tourist and an
African boy masquerading as a beggar. The same boy is relating this
conversation to other Africans:

Boy: Then one day, myself and this girl were sitting
outside New Stanley. As we were talking, a fat
American came loaded with baggage:

(boy):   "Saidia maskini, sah
[help the poor]
Me and my sister
can carry your bags."

(tourist):   "Here, you take this, boy. And your sister can
take this, okay? Good boy!
(walking along) "A beauddiful country . . . a
beauddiful ciddy . . . and beauddiful people, eh?
"Take the baggage to that taxi over there.
"Understand? Good.
"Ahsonde soona!"
[*asante sana*=thank you very much] [16-17]

The entire conversation is related by the boy who was begging.
He uses Pidgin-Swahili with the tourist, then switches to English, as
it would be unlikely for a tourist to understand more than a few
phrases. Because the African wants money from the American, he
switches to the American's mother tongue. In relating this conversation to friends, the boy is imitating the American's speech. The

particular use of *boy* by the tourist is more representative of (Southern) Americans than of Kenyan settlers. "American" pronunciation is reflected in the use of double *d*'s in *beauddiful* and *ciddy*. When the tourist speaks Kiswahili, it also has an American accent (*asante sana* → *ahsonde soona*). Racial dynamics are again conveyed by the commands given the African.

5) Conversation between Kimathi and Indian trader:

Indian: In India--a, ve got our independent. Preedom. To make money. This here, our true priend. Not racialism. Leaves your custom alone. You can pray Budha, pray Confucius, pray under the trees, pray rocks, vear sari . . . your culture . . . songs . . . dances . . . ve don't mind . . . propided . . . ve make money . . . priend . . . priend.

Kimathi: Some of our people passed through India on their way from Burma. Calcutta. Delhi. Bombay. They told of hungry peoples, beggars on pavements . . . wives selling themselves for a rupee . . . Have they now said "no" to poverty?

Indian: Ve trying. Little. Little. But ve hawe our religion. Ve hawe our plag. Ve hawe national anthem. And now ewen Indian Bankers. Ha! Ha! [39]

This conversation takes place in English; both characters are speaking it as a second language, but here the marked version is that of the Indian. Rapid speech and intonational differences are indicated by short sentences, fragments, and repetitions. There are also syntactic irregularities, and phonological deviation is represented by orthographic differences. Contrast this with Kimathi's lyrical style. He is the more reflective, questioning character; there is no need to linguistically stigmatize him. He is the mentor in the play; his ideas require conveyance in a clear, fluent style. His speech is thus unmarked linguistically.

Conclusion

The preceding sections have represented preliminary analyses of the functions of English in Kenya and aspects of its form which differentiate it from native speaker varieties. In addition, I have discussed how several Kenyan creative writers have portrayed the functional interrelationship of English with other Kenyan languages. I have attempted to show that English is a dynamic, functioning language in Kenya, and that as a result syntactic, semantic, and lexical nativization has occurred, producing an English that may be called Kenyan. This is not necessarily an argument for a new, non-native model of English in the schools; Kenyan English is not yet popularly accepted as a variety on its own. But it is hoped, at the least, that this discussion will lead to an understanding of why English in Kenya differs from native English varieties, rather than to considering it merely an aberration.

NOTES

1. "Variety" (following Kachru 1966) refers to a form of a language that developed in a particular context, the parameters here being societal and geographical. Consequently, Kenyan English can be differentiated from Indian English, New Zealand English, etc.

2. Angogo and Hancock's "types" (1980: 71)are as follows, "[which are] intended to serve for East, as well as West Africa": I) native English of African-born whites and expatriates; II) native English of locally born Africans; III) non-native English spoken fluently as a second language (in several styles); IV) non-native English spoken imperfectly, as a foreign language (in several styles).

3. Following Kachru's description of the *Indianness* in Indian English (1965: 392), *Kenyanness* will here refer to those features distinguishing English in Kenya from the *Englishness* of British English or the *Americanness* of American English.

4. The following is a list of authors and titles of works cited by initials and page numbers in the examples:

(JMG) Green, Robert, ed. N.d. *Just a Moment, God! An Anthology of Prose and Verse from East Africa.* Nairobi: East African Literature Bureau.

(VD) Kibera, Leonard. 1970. *Voices in the Dark.* Nairobi: East African Publishing House.

(EC) lo Liyong, Taban. 1970. *Eating Chiefs: Lwo Culture from Lolwe to Malkal.* London: Heinemann.

(PB) wa Thiong'o Ngugi. 1977. *Petals of Blood.* London: Heinemann.

(RB) Ngugi, James [same author as above]. 1965. *The River Between.* London: Heinemann.

(SL) wa Thiong'o, Ngugi. 1975. *Secret Lives.* London: Heinemann.

(TTT) ———— . N.d. *This Time Tomorrow.* Nairobi: East African Literature Bureau.

(DK) ———— and Mugo, Micere Githae. 1976. *The Trial of Dedan Kimathi.* London: Heinemann.

(PL) Ogot, Grace. 1966. *The Promised Land.* Nairobi: East African Publishing House.

(S) *The Standard.* Nairobi, Kenya. This is a daily newspaper; examples were supplied by sixteen issues published between February and June, 1978. Each issue is cited by date (e.g., S3.9 is March 9).

Key to language abbreviations: Kk = Kikuyu; Ks = Kiswahili; L = Dholuo.
   5. One explanation is that *get* is more proper culturally than *give birth to* or *deliver*, because it is less direct.
   6. Probable transfer from Kiswahili *kusikia*, which means both *listen* and *hear*.
   7. *Mwanaharamu* in Kiswahili refers to an *illegal* child, but also has the connotation of a child who is *bad*.
   8. Forms of address and reference are less direct in Bantu languages than in native varieties of English. The less indirect forms are transferred into Kenyan English. Terms of respect are not translated; some reflect colonial categories of status or racial superiority.
   9. Angogo and Hancock (1980: 92). The report mentioned was written by James Curry, of Heinemann Educational Books, and appeared in the *Guardian*.

REFERENCES

Angogo, Rachael, and Hancock, Ian. 1980. English in Africa: emerging standards or diverging regionalisms? *English world-wide: a journal of varieties of English* 1(1): 67-96.

Bamgbose, Ayo. 1971. The English language in Nigeria. Pp. 35-48 in John Spencer, ed., *The English language in West Africa*. London: Longmans.

Gorman, T. P. 1974a. Patterns of language use among school children and their parents. In Whiteley (1974).

————. 1974b. The development of language policy in Kenya with particular reference to the educational system. In Whiteley (1974).

Hemphill, R. J. 1974. Language use and language teaching in the primary schools of Kenya. In Whiteley (1974).

Hocking, B. D. W. 1974. All what I was taught and other mistakes: a handbook of common errors in English. Nairobi: Oxford University Press.

Kachru, Braj B. 1965. The *Indianness* in Indian English. *Word* 21(3): 391-410.

————. 1966. Indian English: a study in contextualization. Pp. 255-87 in C. E. Bazell et al., eds., *In memory of J. R. Firth*. London: Longmans.

————. 1976. Indian English: a sociolinguistic profile of a transplanted language. *Studies in Language Learning* 1(2).

————. 1977. The new Englishes and old models. *English Teaching Forum* XV (3): 29-35.

————. 1981. The pragmatics of non-native varieties of English. In Smith (1981).

Mazrui, Ali A. 1975. *The political sociology of the English language*. The Hague: Mouton.

Moore, Gerald. 1969. *The chosen tongue: English writing in the tropical world*. London: Longmans.

Native Affairs Department Annual Report. 1936. Nairobi: Kenya National Archives.

Parkin, D. J. 1974. Language switching in Nairobi. In Whiteley (1974).

Smith, Larry, ed. 1981. *English for cross-cultural communication*. London: Macmillan.

Whiteley, W. H., ed. 1974. *Language in Kenya*. Nairobi: Oxford University Press.

8

Chinese Varieties of English

CHIN-CHUAN CHENG

The varieties of English spoken by native Chinese around the world presumably share certain features because of common language background.[1] However, there are differences in the status of English and its function in different areas, such as the People's Republic of China, Taiwan, Hong Kong, Malaysia, Singapore, and Chinatowns in the United States. There are no detailed in-depth studies of any of these varieties, though in recent years some attention has been given to English in certain political settings — for example, in Singapore and Malaysia (Platt 1977) and in Hong Kong (Richards and Luke 1981). Here I will deal with the varieties of English in mainland China. These varieties display a cline of proficiency, beginning with Pidgin (Kachru 1969), while they manifest the different sociopolitical perceptions of the West evident in different stages of Chinese history.

Today, English is the most-studied foreign language in China. In some areas English instruction starts in the third grade of elementary school, and most middle-school students take English to satisfy foreign language requirements (Lehmann et al. 1975; Cheng 1975; Light 1978; Cowan et al. 1979). Adults are also interested in learning English. As Cowan et al. (1979) report, 242,000 students were enrolled in a television English course produced by the "Chinese Television University" in Beijing in 1979. The primary purpose of the study of English — or of any Western language — in the recent past has been essentially "to serve the revolution" (Lehmann et al. 1975) and is now to gain access to Western science and technology. The increased flow of Western tourists and businessmen to China has also made it crucial to use English, though in restricted contexts (Cowan et al. 1979).[2]

In spite of the number of people involved in learning English, there is no English-speaking Chinese community; nor does English serve as an interlanguage among the nation's fifty-five ethnic groups. In this sense, the functions of English are much different in China than in Africa (see Bamgboṣe 1982) and in South Asia (see Kachru 1981). While some Chinese writers — for example, Armand Su —

write primarily in Esperanto, I know of no significant works of literature in English or other foreign languages by Chinese authors living in
China.

English is used primarily in international communication, and
written English in China appears in publications mainly for international consumption. The international function often requires a uni-
fied expression, not only in ideology, but also in language. Therefore
one finds identical or very similar expressions used in various publications. This tendency toward fixed expressions is also noticeable in
spoken English. To an outsider, both spoken and written varieties
appear stilted.

Recently the most outstanding feature of English in China has
been the prevalence of terse and politicized lexical items and phrases.
These terms are unintelligible to outsiders who are not familiar with
the Chinese context. Thus there appears to be a kind of English peculiar to the Chinese culture: one might call it Sinicized English. This
variety has not derived its characteristics from an earlier version of
English in China, nor will it necessarily remain invariant in the future.
My intention here is to show that peculiarities of English in China
reflect the sociopolitical situation there. In examining the history
and the current situations of the Chinese varieties of English, I hope
to demonstrate that when China is inward-searching, the English
there acquires more Chinese elements, and when China is outward-
looking, the English is more Western.

The Earliest Phase

Kachru (1981) characterizes the origin of non-native Englishes
as follows: "The non-native Englishes are the legacy of the colonial
period, and have mainly developed in 'unEnglish' cultural and linguistic contexts in various parts of the world, wherever the arm of
the Western colonizers reached." In the case of China, the Western
powers reached only a few ports, and one linguistic consequence of
that limited contact was the development of pidgin varieties.

The British established their first trading post in Guangzhou
(Canton) in 1664. The development of pidgin English there reflected
the Chinese "Middle Kingdom" conception of the universe. The Chinese held the British, like all "foreign devils," in low esteem, and
would not stoop to learning the foreign tongue in its full form (Hall
1966). The British, on the other hand, regarded the "heathen Chinee"
as beyond any possibility of learning, and so began to modify their
own language for the natives' benefit. Hall (1966) shows traces of an

earlier Cantonese Pidgin Portuguese in Chinese Pidgin English (see also Todd 1974), although Reinecke et al. (1975) remark that such a relationship is in dispute. Whatever the relationship, it is certain that pidgin English apparently took shape in the first quarter of the eighteenth century in Guangzhou. Beginning in 1843, when the so-called Treaty Ports were established, it spread to the southeastern coastal cities and the Changjiang (Yangtze) valley. During the last decade of the nineteenth century, as a consequence of social and political disfavor and of the preference for Standard English, it started to decline. Chinese Pidgin English is now virtually dead, with only marginal use remaining among a few Chinese speakers in the British colony of Hong Kong (Whinnom 1971).

Based on Reinecke's (1937) dissertation, "Marginal Language," Hall (1944) divides the history of Chinese Pidgin English into four phases: original, "classical," expanding, and declining. He further points out that, throughout its life, Chinese Pidgin English was mostly a means of communication between foreign masters and Chinese servants, and a medium used in retail shops catering to foreigners. During the period of expansion, however, it was used between foreigners and upper-class Chinese, as well as by servants and tradesmen.[3]

Chinese Pidgin English deviated considerably from Standard English. For example, consider the following sentence (which I have converted into standard orthography from the phonetic symbols appearing in Hall 1944: 108, 1966: 152): *Tailor, my have got one piece plenty hansom silk; my want you make one nice evening dress.* The use of *my* for *I* and *my* (the latter not shown in this example) was a result of the reduction of English morphology. In Chinese, the possessive is formed by adding a particle to the pronoun; there is no case change, such as from *I* to *my*. Because this is true in all dialects, one may safely infer that the reduction in this instance is a case of interference (or transfer) from Chinese.

Toward Westernization: English as a Tool

At the turn of the present century, the Chinese perceived a great need for modernization, which in essence meant Westernization. Learning foreign languages in their full forms was a prerequisite to acquisition of Western knowledge. At the same time, there was also a great surge of nationalism; pidgin English was occasionally disparaged as "coolie Esperanto" (Reinecke et al. 1975). Hall (1973: 79) explains the decline of pidgin as follows:

In the case of Chinese Pidgin English a standoffish attitude characterized both sides, for the Chinese more than
matched the Europeans in their sense of national superiority. If only two language groups are involved, the side
that feels it suffers loss of status because it speaks pidgin
may come to insist on learning the other side's full language; this happened in China after 1900.

Such an attitude necessitated that English become part of a standard
post-primary curriculum. Some schools even started teaching English
as early as the third grade (Zhu 1978).

In the several decades immediately preceding 1950, English was
equated with British literature, as is also the case in parts of Africa
and South Asia. In schools, especially at the university level, English
learning meant memorizing the works of Shakespeare and other writers of the past; contemporary writings were rarely studied. Zhu (1978)
mentions that English majors could write quaint and sentimental essays in imitation of Charles Lamb, but they were unable to write short
articles to comment on current national and international situations.
Bookish rather than colloquial English was the norm in conversations.
Such a bias against contemporary English existed because the university curricula were transplanted, without much modification, from
the United States and Britain. In those English-speaking countries, it
was only natural to study literature in college. Chinese students, in
contrast, at that time had no opportunity to learn spoken English. In
some missionary schools English was the only language spoken, and
the teachers were often foreigners — but their Chinese students were
few in number. The Chinese situation was, again, not much different
from the Indian (Kachru 1969) or the Nigerian (Bamgboṣe 1982).

In the first half of the twentieth century, China came into more
frequent contact with foreign countries. Many works were translated
from English and other languages into Chinese. English was known
well by a comparatively small educated elite; yet the impact of English on the Chinese language was significant, especially in the written
form. Wang (1955) devotes a lengthy chapter to discussion of "Westernized grammar," expounding mainly on the influence of English
grammar on Chinese. An infusion of new lexical items occurred, along
with modification of some aspects of Chinese syntax. The new lexical
items were formed by transliteration or by compounding words with
similar meanings. This Westernization brought about an increase in
the number of polysyllabic words, for example *modeng* (modern),
moteer (model), *shehui* (society), and *yuanliang* (excuse).

At the syntactic level, the influence of English on Chinese can be exemplified by the length of phrases and the use of passive verb forms. In Chinese, the modifying part comes before the modified; therefore Westernized Chinese sentences often contain long modifiers before the head noun to accommodate English subordinate clauses. In the following, sentence (a) is English, (b) is Westernized Chinese, and (c) is "normal" Chinese (Wang 1955: 282-83):

(a) People who regard literary taste simply as an accomplishment, and literature simply as a distraction, will . . .

(b)

Naxie	ba		wenxue	xingwei	renwei
those	CO-VERB		literary	taste	regard

chunran	yizhong	caiyi,		ba	
simply	a kind	accomplishment		CO-VERB	

wenxue	renwei	chunran	yizhong
literature	regard	simply	a kind

xiaoqianpin	de		*renmen,*	jiang . . .
distraction	POSSESSIVE		people	will

(c) *Yigeren ruguo* ba wenxue xingwei renwei chunran yizhong caiyi, ba wenxue renwei chunran yizhong xiaoqianpin, jiang . . .

The Westernized style puts the head noun *renmen* (people) at the very end of the long modifier. The normal Chinese, however, brings out the subject *yigeren* (a person) at the very beginning and uses *ruguo* (if) to qualify it.

The passive preposition (also called co-verb) *bei* was limited to sentences expressing suffering from some action. The English passive has extended the use of *bei* beyond pejorative to positive senses: *Ta bei juwei zhuxi* (He was elected chairman), or *Ta bei kuajiangle yifan* (He was greatly praised).

Whereas Chinese underwent these changes under the influence of English, the English language in China received little modification. This was the situation when China looked outward for change in the country.

Model for Chinese English

The term "Westernization," used above with reference to Wang (1955), is actually *ouhua,* "Europeanization." For many years the West was Europe, and British English was the standard model. British English has remained more or less the standard since the 1950s, even though the United States had already attained the height of its influence politically, economically, and linguistically. Several factors contributed to the continued dominance of British English. First, Chinese education was very much under the influence of the Soviet system. English curricula were designed on the basis of those of the Soviet Union (Xiong and Cheng 1980), where British English was more or less the standard. Second, there was not much contact between China and the United States. The Cold War, McCarthyism, and the U.S. economic blockade perhaps contributed to a negative feeling toward American English. In contrast, the United Kingdom and China established diplomatic relations early. Furthermore, there have even been a few British citizens on the editorial staffs of English-language publications in Beijing. Until 1979, as Cowan et al. (1979) report, foreign English-language experts were provided primarily by the governments of Britain, Canada and New Zealand. This earlier impact is visible even now, and can be seen in the English edition of the weekly journal *Beijing Review.* The *Beijing Review* indicates what written English is like in China today. The most apparent feature of British English is the spelling; e.g., the use of *-our* for *-or: in honour of* (May 6, 1977, p. 33); *labouring people* (April 28, 1978, p. 10); *scientific endeavour* (April 7, 1978, p. 16). Words such as *programme* also prove this point. The preference for British English is not limited to the one journal. Lehmann et al. (1975), reporting on the visit by the first U.S. linguistics delegation to China in 1974, mention that British English was obviously preferred there, simply a consequence of history and attitude.

Developing Political English According to the Chinese System

As one reads the *Beijing Review,* however, one immediately sees that the British features are overshadowed by the distinct vocabulary of the text: "The gang arbitrarily described the political line and the achievements of 1975 as a 'Right-Deviationist wind to reverse correct verdicts' " (December 29, 1978, p. 13). Sentences like this, as Brumfit (1977) points out, appear to the native English speaker as bizarre in some sense. Indeed, it is hard for the reader who does not know the cultural (especially political) background of contemporary China to comprehend such writings.

Several articles in this volume deal with the "nativization" of English; I will illustrate this phenomenon in the political register of Chinese English, with examples from the *Beijing Review*. The weekly journal, with the Chinese subtitle *Beijing Zhoubao* (Beijing Weekly), has been in existence for more than twenty years. It is now published in English, French, Spanish, Japanese, German, Arabic, and Portuguese editions. The English edition was formerly called *Peking Review*. Beginning on January 1, 1979, all foreign-language publications using the Latin alphabet in China adopted the Chinese *pinyin* romanization system for spelling Chinese names, instead of the customary British Wade-Giles system. *Peking* is now spelled *Beijing,* and so is the title of the journal.[4] The journal usually contains the following sections: weekly chronicle, events and trends, articles and documents (translated from Chinese), special features, "round the world," and "on the home front." The translation is usually done by native Chinese staff members, with native English speakers adding the final touches. The translations represent typical renditions of English in China.

The function of the *Beijing Review,* and of all foreign-language journals in China, is to serve the international community. In discussing the "communicative competence" question, Kachru (1981) argues eloquently for the need to separate the uses of non-native English into local, national, and international contexts. English in China fills no local or national function. While students of English may be required to study the journal and other English-language publications, they are not the intended readership.

During the Cultural Revolution (1966-76), the Chinese people were deeply involved in a series of political movements and struggles, and China was to a large extent cut off from the outside world. In fact, individuals who read foreign materials without official sanction ran the risk of being labeled as *chong yang mei wai* (worship and have blind faith in things foreign). In these years politics were in command; and, since politics were mainly based on threat, during the times of intense struggle one often had to echo what was said in the official newspapers. As the same phrases were repeated time and time again, shorter idioms were formed to substitute for them. These idioms or abbreviated terms became ubiquitous. Naturally, the English language must accommodate itself to a culture as powerful and rich as China's, and to the currents of the time. This phenomenon is essentially what Kachru (1976, 1981) identifies as language pragmatics of non-native Englishes.

The impact of Chinese cultural parameters on English is especially

conspicuous in the joint communique issued on February 1, 1979, in
Washington, D.C., by the visiting Vice-Premier Deng Xiaoping and
President Carter. One sentence declares: "They reaffirm that they are
opposed to efforts by any country or group of countries to establish
hegemony or domination over others, and that they are determined
to make a contribution to the maintenance of international peace,
security and national independence" (February 9, 1979, p. 3). Because *hegemony* was a Chinese code word for "Soviet expansionism,"
and the U.S. side did not want to involve itself in the Sino-Soviet feud,
or domination over others was added to soften the tone. Indeed, during Vice-Premier Deng's visit, Western reporters were busy looking up
the meaning and pronunciation of *hegemony*. At the same time, the
Chinese visitors were painstakingly searching for a Chinese translation
of *rodeo*.

The distinct Chinese cultural element in English is shown mostly
in idioms, phrases coined during political movements, lexical connotations and semantic shifts, and the style of discourse. The editors of
the *Beijing Review* may add explanatory notes for the English reader's
benefit: "There is much that is new on the educational front since the
overthrow of the 'gang of four' and particularly since the reform of
the college enrolment system and the criticism of the 'two estimates'"
(May 5, 1978, p. 6). A footnote explains the "two estimates," but
"gang of four" is supposedly well known, and no further clarification
is given.

The Chinese elements in English may not always require elucidation. First of all, Chinese saying and idioms are usually not annotated:

> When one drinks water, one must not forget where it
> comes from; when we think of these things, how can
> we not show our profound gratitude to our great leader
> Chairman Mao and our respected and beloved Premier
> Chou and cherish their memory? [April 7, 1978, p. 16]

> But they were like "mayflies lightly plotting to topple
> the giant tree." [Ibid.]

The first phrase of the first example is a translation of *yin shui si yuan,*
and the quote in the second example is *fu you han shu,* both idiomatic
expressions in Chinese. Because these direct translations are easy to
understand, no footnotes are called for.[5]

Words such as *bad egg* (from Chinese *huai dan*) for "villain" or
"bad guy," and *running dog* (from *zou gou*) for "lackey," have become standards in Chinese derogatory remarks or polemics. Terms

coined in recent political movements are not readily understandable
from their constituent words, but because they occur so frequently,
no explanations are provided:

> To make the matter worse, the gang cooked up works
> centering on the struggle against "capitalist-roaders"
> in co-ordination with their attempt to usurp Party and
> state leadership under the pretext of "combating the
> capitalist-roaders." [April 28, 1978, p. 8]

> Having destroyed the gang's "iron and steel and hat
> factories" and condemned its crime of savagely attack-
> ing and persecuting them, our cadres are displaying re-
> newed revolutionary spirit. [March 10, 1978, p. 12]

A *capitalist roader* (from Chinese *zou zi pai*) is someone who takes
the road leading to capitalism, i.e., someone who is in favor of a capitalist social system. *Iron and steel and hat factories* (from Chinese
gangtie gongchang maozi gongchang) are where cudgels are made to
beat (to criticize), and caps are fabricated to force upon someone's
head (to label); hence the phrase means "wanton attack." The phrase
right deviationist wind to reverse correct verdicts, given earlier, is a
translation of the Chinese term *youqing fan an feng,* which means the
rightist trends to invalidate the gains of the Cultural Revolution. The
phrases in quotes in these examples were often used without quotes
previously. A regular reader would have no difficulty understanding
them, although a casual reader or a novice would find them incomprehensible. In fact, even Chinese native speakers who live outside
mainland China and who do not follow Chinese political events are
often nonplussed by these terms.

Some phrases often appear in the same order, even though there
is no apparent logical sequence:

> We must grasp the three great revolutionary movements of
> class struggle, the struggle for production and scientific ex-
> periment at the same time . . . [April 28, 1978, p. 4].

> The general task facing our people in the new period of
> development in socialist revolution and socialist construc-
> tion is firmly to carry out the line of 11th Party Congress,
> steadfastly continue the revolution under the dictatorship
> of the proletariat, deepen the three great revolutionary
> movements of class struggle, the struggle for production and
> scientific experiment . . . [March 10, 1978, p. 13].

In the new period of socialist revolution and socialist construction in our country, the realization of the four modernizations is politically the most important thing. [Sep-
tember 8, 1978, p. 10]

In the original Chinese text, *san da geming yundong* (three great revolutionary movements) is usually the only wording, but the *Beijing Review* editors add the explanatory words *of class struggle, the struggle
for production and scientific experiment* to enumerate the three items.
The whole string thus becomes a fixed phrase. Even at the height of
the Cultural Revolution a few years ago, when "continued" or "per-
petual" revolution was very much the theme of the political movements, no change of word order occurred in *socialist revolution and
socialist construction*. These are actually translations from Chinese
phrases which have fixed word orders. Such expressions have become
so frequently used that some Chinese printing houses simply mold
them in one block; as the typesetter picks up the first character, he
conveniently gets the whole phrase.

In terms of lexical connotations, it is well known that in different societies some words have certain social values or stigmas attached
to them. For example, *capitalist* and *bourgeois* are negative, but *communist* and *propaganda* are positive in China: "At the Chinese Communist Party's National Conference on Propaganda Work in 1957,
Chairman Mao made a scientific analysis of the intellectuals in our
country" (July 8, 1977, p. 13). Here *propaganda* has a perfectly respectable meaning.

In terms of syntax, readers may find the *Beijing Review*'s sentences somewhat longer than usual. Indeed, nouns with short modification in Chinese often have to be translated into English with embedded sentences. Moreover, complex sentences appear more often
in political documents, in both Chinese and English. My feeling is
that the syntax of the *Beijing Review* is not particularly Sinicized.
For many years one could find articles in the *Beijing Review* profuse-
ly quoting Chairman Mao's aphorisms; it is also common to find articles recounting situations in the times "before Liberation." Naturally,
these features reflect the current way of life in China.

To recapitulate, English in the *Beijing Review* shows its distinctiveness mainly by way of lexical items. In other parts of the world,
however, as Kachru (1981) clearly shows, the transfer of a non-native
English speaker's native linguistic and cultural elements is not restricted to the lexicon, but appears in syntax as well (see also, e.g., Bokamba 1982, Craig 1982, and Zuengler 1982). The reason for the
lack of a significant transfer of Chinese syntax in the *Beijing Review*

has to do with the fact that the English writings are done by specially trained translators, and the feeling that one should not impose Chinese syntax which would confound the international reader. The lexical items as presented above are clearly culture bound. There is no doubt that some of these items or phrases can be replaced by words appropriate to British or American practice (e.g., *dramatic work* instead of *propaganda work*), but then one risks the loss of authenticity.

Four Modernizations: Moves against Sinicized English

As China diverts its energy to science and technology, massive political movements will diminish. This desire to end excessive political struggle is clearly expressed in a recent document. The Communique of the Third Plenary Session of the 11th Central Committee of the Communist Party of China, adopted on December 22, 1978, emphasizes that the large-scale turbulent class struggles have more or less come to an end, and that the people should direct their work and attention toward the modernization of agriculture, industry, national defense, and science and technology. As political movements diminish, the number of the politicized phrases unintelligible to the casual reader will decrease. Moreover, as a tourist industry develops, China will have to use more words familiar to Westerners.

Moves away from the politicized and stereotyped expressions are currently underway. In the *Beijing Review,* change is the rule, rather than the exception. For example, 1978 saw a reduction in the profusion of quotes from Chairman Mao; furthermore, such quotes are now printed in the regular text type font, rather than in the boldface. Such changes are not unique to the *Beijing Review;* rather, they originated in Chinese-language publications.

Ideas for change in the English language in China have come mainly from English teachers there. Some teachers have recently voiced their views against the use of Sinicized English. China is now eager to learn foreign things and ways, and English teachers are collecting foreign English-language textbooks to aid their compilation of teaching materials.

This move toward modernization is in reaction to the ways of the past decade. As I have pointed out elsewhere (Cheng 1975), social relevance is an important requirement in China's foreign language teaching. Typical content from "social practice" is exemplified in "classroom practice." An extreme interpretation of this requirement said that, if things depicted in the textbook all happened in a com-

munity unknown to the students, that text would be devoid of social reality. Hence we found the lessons in one English textbook (*English,* Volume 2, Intermediate level; Shanghai People's Publishing
House, 1974) to have titles such as "Serve the People," "Carry the
Struggle to Criticize Lin Piao and Confucius Through to the End,"
"Tachai Marches On," "Recounting the Family's Revolutionary History," etc., mainly relating to Chinese society.

The emphasis on one's own society to the exclusion of the foreign culture, as practiced a few years ago in China, is somewhat extreme. Zhu (1978) mentions that the authorities politicized the aims
of foreign language teaching, selecting for reading lists too many writings which were inappropriate to foreign norms, Sinicized, or related
solely to China. In some schools only two months in the entire three
years of training were spent in reading original English materials. To
correct that bias, more materials written in the West have now been
incorporated. For example, in issue number 104 (1980) of the month-
ly magazine *Yingyu Xuexi* (English Language Learning), about half of
the sixty-five pages are devoted to reading materials, and the other
half to articles. Among the readings, only one was a translation from
Chinese and about China ("The Green Pine" by Chen Yi); the others
were written by Westerners or about Western culture: "The Hero" by
Edmondo d'Amicis (rewritten in English), "The Skeleton of the Future" by Hugh MacDiarmid (Christopher Murray Grieve), "A Day's
Wait" (Ernest Hemingway), "Six Humorous Stories" (selected from
L. A. Hill's Intermediate Comprehension Pieces), "The Million Pound
Note" (unsigned), "The Rainmaker" (from Lucky Accidents in Sci-
ence), and "Pipelines" (unsigned).

Some English-language teachers have also voiced their views
against the fixed translations of some Chinese terms which are not
intelligible to foreigners. For example, Xiong and Cheng (1980) mention that *pinnong* should be translated as "peasant of poor origin,"
and that *Uncle PLA man* should not be used at all. In translations
appearing in officially printed materials such as the *Beijing Review,*
these terms have become fixed. The Chinese word *pinnong* is officially translated as "poor peasant"; the Chinese-English dictionary compiled at the Beijing Foreign Language Institute (1978) also gives
"poor peasant" as its definition. This term is in fact a social class designation. But Xiong and Cheng argue that, from a sentence *Zhege pinnong jiating fengyi zushi,* the translation "The family of this poor peasant is well fed and well clothed" does not render the meaning correctly. The translation should therefore be changed. With regard to
Uncle PLA man, they say that foreigners simply cannot derive any
sense from it.

In the area of phonology, Xiong and Cheng (1980) mention that English students in China have used IPA transcriptions in textbooks and dictionaries as guides for pronunciation, rather than listening to native speakers; thus a special kind of pronunciation and intonation has developed. Naturally, there must be a wide range of phonological differences, because of Chinese dialect background and degree of proficiency. However, these registers are not sociolinguistically outstanding, and detailed treatments of them fall outside my present scope.

As the current trend is toward modernization, it is felt that there is a need to teach and use "genuine" and "idiomatic" English (see, e.g., Wei 1978). On the other hand, it is also time to clean up old English translations which render the Chinese meanings inadequately. Wu (1979) shows many incorrect English translations of Chinese terms in the last hundred years. Zhao (1978, 1979) challenges the correctness of the official English version of Chairman Mao's poems. In the near future the Chinese variety of English will certainly move closer to that of the West.

Conclusions

China regarded the people outside its boundaries as barbarians until the seventeenth century. Though for several hundred years China was ruled by the Mongols and the Manchus, no foreign languages were imposed on the Han Chinese. The introduction of English into China in the eighteenth century occurred during a time of self-complacency. The Chinese then did not know much about the outside world, so English was imposed on people with an inward-looking mentality, people who were not eager to learn other tongues. Because the language had to be modified, Chinese pidgin developed.

Then, between 1850 and 1950, Westernization movements emerged, and China began looking outward, aspiring to learn things foreign. Because the English language was a valuable tool for modernization, the Chinese began to learn it in its full form. In turn, Chinese also acquired certain English features.

In the 1960's and 1970's, China was isolated to some extent and was entangled in its own domestic affairs (the Cultural Revolution). It was again a time of inward-looking mentality, euphemistically characterized as self-reliance. Chinese elements took hold of the English language in China. In reaction to the inward-looking Cultural Revolution, the Four Modernizations movement emerged. Chinese elements are gradually giving up their hold in English.

Thus English in China largely reflects the socio-political situations there. The patterns of the Chinese varieties of English are clear: When China is inward-looking, the English there acquires more Chinese elements; when China is outward-searching, English there is more like the norm in the West.

NOTES

1. I thank Bruce A. Sherwood for commenting on an earlier version of this paper, and Wang Yihua for providing me with several journals from China dealing with foreign language teaching.
2. Xu (1978) lists the missions of foreign language teaching in China in the past as (1) to propagate great achievements of New China, (2) to establish contacts with people of various countries by means of foreign languages, (3) to use foreign language as a tool in the struggle with imperialist countries. He says that the newly added mission is to serve the learning of modern science and knowledge.
3. In the past, some writers used the pidgin (or a pseudo form) to create a humorous effect (Reinecke et al. 1975).
4. The *pinyin* system was established in 1958 and has been in use in schools and other areas, but the government decided to use it in foreign-language publications only recently. It was also recently adopted by the United Nations and by the U.S. Board on Geographic Names.
5. The difficulties in translating metaphors into English are discussed in Chen (1979).

REFERENCES

Bamgbose, Ayọ. 1982. Standard Nigerian English: issues of identification. In this volume.
Beijing Foreign Language Institute. 1978. *A Chinese-English Dictionary*. Beijing: Shangwu Yinshu Guan.
Bokamba, Eyamba G. 1982. The Africanization of English. In this volume.
Brumfit, C. J. 1977. The English language, ideology and international communication: some issues arising out of English teaching for Chinese students. *English Language Teaching Documents*, pp. 15-24. London: British Council.
Chen, Wenbo. 1979. Chengyu Yingyi shi xingxiang he yuyi de maodun (Contradictions between image and metaphor in English translation of Chinese idioms). *Waiyu Jiaoxue Yu Yanjiu* (Foreign Language Teaching and Study) 4: 44-51, 23.
Cheng, Chin-Chuan. 1975. Trends in foreign language teaching in the People's Republic of China: impressions of a visit. *Studies in Language Learning* 1(1): 153-62.
Cowan, J. Ronayn; Light, Richard L.; Mathews, B. Ellen; and Tucker, G. Richard. 1979. English teaching in China: a recent survey. *TESOL Quarterly* 13(4): 465-82.
Craig, Dennis R. 1982. Toward a description of Caribbean English. In this volume.
Hall, Robert A., Jr. 1944. Chinese Pidgin English grammar and texts. *Journal of the American Oriental Society* 64(3): 95-113.

————. 1966. *Pidgin and creole languages.* Ithaca: Cornell University Press.

————. 1973. Pidgin languages. Pp. 91-114 in *Varieties of present-day English,* ed. Richard W. Bailey and Jay L. Robinson. New York: Macmillan.

Kachru, Braj B. 1969. English in South Asia. In *Current trends in linguistics,* V, ed. Thomas Sebeok. The Hague: Mouton.

————. 1976. Models of English for the Third World: white man's linguistic burden or language pragmatics? *TESOL Quarterly* 10(2): 221-39.

————. 1981. The pragmatics of non-native varieties of English. In Smith, ed., 1981.

Lehmann, Winfred P., et al. 1975. *Language and linguistics in the People's Republic of China.* Austin: University of Texas Press.

Light, Timothy. 1978. Foreign language teaching in the People's Republic of China. In *On TESOL '78: EFL policies, programs, practices,* ed. Charles Blatchford and Jacquelyn Schachter. Washington, D.C.: TESOL.

Platt, John T. 1977. A model for polyglossia and multilingualism (with special reference to Singapore and Malaysia). *Language in Society* 6: 361-78.

Reinecke, John E. 1937. Marginal language. Ph.D. dissertation, Yale University.

————; DeCamp, David; Hancock, Ian F.; Tsuzaki, Stanley M.; and Wood, Richard E. 1975. *A bibliography of pidgin and creole languages.* Honolulu: University of Hawaii Press.

Richards, J., and Kang-Kwong, Luke. 1981. English in Hong Kong: functions and status. Paper presented at the seminar on varieties of English, RELC, Singapore, April, 1981.

Shanghai Peoples Publishing House. 1974. *English: intermediate level.*

Smith, Larry E., ed. 1981. *English for cross-cultural communication.* London: Macmillan.

Todd, Loreto. 1974. *Pidgins and creoles.* London: Routledge and Kegan Paul.

Wang, Li. 1955. *Zhongguo Yufa Lilun* (Theory of Chinese grammar). Beijing: Zhonghua Shuju. (Original edition, 1944, Shanghai: Shangwu Yinshu Guan.)

Wei, Yuanshu. 1978. Qiantan waiyu jiaoyu xiandaihua (Plain talks on modernization of foreign language teaching). *Waiguo Yu* (Foreign Language) 2: 1-2.

Whinnom, Keith. 1971. Linguistic hybridization and the "special case" of pidgins and creoles. In *Pidginization and creolization of languages,* ed. Dell Hymes. London: Cambridge University Press.

Wu, Jingrong. 1979. Women zouguo de daolu (The path we have taken). *Waiyu Jiaoxue Yu Yanjiu* (Foreign Language Teaching and Study) 3: 1-6, 40.

Xiong, Delan, and Cheng, Musheng. 1980. Waiyu jiaoxue poqie xuyao gaige (Foreign language teaching urgently needs to be reformed). *Guangming Ribao* (Guangming Daily), April 4, 1980, p. 2.

Xu, Guozhang. 1978. Lun waiyu jiaoxue de fangzhen yu renwu (On the policy and mission of foreign language teaching). *Waiyu Jiaoxue Yu Yanjiu* (Foreign Language Teaching and Study) 2: 6-15.

Zhao, Zhentao. 1978. Jiu Mao Zhuxi shici Yingyi ben tantan yiwen zhong de jige wenti (Discussion on some problems of translation with respect to the English edition of Chairman Mao's poems). *Waiyu Jiaoxue Yu Yanjiu* (Foreign Language Teaching and Study) 1: 21-26.

————. 1979. Zai tan Mao Zhuxi shici Yingyi ben yiwen zhong de wenti (Problems of translation in the English edition of Chairman Mao's poems revisited). *Waiyu Jiaoxue Yu Yanjiu* (Foreign Language Teaching and Study) 2: 7-12, 6.

Zhu, Shuyang. 1978. Luetan waiyu jiaoxue de yixie jingyan he gaijin yijian (Discussion on foreign language teaching experience and ideas for improvements). *Waiyu Jiaoxue Yu Yanjiu* (Foreign Language Teaching and Study) 2: 16-22.

Zuengler, Jane. 1982. Kenyan English. In this volume.

9

English in a South Indian Urban Context

KAMAL K. SRIDHAR

This paper discusses the use of English vis-à-vis Hindi and the mother tongue (Kannada) in the state of Karnataka in South India.[1] My discussion is based on the results of an empirical survey involving university students and employees in the public and private sectors. The results of this survey, a pilot project though it was, are interesting and important in three respects. First, this is one of few empirical studies of the language situation in Karnataka in particular, and in India in general. Second, it helps us understand the complementarity of role distribution among languages in a multilingual society. And third, it helps us assess the success of institutional efforts in language planning in India.

Previous studies on bilingualism and multilingualism have explored various aspects of what, to some Western minds, has seemed to be a curious and abnormal phenomenon. Studies such as those of Darcy (1946) showed that the performance of children from bilingual environments is substantially below the level of their monolingual English-speaking peers, particularly on tests requiring verbal skills. Brown, Fournier, and Moyer (1977), in a study focusing on science concepts and Piagetian concrete reasoning, found that "the Mexican American children in this study scored significantly lower on both tests than the Anglo American children. . . . The lag in development between the two groups . . . appears to be about 2+ years" (1977: 331-32). The above studies have been critiqued for their research format, technical aspects, etc., in the works of De Avila and Havassy (1974) and Kohlberg and Mayer (1972).

Current research emphasizes the positive aspects of bilingualism, and the indications are that rather than causing intellectual deprivation, the benefits of bilingualism are remarkable. Recent works drawn from a variety of fields such as linguistics, psycholinguistics, learning, developmental psychology, and organizational sociology suggest that bilingual children may be potentially more intellectually advanced with respect to concept formation and general mental flexibility than their monolingual counterparts. Studies by Lambert and

Tucker (1972) and Edwards and Casserly (1973) involving French-
English bilingual children in Canada suggest that French immersion
facilitated certain mathematical skills; furthermore, increased exposure of basically Anglophone children to a second language "benefits not only the acquisition of the second language, but also the
development of the mother tongue" (Tremaine 1975: 2).

In another study, Feldman and Shen (1971) compared the cognitive abilities of bilingual Chicano and Anglo-American Head Start
children. The experimental tasks were taken from Piaget. The results
indicated that bilingual children significantly outperformed the
monolinguals on all tasks in the study. Other studies, such as those
by Ianco-Worall (1972), Been-Zeev (1972), and Cummins and
Guilustan (1973) seem to support the above claim.

Studies by Lambert and Tucker (1972) and associates have
dealt with the cognitive basis of bilingualism as well as with its
social psychology, in particular language attitudes. Numerous studies
following the pioneering ones of Einar Haugen (1953) and Joshua
Fishman (1971) have discussed language maintenance among bilinguals. An even larger number of studies have examined the impact
of bilingualism on the structure of the languages in contact, in the
tradition of Uriel Weinrich (1953), Henry and Renée Kahane (1979).
The formal and functional properties of mixed varieties in contexts
of stable bilingualism have been explored by Kachru (1978) and
Gumperz and Hernandez (1978). Fishman (1972), Spolsky (1972),
Trueba (1977), and Andersson (1970) have written on the educational aspects of bilingualism. Finally, and most relevantly for our
purposes, there have been a number of studies examining the role
of different languages in multilingual societies. Since the present
article falls in this last category, it is useful to briefly review some
of these.

Since bilingualism is generally considered to be an abridged
version of multilingualism, we may take into account a few of the
studies on language choice among bilinguals. Greenfield and Fishman (1971) discuss the roles of Spanish and English in the Puerto
Rican community in New York City. Spanish is associated with values such as intimacy and solidarity and is used primarily in domains
such as family and friendship, while English is associated with values
such as status differentiation and is used in domains such as religion,
education, and employment. We can distinguish between what may
be termed "affective" and "utilitarian" domains.

Cooper and Carpenter's "Linguistic Diversity in the Ethiopian
Market" (1972) is an extensive study of languages used in twenty-

three Ethiopian markets. There is no evidence that Amharic, Arabic, or any other language has emerged as a lingua franca for trade. The authors conclude by observing that in the linguistically diverse contexts of these Ethiopian markets, transactions were facilitated by the traders' multilingualism, rather than by the emergence of a trade lingua franca.

Ferguson's study entitled "The Role of Arabic in Ethiopia" (1970) deals with Arabic in relation to English, Amharic, and French. Ferguson's emphasis is slightly different from that of the present study in that he is concerned primarily with Ethiopians' attitudes toward the possible roles of the various languages, rather than with the distribution of these languages in various domains. Ferguson's research technique is similar to the present one, however, in using a questionnaire for gathering data.

Whiteley's *Language in Kenya* (1974) reports the results of an extensive survey of language usage in multilingual Kenya. The situation he describes bears many interesting parallels to that of India. In Kenya, a number of factors have contributed to a situation in which the use of a particular language has come to be characteristic of a particular social domain, in much the same way that domains are characterized in England by varieties of English. The languages themselves have taken on the complex of emotions, prestige, etc., associated with the domains. Local languages like Kamba or Kipsigis may be linked with the rural homestead or with traditional values; Swahili may be linked with town life, trade, and certain kinds of jobs; English is associated with government service, the professions, and high-status jobs.

Most germane to the present study are the linguistic surveys conducted by Pandit (1978) and Kachru (1976). Pandit's "Language and Identity: The Panjabi Language in Delhi" reports the results of a survey questionnaire administered to undergraduate students of a women's college in New Delhi. The data indicated the relative usage of English, Panjabi, and Hindi in affective domains (domestic, neighborhood, religion) as well as in utilitarian ones (e.g., education, mass media, reading, and writing) by Hindu, Sikh, and Muslim students. Pandit's data indicate the relatively higher usage of English in utilitarian domains, and of the mother tongue in affective domains.

Kachru's study deals with the use of English among the students and faculty of English departments in Indian universities. This study also used the questionnaire method, and part of it deals with the use of English in some selected domains. Although Kachru's study indicated a preference for English in what I have termed "utilitarian" domains, these results, by virtue of the circumstances in which the study was conducted, have some limitations. First, the population consisted of people professionally committed to the use of English. Second, the population was drawn mainly from large metropolitan areas such as Bombay, Delhi, Madras, and Hyderabad. Third, the questions did not involve a comparison between English and other languages in different domains. Finally, no correlational analysis was made; hence a finer isolation of variables has not been possible.

The present study is an expansion of Kachru's, more limited in some respects, and broader in others. It is limited in the sense that only one Indian state is involved; also, no attempt is made to elicit attitudes toward the different varieties of English, or to determine what role that language should play in India. However, it is broader in that it represents both student and worker populations; the former includes students from a variety of disciplines (excluding English literature). Within the worker population, a wide variety of occupations is represented. Therefore the results of this study complement Kachru's.

My data come from two questionnaires administered to two distinct populations in the summer of 1977. The first set of subjects consisted of undergraduate students studying for the degrees of Bachelor of Arts, Bachelor of Science, or Bachelor of Commerce in four private colleges, two in the state capital and semi-metropolitan city of Bangalore, and two in the medium-sized city of Shimoga. A second questionnaire was administered to public and private employees in Bangalore. This population consisted of (1) white-collar employees of the Karnataka Government Insurance Department; (2) federal government employees of the Indian Posts and Telegraphs Department at the General Post Office in Bangalore; (3) employees of the Life Insurance Corporation of India — a nationalized (public sector) undertaking; (4) employees of the Public Works Department (engineering division) of the Government of Karnataka; and (5) employees of a prosperous private engineering consultant firm. This population included both highly educated and skilled professionals and middle-level (clerical) employees.

The student questionnaires dealt with the following topics: demographic data; fields of specialization; the current and previous medium of instruction, and reasons for the choice; educational level and occupation of parents; languages in which the students claimed competence, and their degrees of competence; job aspirations of the students; preference for English, Hindi, or mother tongue in the following domains: (1) mass media (radio, newspapers, and magazines) and (2) a number of interpersonal situations. This last category specified the following: with family, friends, teachers, neighbors; with relatives at marriages and socio-religious functions; with office or bank employees; while discussing politics, technical topics, etc., and while visiting another state in India. The rationale for eliciting all these different kinds of data was that each factor might be a significant variable affecting patterns of language choice. The second questionnaire involved roughly the same demographic data, except information was also gathered about the subjects' occupations and incomes, and the domains concentrated on occupational interaction (while talking with colleagues and superiors, with subordinate staff, with public customers, etc.).

A total of 299 students and 88 employees responded to the questionnaires. Analysis of the responses is still in progress; therefore, I have not been able to extract all the significant results, specifically correlational patterns. However, from the analyses performed so far, a very interesting pattern of language usage has begun to develop.

First, let us look at the percentage of students who preferred English to their mother tongue as the medium of instruction at the high school level. Although this choice was available to all the students, 68 percent chose English, 27 percent mother tongue, and only 5 percent other languages, including Hindi/Urdu. The reasons for this choice become apparent when we analyze the students' response to another question: "What will be your opportunities if your education was through (1) English, (2) Hindi-Urdu, (3) mother tongue, and (4) the state language, if it is not the same as your mother tongue?" The responses are given in Table 1.

Table 1. Job Prospects and the Language of Training (%)

Languages	None	Good	Very good	Excellent	No answer
English	1	20	16	52	11
Hindi/Urdu	18	20	7	0	45
Mother tongue	8	20	12	16	44
State language	20	11	6	3	60

The majority (52 percent) said that their job prospects would be excellent if their education was through English; the mother tongue placed a very distinct second. No student felt the same way about Hindi/Urdu; indeed, 18 percent thought their job prospects

would be nil with Hindi/Urdu. This preference for English is consistent with the educational goals and job preferences of the respondents: 85 percent indicated a desire to pursue a master's degree or
higher; as for job preference, 31 percent wanted to become bank
managers, 15 percent college or university teachers, 14 percent high-
level officers in the Indian Administrative Service, and 10 percent
lawyers. These educational goals and preferences reflect the ubiquitous desire for upward mobility. (The educational level of the parents of 81 percent of the respondents is a B.A. degree or lower.)

Let us now turn to the question of language competence. Table
2 presents the percentage of students who claim proficiency in the
languages specified below in various domains.

Table 2. Students Claiming Proficiency in Various Languages (%)

| | Proficiency | |
Language	None	Enough for most conversations
English	—	29
Hindi/Urdu	19	11
Mother tongue	—	63
State language (if other than mother tongue)	—	18

Next to the mother tongue, the language in which most people
claim proficiency is English (nearly 30 percent); as many as 19 percent claim no proficiency in Hindi/Urdu. These results throw much
light on the sociolinguistic status of English compared to Hindi/Urdu
in South India. It is a well-known sociolinguistic phenomenon that
when a language commands prestige in a society, even those who have
minimal or marginal proficiency in that language are eager to claim to
know it; for example, it is very common in India to find even those
who have had only four to six weeks' instruction in French or German listing it among the languages they know. The poor showing of
Hindi/Urdu vis-à-vis English correctly reflects the attitudinal barrier
that Hindi must overcome in the South before it can claim to be a
pan-Indian language.

Now to turn to the actual use of English, mother tongue, and
Hindi/Urdu in Karnataka. The first domain we shall consider is the
mass media — newspapers and radio. The response to the question
of the language of the printed media is given in Table 3.

The readership of English-language newspapers is slightly more than that of Indian-language newspapers, whereas the readership of English and Indian-language magazines is about equal. This confirms my intuitive observation that educated Indians rely largely on English-language newspapers and magazines for state and local news and for light general reading, respectively. Unfortunately, the table does not give a language-by-language breakdown of the Indian-language newspapers and magazines. However, respondents did list the periodicals they regularly read; from this it is clear that most periodicals are in Kannada and other regional languages, and that the role of Hindi/Urdu in this domain is marginal.

Table 3. Students Who Read English and Indian Language
Daily Newspapers and Magazines (%)

| | Number of periodicals read | | | | | |
	1	2	3	4	5	Above 5
English-language newspapers	56	14	10	—	—	20
Indian-language newspapers	50	12	7	1	1	29
English-language magazines	30	14	17	4	1	34
Indian-language magazines	29	21	19	3	1	27

It is interesting to contrast the pattern of English use in this domain with that reported in Kachru's (1976) study. Kachru found that as many as 71 percent of the respondents "always" read newspapers and magazines in English; in my study, the figure is 56 percent. For general reading, Kachru's figure was 64 percent; mine is only 30 percent. The difference may be attributed to the fact that Kachru's subjects were all students majoring in English literature, whereas my subject population is more diversified. Nevertheless, the percentage of students reading newspapers and magazines in English in the present sample remains extremely impressive, testifying to the powerful role of English in the mass media.

The next question referred to the language of radio news broadcasts. Seventeen percent of the students claimed to listen to English-language newscasts exclusively, and 16 percent to newscasts in the mother tongue exclusively. As many as 61 percent claimed to listen to both. A high percentage of these latter responses may be explained by the fact that 88 percent of the students' mothers had an educational level of matriculation (secondary school) or less; in such families it is typical for both English and the mother tongue to be used.

The use of languages in interpersonal domains is summarized in Table 4. These domains may be broadly divided into two classes: the intimate or affective domains (items A-D) and the formal or utilitarian ones (items E-I). As predicted, in intimate domains the language(s) used regularly are the mother tongue and English, in that order. The language most rarely used is Hindi/Urdu. One interesting result might be worth noting: while there is a big gap between the use of English and the mother tongue in most of the intimate domains, the gap is very narrow when it comes to interaction with friends. This may be due to shared educational status, goals, and interests.

Table 4. Students Who Use Mother Tongue, English, and Hindi/Urdu in Social Interaction (%)

Domain	Language	Regularly	Rarely
A. Family	English	15	29
	Mother tongue	87	1
	Hindi/Urdu	3	54
B. Friends	English	42	8
	Mother tongue	53	12
C. Neighbors who can speak your	English	17	24
language	Mother tongue	65	6
	Hindi/Urdu	4	48
D. Friends and relatives, during	English	24	15
weddings, etc.	Mother tongue	71	3
	Hindi/Urdu	5	47
E. Teachers	English	57	3
	Mother tongue	24	26
	Hindi/Urdu	2	57
F. Strangers on the bus	English	47	11
	Mother tongue	35	11
	Hindi/Urdu	5	48
G. Office and bank employees	English	57	8
	Mother tongue	26	17
	Hindi/Urdu	2	49
H. Political and technical discussions	English	42	8
	Mother tongue	41	12
	Hindi/Urdu	4	50
I. While visiting another state in	English	64	6
India	Mother tongue	17	27
	Hindi/Urdu	15	32

Turning to the formal or utilitarian domains, one finds that English is consistently preferred over the mother tongue and Hindi/ Urdu. The preference for English when interacting with teachers shows that English is still very much the language of higher education; it also probably reflects the fact that the mother tongue lacks the technical registers used in academic discussions. (The negligible difference between the use of English and the mother tongue for political and technical discussions is almost certainly due to a defect in the testing instrument. If I had separated political from technical discussion, I am sure the pattern of response would have been quite different. Politics is discussed informally in India, and lexical borrowings in the regional languages make the code adequate for this function. Technical discussion, on the other hand, more often results in code-switching, since code-mixing is not adequate.)

Proceeding next to the domain of interaction with office and bank employees, we again notice a preference for English. This may be due to two factors. First, despite the efforts of state and central governments, English is still very much the language of administration. Second, English is felt to be the language of power, a language of prestige. By and large, it is easier to get things done in a government office or a bank if one speaks English than if one speaks the mother tongue. Again, notice the poor showing of Hindi/Urdu in this domain.

Finally, consider the responses under Item I, which show the roles of English, Hindi/Urdu, and the mother tongue as interstate link languages. Again English is preferred, and the frequency of mother tongue use goes down, not unexpectedly; but what is interesting is the considerably better rating of Hindi/Urdu — for the first time the figures are in double digits. The 15 percent rating of Hindi/ Urdu does not compare with the 64 percent rating of English as a link language; furthermore, the rating given to Hindi/Urdu would probably be given to any other regional language, if the question had specified the state where that language was spoken. This hypothesis is confirmed by the fact that the rating for Hindi/Urdu actually remains lower than that of the mother tongue.

The preceding discussion demonstrates a clear and identifiable pattern of language distribution in various domains. The mother tongue is dominant in intimate or affective domains, whereas in formal or utilitarian ones the language of choice is English. All the functions investigated in this study are adequately (and almost exhaustively) handled by the mother tongue and English. Hindi/Urdu plays a very marginal role.

When comparing the patterns of language use by students with those of employees (see Table 5), again we note the clear preference for the mother tongue in the intimate domain (66%). In domains B and E — that is, with colleagues and superiors, and with customers who do not speak the respondent's mother tongue — the preference is again overwhelmingly for English. The response in Item C is very interesting: with subordinate staff (which in the context of this survey must refer, by and large, to clerks and "attenders") the roles of the languages are *reversed:* English is used least (probably only with clerks and typists), and the mother tongue most frequently (48 percent). Hindi/Urdu is used more in this domain than in any other. The relative ranking of the three languages is a good indicator of their status in the attitudinal hierarchy. There is one apparently puzzling result under Item D, however: as many as 27 percent of the respondents claim to use Hindi in this domain, although the number of respondents with Hindi as their mother tongue is only 2 percent.

Table 5. Employees Who Use English, Mother Tongue, and Hindi/Urdu in Professional Contexts (%)

Domain	Language	Regularly	Rarely
A. Friends	English	33	6
	Mother tongue	66	3
	Hindi/Urdu	25	6
B. Colleagues and superiors	English	64	3
	Mother tongue	31	19
	Hindi/Urdu	16	7
C. Subordinate staff	English	22	25
	Mother tongue	48	14
	Hindi/Urdu	30	5
D. Customers who speak mother tongue	English	38	9
	Mother tongue	45	13
	Hindi/Urdu	27	6
E. Customers who don't speak your language	English	74	1
	Mother tongue	5	25
	Hindi/Urdu	14	14

This last finding is consistent with another very general effect noticed in the employees' responses. Although Hindi is used less frequently than English and the mother tongue in most formal domains, it is nevertheless used more frequently by employees than by students. This may be due in part to two factors: first, only about half of the employees claim to know Kannada (including 43 percent who are native speakers); second, most respondents are employed in nation-wide public or private enterprises and hold transferable jobs. It is clear that Hindi/Urdu is perceived as better suited than English to serve as a low-level lingua franca.

Summarizing the findings from the employees' responses, we see that, as with the students, the mother tongue is used primarily in the intimate domain; English is the language of choice in professional contexts, except with subordinate staff; English is also the preferred language with customers when there is no shared language; and Hindi is the language of interaction with subordinate staff, after the mother tongue.

I believe the data and analysis presented here give us a clear, empirically based picture of language use and language attitudes in a developing multilingual society. The findings confirm the recurrent pattern of use of the mother tongue in intimate or affective domains. These data also provide strong empirical evidence to support the claims made about the role of English in present-day India. We have seen its importance in the domains of mass media, academic and professional interaction, administration, and interstate communication. We have also seen its power and prestige in terms of job opportunities. In contrast, the mother tongue and Hindi/Urdu are less versatile. Hindi/Urdu in particular seems to be of marginal communicative value for students and employees in Karnataka.

All these findings "make sense" when viewed in light of what Kachru (1976) has called the pragmatic role hierarchy in the multilingual's repertoire. In this model, the position of a given language in the multilingual's repertoire hierarchy is determined by very pragmatic considerations. The more roles a language can open up for the speaker, the higher its position. Students and professionals in Karnataka feel that English equips them for the largest number of socially valued roles; next comes the mother tongue. Efforts of propagandists for Hindi, including the federal government, have not succeeded in translating a constitutional mandate into a pragmatic reality for the people of South India.

NOTE

1. I wish to express my gratitude to U.V. Vishvanath and S.N.K. Rao for their help in gathering the data in India. My sincere thanks to Frank Anshen, Stewart Jones, Braj B. Kachru, Henry Kahane, Richard Smock, and S. N. Sridhar for their comments and suggestions.

REFERENCES

Andersson, Theodore, and Boyer, Mildred. 1970. *Bilingual schooling in the United States.* Detroit: Blaine-Ethridge Books.

Baratz, J., and Baratz, J. 1970. Early childhood intervention: the social science base of institutional racism. *Harvard Educational Review* 40.

Been-Zeev, S. 1972. The influence of bilingualism on cognitive development and cognitive strategy. Ph.D. dissertation, University of Chicago.

Brown, R. L.; Fournier, J. F.; and Moyer, R. H. 1977. A cross-cultural study of Piagetian concrete reasoning and science concepts among rural fifth-grade Mexican and Anglo-American Students. *Journal of Research in Science Teaching* 14.

Cooper. R. L., and Carpenter, Susan. 1972. Linguistic diversity in the Ethiopian market. In Fishman (1972).

Cummins, J., and Guilustan, M. 1973. Some effects of bilingualism on cognitive functioning. Edmonton: University of Alberta. Mimeo.

Darcy, N. T. 1946. The effects of bilingualism upon the measurement of the intelligence of children of preschool age. *Journal of Educational Psychology* 37 (1): 21-43.

De Avila, E. A., and Havassy, B. H. 1974. The testing of minority children. *Today's Education.* Nov.-Dec., pp. 72-75.

Edwards, H. P., and Casserly, M. C. 1973. Evaluation of second language programs in the English schools. *Annual Report 1972-73.* Ottawa: Ottawa Roman Catholic Separate School Board.

Feldman, C., and Shen, M. 1971. Some language-related cognitive advantages of bilingual five-year-olds. *Journal of Genetic Psychology* 118: 235-44.

Ferguson, C. A. 1970. *Language structure and language use.* Palo Alto: Stanford University Press.

Fishman, J. A. 1971. *Bilingualism in the barrio.* Bloomington: Indiana University Press.

———, ed. 1972. *Advances in the sociology of language,* vol. 12. The Hague: Mouton.

Greenfield, L., and Fishman, J. A. 1971. Situational measures of normative language views of person, place and topic among Puerto Rican bilinguals. In Fishman (1971).

Gumperz, John, and Hernandez, Edward. 1978. Cognitive aspects of bilingual communication. *Language-Behavior Research Laboratory Working Paper No. 28.* Berkeley: University of California. Mimeo.

Haugen, Einar. 1953. *The Norwegian language in America: a study in bilingual behavior.* Philadelphia: University of Pennsylvania Press.

Ianco-Worrall, A. D. 1972. Bilingualism and cognitive development. *Child Development* 43: 1390-1400.

Kachru, Braj B. 1976. Models of English for the Third World: white man's linguistic burden or language pragmatics? *TESOL Quarterly,* 10(2): 221-39.

——— , 1978. Toward structuring code-mixing: an Indian perspective. In Braj B. Kachru and S. N. Sridhar, eds., *Aspects of sociolinguistics in South Asia* (special issue of *International Journal of the Sociology of Language* 16: 27-44).

Kahane, Henry, and Kahane, Renée. 1979. Decline and survival of Western prestige languages. *Language* 55(1): 183-98.

Kohlberg, G. L., and Mayer, R. 1972. Development as the aim of education. *Harvard Educational Review* 42: 4.

Lambert, Wallace E., and Tucker, G. Richard. 1972. *Bilingual education of children: the St. Lambert experiment.* Rowley, Mass.: Newbury House.

Pandit, Prabodh B. 1978. Language and identity: the Panjabi language in Delhi. In Braj B. Kachru and S. N. Sridhar, eds., *Aspects of sociolinguistics in South Asia* (special issue of *International Journal of the Sociology of Language* 16: 93-108).

Spolsky, Bernard. 1972. *The language education of minority children.* Rowley, Mass.: Newbury House.

Tremaine, Ruth V. 1975. *Syntax and Piagetian operational thought.* Washington, D.C.: Georgetown University Press.

Trueba, Henry T. 1977. Bilingual-bicultural education: an overview. In Robin, L., ed., *Handbook on curriculum.* Boston: Allyn and Bacon.

Weinreich, Uriel. 1953. *Languages in contact: findings and problems.* New York: Linguistic Circle of New York.

Whiteley, W. H. 1974. *Language in Kenya.* Nairobi: Oxford University Press.

10
Singapore English: Rhetorical and Communicative Styles

JACK C. RICHARDS

The role of language in a community may be studied from a number of different points of view. Traditionally, linguistics has been concerned with describing the linguistic code of the idealized speaker-hearer in a homogeneous speech community. Language variation was regarded as of little intrinsic interest. More recently, the social significance of language variation has been emphasized. Sociolinguists have stressed the inapplicability of language models based on monolingualism or monodialectalism to situations where a variety of languages or speech levels are in use (Bickerton 1975). In analyzing the acquisition and maintenance of register or dialect differentiation, the functional and symbolic status of different speech varieties has been examined. Halliday's and Labov's work has emphasized the symbolic role of language. Halliday has described the different models of language constructed by a child during language acquisition, corresponding to the different functions for which the child needs language. Labov has studied the symbolic role of language, that is, the role of language in realizing such abstract notions as "nation," "class," or "power," and has given a detailed description of the role of language in conferring "solidarity" in a speech community (Labov 1966). This paper is concerned with the contribution of both pragmatic and symbolic factors to variations within the English language as it is used in Singapore.

Singapore, together with many of her neighbor nations, has experienced major political and social changes in the last thirty years. The struggles for independence and self-government in Singapore, Indonesia, Malaysia, and the Philippines have been accompanied by attempts to construct the concept of *nation* by subordinating regional or ethnic loyalties to wider social and political goals. Thus people with languages and cultures as distinct as Acheh and Bali become one, through a common administrative and political superstructure. What distinguishes a nation, however, from groupings of different ethnic or social groups are shared feelings, intentions, attitudes, beliefs, and loyalties (Sprott 1958). The problems are compounded in a multiracial society, since perception of *nation* is often directed along non-ethnic lines; hence a crucial question in many multiracial states is to find a language or languages that can suitably express the new nationalism.

Language in Southeast Asia is a factor which reflects the degree to which new aspirations, identities, and social groupings have replaced the old, and the recent history of language change in Southeast Asia is a fascinating witness to the role of language in mirroring deeper social processes. In Indonesia, independence saw the rapid demise of Dutch and the ready acceptance of Malay as the national language of the new republic. The willing acceptance of Bahasa Indonesia was itself due to the fact that it was identified with a strong nationalist movement, it was not a significant ethnic language, it already had wide roots as a lingua franca, and it emerged as a national language at a time of violent social upheaval (Hoffman 1973). In Malaysia, there is an ongoing attempt to elevate Malay from an ethnic language to the national language of all ethnic groups. However, the fact that Malay is the language of a significant ethnic group, and the absence of strong nationalist associations with the language, have not given Bahasa Malaysia the same rapid acceptance that Bahasa Indonesia received. Likewise, in the Philippines, difficulties in extricating Tagalog from its ethnic roots, together with strong ethnic loyalties toward other regional languages, have not given ready acceptance to Pilipino, a Tagalog-based language, as the national language.

English in Singapore

In Singapore and in many other former British colonies, a further phenomenon has emerged as a product of social change. This is the evolution of relatively stable local varieties of English which have replaced the colonial linguistic models as norms for much that is communicated in English. In Singapore, English is widely used as a medium of instruction in the schools and as a language of communication outside the schools, but the type of English which is heard from people of all walks of life is rarely identical to British models. Instead, one witnesses a variety of local forms of English, ranging from a simplified and almost pidginized dialect of English, to a formal variety of English differing little in grammar and vocabulary from Standard British English, though with more substantial differences in phonology. A similar situation holds in many other countries which were formerly under British administration (Khubchandani 1973). It seems to be generally true in these situations that, with the formal speech levels, variation in phonology is accepted much more readily than grammatical deviation; however, at the lower ends of the speech range, grammatical deviation is marked. In Singapore, since both forms of English remain distinctively Singaporean, we will refer to this phenomenon as the Singapore English speech continuum. To understand the cause and significance of such variation within Singapore English, we need first to consider language use in Singapore.

Singapore's population of some 2¼ million is approximately 76 percent Chinese, 15 percent Malay, and 7 percent Indian, with the remainder being mainly other South Asians and Europeans. Linguistically the Chinese may speak any of the following: Hokkien, Teochew, Cantonese, Hainanese, Hakka, Foochow, or Mandarin, most of which are mutually incomprehensible. Malay and Tamil are the major languages of the other groups. In the schools, English, Mandarin, Malay, or Tamil may be used as mediums of instruction. In non-English-medium schools, English is taught as a second language; in the English-medium schools, one of the other official languages (Malay, Mandarin, or Tamil) may be taught as the second language. Most of the educated population is thus functionally bilingual or multilingual. How do members of different linguistic groups communicate with each other? The following channels of communication are possible (see Platt 1975, and Kuo 1976).

Chinese to a	Chinese	One of the Chinese languages, or English
	Tamil	Malay or English
	Malay	Malay or English
Malay to	All groups	Malay or English
Tamil to a	Tamil	Tamil, English or Malay
	Chinese or	
	Malay	Malay or English

There have been distinct changes in the choice of language of communication in the last twenty years. Among the Chinese, Hokkien has been a common lingua franca in Singapore. Malay has also been a traditional lingua franca in the region, functioning both as a trade language and as a link between different ethnic groups. The Malay so used (bazaar Malay) differs widely from literary Malay, utilizing a limited range of vocabulary and omitting many of the prefixes and suffixes used to mark formal Malay. Choice of language for Chinese is determined both by situational and ethnic constraints. A Chinese speaking to a member of his own language group could use either English or the vernacular. When addressing a member of a different ethnic group, he could choose between Mandarin, English, Hokkien, or bazaar Malay, depending on the degree of familiarity with the languages concerned and the formality or informality of the situation. Mandarin and English tend to be used in formal situations, while Hokkien and bazaar Malay are used in informal settings. In pre-World War II days, when English-medium education was reserved for a privileged few, there was much less demand for English outside the classroom and a much greater use of bazaar Malay and Hokkien as lingua francas. Since independence, the percentage of the population which has had English-medium education or been taught English as a second language in school has greatly expanded; hence English has moved out of the classroom to become a widely used language in all spheres of life. The expansion in educational facilities, increased use of English both within and outside the educational system, the wider use of English in an expanded economy based on industry, trade, banking, and finance, together with the need for younger Singaporeans to identify themselves as Singaporeans (rather than as overseas Chinese, overseas Indians, etc.) are major forces influencing the way local varieties of English have become part of the Singapore language scene. The way English is spoken becomes part of the process by which personal and national identity is expressed, ethnic identity being largely realized through use of the mother tongue. The processes of linguistic adaptation and innovation which result from these new personal and social functions for English may be referred to as aspects of the "indigenization" or "nativization" of English.

Indigenization/Nativization of English

The terms "indigenization" and "nativization" have been used to describe the divergence of varieties of a language from a "parent" source (Kachru 1981; Moag 1977). Whinnom uses the term "hybridization" with similar meaning. Kachru describes Persianized Hindi and Indianized English as two instances of nativization. In a series of major articles he has documented the linguistic processes which account for nativization of a language, with particular reference to the nativization of English in India. "During almost three hundred years of contact with Africa and Asia, English has completely been embedded in the local contexts and has slowly gone through the process of nativization" (Kachru 1981). Nativization in this

sense describes the emergence of linguistic features in new varieties
of English which are *categorical*. It describes features of the code. It
hence refers to permanent additions or modifications to the code of
the language which reflect the force of cultural embedding. Thus,
while acknowledging variations in Indian English according to region,
ethnicity, and proficiency, Kachru has concentrated on describing
the major categorical (i.e., non-variable) features of Indian English.
The "Indianness" of Indian English is thus described in terms of linguistic manifestations — at the level of phonology, lexis, grammar,
and semantics — of distinct cultural, affective, and situational aspects
of Indian society and culture. "The linguistic study of the following
features of South Asian English has proved useful not only in understanding the formal features of the texts, but also in relating these to
typically Indian contexts: (a) Register variation, (b) Style variation,
(c) Collocational deviation, (d) Semantic shifts, (e) Lexical range"
(Kachru 1969: 656). Kachru has documented the range of linguistic
innovations found in both written and spoken Indian English, and
he has found a wide variety of linguistic evidence for nativization,
some of the processes of which he refers to as contextualization,
hybridization, and register extension.

Categorical and Variable Features

Focussing on categorical features of varieties of English leads
to description of the linguistic features which characterize the speaker of both native and "nativized" varieties of English, enabling the
identification of the "Canadianness" of Canadian English, the "Indianness" of Indian English, and so on. In addition to categorical
features, however, there are also major *variable* features in Singapore
English which contribute as significantly as categorical features to
the distinctiveness of this indigenized variety of English. A number
of linguistic features are observed to occur variably in the speech of
individuals. In certain situations and with certain interlocutors, for
example, a speaker may code-switch between Hokkien and English
throughout an entire speech event. Or a speaker may switch effort-
lessly from a variety of English which is close to Standard British
English, to a variety of English which is quite different. The different varieties of English in the Singapore English speaker's speech
repertoire result from variable rules for major features of phonology
and syntax. We also observe variability at the lexical level. A word
from a local language may thus temporarily displace an English word
for certain types of speech events, the English word reappearing for
other speech events. I will refer to such manifestations of variable

features in the speech of speakers of many nativized varieties of English as *lect shifting*. Lect shifting hence describes the selection of a variable (rather than a *categorical*) feature from the speech code of the individual for particular types of speech events. Lect shifting is a major and distinctive characteristic of many indigenized varieties of English.

Rhetorical and Communicative Styles

An adequate description of the processes of nativization that have led to the development of Singapore English should include both the linguistic and the functional dimensions of language nativization. It would be inadequate to characterize Singapore English as simply resulting from structural and phonological convergence of relevant linguistic features of English through contact with other languages; while such an approach might explain the formal linguistic characteristics of Singapore English, it would fail to explain the affective and social significance of the linguistic phenomena involved. What characterizes the development of new varieties of English is the functional motivation for the employment of new linguistic codes. Indian English, Singapore English, Nigerian English, etc., would not gradually be achieving legitimacy if they did not have distinct functional uses and requirements that could not be met by imported varieties of English. To understand the significance of the processes of indigenization, we thus have to consider the functional values represented by the particular forms of English which the Singaporean employs.

Numerous approaches to the functional analysis of language use have been proposed in recent years, and while serious problems present themselves when we attempt to interpret functional categories from linguistic data, the use of a functional approach appears to be essential in accounting for language nativization. Haugen adopts a basically functional approach in discussing the divergence of American Norwegian (the variety of Norwegian spoken among Norwegian migrants to America) from standard Norwegian (Haugen 1977). Haugen makes a distinction between two contrasting norms for language available to members of a community. One, the rhetorical norm, is the standardized variety of the language, codified in grammars and sanctified by its use perhaps as a model for written language. It is thus the educated model of language, typically regarded as grammatically "correct" and used as a model for teaching in school. In contrast, a different model of language is represented by

what Haugen refers to as the *communicative norm,* which is the
variety of language used in daily social interaction and which reflects
the speaker's situational and communicative needs. In Haugen's example, the communicative norm of the Norwegian immigrants to
America was a type of contact variety of Norwegian which had developed in America and which was much despised by purists. The rhetorical norm was the standard variety of Norwegian, particularly as
it was spoken in Norway. Judged by the external norm, the new communicative norm for Norwegian was often denied linguistic legitimacy. "Those who cling categorically to the rhetorical norm either
deride or deplore contact dialects and even go so far as to deny that
there is any norm whatsoever in their usage" (Haugen 1977: 94).

The concept of rhetorical and communicative norms provides
a useful perspective on the processes of indigenization. Whereas, in
Haugen's case, indigenization of Norwegian refers to *diachronic*
changes in the language code, as a result of which the source-language
norms came to be regarded as having rhetorical functions (and values)
and the new contact variety of Norwegian as having communicative
functions (and values), in the case of indigenized varieties of English
the contrast between rhetorical and communicative exists at the
synchronic level. It is a characteristic of *users* of the code. Consequently I shall here use the terms *rhetorical styles* and *communicative styles* to refer to contrasting styles of speaking within an individual's speech repertoire, and use the terms *rhetorical norms* and
communicative norms to refer to the community's accepted norms
for formal and informal speech.

Members of the English-speaking communities in these countries can be said to possess variable linguistic rules to mark distinctions between rhetorical and communicative styles of speaking. The
favored speech variety for formal communication (the acrolect) can
be regarded as the rhetorical norm of the community. The speech
variety accepted for informal communication (the mesolect) can be
regarded as the communicative norm of the community. *Lect shifting* refers to the use of variable linguistic rules to mark differences
between rhetorical and communicative styles. All speech communities make use of lect shift rules, and distinctions between rhetorical
and communicative styles are presumably universal. What calls for
special comment in the case of indigenized varieties of English is the
generation of new varieties of English markedly different from the
source varieties, to meet the need for new rhetorical and communicative styles. Individual speakers have a command of contrasting
speech styles, while within the community as a whole there is a

continuum of speech varieties. The acrolect represents the idealized rhetorical norm for the community; the mesolect is the idealized communicative norm. The basilect may represent an actual communicative style, but it is scarcely recognized as a norm.

Functional Distinctions between Rhetorical and Communicative Styles

While the linguistic means used in different nativized varieties of English to distinguish rhetorical and communicative styles evidence considerable diversity, they can be seen to represent a common and perhaps universal set of functional contrasts. Let us therefore consider the functional structure of the distinction between rhetorical and communicative styles proposed here, before considering the linguistic processes employed to mark this contrast in Singapore English.

The functional basis for distinguishing rhetorical and communicative styles depends on the recognition of contrasting values and differences in affective content for different types of speech events. Differing ranges of illocutionary force for different classes of speech events can be summarized in the following sets of binary scales, without necessarily suggesting that such labels are mutually exclusive or easy to define.

Rhetorical style		Communicative style
Characteristics of the speech event		
Public	. . . .	Private
Formal	. . . .	Informal
High	. . . .	Low
Distant	. . . .	Intimate
Impersonal	. . . .	Personal
Careful	. . . .	Casual
	etc.	

The use of variable linguistic rules to mark functional contrasts of this sort has been discussed by Labov: "We here make use of the distinction between a variable rule and an independent obligatory one in a new way: the variable rule has a communicative function — 'stylistic,' 'expressive,' or 'emphatic' . . . while the invariant rule has none, it merely facilitates the expression of choices already made" (Labov 1972: 237).

A rhetorical style is hence a speech variety used for speech events which have the functional status of *Public, Formal, High,* etc., and a communicative style a speech variety used for speech events which have the contrasting functional status of *Private, Informal, Low,* etc. The defining characteristics of speech events giving them rhetorical versus communicative status depend, in turn, on characteristics which are related to speaker, role, setting, topic, and other variables. The distinction made here between rhetorical and communicative styles is an overarching one which subsumes a number of implicit contrasts within the ethnography of communication.

The processes by which English becomes nativized in a new cultural setting include the generation of new rhetorical *and* communicative speech varieties. Historically, indigenization takes place in situations where the functions of English experience a gradual shift within a society, as English becomes a language of personal interaction within a community and as it comes to take on more and more communicative functions. The nativization of English requires the development of new codes for both rhetorical and communicative functions, and the existence of variable rules allows the functionally distinct contexts for language use to be formally marked.

A range of different linguistic resources can be employed in nativized varieties of English to mark the shift from a rhetorical to a communicative style. The following processes have been observed in Singapore English.

Phonological Shift

Variable phonological rules are perhaps the commonest indication of a shift from a rhetorical to a communicative style. Tay (1978) identifies a number of variable features in the pronunciation of speakers of Singapore English:

Decrease in aspiration: voiceless stops may be weakly aspirated or unaspirated in all positions.

Simplification of consonant clusters: final consonant clusters in words like *went, just, ask* may be reduced to the first consonant of the cluster.

Replacement of final stops: final stops may be replaced by glottals.

Other variable phonological features noted by Tay include

changes in vowel and diphthong quality, stressing, and intonation.

Grammatical Shift

A marked feature of many indigenized varieties of English is variable use of grammatical features to mark the shift from a rhetorical to a communicative style. This is sometimes referred to as lect shifting, and an upper, middle, and a lower lect are sometimes referred to. Empirical studies of lectal variation in such settings as Guyana (Bickerton 1975) and Singapore (Platt 1975) suggest, rather than three lects, a continuum of grammatical features, with different members of the community controlling different sections of the continuum as part of their speech repertoire.

Platt (1977) identifies a number of variable grammatical features found in the mesolectal variety of Singapore English, including the following:

Variable lack of marking for past tense:
My father bring my mother over.
I attend(ed) night school.
From there I pick(ed) up my English.

Variable lack of realization of third-person tense marking:
He mix a lost with them.
My mother sleep in there.

Deletion of it:
If by bus — is very convenient.
You see — is compulsory.

Morpheme Addition

The English spoken by Singaporeans displays other unique features which serve to mark a shift from a rhetorical to a communicative style. One of the most distinctive is the variable employment of morphemes from local languages attached to English sentences to mark a communicative style. In Singapore English, a final sentence-particle *la,* probably of Hokkien origin, is extensively used when English is employed in informal settings and where the speech event calls for solidarity, rapport, etc. The *la* particle in Singapore English is seen in the following examples from Richards and Tay (1977):

That depend on you *la,* if you want to take off one day, or your office give you, that up to you *la.*

Must go *la.*
I said no *la.*
Cannot *la.*

Lexical Shift

Lexical shift refers to the replacement of a known English word by a word from a local language when the speech event calls for a communicative style. This is distinct from *lexical borrowing,* which refers to terms from local languages which have entered the speech code but which do not carry particular communicative or affective value and for which no English equivalent exists. In Singapore the word *satay,* taken from Malay, refers to a particular type of barbecued meat. Because no English word exists for this type of meat, this is a case of lexical borrowing. This is a different situation, however, from the variable use of lexical items from local languages in many indigenized varieties of English. In Singapore English, for example, the Malay word *makan,* which refers to food and eating, may be used to replace the English words *food* or *eat* or *eating* when a communicative style is employed. *Let's have something to eat* may become *let's go for makan* in the communicative style. The following are examples of items subject to lexical shift in Singapore English.

Rhetorical norm:	*Communicative norm:*
ride	tumpang
"Good God"!	allama
a primitive place	an ulu place
busybody	kaypoh
help	tolong

The choice of a word from a local language, rather than the English word, would appear to make the speech event more colloquial and informal, or more virile and "genuine."

Code-Switching

A further linguistic device employed in nativized varieties of English to signal a shift from the rhetorical to the communicative style is the use of rapid code-switching. While code-switching is a phenomenon found in many bilingual and multilingual communities, I am distinguishing the commonly described diglossic code-switching from code-switching as a special way of marking a communicative style. In diglossic code-switching, code alternation is largely of the situational type. Distinct varieties are employed in certain settings (such as home, school, work) associated with separate bounded kinds of activities (public speaking, formal negotiations, special ceremonies, verbal games, etc.) or spoken with different categories of speakers (friends, family members, strangers, social inferiors, government officials). Although speakers in diglossia situations must know more than one grammatical system to carry on their daily affairs, only one code is employed at any one time (Gumperz 1978: 3).

This is a type of code-switching quite distinct from a phenomenon that has emerged in a number of situations where English has become indigenized. In Singapore, a different type of code-switching takes place when speakers are fluent in English-Cantonese, English-Mandarin, or English-Hokkien, for example, and regularly use both languages in the course of their daily routines. Particular types of speech events may use a mixed code based on alternate sections of English-Cantonese, English-Mandarin, or English-Hokkien. Gumperz comments on the special features of this type of code switching:

> The exchange forms a single unitary interactional whole. Speakers communicate fluently, maintaining an even flow of talk. No hesitation pauses, changes in sentence rhythm, pitch or level of intonation contour mark the shift in code. There is nothing in the exchange as a whole to indicate that speakers don't understand each other. Apart from the alternation itself, the passages all have the earmarks of ordinary conversation in a single language (Gumperz 1978: 1).

A similar variety of code-mixed English-Tagalog widely used in the Manila area of the Philippines is commonly known as *mix-mix*. The following examples of mix-mix are taken from a family conversation recorded in Singapore; they illustrate English/Hokkien mix-mix (Example 1) and English-Cantonese (Example 2).

(1) "Boy, hopeless. *Kon si mit tiok tui lang 'choa' eh.* Not original. Damn *sia sui.* Everything follows the girl. Where got future?"

(2) "I am very certain that during emergencies he *siong gau toa.* I saw him *mang sai ti* sockets."

Gumperz (1978) gives a functional/semantic account of this type of code-switching, and likewise attributes the motivation for it to the need for an effective communicative style:

> It is this overtly marked separation between in- and out-group standards which perhaps best characterizes the bilingual experience. . . . What distinguishes the bilingual from his monolingual neighbor is the juxtaposition of styles: the awareness that his own mode of behavior is one of several possible modes, that interpretation of what a speaker intends to communicate depends on the style of communication. . .(Gumperz, 1978: 6).

I hence regard code-switching of the "mix-mix" type as part of a continuum of linguistic mechanisms which can be employed for the same communicative/functional effect. The non-mixed code is taken as a marker of rhetorical style, and code-switching has a "softening" effect on the speech event, signaling the affective values associated with the communicative style.

Conclusion

The emergence of nativized varieties of English such as Singapore English demonstrates the relevance of a remark made by Fishman, Ferguson, and Das Gupta in their preface to *Language Problems of Developing Nations:*

> Languages do not really exist except as part of a matrix of language varieties, language behaviors, and behaviors toward language. Any attempt to describe "a language" without recognizing its actual matrix position and any attempt to influence language learning or literacy without questioning what they signify for the language-and-behavior matrix of the prospective learners is to preserve or protect one's own ignorance in connection with those very matters towards which one's expertise would be directed (Fishman et al. 1968: I).

Description of nativized varieties of English must hence include the extent of linguistic variation *within* a particular variety of English, as well as attempting to understand and identify the social meaning of such variation. Such information is vital both to the planning of language teaching and for the interpretation of the results or effects of language instruction. The concept of rhetorical and communicative styles discussed here is an attempt to capture different values, statuses, and functions for speech varieties as reflected in the employment of variable linguistic rules within nativized varieties of English, and draws attention to the role of language in the expression and structuring of social meaning.

REFERENCES

Bickerton, Derek. 1975. *Dynamics of a Creole system.* London: Cambridge University Press.

Fishman, Joshua, et al. 1968. *Language problems in developing nations.* New York: John Wiley.

Gumperz, John J. 1978. The sociolinguistic significance of conversational code-switching. *RELC Journal* 8: 1-34.

Haugen, Einar. 1977. Norm and deviation in bilingual communities. In Peter A. Hornby, ed., *Bilingualism.* New York: Academic Press.

Hoffman, J. E. 1973. The Malay language as a force for unity in the Indonesian archipelago, 1815-1900. *Nusantara* 4: 19-35.

Kachru, Braj B. 1969. English in South Asia. In T. Sebeok, ed., *Current trends in linguistics.* The Hague: Mouton.

———. 1976. Indian English: a sociolinguistic profile of a transplanted language. *Studies in Language Learning* 1(2): 1-49.

———. 1981. The pragmatics of non-native varieties of English. In *English for cross-cultural communication,* ed. Larry E. Smith. London: Macmillan.

Khubchandani, Lachman M. 1973. English in India: a sociolinguistic appraisal. *International Journal of Dravidian Linguistics* 11(2): 211.

Kuo, Eddie C. Y. 1976. A sociolinguistic profile of Singapore. In R. Hassan, ed., *Singapore: a society in transition.* Kuala Lumpur: Oxford University Press.

Labov, William. 1966. The effect of social mobility on linguistic behaviour. *Sociological Enquiry,* spring issue.

———. 1972. *Sociolinguistic patterns.* Philadelphia: University of Pennsylvania Press.

Moag, Rodney F., and Louisa B. Moag. 1977. English in Fiji: some perspective and the need for language planning. *Fiji English Teacher's Journal* 13: 2-26.

Platt, J. T. 1975. The Singapore English speech continuum and its basilect "Singlish" as a "Creoloid." *Anthropological Linguistics* 17(6): 363-75.

———. 1977. The sub-varieties of Singapore English: their sociolectal and functional status. In William Crewe, ed., *The English language in Singapore.* Singapore: Eastern Universities Press.

Richards, Jack C., and Tay, Mary. 1977. The *la* particle in Singapore English. Pp. 141-56 in William Crewe, ed., *The English language in Singapore.* Singapore: Eastern Universities Press.

Sprott, W. J. H. 1958. *Human groups.* Middlesex: Penguin Books.

Tay, M. W. J. 1978. The uses, users and features of English in Singapore. Paper presented at the Conference on English as an International Auxiliary Language, Honolulu, April 1-15, 1978.

Whinnom, Keith. 1971. Linguistic hybridization and the 'special case' of pidgins and creoles. In Dell Hymes, ed., *Pidginization and creolization of languages.* Cambridge: Cambridge University Press.

11

English in Japanese Communicative Strategies

JAMES STANLAW

An outsider might say the English language in Japan has not developed into an institutionalized variety (Kachru 1981), as it has in South Asia or parts of Africa. Japanized English — or, as some prefer, "Japlish" (Pierce 1971) — is essentially a performance variety.[1] But to an insider, the function of English cannot be isolated from communicative strategies in Japanese society. The use of English loanwords is an integral part of one such strategy. I shall illustrate this point by focusing on the form and function of English borrowing in Japanese today. The Japanization of such borrowing exemplifies what has been termed "nativization" by linguists (Kachru and Quirk 1981) or "acculturation" by anthropologists.[2]

The extent of this borrowing, its historical roots, and the use of English in the Japanese school system will be briefly discussed below. The processes of nativization of English will be described, with examples, in the next sections, and current research will be mentioned. I will conclude with some speculations as to why English borrowings are so extensively used as a communicative strategy in Japanese.

Historical Contact

Language contact in Japan goes back at least a thousand years. Buddhism and Chinese scholars arrived in the ninth century. Numerous foreign languages have been found in Japan ever since (Umegaki 1978), even during the period of isolation (*sakotu*) from 1640 to 1853, when Dutch traders were still allowed to land at the island of Deshima in Nagasaki Bay.

According to Umegaki (1978: 32), the various cultural and linguistic contacts between Japan and the rest of the world may be summarized in the following six phases. The first phase (9th to 13th century) was the period of Buddhist impact, with an emphasis on Chinese learning and linguistic exposure to Chinese and Sanskrit. The second phase (14th to 16th century) brought Christianity through European contact, and some exposure to Portuguese. The third phase

(17th to 18th century) was essentially a period of isolation, though there was contact with Dutch learning and language. The fourth phase (19th century), the period of Meiji enlightenment, saw renewed contact with Western culture and exposure to English, German, and French. The fifth phase (early 20th century) initiated the contact with contemporary Western culture; it saw the development of Taisho democracy and the rise of Japan as an important world power. The last phase (late 20th century) opened Japan to world culture and economic importance, and it has seen a more open attitude toward world languages, especially English.[3]

There have been periods of contact with the English language since Will Adams[4] was stranded near Edo in 1600. However, Commodore Perry's arrival in 1854, and the social unrest in Japan at the time, instigated a Japanese interest in learning English well enough to read Western books and to speak with these new visitors. This curiosity brought many English words into the Japanese vocabulary, and English quickly replaced Dutch as the language used to learn about the West. In his autobiography Fukuzawa, an influential Meiji-period educator and writer, stated that "As certain as day, English was to be the most useful language of the future" (1899: 98). Serious attempts to designate English the official language of Japan were made by "public figures of such great prestige that their recommendations could not help having a considerable impact," even though implementation of these proposals was impossible (Miller 1977: 41-42). One such advocate was Mori Arinori, the first minister of education, who claimed that "our meager language, which can never be of any use outside of our islands, is doomed to yield to the domination of the English tongue, especially when the power of steam and electricity shall have pervaded the land" (quoted in Sonoda 1975: 17).

As contact between Japan and the West increased, there was an influx of British and American technical advisors; likewise, Japanese students and statesmen traveled abroad. An immense fascination with Western customs and ideas facilitated the adoption of English loanwords. In 1867 the American missionary James Hepburn printed *A Japanese and English Dictionary; with an English and Japanese Index* and introduced the romanization system which is still the most popular today. Many schools taught English, and it became fashionable for Japanese students to intersperse their conversations with English words (Sonoda 1975: 16).

The Taisho period (1912-26) was marked by an increase in the number of English borrowings and the fall into disuse of loanwords from other languages, most noticeably Dutch and Portuguese (Ueno

1968). While most of the English loanwords of the Meiji period had
to do with Western culture, many of those of the Taisho period had
to do with everyday topics: *takushī* (taxi), *rajio* (radio), *sararīman*
(salaried man).

With the rise of militarism and nationalism in the 1930s and
World War II, the government tried to purge Japan of all foreign influences. The commonly understood *anaunsā* (announcer) was replaced by the esoteric *hōsō-in* (literally "broadcast person"), and
rekōdo (record) was supplanted by *onban* (literally "euphonic
board").

English regained its former level of popularity and prestige immediately after World War II, and the Occupation spurred even more
linguistic borrowings. Political and economic opportunities led
many Japanese to learn at least some English, or an incipient pidgin
called "Bamboo English" (Miller 1967: 262; Norman 1955). Another
variety of postwar pidgin, termed *pangurisshu* (from *pansuke*, "street-
walker," plus *ingurisshu*, "English"), was used for verbal communication "between non-Japanese-speaking foreigners and the extensive
world of their local lady friends of every variety and description"
(Miller 1967: 263).

Since the Occupation, the use of English has continued to grow.
There are now loanword dictionaries of all sizes and descriptions,
with the largest and most reliable, Arakawa's *Kadokawa gairaigo jiten*
(1977), containing over 27,000 entries. Today, almost all advertising
uses loanwords of English origin. For example, Horiuchi (1963: 49)
found only one advertisement – for a typical Japanese food – that
used no English loanwords or phrases when he examined advertisements for one month in the widely circulating *Asahi* newspaper. But
perhaps the best indication of the current acceptability of loanwords
appeared in Prince Mikasa's entry in the 1965 Imperial Court poetry
contest. Since even traditional Chinese loanwords are usually avoided
in this literary style, it was quite significant that the prince used the
term *beruto-konbea* (conveyer belt) in his poem. In 1976 the emperor
used the phrase *hiroki damu miyu* (a view of the broad dam) in his
own entry (Passin 1980: 73). As Miller (1967: 267) says, this cannot
help but "teach us a profound lesson about the degree to which loanwords of every variety, especially from English, have permeated modern Japanese life."

Types of Japanese English: The "Cline of Proficiency"

Among the Englishes described in this volume, the variety spoken in Japan is unique. It is not an official language, a lingua franca, or a second language in the same sense as in the other contexts described here. It is not a remnant of colonialization[5] or the legacy of zealous missionaries, and though it is taught in the schools it has never been institutionalized[6] (as, say, in India or Nigeria) to function as the primary language of higher learning. English is required on college entrance exams, and a typical Japanese student may study it for six to ten years; still, few Japanese actually *speak* English well enough to converse with foreigners beyond a rudimentary exchange of greetings.[7] Almost every bookstore has an "English corner" offering hundreds of the latest texts, annotated novels, tapes, and learning aids. Major newspapers print extra weekly supplements for studying English, and several popular journals are devoted to the subject.[8]

There is, therefore, a *cline of proficiency* in the use of English in Japan, ranging from people fluent in both spoken and written discourse to those who know only a few vocabulary items. Though most Japanese people are not fluent in English, and the variety they use may be essentially a performance variety rather than an institutionalized variety, anyone with even cursory exposure to Japan knows that English plays an important role in their everyday lives.

Sources of English Borrowing

English loanwords can be heard in Japan in everyday conversation, on television and radio programs or announcements, and in political speeches. Newspapers,[9] popular magazines, and books all use loanwords. They may appear as section headings, such as *opinion pēji* (opinion page); in titles, like *sandē sukūru* (Sunday school); and in the main body of the text. Technical and professional journals use English loanwords for a specialized vocabulary, e.g., *sōrā furea* (solar flares), *tenshon* (tension — of metals), *nyū refuto* (new left).

The vocabulary of sports borrows from English quite readily, though often with a slight Japanese twist on the words involved, e.g., *sekando ōbā* (over second), *sayonara hōmu ran* (a game-ending home run). Men's magazines also use numerous English loanwords, especially when dealing with sexual topics. For instance, in the weekly magazine *Purēbōi* (a Japanese version of the American *Playboy*) one finds such items as *būbusu* (boobs), *majikku pawā* (magic power — aphrodisiacs), and *datchi waifu* (Dutch wife — an inflatable bed partner). Many English loanwords also appear in the adult *manga*, the men's comics genre unique to Japan.

One of the most interesting and prevalent uses of English is on personal "artifacts" — T-shirts, sweaters, handbags, and other belongings. When an English word is borrowed orally into Japanese, it undergoes substantial phonological modification, even if it is a proper name. When the word is then printed in a book or newspaper, this modification is reflected in a special Japanese syllabary called *katakana*,[10] used for foreign terms. When words are borrowed on T-shirts, however, they are not modified phonologically or written in *katakana*.

English borrowings are often seen on things other than apparel. Women's purses are sometimes decorated with cartoon characters like Snoopy or Popeye, and men's bags often bear sports names or sports-related terms (*champion*, or *official team*). One common word is *cityboy*, meaning a debonair, sophisticated young man, used somewhat like the American term "playboy."[11]

English, then, is used in a variety of contexts by a variety of speakers in a variety of ways, depending on the strategy and context of communication.

Range and Context of English Borrowings

In 1931 Sanki Ichikawa predicted, "The influence of foreign languages — especially English — on Japanese is of such importance that probably not only words and expressions will continue to be borrowed in greater numbers but even the structure and grammar of the Japanese language will be considerably modified." He found that Japanese had borrowed more than 1,400 words, most of which were "quite naturalized in Japanese" (1931: 141). The following (albeit extreme) example, given by Matsumoto forty years later (1974: 5), shows extensive use of English loanwords in Japanese:

> We, that is, the Matsumoto family, live in a *manshon,* too. At this moment, I am watching *beisu-booru* on *terebi.* My wife is out shopping at a *depaato,* and later she will stop at a *suupaa* to get *pooku choppu, pan, bataa, jamu,* and perhaps some *sooseiji* for breakfast. My daughter has gone to the *byuuchii saron* to get a *paama.* Oh, the *terehon* is ringing.
>
> We cannot live a day in Japan today without these loan words. Language purists lament the fact. The nationalists would wipe out all foreign-sounding words from our vocabulary. But where will they be without *takushii, terebi, rajio, tabako, biiru, shatsu, beruto* and *meetoru*?

According to the National Language Research Institute's 1964 study of ninety different magazines published in the early 1950s, almost 10 percent of Japanese vocabulary items come from Western languages. Of these borrowed Western words, 80.8 percent come from English, which suggests that approximately 8 percent of the total Japanese vocabulary is derived from English (Higa 1973: 79).[12] Miller (1967: 249) speaks of the "total availability" of the English vocabulary for borrowing into Japanese: today, "virtually any English word in the book is fair game in writing or in public speaking."

There is also a cline of "foreignness" for English loans. Words like *rajio* (radio) and *tabako* (cigarette) seem to be regarded as completely Japanese by native speakers; in contrast, many of the latest loanwords occurring in advertising or professional journals are short lived or have limited circulation. English terms may be brought in to fill certain "lexical gaps," as in the case of *tĩn'ējā* (teenager) or *haitĩn* (high teen — a person 16 to 19 years old), instead of the Japanese term *jūdai* (meaning anyone 10 through 19). However, it is clear from the examples above that the filling of lexical gaps is only one reason for the English borrowing process. It is also clear that semantic borrowing is independent of the existence of the term in either language.[13]

Kachru (1978a) explains the "lexical sets" of borrowed items with what he terms "contextual units." In a language contact situation, especially where more than two languages are involved, the borrowing may depend on register or style. There may be a mutual expectancy or dependency between the lexical borrowing from a particular language and a specific register. For example, in Hindi, Persian loanwords may be used in legal contexts, Sanskrit ones in literary or philosophical writings, and English ones in technical or political registers. It is difficult to demonstrate such clearcut distinctions for the use of English in Japanese. English loanwords can be used by anyone, regardless of age, sex, or education, though certain technical or scholarly terms might be limited to specialists. Some registers, such as advertising, are thought to be permeated with English (Horiuchi 1963; Quackenbush 1974). While most written and oral advertisements do use loanwords, how much this varies from other registers is still an empirical issue.

Processes of Nativization

Phonology[14]

The process of phonological assimilation of English loanwords into Japanese has been discussed extensively by both Japanese (e.g., Isshiki 1957; Kawakami 1963; Ohye 1967a, 1967b; Sonoda 1975;

Umegaki 1978) and Western scholars (e.g., Gauntlett 1966; Lovins 1973; Neustupný 1978; Pierce 1971; Quackenbush 1974). Therefore, only a few illustrations will be given. No consonant clusters exist in Japanese, so vowels are inserted between two consonants in borrowed English words; e.g., *kurisumasu* (Christmas), *makudonaruzu* (MacDonald's). A word may not end in a consonant except for the syllabic *n*; e.g., *resutoran* (restaurant). English /r/ or /l/ sounds are usually manifest as Japanese /r/ in the loanword; e.g. *raito* (light, right).[15] These are some of the phonetic characteristics considered typical of English words brought into Japanese.

Morphology

Japanese is a loose SOV language, highly agglutinative and marked for case. Verbs must be sentence-final, but there is optionality in the placement of agent, patient and locative or time phrases, though usually subjects or topics come at the beginning of the sentence. Like other SOV languages, Japanese is post-positional. A typical sentence pattern might be:

sumisu –	*san*	*wa*	*yūbe-no-nyūsu*	*o*	*mi-mashita*	*ka*
proper name	honorif.	topic marker	noun	object	verb tense	interrog. marker
Smith			last night's news		watched	?

Mr. Smith, did you watch the news last night?

The majority of English loanwords are nouns[16] (Hinds 1974: 93; Sonoda 1975: 173), and most nouns are taken into Japanese in the singular form, even though their use may have required the plural in English — e.g., *surī-sutoraiku* (three strikes), *foa-bōru* (four balls). When an English loanword is borrowed as a noun, it is usually unchanged, and will behave syntactically and morphologically like other Japanese nouns.

terebi	*o*	*mi–*	*mashita*	*ka*
loan	case marker	verb	tense	interrog. marker
television		watched		?

Did you watch TV?

If a loanword is to be used as an adverb, it takes the particle *ni* and does not decline using *-ku,* as do adverbs derived from true Japanese adjectives.

kare	wa	songu	o	naisu -	ni	utau
3rd pers.	topic	loan	case	loan	case	verb
masc.pron.	marker		marker		marker	
he		song		nicely		sings

He sings nicely.

If an English loanword is to be used as an adjective, it is marked with the particle *na* and rarely takes the true adjective ending -*i* or its declensions.[17]

kare	wa	nau -	na	hito	desu	ne
3d pers.	topic	loan	part.	noun	copula	sent.
masc.pron.	marker					part.
he		"now"		person	is	right?

He's a real modern "with it" person, isn't he?

Sonoda (1975: 190) gives several other examples of English loanword adjectives: *chāmingu-na* (charming), *romachikku-na* (romantic), *derikēto-na* (delicate), *gurotesuku-na* (grotesque), *supesharu-na* (special). Sonada also mentions that degrees of comparison are syntactically indicated in Japanese by the use of the free-form morphemes *motto* (more) and *ichiban* (most). Thus, comparative phrases involving loanwords might be something like *motto senchimentaru* (more sentimental [than] . . .) or *ichiban senchimentaru* (the most sentimental [among] . . .).

Syntax

Most loanwords which can be used as verbs take the auxiliary suffix *suru* (do), as in *appu-suru* (to improve, go up) or as in the following example:

dō	desu,	tenisu -	o	shimasen		ka
idiom		loan	case	suru +		interrog.
			marker	tense		marker
What-do-you-say		tennis		to do		?

What would you think about having a game of tennis?

Other examples include *gorofu-suru* (to play golf) or *gōru-in-suru* (goal in — to fulfill, for example, the goal of getting married).[18]

Personal pronouns do exist in Japanese, but until recently they had never been used as much as in English. Names, kinship terms, or titles are used instead of *kare* (he) or *anata* (you). An increase in personal pronoun usage has been attributed to the influence of English

(Passin 1980: 14-23); still, there never seems to have been a case where a personal pronoun has been borrowed as the subject of a sentence.[19] There are a few — but very popular — phrases where the personal pronoun *mai* (my) is used to modify a noun, as in *mai kā* (my car),[20] *mai kā zoku* (those who drive their own cars), or *mai hōmu*. Passin (1980: 24-29) believes that this term highlights a new social and psychological point of view in Japan, that of the assertion of individuality. Thus the productiveness of the *mai* prefix is not surprising, and can be seen to be extended to such things as *mai pēsu* (at my own pace), *mai puraibashii* (my privacy), or *mai seihin* (my product).[21]

Vocabulary

There are several ways in which Japanese incorporates new English vocabulary items. One common method is to adopt the English loan with the required phonological modification, but with little change in its form or structure; e.g., *takushī* (taxi), *basu* (bus), *tabako* (cigarette).[22] However, several other processes involve either restricting or expanding the original meaning in English (Sonoda 1975; Hinds 1974; Ozawa 1970; Miura 1979; Matsumoto 1974; Fukao 1979; Yokoi 1978).

Truncation, or shortening, is a very popular means of using an English word. Often the meaning remains unchanged; e.g., *sūpā* (supermarket), *terebi* (television), *depāto* (department store), and *demo* (demonstration). Sonoda (1975: 198) claims that, if a borrowed word contains two morphemes, the part most likely to be dropped is the one which plays the grammatical role, and not the semantically important segment — e.g., *sarariman* (salaried man), *kōn bīfu* (corned beef), *sukī* (skiing). If there are several syllables in a word, or if several nouns are involved, the reduction is usually made in the non-initial nouns or syllables.

Another common way of shortening is through acronyms, e.g., *ō-eru* (office lady), *pī-āru* (public relations), *ō-bī* (old boy), *dī-pī-ī* (developing, printing, and enlarging), *shī-emu* (commercial message), *dī-kē* (dining kitchen). This process seems to be shared with other non-native Englishes (see Kachru 1966). These acronyms may be totally new Japanese creations, as in *OL,* the term for the modern Japanese working girl, or *DPE,* the sign that appears in every photography store window. They may also be used as modifiers of other nouns, as in *CM songu,* a jingle used on a television or radio commercial. Abbreviations may also be taken from English, but the meanings may be somewhat altered; *PR* in Japanese refers to advertising.

Sometimes even native Japanese words will be abbreviated in roman letters, and will be spoken of, and pronounced, in that way. *NHK* (standing for *Nippon-Hoso Kyōkai*) is the common way to refer to the national public television of Japan. Another example, *H* (pronounced *etchi*), comes from the Japanese term *hentai* (perverted) and means something dirty, or an unusual interest in sex.

Native affixes are easily applied to foreign words (Weinreich 1953: 31), and in this way many English loanwords are used in Japanese. Consider, e.g., *amerika + jin* (an American person), *shin + kanto + ha* (neo-Kantianism), *Kātā-shiki* (Carter's style), *dai-sutoraiki* (large strike), *amerika + sei* (made in America). There are also some cases where English affixes can be applied to native Japanese terms, as in *puro yakyū* (pro baseball), or *shaber + ingu* (talking). These may also be applied to loanwords as well, as in *semi + sofuto + karā* (semi-soft collar).

Sonoda (1975: 214) claims that compounding is the most productive method of expanding the borrowed English vocabulary. He believes that two-thirds of the borrowed items have been formed in this way,[23] e.g., *ero-guro-nansensu* (erotic grotesque nonsense), *ōrudo misu* (old miss — a spinster), *masu komi* (mass communications), *wan pīsu* (one-piece dress).

Blendings are special compounds where one element is an English loanword and the other a native term, e.g., *nūdo shashin* (nude picture), *meriken ko* (American powder — flour), *denki sutando* (standing desk lamp). English loanwords may also include a phrase or a fixed collocation, e.g., *ofu dei* (off day), *tēburu supīchi* (table speech — after-dinner speech), *atto hōmu* (at home), *ai rabu yū* (I love you). (See also Kachru 1982 and Zuengler 1982.)

For some concepts brought into Japan from the West, the old literal Japanese translation of the term is eventually replaced by the English loanword. *Entaku* (taxi) becomes *takushī, kōshaki* (elevator) becomes *erebētā,* and *higyō* (strike) becomes *sutoraiki* (Sonoda 1975: 231).

The Semantics of English Borrowing

Semantic Restriction

Sonoda (1975) and Ozawa (1970, 1976) have suggested some typologies for the semantic borrowing of English loanwords. In the first case, the meaning of the English word is restricted when it is brought into Japanese. *Rikuesuto* (request) in Japanese is used only in asking a band to play a certain song; *mishin* (machine) refers only to a sewing machine; *manshon* (mansion) is applied only to high-rise condominiums; *naitā* means a night baseball game; *kappu* (cup) is a prize won in a contest; *nega* (negative) refers only to photographic processing.

Semantic Shift

A semantic shift may occur in the connotation or nuance of a borrowed English loanword, as in *madamu* (proprietress of a bar), *miruku* (condensed milk — milk for coffee), or *nēmu* (name, embroidered on a personal article). *Mōningu* is short for *mōningu-sābisu* ("morning service," a restaurant's breakfast special) or is used in special compounds like *moningu shō* (morning show).

Semantic Extension or Redefinition

Sometimes a loan will undergo a complete change in meaning from the way it is used in English.[24] *Haiyā* (hire) refers to a chauffeur-driven car; *ōrai* (all right) is shouted when helping a vehicle back up; *uetto* (wet) means sentimental or soft-hearted, while *dorai* (dry) means unsentimental or businesslike. Loanwords are also used to create new terms from nonexistent sources,[25] e.g., *bēsu-appu* (base up — an increase in the standard of living), *chīku dansu* (cheek dance — ballroom dancing), *rūmu kūrā* (room cooler — air conditioner), or *Dekansho* (Descartes, Kant, and Schopenhauer) (Hinds 1974: 94). English loanwords may occasionally be used as slang expressions, e.g., *panku* (puncture — to deliver a baby), *sukuramburu* (scramble — the flow of people crossing a busy street after the stoplight has changed), *rimo-kon* (remote control — a husband who goes straight home after work is *rimo-kon*-ed [Matsumoto 1974: 24]).[26]

Sociolinguistic Functions of English

There is a large body of theoretical literature on language contact dealing with the use of a language in linguistically plural contexts (Haugen 1950, 1953; Vogt 1954; Weinreich 1953). Case studies describing this behavior in actual speech situations also abound (Hymes 1964; Fishman 1968, 1972; Gumperz and Hymes 1972; Scherer and Giles 1979). However, little attention has been paid to these factors in examining the way English loanwords are used by Japanese people in speech, on artifacts, and in written sources, or to the way English loanwords are nativized by being brought into the cognitive system of Japanese speakers.[27] This section constitutes a preliminary attempt to describe some of these processes.

Among Japanese college students, there seems to be a tendency for men to use more loanwords in academic discussions than in everyday speech. In one experiment the number of English loanwords used by three male university students was noted over a period of several days. The total number of loans used in academic contexts was also tallied. "Academic context" was defined as discussion germane to their field with either majors or non-majors, discussions with classmates about classroom or department activities, or mention of department, classroom, or major topics to others not involved in, or directly discussing, their discipline. One student was in medical school; his data were collected over a fourteen-hour period. Two other students, upper-classmen in political science and economics, were observed for eight hours and five hours, respectively. Data were gathered in natural settings with the investigator present as an observer or, sometimes, a participant. No attempt was made to guide the conversation or intentionally elicit English loanwords. Data and notes were collected obtrusively, so estimates occasionally had to be made.

Table 1. English Loanwords Used by Japanese College Students

		Male students			Female students	
		Medicine	Political Science	Economics	Psychology	Business
Total	hours	14	8	3	6	3
	# loans	210	192	41	114	138
Non-academic settings	hours	10.5	2.75	1.5	4.25	2
	# loans	96	69	17	65	74
	%	46	36	41	57	54
Academic settings	hours	3.5	5.25	1.5	1.75	1
	# loans	114	123	24	49	64
	%	54	64	59	43	46

All three male informants seemed to use loanwords slightly more often when speaking about academic topics; in contrast, the women informants tend to use English loanwords *less* often when talking about things related to their major.

Several difficulties arise if one attempts to draw definitive conclusions from frequency counts such as these. There are the obvious methodological problems of the number of subjects, equal proportions of men and women, and various rates of speech between indi-

viduals in a conversation. Different majors may have different tendencies to use loanwords (see Ichikawa 1931).[28] The frequency of
loanword usage may also depend on the speaker's knowledge of English. Finally, in the broad category of non-academic topics there
may be any number of occasions when loanwords *are* used frequently. For example, loanwords pervade — and seem almost necessary
for — men's discussions of baseball, tennis, golf, horse racing, and
the Olympics. In these contexts two or three loanwords per sentence
are not uncommon. Both younger and older female informants tend
to use English loanwords when discussing topics like the latest fash-
ions or cosmetics, or when talking about romantic intrigues (real or
fictional) or speaking of marriage plans.

A more fruitful approach to these variables involves examining
the dynamics of the situation. For example, Brown and Gilman
(1960) have shown that language can be a measure of solidarity; so
the use of English loanwords in a conversation might depend on
the closeness of the relationship between the speakers. An American
anthropologist in Japan can find it rather difficult to make an accurate estimate of the strength of a friendship between two individuals,
especially after knowing some informants for only a few weeks or
months. However, there does seem to be some pressure not to use
large numbers of English loanwords at first meetings. Several informants have indicated that when people whom they do not know
sprinkle their conversations with too much English, the speech may
sound affected, especially if the loans are complicated or esoteric.

Brown and Levenson (1978) have noted that code-switching
and the use of slang or jargon are strategies for communicating needs
or desires. Such observations might be supported by the language of
the Japanese *sarariman* (white-collar workers, or rising business execu-
tives) in their middle or late thirties. When describing products or
making sales presentations, their speech is filled with English loanwords. These are not limited to specialized technical terms, where
the Japanese equivalents might be awkward or uncommon.

Japanese people in general, and men in particular, seem to use
English loanwords more than Japanese terms when speaking of ro-
mance, sex, or male or female companions. In some cases new words
like *bōi furendo* (boyfriend), *gāru furendo* (girlfriend), or *gāru hanto*
(girl hunting) are being used where there were no satisfactory Japanese equivalents. A new term may be coined, based on an English loanword, as in *rabu-hoteru* (a hotel that rents by the hour, afternoon, or
evening and is openly used by lovers for romantic rendezvous). However, many other loanwords are borrowed from English but added to

a Japanese term or otherwise given a Japanese twist. Such a case is *onna-petto* (from Japanese "woman" and English "pet"), meaning the object of someone's sexual fantasy, or *gē-bōi* (gay boy), meaning any male homosexual. Instead of the Japanese *shuin* (masturbation), which is rather clinical, Japanese young men commonly use *masutā-bēshiyon* or *onani* (from "onanism"). A book may even bear the title *How to Onani.* Less charged terms dealing with relationships are also beginning to use loans, e.g., *hazu* (husband), *waifu* (wife). When asking a girl out, a young man will most likely use the word *dēto* (date), and he will use an English loanword if he refers to a sexual topic or makes an off-color remark (e.g., *pinku mūdo* [pink mood] when referring to something with sexual overtones).

A few other situations should also be mentioned; for example, contemporary music, entertainment fields, and news broadcasting. Also, most people use slightly fewer loanwords when conversing with elders than when speaking with those their own age or younger. Certain social factors tend to imply differential loanword use, though compounding of variables makes clear conclusions difficult to draw. Teenagers tend to use more loanwords, perhaps because of certain topics of conversation — sports, cars, boyfriends and girlfriends.

The more important conclusion to be drawn from these data is that some people use more loanwords than others just as part of their individual personality or speaking style, and depending on the context. The data do not support the view that a person's sex determines the frequency of loanword use. In the study mentioned above, the ratio of loanwords used to total time investigated was 15, 24, and 13.6 for the men, and 19 and 46 for the women. The average was 20.4 per hour. The frequency of use depends on the person, style, and topic.

English in Education and the Media

The formal study of English in Japan is extensive. There are over 50,000 English teachers, though the ability of many is questionable (Reischauer 1977: 399). According to policies established by Japan's Ministry of Education, all middle school and most senior high school students should study a foreign language. Hayes (1979: 365) points out that approximately 99 percent of middle school students begin studying English in seventh grade. About 70 percent of the high school students continue studying English, as do 20 percent of those who attend college. If a middle school student (seventh through ninth grade) plans on entering a university, he must have had

525 hours of English instruction. A terminal high school student will
have had 315 hours. Along with the instruction given in the public
schools, there are hundreds of private English language academies of
varying competence and repute, as well as many *juku* (cram schools
for entering a university) which offer English language and literature
as subjects. Even in the early grades, lessons on Japanized English are
given. For example, Fukao (1979: 234) mentions the following items
that had to be identified on a recent fifth-grade test: *aidea* (idea), *kon-
torasuto* (contrast), *nansensu* (nonsense), *menyū* (menu), *mania* (mania), *raibaru* (rival), *sensu* (sense), *popyurā* (popular), *rūzu* (lose),
kyatchi-furēzu (catch phrase).

English loanwords are very popular in Japanese broadcasting,
and they are not limited to advertising. For example, on daytime TV
game shows, contestants are often asked to identify English loanwords.
Such words are also found in program openings, closings, and in conversations on talk shows. Tokyo area television stations recently began
"dual broadcasting," transmitting some programs in both Japanese
and English. In homes possessing one of the newer television sets, either language can be tuned in.

All indications are that the use of English loanwords is at least
as extensive in books, newspapers, and magazines as it is in everyday
speech.[30] The following headlines are just a few of the ones that used
loanwords in a single edition of a typical daily newspaper:[31] *gasu
more – ni kai renzoku* (Gas Leak – Second Time in a Row); *hotto
jamu '80, faitingu jamu – mūdo jōjō, yagai no kaihōkan mo* (Hot
Jam 80, A Fighting Jam – The Best Mood, and an Open Outdoor
Feeling [referring to a concert]); *gyamburu, sake, shakkin . . . kyat-
chā – "yakyū suki" no ura no kao* (Gambling, Drinking, Debts . . .
Catcher Who "Loves Baseball" Shows Another Face).

Many of the data published in the research literature have been
based on printed sources (Bailey 1962; Hirai 1978; Ozawa 1970,
1976; Sonoda 1975; Umegaki 1978). As mentioned before, certain
genres,[32] such as magazines dealing with sex and the men's comic
books, use an inordinate number of English loanwords. In these magazines one finds English loanwords written both in roman letters and
in *katakana* syllabary (e.g., *samā* big *purezento* [summer big present]
depicts a nude girl holding a pistol). The *manga* comics seem to do
this with greater regularity; in this sense the *manga* might be a sort
of blend between the usually *katakana*-using print medium and the
roman-letter-using artifacts.

Attitudes toward English Borrowing

The reasons for the expansion in the Japanese vocabulary are of interest in both theoretical and applied settings. There are several possible reasons why English loanwords are so popular.

Bruner, Goodnow and Austin (1956) claim that the human thinking process divides the world into "conjunctive" concrete concepts and "relational" concepts; the latter exist only with respect to each other. Higa (1975: 85) believes this may explain why seemingly unnecessary English words are borrowed into Japanese, at least for the dialect spoken in Hawaii. Presumably he means that when a word is introduced which has no exact equivalent in Japanese ("curry"), the other related words (such as "rice") also tend to be borrowed, regardless of whether Japanese equivalents already exist. However, this statement seems to oversimplify a highly complex interaction between the social-situational, the symbolic, and the cognitive levels of the use of English loanwords by Japanese speakers. To follow up on this example, in Japan today two words for rice are commonly used: *gohan,* a native term, and *raisu,* a loan from English. The preference for one word over another may depend on style (Makino 1978; Sibata 1975) or on any number of other sociolinguistic variables. *Raisu* seems to be used for food of non-native origin (as in *raisu karē*), while native foods use *gohan* (as in *tori gohan* [chicken and rice], *kaki gohan* [oysters and rice], or *kuri gohan* [chestnuts and rice]). This might imply that *raisu* and *gohan* are used in two different contexts, and that they probably involve different feelings or connotations as well. There also seems to be a tendency to use the word *gohan* in traditional Japanese-style restaurants (*shokudō*), while *raisu* may be used in a *resutoran,* a large, modern Western-style restaurant. Lest one assume that *raisu* is always used with foreign dishes or occasions while *gohan* is used otherwise, the data are not consistent. Some informants claim that *raisu* should be used with homemade foods served in small local restaurants, while modern medium-sized restaurants will use *gohan.* The specific ways in which reference and situation interact are some of the most important and interesting topics for research in the Japanese-English contact situation, and they still need to be untangled.

English loanwords may also be brought into Japanese through the use of advertising.[33] This is the most common reason given by informants when they are asked why so many English words appear in Japanese. Japanese companies spend almost $5 billion a year on advertising, second only to the United States' $33 billion (Dunn and Barban 1978: 696). Of that amount, over half is spent on print media. However, the quantity of goods from Japan entering the United States

is greater than the quantity of American goods exported to Japan —
yet almost no Japanese loans appear in English.[34] True, different
sociolinguistic mechanisms might be operating for the two countries.
But as yet no one has offered any evidence that advertising is the
cause (rather than a reflection) of the use of English loanwords by
Japanese speakers.[35]

Though there may be elements of prestige involved in the use
of loanwords, there are also pressures which act against their use.
Many Japanese people believe that loanwords are overused. For example, consider the following dialogue from a beginning Japanese
language text (Yoshida et al. 1973: 286):

> Kono aida, *"kūru-na tatchi* de *hādo-na akushon* o *dairekuto-ni
> sābisu-suru Naporeon Soro"* to iu eiga no senden ga arimashita.
> Ichi-do kiita dake de dō iu imi ka wakarimasu ka?

> The other day I saw this ad saying, *"Napoleon Solo — direct
> served hard action* with a *cool* touch."* How are you supposed
> to understand that the first time through?

The use of English loanwords has no official support. The Ministry
of Education's Department of National Language, as a matter of policy, "has never published anything that contains loanwords of Western origin" (Sibata 1975: 169).

Dolgin, Kemnitzer and Scheider (1977) claim that certain "negative" symbols (in this case, some native Japanese words) might be
"displaced" by less threatening symbols (English loanwords). Evidence to substantiate this claim can be seen in the high frequency of
loanwords used when sexual topics are discussed. Some informants
also claim that *tibi*[36] (tuberculosis) is preferable to the native Japanese term *kekkakubyo*.[37] (See Annamalai [1978] and Kachru [1978a,
in press] for discussions of the Indian situation.)

Individual speakers use English loanwords in highly creative and
personal ways, as this example indicates (Sibata 1975: 170):

> In the script I found the expression "flower street." I then
> asked the script writer what it meant and where he picked
> up the expression. The reply was: "I just made it up myself."
> I was subsequently told that the meaning had to do with the
> decoration of flowers, a decoration movement that was going
> on at the time. I no longer recall the exact meaning, but there
> can be no mistake that Japanized "English," such as "happy
> end" or "flower street," was introduced into the Japanese
> lexicon by people . . . in a more or less similar fashion.[38]

However, not all inventions gain acceptance; nor is this a practice indulged in by everyone. The educational system in Japan gives all students some inkling of English vocabulary and grammar, perhaps enough to provide a common ground for individual expression and creativity, or to allow for a choice of new linguistic strategies. For example, the young lady who has *Dream Girl* embroidered on her sweater might be making a statement about herself that she would find it difficult to make otherwise, given the prevailing Japanese social and linguistic conventions.

The impact of language on an individual in Japan should not be underestimated. This linguistic pressure is sometimes discussed in the media. In the 1970 award-winning bestseller, *Nihonjin to Yudayajin (The Japanese and the Jews)*, Ben-Dasan (1970: 186) points out that both the learned discourse of a conservative college professor and the radical arguments shouted over loudspeakers by leftist students employ the same level of courteous language considered appropriate for someone addressing a group of people. In 1980, members of the Japanese National Debate Team told me that such argumentation was almost impossible to conduct in Japanese, especially for women. To their knowledge, all debating societies in Japan conduct their contests in English. These examples imply that the Japanese language places constraints on individual language usage. Perhaps one way to circumvent these inhibitions is through the use of loanwords.

The semantic range of some loanwords varies among different Japanese speakers. This may allow for some ambiguity, with its consequent play on connotations whenever loanwords are used.[39] Such ambiguity and appeal to connotation is not unusual in Japanese language and literature. Loanwords may provide another linguistic mechanism involving these devices.[40]

Japanese English and Other Non-Native Englishes

Bamgbose (1982) postulates a typology to identify varieties of Nigerian English. He posits four levels (from pidgin English to university speech) and four varieties (from extreme phonological/syntactical imposition of the native language on English, to speech identical to that of a native Standard English speaker). However, few of these observations are helpful in the Japanese case. Japan was never colonized by the British, who elsewhere left a linguistic legacy in the form of civil service requirements, government legislation, or a prestige language. Such factors encouraged people to become fluent in spoken and written English. English was never the language of the

Japanese public school system, though there were intellectual incentives to acquire at least a reading knowledge. Most important, Japan has never had the cultural and linguistic pluralism which made English convenient as a lingua franca (at least) or a national language (at most).[41] In short, English in Japan never became institutionalized.

The major difference between Japanized English and most other non-native varieties is the degree to which members of the population are fluent speakers. In numerous other countries, many people can speak a simplified pidgin English and a large number possess varying degrees of fluency. In Japan, while the number of highly fluent speakers may be smaller, all people have some ability to use English linguistic resources. Except in special instances (such as among Hawaiian-Japanese), pidgin English per se is not found because it is not needed. Japanese English mainly emphasizes vocabulary items and phrases (many of which are highly productive), rather than morphology or syntax.[42]

The investigation of language contact between Japanese and English is a subject of great import for both theoretical and applied linguistics. The unique use of English loanwords by Japanese people defies most of the classic typologies proposed by Haugen (1950, 1953), Weinreich (1953), Ferguson (1959), or Vildomec (1963). It also stands outside the bounds of Gumperz's (1964) code-switching, where alternating sentential language changes accompany a change in the speech situation, or Kachru's (1978b) code-mixing, where language changes are found in a single sentence in the same speech situation. Perhaps the most practical theoretical approach for the Japanese case involves internal versus external switching, as described by Oksaar (1976) and Hatch (1976), where internal switching depends on social factors and external switching on the fluency of the speaker, his ability to use various emotive devices to establish tone, and his ability to respond to the interlocutor. Uyekubo (1972) and Ervin-Tripp (1967) have shown how important these factors are for the speech of Japanese bilingual children and adults and for Japanese monolinguals, respectively.[43]

Conclusion

I have presented some factors that affect the use of English loanwords in Japanese, and have suggested some ways in which Japanese speakers use these words as a communicative strategy or rhetorical device. Certain social factors seem to indicate differential loanword usage, but the dynamics of the individual personality, the particular speech situation, and the general social context are of at least equal importance. Loanwords may provide a different set of linguistic symbols which might carry neutral or ambiguous meanings, connotations, or affective content. This unique "English" in Japan affords the individual an expanded range of linguistic means to achieve a variety of social ends — without necessarily becoming completely bilingual.

Research on the use of English in Japanese is continuing. Several popular claims about loanwords (e.g., that referents of English loanwords represent things new and modern; that English loanwords are used to intellectually impress others) need rigorous empirical investigation. The semantics of "hybrid innovations" (Kachru 1975) — lexical items which consist of an element from a native language along with a component from English — occur frequently in Japanized English but have not been thoroughly studied. Another area which merits attention involves the linguistic constraints (Pfaff 1979; Kachru 1978b) that operate on English loanwords. Is there a limit to the number of English vocabulary items which the Japanese language can tolerate? Why do some items flourish, while others disappear?[44] Some work has been done on the semantic and cognitive aspects of English loanwords, but only on limited topics (e.g., Hinds 1974; Sanches 1977).[45] Japanese-English bilingualism has begun to be explored among adult learners (Ervin-Tripp 1967), bilingual and monolingual children (Uyekubo 1972; Yoshida 1978), and Japanese-American pidgin speakers in Hawaii (Higa 1975; Nagara 1972), suggesting that these areas might also be profitably pursued by those studying English loanwords in Japanese.

Much work still needs to be done in relating this switching or mixing to other aspects of Japanese communicative behavior, such as kinesics, paralanguage, and nonverbal communication. We cannot yet predict where and when an English loanword will be used, who will use it, and what strategies he intends to implement while doing so. It is also unclear how any of the special subcultures of Japan — the Korean minority, the *burakumin* (Japan's "untouchable" caste), or the *yakuza* (ritualized underworld society) — react to or utilize English loanwords. So far, all that is really understood is that the use of English is widespread and is apparently affected by situational and social factors, and that these variables are terribly conflated.[46]

NOTES

1.   This research was based on data collected during the summers of 1979 and 1980 in Japan, supported in part by a summer research grant from the

University of Illinois. I thank this committee and its chairman, R. T. Zuidema, for their invaluable assistance. I also thank Joseph B. Casagrande, Janet W. D. Dougherty, Braj B. Kachru, Mariko Kaga, Seiichi Makino, and David W. Plath for their help in discussing topics and problems relating to this study and for reading earlier drafts.

2. This use of the term "acculturation" is somewhat unusual; I beg indulgence from fellow anthropologists. For discussions in English on the general structure of Japanese, see Inoue (1979) and Miller (1967).

3. Ohno (1970: 80) speaks of the influence of Korean borrowings before the 9th century: "The original stimulus to the cultural development of the *Yayoi* [300 B.C. to approximately 300 A.D.] probably came from South Korea." There are many accessible texts in English on the history of Japan, including George Sansom's three-volume *History of Japan, To 1334, 1334-1615, 1615-1867* (Stanford: Stanford University Press, 1958). For the post-contact period, see Edwin Reischauer's *The United States and Japan* (New York: Viking Press, 1965) and W. G. Beasley's *The Modern History of Japan* (New York: Praeger, 1963). For a discussion of the Dutch influence on the Japanese language, see Vos (1963).

4. On whom the novel *Shōgun* is (very loosely) based. See P. Rogers, *The First Englishman in Japan* (London: Harwill, 1956), or any of the half-dozen novels based on the incident, such as R. Blacker's *The Needle Watcher: The Will Adams Story; British Samurai* (Tokyo: Tuttle, 1973).

5. English was well on its way to becoming an influence on the Japanese language long before the post-World War II Occupation.

6. As Fukuzawa (1899: 213) pointed out, English became a popular subject for students, even replacing the traditional Chinese studies, but it never became the official language of instruction.

7. Educated people may be quite competent *readers* of English, however.

8. There are also four daily English-language newspapers readily available. Interestingly, there are more English-language newspapers published in Tokyo than in Chicago.

9. Passin (1980:48) counted 1,300 separate foreign loans in a random issue of *The Yomiuri* newspaper.

10. The Japanese writing system has four sets of symbols: *kanji* (Chinese-based ideographs) for most common lexemes, a syllabary of 46 basic symbols called *hiragana* used for inflections and other morphemes, an angular version of the *hiragana* called *katakana* used as an italics and to write foreign names, and *romanji*, a phonemic transliteration. Occasionally a foreign name or word will be written in *hiragana*, as in *bai-bai* (bye bye) at the end of a television program.

11. The use of English loanwords on artifacts will be discussed at a later date.

12. Mackey (1979) does caution us against taking the percentage of loanwords as a measure of language influence or dominance in a contact situation. However, even with these reservations, the number of English loanwords is quite large. For other statistics on the extent of English loanword usage (though limited to only frequency counts of items found in dictionaries), see Ozawa (1970; 1976).

13. Some scholars (e.g., Pierce 1971) use the term "Japlish" to refer to parts of the nativization processes discussed in this paper. However, one should not be misled into thinking that this is a variety of English equivalent to, say, Chicano English or Indian English.

14. For a complete description of Japanese phonology, including some remarks on the phonology of foreign words, see McCawley (1968).

15. The basic Japanese phonemes are *a, i, u, e, o, k, s, t, n, h, m, y, r, w* and syllabic *n*. The vowels are "Italian" vowels, and most consonants are pronounced somewhat as in English. Vowel length (indicated by repeating the symbol or using a raised bar) and consonant gemination (indicated by repeating the symbol) are also phonemic. The sounds *k, s, t, n, h, m,* and *r* can form clusters with the semipalatal *y*. The series *k, s,* and *t* have voiced correspondents, and *b* and *p*, thought to be derivable from *h*, are also present. As Japanese romanization is basically phonemic, the slashed bar symbols have been omitted. Though the sounds *fa, fi, fo,* and *fe* do not occur in native Japanese words (only *fu* is found naturally in this consonant-vowel series), these sounds are found in English loanwords. They are written in *katakana* using the symbol for *fu* plus a subscripted vowel sign. The Japanese *r*-sound is midway between the English /l/ and /r/ (see Sonoda 1975: 145-46). For a detailed discussion of all the constraints on gemination in English loanwords, see Lovins (1973: 81-98).

16. Strictly speaking, the categories "noun," "verb," etc., as used in English are inadequate for Japanese. See Martin (1975).

17. Words of Chinese origin which have been borrowed into Japanese in the past also take this *na* marker: *kirei-na hana* (pretty flower), *shizuka-na machi* (quiet town). Loanwords may, on occasion, take the *-i* adjective marker, as in *now-i onna* (a "now"/contemporary woman).

18. This compounding process seems to be a common way of taking certain English elements into a host language. For example, Kachru (1978a: 36) gives, among others, these instances from Hindi: *begin karnā* (to begin), *worry karnā* (to worry), *control karnā* (to control). Pandharipande (1981) gives similar examples from Marathi: *atæk yene* (to get an attack), *šɔk basṇe* (to get a shock). One possible reason why such a process is so productive in these languages is that using these compound verbs may express meanings related to the manner in which the acts are performed, thus allowing this device to be used to express attitudinal meanings (Y. Kachru and Pandharipande 1980: 122).

Apparently, as mentioned by Henderson (1948: 39), case markers in this form are often ignored when applied to English loanwords. For example, *rabu suru* should mean "to love" and *rabu o suru* should mean "to make love." However, both seem to be used interchangeably. Likewise, "to like" should be *raiki suru*, but the peculiar *raiki o suru* is also heard.

19. Sonoda (1975: 177) claims that *yū* (you) can occur as an object, subject, or possessive, as in *yū wa dochira kara kita* (Where do you come from?). I have never heard such an example.

20. Cf. *boku no mai-kā* (my "my-car").

21. This summary does not mean to imply that there are no other grammatical aspects of English word borrowing in Japanese. Much research still needs to be done. For example, Kachru (1978b) has shown some of the grammatical constraints operating on the borrowing of English into Hindi, and Warie (1977) has discussed such problems in Thai. Sridhar and Sridhar (1980) have demonstrated similar syntactic constraints on English borrowing in Kannada and Spanish. For a general theoretical discussion on these topics, see Wentz (1977).

22. Makino has mentioned that visual effects might also be operating in the use of English loanwords. For example, *tabako* (cigarette) is written in *hiragana*, while most other loanwords are written in *katakana*, perhaps indicating the extent to which *tabako* has become adopted. Yotsukura (1971: 116) points out that "news" was taken in as *nyūsu*, not *nyūzu*, because this word, like most English loanwords, was borrowed by sight rather than by sound.

23. Horiuchi (Passin and Horiuchi 1977: 39-41) discusses more than two dozen compounds involving the English word "love."

24. Garneau (1975) terms these "misleading transfer items" and demonstrates how a similar phenomenon is operating in French.

25. Another fascinating aspect of vocabulary nativization in Japanese is seen in the borrowing of place names in sign language (Peng and Clouse 1976). For example, in the sign for New York City (*nyū yōku* in spoken Japanese) the right-hand configuration is finger-spelled *y* of English, intending the *y* of York. The rest of the sign is in regular Japanese sign language.

26. In some cases English words enter Japanese as verbs, after they have been shortened and the -*ru* verbal suffix has been added (Hinds 1974: 94; Seward 1968: 99; Miura 1979: 39-40), e.g., *taku-ru* (to go by taxi), *nego-ru* (to negotiate), *demo-ru* (to demonstrate). After such modification, the new term may be conjugated as a normal Japanese verb, as in *ima kare to negotte imasu* (I'm negotiating with him now). Such items are not common.

27. Little work on Japan has been done by cognitive anthropologists except in confined areas such as kinship studies (see Wallace and Atkins 1965).

28. Ozawa (1976) has updated Ichikawa's data, though he has used only a dictionary as his source.

29. For women, too, presumably — though this was not studied. The use of loanwords (if any) in traditional Japanese sports like *sumō* (Japanese stylized wrestling) or *kendō* (bamboo-sword fighting) was not investigated, either.

30. As an example Horiuchi (1963: 52) gives the following reply, printed by the *Asahi* newspaper, in response to a question about the number of loanwords used in a previous issue: "As a rule, foreign words are to be printed in *kana*. Words which we feel to be strange to the average reader and words which in our estimate are still unfamiliar to the public are usually withheld; the newspaper should try to reach as wide a range of readers as possible by using a vocabulary easy to grasp. Of late the use of 'foreign' words has grown by leaps and bounds. Sometimes the total will be as many as 60-70 to a page. This is a conspicuous phenomenon in the case of articles with close affiliations with the home, sports, arts, radio and TV, and advertisements. Post-war Japan has met with a deluge of technical terms relating to thought, science, techniques, and merchandise. These have seldom been translated nor have *kanji* been adapted to them, and apparently without a second thought the Japanese have taken them on as they thought the words to be. To all intents and purposes we appear to be a foreign-word loving people. Anything in *kana* looks sweet and fresh. We bow to it and value it overmuch."

31. *The Yomiuri*, August 16, 1980.

32. Though some Japanese authors do write in English (e.g., Kawasaki's *Alien Rice*) their number hardly rivals the scores of Indian and African authors who write in English.

33. This manifests itself in some very interesting product names, such as a coffee creamer named Creap or a soft drink named Calpis. Seward (1968: 67) mentions some earlier examples: Pecker mechanical pencils, Rony Wrinkle rubber prophylactics, Puddy prepared pudding mix, Violent blue jeans. For a French example of how English loanwords are borrowed in advertising, see Knepler (1976).

Plath also points out that some names for products in Japan involve bilingual punning or word-play. For example, the name of the popular Japanese whiskey *Suntory* might be a pun on Torii, the name of the three brothers who founded the company. (A Japanese word for "three" is *san*.) Plath also notes that almost all cigarette brand names are in English (e.g., Peace, Mild Seven, Hi-Lite, Cabin).

34. Of course, some Japanese loans, such as *sukiyaki, kimono, harakiri,* and *kamakazi*, appear in English. Miura (1979: 173-75) lists about 75-100 examples, ranging from the very common to terms used only by specialists in a Japanese craft or art.

35. Makino (1978) suggests that Japanese people have an empathy hierarchy toward individual vocabulary items. They are thought to be most empathetic to *Yamato* (native Japanese) words, less empathetic to Chinese loanwords, and non-empathetic toward Western loanwords.

36. Makino has mentioned that this might be because of the similarity to the older German clinical term *tēbē*.

37. Kachru (1978a) terms this process in code-mixed situations as "neutralization." It is still not clear whether the mechanisms by which English loanwords are borrowed into Japanese fulfill all the necessary conditions of code-mixing.

38. One other thing the scriptwriter might have had in mind was the term *hana-dori* (flower road), used to refer to the long platform by which *kabuki* players entered the stage from their positions near the audience. Plath also notes that the main thoroughfare running through downtown Kobe was known as *furawā rōdo* for many years.

Kachru (1978a) claims that in such mixed situations there is a cline of acceptability of mixed forms, ranging from normal code-mixing to unusual "odd-mixing." These parameters, motivations, and criteria have yet to be clearly isolated for English loanwords in Japan.

39. E.g., the name of the famous Japanese singing duo *pinku redi* (Pink Lady). The color conjures up the same feelings of sensuality as does red or pink in English. But when these two girls give interviews in the popular press, they always present a very wholesome image.

40. In the "folk beliefs" of most Westerners, the Japanese are thought to be the world's great imitators. The popular media indicate that many Japanese now believe this, too. However, no satisfactory definition of imitation has ever been proposed, nor have any tests been suggested on how to find it. It is difficult, then, to claim imitation as a possible reason for the large number of loanwords in Japanese without falling into a circular argument.

41. See Kachru (1981) for a description of the Indian situation.

42. As Horiuchi (1963: 51) said, "English is often so near and yet so far from the grasp of the average Japanese citizen."

43. How children acquire loanwords in Japanese has yet to be investigated. It is not known whether television, school, friends, or other factors are the most crucial in imparting this English vocabulary. See Yoshida 1978; Weitzman 1967.

44. E.g., certain loans like *moga* (from the initial sounds of "modern girl," meaning a 1920's flapper) became fashionable but rapidly faded (Miller 1967: 249-50). Plath suggests that the current *za shitī* (the city, i.e., Tokyo) might be another such instance.

45. Hinds examined differential responses to native color terms and English loanwords for color. Sanches studied, in part, how Japanese numerical classifiers were not extended to cover certain English loans.

46. Other references of interest include Baird (1971), Inui (1958), Kunihiro

(1967), Mori (1972), Nagasawa (1957), Nishiwaki (1961), Pae (1967), Yazaki (1964), and Yokoi (1973). Loanword dictionaries in Japanese are Arakawa (1977), Nikaido (1980), Oka (1980), Sanseidō Henshū-bu (1979), Shinsei Shuppankai Hen-shū-bu (1978), Yoshizawa (1979), and Yoshizawa and Ishiwata (1979). Landy and Horiuchi (1978) and Masuda (1974) are also useful. English glossaries of some English loanwords in Japanese can be found in Bailey (1962), Matsumoto (1974), and Miura (1979). A later edition of the *Kokuritsu Kokugo Kenkyūjo* study has been released as *Denshikeisanki ni yoru shimbun no goi chosa [A Computer Study of Contemporary Newspaper Vocabulary]* (Tokyo: Shūei Shuppan, 1970).

The transliterations used in this article are based on the *Hyojunshiki*/Hepburn system (but with long vowels indicated by a raised bar), rather than the less popular *Sin-kunreisiki* or *Nipponsiki* systems. This would be of little interest to the non-specialist, were it not for the fact that a few names in the bibliography are inconsistent with the text transcriptions and might puzzle readers doing further research. All citations and quotes are given as in the original (e.g., Sibata or Ohno, vs. Shibata or Ōno, which would be consistent with the text).

REFERENCES

Annamalai, E. 1978. The Anglicized Indian languages: a case of code-mixing. *International Journal of Dravidian Linguistics* 7(2): 239-47.

Arakawa, Sōbe. 1977. *Kadokawa gairaigo jiten, dai-ni-han* [Kadokawa loanword dictionary. 2nd ed.] Tokyo: Kadokawa Shoten.

Bailey, Don C. 1962. *A glossary of Japanese neologisms.* Tucson: University of Arizona Press.

Baird, Scott. 1971. Contact: English with Japanese. *The Study of Current English* 25(15): 23-28.

Bamgbose, Ayọ. 1982. Standard Nigerian English: issues of identification. In this volume.

Ben-Dasan, Isaiah. 1970. *The Japanese and the Jews.* New York: Weatherhill.

Brown, Penelope, and Levinson, Stephen. 1978. Universals in language usage: politeness phenomena. Pp. 56-310 in E. Goody, ed., *Questions and politeness: strategies in social interaction.* Cambridge: Cambridge University Press.

Brown, Roger, and Gilman, Albert. 1960. The pronouns of power and solidarity. Pp. 302-35 in *Psycholinguistics: selected papers of Roger Brown.* New York: Free Press.

Bruner, J.; Goodnow, J.; and Austin, G. 1956. *A study of thinking.* New York: John Wiley.

Doglin, J.; Kemnitzer, D., and Schneider, D., eds. 1977. *Symbolic anthropology.* New York: Columbia University Press.

Dunn, S. W., and Barban, A. M. 1978. *Advertising: its role in modern marketing.* New York: Dryden Press.

Ervin-Tripp, Susan. 1967. An Issei learns English. *Journal of Social Issues* 23: 78-90.

Ferguson, Charles A. 1959. Diglossia. *Word* 15: 325-40.

Fishman, Joshua, ed. 1968. *Readings in the sociology of language.* The Hague: Mouton.

———— . 1972. *Advances in the sociology of language*, II. The Hague: Mouton.

Fukao, Tokiko. 1979. *Katakana kotoba* [Words in Katakana]. Tokyo: Saimaru Shuppankai.

Fukuzawa, Yukichi. 1899. *The autobiography of Yukichi Fukuzawa*. New York: Schocken Books, 1972.

Garneau, Jean-Luc. 1975. Anglo-French misleading transfer items: a semantic analysis. Pp. 567-83 in P. Reich, ed., *The second LACUS forum*. Columbia, S.C.: Hornbeam Press.

Gaunlett, O. J. 1966. Phonetic discrepancies in Japanese loanwords. *The Study of Sounds* 12: 308-26.

Gumperz, John. 1964. Linguistic and social interaction in two communities. *American Anthropologist* 66(2): 137-54.

————, and Hymes, Dell, eds. 1972. *Directions in sociolinguistics: the ethnography of communication*. New York: Holt, Rinehart and Winston.

Hatch, Evelyn. 1976. Studies in language switching and mixing. Pp. 201-14 in W. McCormack and S. Wurm, *Language and man: anthropological issues*. The Hague: Mouton.

Haugen, Einar. 1950. The analysis of linguistic borrowing. *Language* 26: 210-31.

———— . 1953. *The Norwegian language in America: a study in bilingual behavior*. Philadelphia: University of Pennsylvania Press.

Hayes, Curtis. 1979. Language contact in Japan. Pp. 363-76 in Mackey and Ornstein (1979).

Henderson, Harold. 1948. *Handbook of Japanese grammar*. Boston: Houghton Mifflin.

Higa, Masanori. 1973. Sociolinguistic aspects of word borrowing. *Topics in Culture Learning* 1: 75-85. Reprinted in Mackey and Ornstein (1979).

———— . 1975. The use of loanwords in Hawaiian Japanese. Pp. 71-90 in Peng (1975).

Hirai, Masao. 1978. *Henna kotoba, tadashī kotoba* [Strange words, correct words]. Tokyo: Kyōiku Shuppan.

Hinds, John. 1974. Make mine BURAKKU. *Language Research* 10(2): 92-108.

Horiuchi, Amy. 1963. Department store ads and Japanized English. *Studies in Descriptive and Applied Linguistics* (2): 49-67. Tokyo: International Christian University.

Hymes, Dell, ed. 1964. *Language in culture and society*. New York: Harper and Row.

Ichikawa, Sanki. 1931. Foreign influences in the Japanese language. Pp. 141-80 in I. Nitobe et al., eds., *Western influences in modern Japan*. Chicago: University of Chicago Press.

Inoue, Kyoko. 1979. Japanese: a story of language and people. Pp. 241-300 in T. Shopen, ed., *Languages and their speakers*. Cambridge, Mass.: Winthrop.

Inui, Ryoichi. 1958. *Kokugo no hyogen ni oyoboshita Eigo no eikyō*. [English impact on expressions in the national language]. Tokyo: Mombushō.

Isshiki, Masako. 1957. A comparative analysis of English and Japanese consonant phonemes. *The Study of Sounds* 8: 391-416.

———— . 1965. A contrastive analysis of English and Japanese vowel phonemes. *The Study of Sounds* 11: 193-212.

Japanese Ministry of Education (Mombushō). 1955. *Gairaigo no hyōki* [Representations of loanwords]. Tokyo: Meiji Tosho Shuppan Kabushiki Kaisha.

Japanese National Language Research Institute (Kokuritsu Kokugo Kenkyūjo).

1964. *Gendai zasshi kyūjusshu no yōji yōgo* [Vocabulary and Chinese characters in ninety magazines of today]. Tokyo: Shuei.

Kachru, Braj B. 1966. Indian English: a study in contextualization. Pp. 255-87 in C. Bazell et al., *In Memory of J. R. Firth*. London: Longmans.

———. 1975. Lexical innovations in South Asian English. *International Journal of the Sociology of Language* 4: 55-74.

———. 1978a. Toward structuring code-mixing: an Indian perspective. *International Journal of the Sociology of Language* 16: 27-46.

———. 1978b. Code-mixing as a communicative strategy in India. Pp. 107-24 in J. Alatis, ed., *International dimensions of bilingual education*. Washington: Georgetown University Press.

———. 1981. The pragmatics of non-native varieties of English. In L. Smith, ed., *English for cross-cultural communication*. London: Macmillan.

———. 1982. Models for non-native Englishes. In this volume.

———. In press. *The Indianization of English: the English language in India.* New Delhi and New York: Oxford University Press.

———, and Quirk, Randolph. 1981. Introduction to L. Smith, ed., *English for cross-cultural communication*. London: Macmillan.

Kachru, Yamuna, and Pandharipande, Rajeshwari. 1980. Toward a typology of compound verbs in South Asian languages. *Studies in the Linguistic Sciences* 10(1): 113-24.

Kawakami, Shin. 1963. *Gendaigo no hatsuon* [The pronounciation of today's language]. *Koza gendaigo* 1: 184-210.

Knepler, Myrna. 1976. Sold at fine stores everywhere, naturellement: a look at borrowed words in French and American magazine advertising. Pp. 309-18 in E. Blansitt, Jr., ed., *The third LACUS forum*. Columbia, S.C.: Hornbeam Press.

Kunihiro, Tetsuya. 1967. *Kōzoteki imiron − nichi ei ryōgo taishō kenkyū* [Structural semantics: a contrastive study of Japanese and English]. Tokyo: Sanseidō.

Landy, Eugene, and Horiuchi, Katsuaki. 1978. *Amerika zokugo jiten* [American underground dictionary], 5th ed. Tokyo: Kenkyūsha.

Lovins, Julie. 1973. Loanwords and the phonological structure of Japanese. Ph.D. dissertation, University of Chicago. Reprinted, Bloomington: Indiana University Linguistics Club, 1975.

McCawley, James. 1968. *The phonological component of a grammar of Japanese.* The Hague: Mouton.

Mackey, William. 1979. Toward an ecology of language contact. Pp. 455-60 in Mackey and Ornstein (1979).

———, and Ornstein, Jacob, eds. 1979. *Sociolinguistic studies in language contact*. The Hague: Mouton.

Makino, Seiichi. 1978. *Kotoba to kūkan* [Language and Space]. Tokyo: Tokai Daigaku Shuppankai.

Martin, Samuel. 1975. *Reference grammar of Japanese*. New Haven: Yale University Press.

Masuda, Koh. 1974. *Kenkyusha's new Japanese English dictionary*. 4th ed. Tokyo: Kenkyūsha.

Matsumoto, Toru. 1974. *The random dictionary: a glossary of foreign words in today's spoken Japanese*. Tokyo: Japan Times, Ltd.

Miller, Roy Andrew. 1967. *The Japanese language*. Chicago: University of Chicago Press.

————. 1977. *The Japanese language in contemporary Japan.* Washington: American Enterprise Institute for Public Policy Research.

Miura, Akira. 1979. *English loanwords in Japanese: a selection.* Tokyo: Tuttle.

Mori, Hiroki. 1972. *Nihongo no naka no Eigo* [English in Japanese]. Tokyo: Hyōgensha.

Nagara, Susumu. 1972. *Japanese pidgin English in Hawaii: a bilingual description.* Honolulu: University of Hawaii Press.

Nagasawa, Jiro. 1957. A study of English-Japanese cognates. *Language Learning* 8: 53-102.

Neustupný, J. V. 1978. *The phonology of loanwords in Japanese.* Pp. 74-100 in his *Post-structural approaches to language.* Tokyo: University of Tokyo Press.

Nikaido, Tetsuo. 1980. *Gairaigo jiten: Shin Gairaigo Kenkyūkai Hen* [Loanword dictionary]. Tokyo: Nittō Shoin.

Nishiwaki, Hiroshi. 1961. Morphological problems in linguistic borrowing. *Studies in Descriptive and Applied Linguistics* 1: 28-42.

Norman, Arthur. 1955. Bamboo English: the Japanese influence upon American speech in Japan. *American Speech* 30: 44-48.

Ohye, Saburo. 1967a. The mora phoneme /q/ in English loanwords in Japanese. *The Study of Sounds* 13: 111-21.

————. 1967b. Some phonological problems in language contact. *The Study of Sounds* 13: 83-90.

Oka, Michio, ed. 1980. *Jōyō gairaigo shin jiten* [New daily use loanword dictionary]. 6th ed. Tokyo: Gotō Shoin.

Oksaar, Els. 1976. Implications for language contact for bilingual language acquisition. Pp. 189-200 in W. McCormack and S. Wurm, eds., *Language and man: anthropological issues.* The Hague: Mouton.

Ohno, Susumu. 1970. *The origin of the Japanese language.* Tokyo: Kokusai Bunka Shinkokai.

Ozawa, Katsuyoshi. 1970. A study of English loanwords in the Japanese newspaper *The Yomiuri.* M.A. thesis, Louisiana State University.

————. 1976. An investigation of the influence of the English language on the Japanese language through lexical adaptation from 1955-1972. Ph.D. dissertation, Ohio University.

Pae, Yang Seo. 1967. English loanwards in Korean. Ph.D. dissertation, University of Texas.

Pandharipande, R. 1981. Nativization of loanwords: the case of Marathi. Manuscript.

Passin, Herbert. 1980. *Japanese and the Japanese.* Tokyo: Kinseido.

————, and Horiuchi, Katsuaki. 1977. *Japanese and the Japanese.* Tokyo: Kinseido.

Peng, Fred C. C., ed. 1975. *Language in Japanese society.* Tokyo: University of Tokyo Press.

————, and Clouse, Debbie. 1976. Place names in Japanese sign language. Pp. 295-308 in R. Di Pietro, ed., *The third LACUS forum.* Columbia, S.C.: Hornbeam Press.

Pfaff, Carol. 1979. Constraints on language mixing: intersentential code-switching and borrowing in Spanish/English. *Language* 55: 291-318.

Pierce, Joe. 1971. Culture, diffusion and Japlish. *Linguistics* 76: 45-58.

Quackenbush, Edward. 1974. How Japanese borrows English words. *Linguistics* 131: 59-75.

Reischauer, Edwin. 1977. *The Japanese.* Tokyo: Tuttle.

Sanches, Mary. 1977. Language acquisition and language change: Japanese numeral classifiers. Pp. 51-62 in B. Blount and M. Sanches, eds., *Sociocultural dimensions of language change.* New York: Academic Press.

Sanseidō Hen-shū-bu. 1979. *Konsaisu gairaigo jiten* [Concise loanword dictionary]. 3rd ed. Tokyo: Sanseidō Kabushiki Kaisha.

Scherer, Klaus, and Giles, Howard, eds. 1979. *Social markers in speech.* Cambridge: Cambridge University Press.

Seward, Jack. 1968. *Japanese in action.* New York: Weatherhill.

Sibata, Takeshi. 1975. On some problems in Japanese sociolinguistics: reflections and prospects. Pp. 159-74 in Peng (1975).

Shinsei Shuppankai Hen-shū-bu. 1978. *Shin gairaigo jiten* [New loanword dictionary]. Tokyo: Shinsei Shuppankai.

Sonoda, Koji. 1975. A descriptive study of English influence on modern Japanese. Ph.D. dissertation, New York University.

Sridhar, S. N., and Sridhar, Kamal K. 1980. The syntax and psycholinguistics of bilingual code-mixing. *Studies in the Linguistic Sciences* 10(1): 203-15.

Ueno, Kagefuku. 1968. Seiyō gairaigo [Western loanwords]. In *Nihon no Eigaku hyakunen* [One Hundred Years of English Studies in Japan], ed. Nihon no Eigaku Hyakunen Henshūbu, I, 543-73; II, 341-64.

Umegaki, Minoru. 1978. *Nihon gairaigo no kenkyū* [Studies on Japanese loanwords]. 4th ed. Tokyo: Kenkyūsha.

Uyekubo, Aiko. 1972. Language switching of Japanese-English bilinguals. M.A. thesis, University of California at Los Angeles.

Vildomec, Veroj. 1963. *Multilingualism.* Leyden: A. W. Sythoff.

Vogt, Hans. 1954. Contact of language. In A. Martinet and U. Weinreich, *Linguistics Today.* New York: Linguistic Circle of New York, Columbia University.

Vos, Frits. 1963. The Dutch influence on the Japanese language. *Lingua* 12: 34-88.

Wallace, Anthony F. C., and Atkins, John. 1965. The case of a Japanese informant. Pp. 404-18 in S. Tyler, ed., *Cognitive anthropology.* New York: Holt, Rinehart and Winston.

Warie, Pairat. 1977. Some aspects of code-mixing in Thai. *Studies in the Linguistic Sciences* 7(1): 21-40.

Weinreich, Uriel. 1953. *Languages in contact.* The Hague: Mouton.

Weitzman, Keiko Hirano. 1967. A study of the influence of the Japanese phonemic structure in the English of Japanese Americans. *Studies in Descriptive and Applied Linguistics* 4: 131-41.

Wentz, James. 1977. Some considerations in the development of a syntactic description of code-switching. Ph.D. dissertation, University of Illinois.

Yazaki, Genkurō. 1964. *Nihon no gairaigo* [Japanese loanwords]. Tokyo: Iwanami Shoten.

Yokoi, Tadao. 1973. *Gairaigo to gaikokugo: pazuru ni yoru gogaku nyūmon* [Loanwords and foreign languages: an introduction to language study through puzzles]. Tokyo: Gendai Jānarizumu Shuppankai.

———. 1978. *Gairaigo no goten* [Dictionary of loanword mistakes]. Tokyo: Jūkoku Minsha.

Yoshida, M. 1978. The acquisition of English vocabulary by a Japanese-speaking child. Pp. 91-100 in E. Hatch, ed., *Second language acquisition.* Rowley, Mass.: Newbury House.

Yoshida, Yasuo et al. 1973. *Japanese for today*. Tokyo: Gakken.
Yoshizawa, Norio. 1979. *Zukai gairaigo jiten* [Illustrated loanword dictionary]. Tokyo: Kadokawa Shoten.
————, and Ishiwata, Toshio. 1979. *Gairaigo no gogen* [Etymology of loanword origins]. Tokyo: Kadokawa Shoten.
Yotsukura, Sayo. 1971. Review of *The Japanese language*, by R. A. Miller. *Linguistics* 76: 103-32.
Zuengler, Jane. 1982. Kenyan English. In this volume.

12

Toward a Description
of Caribbean English

DENNIS R. CRAIG

Although at least 90 percent of the population in the historically
British Caribbean use some form of Creole language as the everyday
medium of informal communication, the English language remains
the sole official language and vehicle of literacy in the score or so of
relevant territories: Guyana, Trinidad and Tobago, Grenada, Barbados, St. Lucia, Dominica, the Virgin Islands, St. Vincent, Antigua,
Montserrat, St. Kitts, Nevis, Anguilla, Turks Islands, Cayman Islands,
the Bahamas, Belize, and Jamaica. The English language therefore has
an importance within the Caribbean region that far surpasses the pro-
portional weight of the population that habitually speaks it, and it
remains the model of formal-occasion speech even for Creole speakers.

An inescapable fact of life in the Caribbean is the coexistence
and intermingling of English and Creole. There is a constant diglossia
in most speakers, determined by social situations and the varied impressions that speakers might wish to communicate from one moment to the next. In this constant linguistic shifting, English remains
the code for signaling formality, social distance, greater importance
in the social hierarchy, education, intelligence, and other such impressions.

If, for theoretical purposes, we regard English and Creole as
discrete and different, each form of language shows the influence of
the other in the details of its form. LePage (1960), speaking of the
differences between Jamaican-English and English-English usage, classified the peculiarities of Jamaican usage as follows:

Words which have become obsolete in England.
Words used in a sense which has become obsolete in
England.
Borrowings from dialect, non-standard English.
Words adapted to a new sense in Jamaica.
Words whose pronunciation has been changed so radically
that they must be regarded as Jamaicanisms.
Words which may serve a greater number of grammatical
functions than in England — e.g., as transitive verbs used
only intransitively in England.

Malapropisms.
Compounds or iteratives formed on English stems, often
by analogy with Africanisms (LePage 1960: 119).

These categories of special characteristics, though originally formulated for Jamaica, may however be taken as descriptive of Caribbean
English as a whole, and we may add to them two further categories:

Words that have an African origin.
Phrases which are relexifications or calques of African
forms of expression.

These two further categories seem necessary as complements to those
of LePage in order to represent adequately the nature of the African
survivals in Caribbean English. Allsopp (e.g., 1958, 1972a, 1972b,
1976) has for many years been the most consistent researcher into
the latter survivals, and into the form and functions of what can be
regarded as Caribbean English. The major portion of his work on linguistic items that are acceptable as English to native Caribbean speakers but not similarly acceptable to other English speakers is planned
to result in a "Dictionary of Caribbean English Usage," currently in
progress. Further comment on African survivals will be made subsequently in relation to Allsopp's work.

The continued coexistence of Caribbean Creole and Caribbean
English provides the foundation for what must be regarded, apart
from items that would fall into one of the categories stated above,
as a salient characteristic of Caribbean English; viz., a tendency of
even the most highly educated speakers to produce occasional creolisms in morphology and syntax. This happens on even the most formal occasions and can be found in both speech and writing. It happens so frequently that there is justification for regarding it now as a
"standard" characteristic. Occasionally, however, these creolisms (as
well as other characteristics which, because of the existence of Creole,
are mistakenly identified as creolisms) are pointed out by linguistic
purists, though not often with the touch of political sarcasm that is
evident in the example below, which appeared in a Jamaican newspaper recently.

The Sunday Gleaner, June 18, 1978

SWEET and SOUR

... by Wormwood

• *Why "US"?*

Minister of Finance Eric Bell showed a disregard of the
rules of English grammar which used to be imparted at
schools some years ago, when he said "If we fail, it is not
us who fail, it is the country." Why not the expected "we"?
How did this objective, or accusative, case come into the
picture?

It is freely admitted that there are far more important
things to be done at the present time than follow what
may be arbitrary rules of grammar. Nevertheless, if one
begins to ignore these, the public may start asking, "Can
the Minister be trusted?"

The answer may be that each man is a law unto himself —
and that is exactly the point. Will they, particularly the
Minister, break moral laws as well?

A literary example of the pervasiveness of Creole influences
that is somewhat different from the preceding is cited by Ramchand
(1970: 43):

> West Indian writers, as speakers of WIS [West Indian
> Standard], are also speakers of dialect [i.e., Creole].
> A grammatical lapse which illustrates this in an acci-
> dental way is to be found in a short story *Afternoon in
> Trinidad* by Alfred H. Mendes. At one point in the story,
> Dodo a cab-man suspects that his woman Queenie has been
> two-timing him. "One night he *ask* Queenie about it and
> she denied it so convincingly that all he *could say was* that
> he had found it strange that she *was* on speaking terms
> with Corinne and Georgie." . . . Mendes' grammatical lapse
> "he *ask*" is made glaring by the correctness of his other
> verbs.

Ramchand's own English — the use of the terms *dialect, cab-
man* — betrays him as the West Indian that he is, but does so at the
level of lexis or idiom which will be referred to subsequently. The
example he cites, however, has to do with morphology and syntax. Since examples of the latter kind represent the sporadic in-
cursions of Creole grammar into Caribbean English, they will be
found spread over those aspects of English morphology and syntax that are contrastive with Creole: inflections of case and number in pronouns and nouns, tense and number inflections of verbs,
the ordering of tenses, the use of definite and indefinite articles,
negation, question forms, and other significant characteristics.

One such example from a popular Jamaican newspaper (*The*

Star, December 4, 1978) is shown here. The example had obviously passed the scrutiny of several educated persons before it appeared in print, and it caused no public comment after it appeared; rather, it successfully communicated an item of news that subsequently gave rise to some public discussion. In short, for many persons in the public at large it represents an accepted written standard. Yet, on close examination, it contains the following non-standard features: 1) absence of marking of plural and possessive in some nouns; 2) absence of the definite or indefinite article, as in *took part in class boycott;* 3) misuse of words, e.g., *exempting;* 4) peculiarities of usage, such as *permitted back to school, very angry of;* and 5) an avoidance of the possibilities of sequencing past, present-perfect, and past-perfect tenses (*were, have been, had been*).

Unlike the morphological and syntactic features, the lexical and idiomatic peculiarities of Caribbean English tend to pass completely unnoticed by native speakers, even when they attempt (as Ramchand did, above) to look critically at Caribbean language. Whereas morphology and syntax are describable by rules that become known to the layman through popular education, the same is not equally true of lexis and idiom. It comes as a shock when the Caribbean layman finds that his grammatically correct speech is sometimes misunderstood by non-Caribbean speakers of English.

STUDENTS SENT HOME

SAVANNA LA MAR

Dec. 1: (From our correspondent)

Fourth Formers at Savanna La Mar High School in Westmoreland were all sent home on Friday following a *STAR* report that they boycotted classes.

Reports are that the students in Fourth Form have been sent home since no one would tell the school the name or names of students who have reported the class boycott to the *STAR.*

Some students said that although they took part in class boycott they have no knowledge how the *STAR* got the report yet they have been sent home.

Some parents became very angry of the action of the school in sending home their children just because the newspapers carried a report of the students boycott and that a number of them as parents were planning to take legal actions against the Savanna la Mar High School for exempting their children from classes if students are not permitted back to school by today.

Another group of students said that up to that time no
one honestly knew how the story was leaked to the *STAR*,
but that the Fourth Formers had written a letter to the
School Board with a number of students' name signed to
it, asking the School Board to intervene as a result of the
problems they were facing at the school. However, before
this letter could get to the School Board it managed to get
in the hands of the Acting Principal, Miss G. Brown.

Some students said they were shamefully driven through
the gates of the school and the gate locked behind them.

One dominant influence on lexis and idiom is undoubtedly the
African substrate languages which underlie Caribbean Creole. This
influence has persisted, particularly with respect to idiom, not so
much by the survival of actual African words and phrases in either
Caribbean Creole or Caribbean English (although a considerable number of the latter exist); rather, it has persisted as a form of English
calquing on originally African forms of expression. Allsopp (1976),
examining the latter phenomenon, shows that many characteristic
phrases in Caribbean Creole which tend to be retained in phonologically more Anglicized forms in Caribbean English are directly
parallelled by idioms in West African languages. For example: *hard
ears,* adj. (persistently disobedient, stubborn); *to cut your eye* (make
a contemptuous gesture with the eye); *bad* (very much, very well);
a little more somebody would have + past participle (somebody was
on the point of —ing).

Allsopp points out, however, that a large number of other idioms are not parts of Internationally Received English but are parts
of Caribbean English; so far these seem to have no parallels in African languages. It could be that such parallels will be discovered
through further research on African languages; but it also seems possible that some of the missing parallels in Allsopp's list might be derivable from other sources.

An interesting indication favoring the latter possibility, which
conforms with the characteristics categorized by LePage (1960: 119)
and listed above, is to be seen in McLaughlin (1971). Using mainly *A
Scots Dialect Dictionary* by Alexander Warrack, McLaughlin compiled a list of Scottisms that appear in Jamaican Creole. His list is
reproduced below.

√ *again* (adv.) at another indefinite time DJE 1
√ *backtalk* (n.) sauciness
√ *back* (n.) back premises or yard
√ *baiss* (v.) beat or drub OED (baste v.3)

√ *batie* (adj.) round, plump DJE (bati the buttocks batie SND)
√ *before* (prep.) rather than DJE
  belly-god (n.) glutton DJE
√ *bit* (n.) a piece of money DJE
  black-strap (n.) molasses
√ *botheration* (n.) annoyance DJE
  breder (n.) brother DJE
√ *bruck* (v.) to break DJE
  buck (v.) butt DJE (which however connects it with US)
  bugaboo (n.) a hobgoblin DJE
√ *bust* (v.) beat DJE
  choyse (v.) choose DJE
  claut (n.) a blow
  crabbit (adj.) cross DJE
√ *craw* (n.) crop of a bird OED
  crud (n.) curd
√ *dead-house* (n.) mortuary
  difficil (adj.) reluctant
√ *dilly-dally* (v.) to spend time idly DJE
√ *dock* (v.) to cut the hair DJE
  eddikat (pl. adj.) educated
√ *erruction, ruction* (n.) a quarrel or disturbance
√ *facie* (adj.) insolent, impudent DJE
  fash (v.) to vex oneself
√ *for* (conj.) because
√ *gallivant* (v.) to gad about OED
  ganzey (n.) a jersey DJE
√ *gawlin* (n.) a sea bird
  gesning (n.) the reception of a guest
√ *gie* (v.) to give DJE
√ *gone* (adv.) ago, since CJE
√ *grudgeful* (adj.) unforgiving DJE
  gutsy (adj.) greedy
  g'wa (int.) an exclamation of surprise
√ *ha* (v.) have DJE
  habile (adj.) competent, liable (poss. the source of ably − DJE)
  haig (n.) a violent, ill-tempered woman
  higgle (v.) to argue DJE
  hallow-baloo (n.) an uproar OED
√ *hanky* (n.) a handkerchief
  hape (n.) a halfpenny
  hardfood (n.) dry victuals DJE

√ *heap* (n.) a great deal
Jack-and-the-lantern (n.) Will-o-the-wisp
√ *jag, jog,* (v.) pierce, prick with a sharp instrument (poss. infl.
   jook DJE)
larach (n.) a heap of ruins (prob. loroks DJE)
√ *lick* (v.) to strike DJE

Phrases:

√ betwixt and between
√ dead and gone
√ enquire for
√ like as
√ look in on
√ make off
√ put hand on
√ same-like

For the present discussion, McLaughlin's list of Scottisms is significant in two respects. First, although the list was compiled relative to Jamaica alone, it turns out that most of the items, those before which a tick (√) is placed, also to my knowledge occur in Guyanese and some other Eastern Caribbean Creoles. If McLaughlin is correct relative to Jamaica, then one must conclude that the influence of eighteenth- and nineteenth-century Scottish dialects is significantly present in the Creoles of the Eastern Caribbean as well. Even if (as McLaughlin herself admits) many of the items in the list are not confined to Scottish dialects but can be found in other British dialects as well, the important point is that these British dialectal peculiarities survive throughout the Caribbean.

Second, although the list was constructed solely with reference to Creole, all of its items have become parts of Standard Caribbean English, except for items such as *batie* (which would be regarded as vulgar or obscene), *breder, ha, gie* (which would be regarded as non-standard pronunciations), and *bruck* and *teeth* (which would be regarded as ungrammatical intrusions from Creole). Obviously these exceptions form a very small proportion of the list. Apparently in their formative years both Creole and Caribbean English must have come under the influence of the same external dialects. A listing of Scottish dialectal items more extensive and less tentative than McLaughlin's might provide more correspondences, especially where phrases and idioms are concerned.

The discussion here has been restricted to Scottish dialects, but there is no reason to assume that similar observations cannot be made in relation to other British dialects, including non-standard English ones, that might have been spoken during the past two centuries by British migrants to the Caribbean. The total picture is likely to be very complex, with several disparate influences interacting to produce the whole in any single Caribbean territory. When all territories, with their different patterns of settlement and population compositions, are taken into consideration, they constitute a rich research area that is practically untapped so far as Caribbean English (as distinct from Creole) is concerned.

The evidence so far has had to do with lexis and idiom, morphology and syntax. There is every indication that the situation with respect to phonology is just as complex, with influences from West Africa, Britain, and Europe interacting according to patterns of settlement and composition of population. For a simple understanding of the situation, it may perhaps be best to classify phonological characteristics into three theoretical types: 1) those characteristics that distinguish Caribbean English from Southern British RP; 2) those characteristics that distinguish between Caribbean national varieties; 3) the residue left when the other two types are specified. These comprise the characteristics common to Caribbean English and Southern British RP. To illustrate these three types of phonological characteristics, narrow transcriptions of Jamaican, Trinidadian, and Barbadian voices reading Aesop's fable "The North Wind and the Sun," and the RP transcription of this fable given in the *Principles* of the International Phonetic Association (1963), are shown below.

One variety of Southern British

²ð̥ə ³'nɔːθ ²'wɪnd ¹ɐnd ¹ð̥ə ²'sʌˤn ¹wə ¹dɪs²'pjuˑ¹tɪn ²'wɪtʃ ¹wɐz ¹ð̥ə ²'strɒˑŋ¹gɐ, ²wen ¹ɐ ²'traˑvᵊ³ɫɐ ²keˑm ¹ɐ²'lɒŋ ²'rapt ¹ɪn ¹ɐ ²'wɔːm ²'klɔːk. ²ð̥eˑ ²ɐ³'griːd ¹ð̥ɐt ¹ð̥ə ²'wɒn ³'hu ³'fəːst ¹sʌk²'siˑ²ded ¹ˑɪn ²'meːk²ʊŋ ²ð̥ə ²'trɐˑvᵊ¹lɐ ³'teːk ¹hɪz ³'klɔːk ²ɔːf ¹ʃɒd ¹bɪ ¹kʌˤn²'sɪd²ɐd ²strɒˑŋ¹gɐ ¹ð̥ɐn ¹dɪ ²'ɒð̥¹ɐ. ²'ð̥ɛn ¹ð̥ə ¹ˑnɔːθ ²'wɪnd ³'bluː ¹ɐz ²'haːd ¹ɐz ¹hɪ ²'kɒd, ¹bʌt ¹ð̥ə ²'mɔːʳ ¹hi ³bluː ¹ð̥ə ²mɔːʳ ¹ˑklɔːs²li ¹dɪd ¹ð̥ə ²'traˑvᵊ²ɫɐ ³'foːɫd ²hɪz ²'klɔːk ¹ɐ²'rɔɒŋd ¹hɪm; ¹ɐnd ¹ɐt ²⁻¹ˑlaːst ¹ð̥ə ¹ˑnɔːθ ˑwɪnd ²geːv ²ˑʌˤp ¹dɪ ¹ɐ²'tɛmpt. ³ð̥ɛn ²ð̥ə ³'sʌˤn ²'ʃɒn ²'ɔɒt ²'wɒːm¹li, ¹ɐnd ¹ɪ²'miːˑ³djeˤ²t²li ¹ð̥ə ²'trɐˑvᵊ²ɫɐ ³'tɒk ²'ɔːf ¹hɪz ²⁻¹ˑklɔːk. ¹ɐnd ³soː ¹ð̥ə ³'nɔːθ ²'wɪnd ¹wɐz ¹oˑ'blaɪdʒd ¹tɒ ¹kʌˤn²'fɛs ¹ð̥ɐt ¹ð̥ə ²'sʌˤn ¹wɐz ¹ð̥ə ²'strɒˑŋ¹gɐ ¹ɒv ð̥ə ²tuː.

(*Principles* of the International Phonetic Association 1963)

One variety of Jamaican

²ð̞ɪ ³'nɔrt ²'wɪnd ¹ɐn ¹ð̞ɪ ²'sʌn ¹wər ¹dɪs²'pju·¹tɪn ²'wɪtʃ ¹wɐz ¹ð̞ɪ
²'strɒŋ¹gɐ, ²wɛn ¹ɐ ²'trav¹lɐ ³kʲem ¹ɐ²'lɒŋ ²'rapt ¹ɪn ¹ɐ ²'wɔrm
²⁻³'klᵘo·k. ²ð̞ʲe· ²ɐ³'griːd ²ð̞ɐt ²ð̞ɪ ³wʌn ²hu ³'fʌrst ²sʌk¹'si·¹dɪd
²ɪn ²'mʲe·²kɪn ²ð̞ɪ ²'trav¹lɐ ³'tʲe·k ²hɪz ³'klᵘo·k ²ɒ·f ²ʃɒd
²bɪ ³kʌn²'sɪd¹ɐrd ²'strɒŋg¹ɐ ¹ð̞ɛn ¹ð̞ɪ ³'ɒð̞²ɐ. ²'ð̞ɛn ²ð̞ɪ ³'nɔrθ
²'wɪnd ²'bluː ¹ɐz ²'haʳd ²ɐz ²hi ²⁻¹'kɒd, ¹bʌt ¹ð̞ɪ ²'mo·r ³hi
²'bluː ¹ð̞ɪ ²'mo·r ²'klᵘo·s¹li ¹dɪd ¹ð̞ɪ ²'trav¹lɐ ²fᵘo·łd ²ɪz ²⁻¹'klᵘo·k
²ɐ²'rɔɔn ²⁻¹ɪm; ²ɐn ²ɐt ²⁻¹'laːs ¹ð̞ɪ ²'nɔ·ʳt ²'wɪn ¹gʲe·v ²'ʌp
¹ð̞ɪ ¹ɐ²'tɛmpt. ²ð̞ɛn ¹ð̞ɪ ²'sʌn ¹'ʃʌn ²'ʌɒt ²'wɒ·ʳm³li, ²ɐn
¹ʲ²'miː³dj²et²li ¹ð̞ɪ ²'trav²lɐ ³'tɒk ²'ɒ·f ¹ɪz ²⁻³'klᵘo·k. ¹ɐn ²sᵘo·
¹ð̞ɪ ³'nɔrt ²'wɪn ¹wɐz ¹ɐ²'blaɪdʒd ¹tɐ ²kʌn¹'fɛs ¹ð̞ɐt ¹ð̞ɪ ²'sʌn
¹wɐz ¹ð̞ɪ ²'strɒŋg¹ɐ ¹ʌv ²ð̞ɪ ²'tuː.

(RM/ /F/Jamaica)

One variety of Trinidadian

ðə 'nɔ·θ 'wɪnd ənd ðə 'sʌn wə dɪs'pju·tɪŋ 'wɪtʃ wəz ðə
'strɒŋgɐ, wɛn ə 'trævlɐ keɪm ə'lɒŋ 'ræpt ɪn ə 'wɔːm 'klɒɒk.
ðeɪ ə'griːd ðət ðə 'wʌn hu· 'fɜːst sək'sɪ·dɪd ɪn 'meɪkɪŋ ðə
'trævlɐ 'teɪk hɪz 'klɒɒk ɒf ʃɒd bɪ kən'sɪdəd 'strɒŋgə ðən ð̞ɪ
'ʌð̞ə. 'ð̞ɛn ð̞ə 'nɔ·θ 'wɪnd 'bluː əz 'haːd əz i· 'kɒd, bət ð̞ə 'mɔː
hi· 'bluː ð̞ə 'mɔː 'klɒɒslɪ dɪd ð̞ə 'trævlɐ 'foːłd hɪz 'klɒɒk
əraɒnd hɪm; ənd ət 'la·st ð̞ə 'nɔ·θ 'wɪnd 'geɪv 'ʌp ð̞ɪ ə'tɛmpt.
'ð̞ɛn ð̞ə 'sʌn 'ʃɒn 'aɒt 'wɔːmlɪ, ənd ɪ'mi·djətlɪ ð̞ə 'trævlɐ 'tɒk
'ɒf hɪz 'klɒɒk. ənd 'sɒɒ ð̞ə 'nɔ·θ 'wɪnd wəz ə'blaɪdʒd tə
kən'fɛs ð̞ət ð̞ə 'sʌn wəz ð̞ə 'strɒŋgər əv ð̞ə 'tuː.
file 20

(EM/28/F/Trinidad)[1]

One variety of Barbadian

¹də ²'nɔrθ ³wɪnd ¹ɐ̞n ¹də ²'sʌn ¹wʌʳ ¹dɪs²'pju·¹tɪn ²'wɪtʃ ¹wʌz ¹zə
²'strɔŋ¹gʌ, ²wɛn ¹ʌ ³'trav³łʌ ²kɐ̞ːm ¹ɐ²'lɒŋ ²'rapt ¹ɪn ¹ʌ ²'wɔrm
²⁻¹'klɒːk. ²de· ²ʌ⁴'griːd ²dɐ̞t ²də ²'fʌ̣rs ²huː ¹sʌk²'si·²dɪd ¹ɪn
²'mɐ̞ːʳkɪn ¹də ²'trav²łʌ ²'tɐ̞ːk ²hɪz ³'klɒːk ²ɔ·f ¹ʃɒd ¹bɪ
¹kʌn²'sɪd²ʌʳd ²'strɔŋ²gʌ ¹dən ¹ð̞ɪ ³'ɔ²dʌ. ⁴'dɛn ²də ²nɔrθ ³'wɪnd
²'bluː ¹ʌz ²'haɽd ²ʌz ²hi ²⁻¹'kɒd, ¹bʌt ¹də ²'mɔːr ³hi ⁴'bluː ¹də
²mɔːr ²'klɔːs²li ¹dɪd ¹ð̞ə ²'trav²łʌ ²foːłd ¹hɪz ²klɔːk ²'rʌɒnd
¹hɪm; ²ɐ̞n ²ɐ̞t ³'laːs ¹də ²'nɔrθ ²'wɪn ¹gɐ̞ːv ²'ʌp ¹dɪ ¹ə²'tɛmp.
³dɛn ¹dɪ ²'sʌn ¹'ʃʌn ²'ʌɒt ²'wɔrm¹li, ²ɐ̞n ¹ʲ²'miː²dj²ɐ̞t²li ¹dɪ
²'trav²łʌ ¹'tɒk ²ɔ·f ¹hɪz ²⁻¹klɔːk. ¹ɐ̞n ²sɔː ¹ð̞ə ²'nɔrθ ²'wɪnd
¹wʌz ¹ʌ³'blɔɪdʒ ¹tʌ ²kʌn¹'fɛs ¹ð̞ɐ̞t ¹də ²'sʌn ¹wʌz ¹zə ²'strɔŋ²gʌ
¹ʌv ²ð̞ə ²⁻¹'tuː.

(JG/31/F/Barbados)

Pitch or tone is indicated only for the Caribbean examples. In addition, the fact that the examples represent the reading styles of speakers in declarative sentences means that the full range of tones and characteristic contours normally perceptible in Caribbean conversation (illustrated in, e.g., Allsopp 1972a) are not present.

The examples indicate that patterns of stress do not differentiate significantly between British and Caribbean English. Pitch or tone distinguishes significantly between the two, however, although in the cited example the characteristic pitch contours of RP are not available to make this clear. There is a broad general similarity between RP and Caribbean varieties in the pronunciation of consonants, except that many Caribbean speakers, including those cited here, are likely to demonstrate some variation caused by the influence of Creole phonology in consonants:

RP	Caribbean variations	
/θ/	/t, θ̠/	(disappearance of
/ð/	/d, ð̠, z/	last element in all
/st, nd . . ./	/s, n.../̄	consonant blends)

Regarding the pronunciation of vowels, there seem to be features that differentiate each of the four varieties. Some other vowel features, however, differentiate between RP on the one hand and all Caribbean varieties taken together on the other, because the latter features tend to be present in RP but absent from all Caribbean varieties. Among the latter features, these are probably the most significant:

RP	Tendency in most Caribbean English	
/eɪ/	/e/	(came, take, gave)
/oʊ/	/oː/	(cloak, fold, so)
/æ/	/a/	(traveler)

The other mentioned vowel features, those that differentiate between Caribbean varieties as well as between the latter and RP, can be verified from the transcriptions. Jamaican speech tends to have back vowels lower, and low front and central vowels more retracted than those of other varieties; there is also a tendency to precede lengthened mid-front or mid-back vowels by a glide from a respectively high front or back vowel. English speakers in Trinidad have a tendency toward absence of post-vocalic /r/, and a tendency toward more rounded forms of low- and mid-back vowels than speakers of other varieties. Those from Barbados tend to have very close forms of most vowels, resulting in a general nasalization and velarization not found in other varieties. Caribbean varieties other than the Jamaican, Trinidadian, and Barbadian seem to contain varying blends of the distinctive features seen in these three.

The preceding outline can do no more than indicate the presence of a largely untapped research area. Since the early 1960's, when the more developed Caribbean territories became independent nations, there have undoubtedly been increasing influences that cannot but contribute toward the stabilization of distinctive regional varieties of English. The folk traditions and Creole language which were repressed in a former era now tend to be recognized and preserved as valuable aspects of the national heritage in specific territories; because of this fact, their continuing future influence tends to be assured. At the same time, however, the continuous expansion of educational opportunity and the accompanying social development mean that the use of standard national varieties of English is becoming more widespread. These varieties are now permitted to develop with less hindrance than ever before from former colonial inhibitions. It is important that such a development be recorded, but to date it still remains less studied than Creole language itself.

NOTE

1. I am indebted to Pauline Christie for checking the transcriptions of the Jamaican and Trinidadian versions of the Aesop fable.

REFERENCES

Allsopp, S. R. 1958. The English language in British Guiana. *English Language Teaching* 12(2): 59-66.

———. 1972a. Some suprasegmental features of Caribbean English. Papers from the Conference on Creole Languages and Educational Development. Paris: UNESCO.

———. 1972b. Problems of acceptability in Caribbean creolized English. Mimeo. Barbados: University of the West Indies.

———. 1976. Africanisms in the idiom of Caribbean English. Papers from the Seventh International Conference on African Linguistics, University of Florida, Gainesville.

LePage, R. B. 1960. An historical introduction to Jamaican creole. In *Jamaican Creole*, ed. R. B. LePage and D. DeCamp. London: Macmillan.

McLaughlin, J. 1971. Jamaican creole — influence of Scottish dialect. Mimeo. Jamaica: University of the West Indies.

Ramchand, Kenneth. 1970. *The West Indian novel and its background.* New York: Barnes and Noble.

13
Caribbean English: Form and Function

LILITH M. HAYNES

In announcing his nation's refusal to assume responsibility for the "small islands" when Jamaica opted out of the short-lived ten-member Federation of the West Indies, the Prime Minister of Trinidad and Tobago — two islands which comprise 1,980 square miles — articulated a position that was readily accepted throughout the Caribbean: "One from ten leaves nought."

Caribbean society was constructed out of European, African, Asian, and the indigenous American societies during the last four centuries, primarily for the production of sugar. We have little evidence that democratic relationships obtained among those participating in slavery and indenture, and the coming of political independence to most territories in the area has not radically altered its bittersweet history. Then, as now, the survival of racial and ethnic groups and the creation of new identities has depended upon the ability of the Caribbean to cater to the whims and hopes of the sugar buyers, to interweave the European with the intrinsic.

The subject of Caribbean English dances, as does much of Caribbean life, along the fine line between jest and seriousness. One from ten leaves . . . not nought, but nine; nine separate individuals. Individuality sits easily with the Caribbean person, who is descended from people sent or recruited to this New World largely because of their individual characteristics. The encouragement of individual expression within and across these small societies does not permit the forms and functions of Caribbean English to fit the schemas defined for other societies, as we shall see below.

It is true that non-verbal Caribbean communication exists; most of us have been admonished by our elders not to *look* at them in *that tone* of voice, or to hurry up and take our arms from their akimbo position, if we wished to avoid dire corporal consequences. Nor is walking while lost in thought recommended in the Caribbean if one wants to keep one's friends: greetings may be exchanged, even with people who are inside their houses, by those passing on the street. George Lamming, the Barbadian writer, has said of himself: "so I made a heaven of noise, which is characteristic of my voice, and an ingredient of West Indian behaviour" (1960: 62). We talk a lot, and we like to talk; but, as Reisman has noted for Antiguans, "to have something to say that is worth hearing and also repeatable implies that it is fairly short, and as a result, there is a process of condensation and allusion at work all the time. One is expected in many contexts to 'catch' the meaning. And conversely there is a feeling that undue explicitness implies a dull person" (1972: 22). The uses to which we put speech and writing in the Caribbean tend to interact, moreover, so that Caribbean English on the international scene often has a standard surface manifestation, but is nonetheless misunderstood. In the sections which follow, I characterize the particularity that is English in the Caribbean by examining a Guyanese patriotic song, Jamaican oral literature, a Trinidadian/Grenadian calypso, an excerpt from the writing of a second-generation American, comments about Antiguans, and some results of field research which I conducted in Barbados and Guyana in 1972.

Caribbean Attitudes toward Caribbean English

Writing about Louise Bennett's Jamaican oral literature, Lucille Mair has pointed out that

Miss Mary Dry-Foot Bwoy is pulled up sharply for the affected accent he brings back with him from abroad, and the community mounts a campaign of ridicule to bring him back into line. But just as real is the disappointment with the son who returns unchanged from his American stay — "and you come back not a piece better than how yuh did goh wey? . . . not even lickle language bwoy? not even lickle twang?" [1969: 8]

This recognition of the validity and identity of Jamaican English was echoed by the Barbadians and Guyanese, who, when asked in 1972 to rate their own English vis-à-vis that of Britain, other West Indian territories, and other countries, indicated that their respective local varieties were about the best. Table 1 outlines the nature of these responses.

When asked whether they could understand these varieties of English, the same respondents exhibited some interesting patterns. A greater percentage of Barbadians than of Guyanese claimed that they always understood Guyanese English, whereas no Barbadians recorded instances in which they had failed to understand their compatriots. Both groups claimed that they understood British English only about half of the time — and sometimes never, as Table 2 shows.

Table 1. Ranking of Best English Varieties

Best Variety	Respondent's Nationality		Total
	Barbadian (N=77)	Guyanese (N=54)	(%)
Own Country	19.5	16.1	35.6
Other West Indian	5.9	0.8	6.7
Great Britain	21.2	10.2	31.4
Other Country	1.7	3.4	5.1
None	12.7	8.5	21.2

Table 2. Intelligibility of Varieties of English

Variety		Respondent's Nationality				
	Barbadian			Guyanese		
	Always	Some-times	Never	Always	Some-times	Never
Barbadian	80.0	20.0	0.0	45.1	51.0	3.9
Guyanese	73.2	23.2	6.6	62.2	35.3	2.0
Other West Indian	23.6	63.9	12.5	43.1	54.9	2.8
British	51.4	47.2	1.4	39.2	58.8	2.0

Table 3. Perceived Geographical Variation in Local Speech

Variation	Respondent's Nationality	
	Barbadian	Guyanese
None	20.0	52.9
1 Distinction	42.7	45.1
2 Distinctions	20.0	2.0
3+ Distinctions	17.3	0.0
S.D. .938		

Table 3 illustrates the greater extent to which Barbadians (who live on an island of 166 square miles) defined geographical variations in their language behavior than did the Guyanese (whose country covers 83,000 square miles).

Paul Layne's university student, whose reply to an examination question concerning the need for a dictionary of Caribbean English revolved around its usefulness in *facilitating tourists* (1972: 31), articulates the stance of those people in the Caribbean who revere or (think that they) speak Educated Southern British English. Many people never give a thought to their language behavior unless they are requested to do so; on such occasions they have identified their language behavior as /brɔkɔp/ or "lacking in language," as Reisman notes for Antigua, or have said that there are "natural" and "proper" varieties, as my research has found. Few people in those territories where English is the official language would say that English is a language which is unknown, or that their language behavior is non-English. However, the relationship between the varieties ascribed to discrete contexts and the actual use of those varieties' formal features in those respective contexts is not symmetrical. For example, Guyanese reported that "natural" speech was appropriate in peer-group or all interactions, or else in expressing anger or ensuring comprehension by subordinates; Barbadians, on the other hand, were evenly divided into two groups, with some feeling that there were no contexts for the use of "natural" speech, and others defining it for use in peer-group interactions. More Barbadians than Guyanese felt that "proper" speech was appropriate in all contexts, and fewer Barbadians than Guyanese felt that there were no contexts for "proper" speech. Guyanese were more inclined to define "proper" speech as the variety to be used with elders and strangers, as Table 4 demonstrates.

Table 4. Contexts for Natural and Proper Speech

Register	Context	Respondent's Nationality	
		Barbadian	Guyanese
Natural	All	8.0	14.5
	Peer group	28.0	41.7
	Special*	25.3	18.8
	None	38.7	25.0
Proper	All	56.0	34.7
	Children	9.3	12.2
	Special**	26.7	40.8
	None	8.0	12.2

*Anger, comprehension by subordinates
**Elders, strangers

Table 5 shows that when these same respondents were asked to identify and explain their own language use during the interview, two-thirds of those who claimed that their interview speech had been "natural" felt that this was their habitual code in this context. The rest reported that this behavior represented an unsuccessful attempt to use "proper" speech. On the other hand, most of those who

Table 5. Self-Report of Interview Speech

| | Respondent's Nationality | | |
Self-Report	Barbadian (N)	Guyanese (N)	Row Total
Natural = Habitual	28.8 (21)	23.4 (11)	26.7 (32)
Natural = Unsuccessful	13.7 (10)	4.3 (2)	10.0 (12)
Proper = Habitual	39.7 (29)	40.4 (19)	40.0 (48)
Proper = Careful	17.8 (13)	31.9 (15)	23.3 (28)

thought that their interview speech had been "proper" claimed that this was the result of habit, and large numbers also felt that they had succeeded in a conscious attempt to use "proper" speech. Indeed, only a third of the respondents would have defined the interview as a context for "natural" speech.

Caribbean English Usage

Syntax

The interaction of "natural" and "proper" formal features in one context is exemplified in the assertion of the Antiguan villager cited by Reisman: "I have some pear trees and when those pears are bearing there is nothing I like more than pear. My mouth water for pear. But when my trees finish bearing, my mind not pan pear — done with that" (1970: 133-34). The calypso which follows illustrates another format for the interaction of the syntactic elements of English in the Caribbean, as it is realized by The Mighty Sparrow:

Stanza 1

/huz di gretIs krIkItʌr ɔn ʌrt ɔr maz? ɛniwɔn kan tɛl ju Its di
gret sʌr garfild sobaz.
ðIs hansʊm babeJʌn lad rɛli noz hIz wərk, batIn ɔr bolIn hiz
dʌ krIkIt kIŋ no Jok! cri čers fɔr kyaptIn sobʌz!
wIn or luz ði spɛktetʌz ar ɔlwez pliz wIt dI gretIs tim ɔn ʌrt,
hu ɛls bʌt di wɛst Indiz?
mɛn laik bʊča, Jo solomɔn kanai an devIs an nʌrs an
roJrigɛz kɔnrad hʌnt an wait, gIbz an dI wIkIt kipʌ
henJrIks./

Chorus

/ɔstreliʌ ju lɔs, di wɛst Indiz Iz bɔs, di črofi bilɔŋ tu ʌs, a se ju
lɔs, an ju no ju lɔ̄s, faiʌ (Chorus 2—/bol/), (Chorus 3—/fə
bān/) ! ɔstreliʌ spik ju main, ɔstreliʌ don main,
ju lɔs, betʌ lʌk nɛks taim./

Stanza 2

/dɛm ɔstreliʌn Jokʌz sen dʌŋ kraš hɛlmIt tu protɛk de
batsmen frʌm hɔl an čarli grIfIt,
ai fɛlt so sɔri fɔr sImsən, hi čraid bʌt In ven, wIt grIfIt an hɔl
wIkIt star təfɔl laik ren,
cri čers fʌ hɔl an grIfIt!
onil wɛnt ɔstreliʌ mekIn bIg raiʌt, wɛn i wʊz fesIn grIfIt an
hɔl hi so blumIn kwaiʌt!
wɛn onil mit ril fas bolIn Iz tʊ si hIm dʌkIn, an dɛn di vɛri gai
telin so mʌč lai tɛlIn dʌ wʌrl hau grIfIt čʌkIn!/

Stanza 3

/frʌm di taim di siriz start In Jāmeka, wi pruv ðat ɔstreliʌ
wʌz strɔŋ, bʌt onli ɔn pepʌ,
di fort tɛs In barbedoz ðe fʊl di skorboᵊd, bʌ rohan an simor
kyari ʌp wi skoᵊ, o lɔd! cri čers fɔr nʌrs an kanai!
spešəl prez tʊ knrad hʌnt ʌʊa opəna, braiʌn devIs, sɔlomɔn,
lans gIbz, henJrIks an bazIl bʊča,
ɔl di bɔiz fɔt galʌntli ʌndʌ sobəz kyaptInsi, so hIp Ip Ip ure,
hIp Ip Ip ure, fɔr ʌ gloriʌs vIktori!/

Sparrow begins with a Standard English *wh-* question, and uses standard syntax throughout the first stanza. However, as we go through
the chorus and second stanza, we begin to encounter syntactic variations such as:

/di črofi bilɔŋ tu ʌs/

/dɛm ɔstreliʌn Jokʌz sen dʌŋ kraš hɛlmIt tu protɛk de
batsmen frʌm hɔl.../

/onil wɛnt ɔstreliʌ mekIn bIg raiʌt/

/wɛn onil mit ril fas bolIn Iz tʊ si hIm dʌkIn an dɛn di vɛri gai
telin so mʌč lai, tɛlIn dʌ wʌrl hau grIfIt čʌkIn/

Stanza 3 begins with similar variations, and gradually returns to standard forms, as in:

/frʌm di taim di siriz start in Jāmeka/

/di fort tɛs In barbedoz ðe fʊl di skorboᵊd/

followed by

/ɔl di bɔiz fɔt galʌntli ʌndʌ sobəz kyaptInsi so hIp Ip Ip ure,
hIp Ip Ip ure, fɔr ʌ gloriʌs vIktori/

In short, the deviant or "natural" is *framed* by the standard or "proper."

Phonology

Although the lexicon of the calypso above is clearly English — and indeed concerns that most English of games, which has been adopted enthusiastically by the Caribbean — the sounds informing these features are less so. Those sounds can affect the texture of the syntax, simultaneously marking the speaker's national identity, as in /māz/ (which may be compared with the findings in Table 6, below), -ed, -s, -t → ∅ #. The score of this calypso is unmistakably Caribbean in its syncopated rhythm, and in its use of treble notes when Sparrow wishes to emphasize his point.

In this set of societies which continually equilibrates clowning and seriousness, the role of stigma is particularly interesting. Stigmatized elements of the sound system exist, as do stigmatized elements in the lexical and syntactic systems, although these latter are more easily distinguished and penalized by linguistic and other authorities. Table 6 shows that the palatalization of /k/ and /g/, and the strong

Table 6. Stigmatized Phonological Variants

Stigmatized Variant	Respondent's Nationality		
	Barbadian (*N*)	Guyanese (*N*)	Row Total (*N*)
/kiaɾ/	70.2 (33)	29.8 (14)	42.3 (47)
/kiač/	81.4 (35)	18.6 (8)	39.4 (43)
/giaɾaj/	100.0 (2)	0.0 (0)	1.9 (2)
/baɾbediʌnz/	57.8 (59)	42.2 (43)	93.6 (102)
/kaɾ/	56.0 (61)	44.0 (48)	99.1 (109)
/səɾpɾaizd/	40.0 (2)	60.0 (3)	4.5 (5)
/ʌndʌɾ/	71.1 (37)	22.9 (11)	43.6 (48)
/tʌɾnamɛnt/	100.0 (5)	0.0 (0)	4.5 (5)
/gaɾaj̆/	50.0 (8)	50.0 (8)	14.5 (16)
/idɪf/	94.3 (33)	5.7 (2)	31.8 (35)
/idɪt/	0.0 (0)	100.0 (16)	14.5 (16)
/kõvᴧ̃/, /kanvɛnt/	68.4 (13)	31.6 (6)	17.4 (19)
/bəeⁱg/	100.0 (52)	0.0 (0)	46.4 (52)
/həeⁱŋ/	88.2 (30)	11.8 (4)	30.4 (34)
/bɔi/	100.0 (4)	0.0 (0)	3.6 (4)
/lɔik/	100.0 (3)	0.0 (0)	2.7 (3)
/səɾpɾɔizd/	100.0 (4)	0.0 (0)	3.6 (4)
/kɔmbɔind/	100.0 (4)	0.0 (0)	3.7 (4)
/ɔiləndz/	100.0 (6)	0.0 (0)	5.4 (6)
/nɔintin/	100.0 (7)	0.0 (0)	6.4 (7)

articulation of /r/ — which are stereotypified for Barbadians and Guyanese — are variously treated by respondents, but that greater uni-
formity exists for the Barbadian stigmata / θ / → /f/.

The oral literature of Louise Bennett has recently been taken to
the British public. While most of the forms she uses qualify as items
of English lexicon, the syntax she uses is more particularly Northern
Caribbean; but the *sounds* of Bennett, delivered in rapid speech,
would cause a Britisher to think he was not listening to an English-
speaker, as the following extract shows. Here, as in the Sparrow
calypso, the artist uses "natural" and "proper" elements interchangeably; she also varies pronunciations of the same item.

/a tIŋ hapən tə mai anti roči di ɔdʌ de dat fraitən ar sə tIl It
kɔ̄z di por ʊman fi start bʌs ar bren sɛ ši a stʌdi latən. latən.
tɛk ʌp latən stʌdIz In ar old eǰ—dat hard, fɔr plɛnti jʌŋ
smadi hu fʌ bren stIl plaiʌbəl a fain It hard fə mɛk latən
laŋwIǰ wId al dI amus an dI Ibus an di umvum an di sia an āl
dɛm tIŋ sIŋk In a dɛm brenz! mʌč mor fI mI por anti roči
hu fʊ mentalIti mʌs gɔt ʌ lIkəl ǰʌnǰʌ gro pʌn It bai nʌu! hɔi!
hausəmevʌ azkɔrdən tə anti roči ši stʌdi ʌp latən sə dat no
ɔrdIneri pjāpjā sIntIŋ wʊn ebəl ti ful ar ʌp agen laik di her
rʌbIn wɛ ši dId a gʌbai di ɔdʌ de bika šI sI It mɔrk kɔkɔs
njusifera, hei hei, wId aliʊm fabivum, hI hei, wat a wʌriz!

di hol tIŋ start bikaz wɔn aᴧ herdresʌr nis dɛm ɔv mai anti
roči gʌ ǰam sIzaz In anti roči hɛd wan fʊl mun taim kʌt af ar
her ɛn dɛm sʌ se dat fʊl mun klIpIns wIl mɛk dI her gro tIk.
bʌdI sIzʌz stʌntId dI her an It wʊda nidʌ di nɔr dʌu, nidʌ
gro tIk nɔr tIn. In fak It wʊdən gro atāl atāl an It ǰʌs
dImInIš. sʌ anti roči wʌz a izi vIktIm wɛn dI sem herdresʌ
nis bwɔifren kʌm a di jārd wId a grIp fʊl av farIn her groIn
rʌbIn an se dat mina sɛl dem. wel dI fʌs ǰar a rʌbIn dat Im
tɛk ʌut a dI grIp dId mark am rIsInus kamInus, bʌt anti roči
riǰek dat wan an ši se It sɔun laik kɔmjunIs an kamInIs brid
kamInIzIm an ši nɔt ebəl fɔ go start gro na kamInIzIm In
ar hɛd bikazan se dat ši her bɔut di hol ip ʌ pipəl hu da fli
fram kamjunIzʌm āl ovʌ dI wʌrl an ši wʊdan laik fI ar lIkəl
čenks a her fI go fli aut ar hɛd, In total baldnIs, jə no wat a
min, so ši nʌ ebəl fI dat ətal. sʊ ši pIk ʌp anada ǰar a her
groIn mark kɔkɔs njusifera wId aljum fapivum dās di wan a
tɛl ju baut alrɛdi.../

As shown in Figures 1-4, where a higher score represents less deviation from the Standard English norm, phonological and syntactic deviation varied widely with the ethnic, geographical, and educational
groupings, as well as among respondents who had undertaken much
or little foreign travel.

Figure 1. Mean Variation in Language Behavior by Ethnic Group

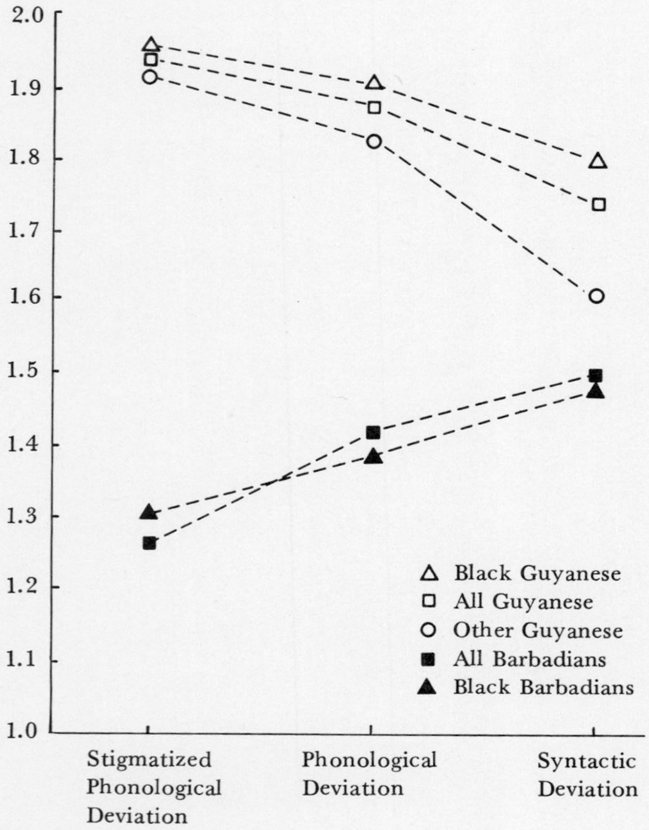

Figure 2. Mean Variation in Language Behavior by Geographical Location

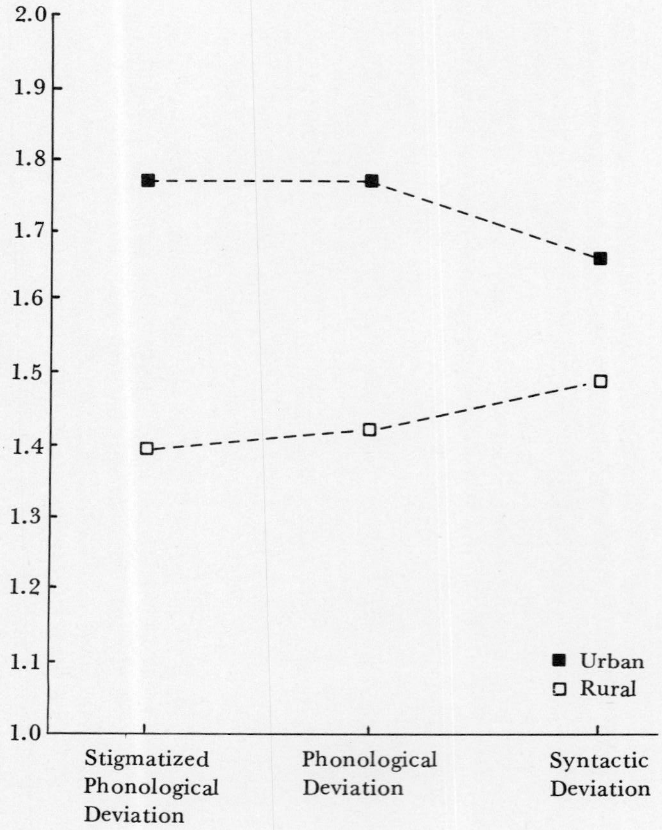

Figure 3. Mean Variation in Language Behavior
by Educational Achievement

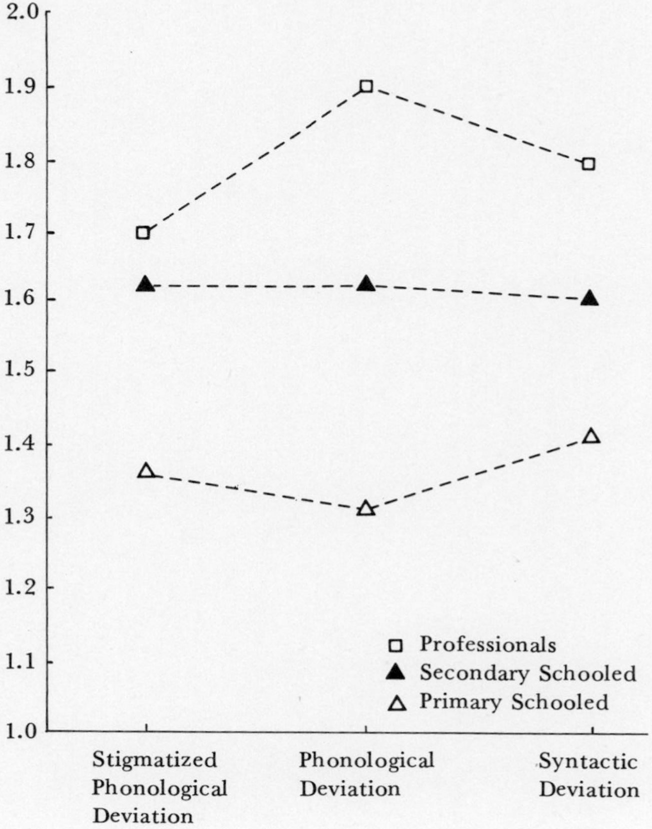

Figure 4. Mean Variation in Language Behavior
by Foreign Travel

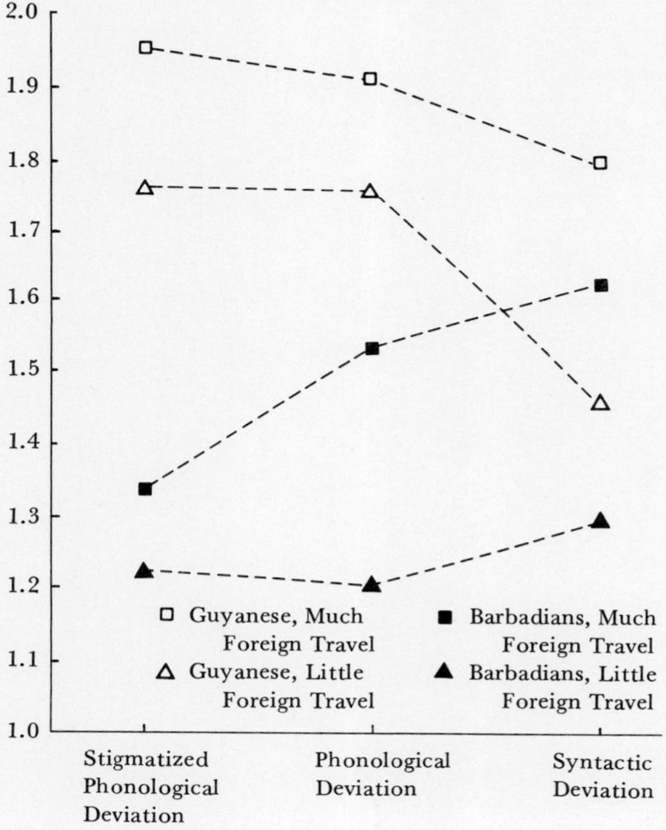

Words and Meanings

An example of what Guyanese children have been doing for decades to a patriotic song indicates how the Caribbean society plays with lexical elements. The song's first stanza and chorus are in Standard English, but with straight faces and lusty voices, accompanied by the Police Force Band on formal occasions (such as those in honor of visiting British royalty), Guyanese children respond with the teasing alternative chorus, whose linguistic elements flirt with Standard English syntax and phonology.

Stanza 1

Born in the land of the mighty Roraima,
Land of great rivers and far-stretching sea;
So like the mountain, the sea, and the river,
Great, wide, and deep in our lives should we be.

Chorus

Onward, upward, may we ever go,
Day by day in strength and beauty grow,
Till at length we, each of us, may show
What Guyana's sons and daughters can be.

Alternative Chorus

Onward, upward, Mary had a goat,
Day by day she tied it with a rope,
Till at lengt' de goat bus' de rope,
And Miss Mary had to run behind it.

At an official university level, in accepting an abstract for a conference, the faculty member feels free to end his letter thus: "I hope to hear from you as soon as possible and I also hope that you will help to make the Conference as uncomplicated and successful as possible" (Roberts 1978: 1). In my written contacts with Americans, English and other Europeans, and Africans, I have found that this type of statement is usually taken to be sharp or insulting; for the Caribbean person, it is merely a statement. That this is taught to children of Caribbean descent even in environments outside the Caribbean is suggested by the following excerpt from *Essence* magazine about the late Geoffrey Cambridge, a black American actor whose parents were Guyanese. In America, this is an angry piece of writing, but to the Caribbean person it is a statement, with no excess emotional baggage:

Nobody played at my father's funeral. Do you know that he was a skilled book-keeper who came to the land of the free and the home of the brave because he really believed America would welcome him with open arms? Well, America *welcomed* him all right, as a ditchdigger for Con Edison. Later he worked his way up to unloading hundred-pound sacks for a food company which so generously sent a ten-dollar tax-deductible bouquet of flowers to the funeral home when his heart gave out. But he did better than my mother. She wasn't as lucky although she was every bit as stupid. A dummy. She came with my father from Canada, wide-eyed, fully expecting America to honor her teaching certificate and years of South American teaching experience. Of course they didn't. But my mama, her dumbness knew no bounds. She kept taking the civil-service exam until some *kind* white civil-service employer clued her in. And even then she couldn't believe that this country would deny jobs to someone because of her color. My mama was some kind of weirdo. She insisted I learn such *wild* things as reading, writing, and arithmetic. She even sent me to Canada to make sure my education would be a proper one. And later when I earned a scholarship to Hofstra College and continued my studies at the City College of New York, that woman's eyes were so proud. But she was dumb. She continued to believe in this country even though it had reduced her to operating sewing machines ten hours a day in some grimy sweatshop. She died on her job, and her employers sent a tax-deductible *sympathy* card. So much for my mother. . . . My parents were Guyanese. We don't scream. We are very proud people. . . . Maybe I've demanded too much, been too insistent. I know I'm intolerant, which is pretty funny for a Black Man, but I cannot tolerate stupidity, dishonesty, and weakness. My parents taught me to hate all three as a child. [*Essence*, October 1975: 51]

At a less public level, Reisman's Antiguan anecdote is also illustrative of English functioning distinctively in the Caribbean: ". . . a strong man in his twenties was sitting on a back step bent over with stomach pains; a girl came up to him and asked with no sympathy at all, 'You sick?' I asked her if she didn't have any sympathy with his pain, to which she answered 'mi want im fu ded!' — I want him to die!" (1972: 17). What she was really saying, of course, was, "Stop making a spectacle of yourself!"

In Caribbean English, meanings for words are not always shared within and across territories: when asked to provide glosses for eleven

words in 1972, respondents in Barbados and Guyana provided the
widely varying results shown in Table 7. Sometimes the gloss represented an attempt to impose a familiar meaning on an unfamiliar
sound (as in *cocoa* for *koker,* or *Guinness* for *genip*), but usually the
words were known to refer to concepts that were quite different.
Whether these words are acceptable as English is yet another point;
my College Edition of the *Random House Dictionary,* for example,
lists only *Old Harry, fast,* and *gypsy,* but the other words — *koker,
akee, bakoo, bram, duppy, ning-ning, quarter-bus,* and *genip,* and
particularly those most identified with Barbados — would also strike
the Caribbean person as English words; some are usually found in official public contexts, as well as in informal private situations, and
their structures do not greatly violate the rules of English morphology. The extent to which they are known, as measured by the numbers of respondents who provided glosses, shows that while *gypsy*
and *fast* are the most widely known, items which do *not* appear in
the dictionary occupy the third to eighth slots, with *quarter-bus*
identified by only 22 per cent of the sample population.

Dialectic

Inter alia, the above sections have characterized English in the
Caribbean as an entity with various identifiable aspects. 1) Varieties
may be identified with discrete geographical locations — such as
Jamaica, Antigua, Grenada, Barbados, and Guyana — each of which
may be considered the best variety by its native speakers, and which
may be variously understandable within and across the different territories. 2) Registers, such as "proper" and "natural," might be ascribed to all contexts of language behavior; their syntactic, lexical,
and phonological elements are seen to co-occur in the same stream of
speech — as in the calypso, the selections from Antigua, and the extract of oral literature cited above. 3) Styles of use are misunderstood
by non-native readers or listeners, as in the examples of the writing
of a university professor and a second-generation American actor,
and the speech of an Antiguan girl. 4) Some words — such as *pyapya*
(inconsequential), *junju* (fungus), *bakoo* (ghost), or *gypsy* (adj., in-
quisitive) — are not recorded in dictionaries of English. Others are
rendered with sounds which are not readily recognizable as English —
/smadi/ (plural of *somebody*), /hausəmɛvʌ/ (however), /hufʌ/ (whose),
/sIntIŋ/ (something), /ar/ (her), — used concurrently with words
known by proficient users of English — *pliable, victim, reject, stunted,
mentality.* 5) Idioms — such as /It wʊda nida di nɔr dʌu/ (It would

Table 7. Sharing of Lexical Values by Respondent's Degree of Foreign Travel
(N=131)

Lexical Value	Barbados		Guyana		Row Total	Word Total
	Little Travel (N)	Much Travel (N)	Little Travel (N)	Much Travel (N)		
Koker (G)						
— sluice gate (G)	0.0 (0)	10.0 (1)	27.1 (13)	72.9 (35)	37.4 (49)	43.5 (57)
— cocoa (E)	70.0 (7)	20.0 (1)	0.0 (0)	0.0 (0)	6.1 (8)	
Akee (U)						
— Melicoccus (B)	50.7 (37)	20.5 (15)	2.6 (1)	17.9 (7)	45.8 (60)	85.4 (112)
— Melicoccus + Blighia (J)	2.7 (2)	26.0 (19)	5.1 (2)	15.4 (6)	22.1 (29)	
— Blighia (J)	0.0 (0)	0.0 (0)	7.7 (3)	51.3 (20)	17.5 (23)	
Bakoo (G)						
— man in bottle[1] (G)	0.0 (0)	12.0 (3)	4.3 (2)	19.6 (9)	9.1 (12)	52.6 (69)
— little man	12.0 (3)	16.0 (4)	6.5 (3)	19.6 (9)	14.5 (19)	
— obeah thing	32.0 (8)	28.0 (7)	17.4 (8)	32.6 (15)	29.0 (38)	
Bram (U)						
— lower-class fete (B)	20.8 (10)	22.9 (11)	5.4 (2)	29.7 (11)	25.9 (34)	64.6 (85)
— successful fete	6.3 (3)	16.7 (8)	5.4 (2)	24.3 (9)	16.7 (22)	
— old bike	0.0 (0)	0.0 (0)	0.0 (0)	18.9 (7)	5.3 (7)	
— loud noise	16.7 (8)	16.7 (8)	2.7 (1)	10.8 (4)	16.0 (21)	
— all of above	0.0 (0)	0.0 (0)	0.0 (0)	2.7 (1)	0.7 (1)	
Old-harry (U)						
— trouble (G)	16.0 (4)	44.0 (11)	20.6 (7)	73.5 (25)	35.8 (47)	44.9 (59)
— drink	8.0 (2)	12.0 (3)	0.0 (0)	0.0 (0)	3.8 (5)	
— drudge	8.0 (2)	12.0 (3)	5.9 (2)	0.0 (0)	5.3 (7)	

Table 7 (continued)

Fast (G)						
— inquisitive (G)	4.3 (3)	4.3 (3)	0.0 (0)	38.8 (19)	19.0 (25)	89.1 (117)
— sexually precocious	13.0 (9)	11.6 (8)	2.0 (1)	2.0 (1)	14.5 (19)	
— speed/abstinence (E)	18.8 (13)	5.8 (4)	20.4 (10)	14.3 (7)	25.9 (34)	
— all of above	15.9 (11)	26.1 (18)	4.1 (2)	18.4 (8)	29.7 (39)	
Duppy (B)						
— dead person (B)	25.0 (18)	20.8 (15)	0.0 (0)	0.0 (0)	25.1 (33)	70.8 (93)
— obeah thing	22.2 (16)	22.2 (16)	4.8 (1)	66.7 (14)	35.8 (47)	
— short person	6.9 (5)	2.8 (2)	19.0 (4)	9.5 (2)	9.9 (13)	
Ning-ning (U)						
— fish (B) hunger pangs (G)	24.5 (13)	18.9 (10)	8.1 (3)	16.2 (6)	24.4 (32)	68.5 (90)
— pains	13.2 (7)	5.7 (3)	10.8 (4)	43.2 (16)	22.9 (30)	
— inconsequential	5.7 (3)	7.5 (4)	5.4 (2)	13.5 (5)	10.6 (14)	
— all of above	9.4 (5)	15.1 (8)	0.0 (0)	2.7 (1)	10.6 (14)	
Gipsy (B)						
— inquisitive (B)[2]	40.0 (28)	37.1 (26)	0.0 (0)	9.3 (4)	44.2 (58)	93.7 (123)
— wanderer	0.0 (0)	2.9 (2)	23.3 (10)	55.8 (24)	35.1 (46)	
— all of above	14.3 (10)	5.7 (4)	0.0 (0)	7.0 (3)	12.9 (17)	
— other gloss	0.0 (0)	0.0 (0)	0.0 (0)	4.7 (2)	1.5 (2)	
Quarter-bus (B)						
— bus ¼ to hour (B)	17.9 (5)	3.6 (1)	0.0 (0)	0.0 (0)	4.5 (6)	22.0 (29)
— bus every hour (B)	53.6 (15)	25.0 (7)	0.0 (0)	100.0 (1)	17.5 (23)	
Genip (G)						
— Melicoccus (G)	25.0 (8)	59.4 (19)	28.0 (14)	72.0 (36)	58.7 (77)	62.5 (82)
— Guinness	15.6 (5)	0.0 (0)	0.0 (0)	0.0 (0)	3.8 (5)	

1. fed bananas and milk, for luck

neither thee nor thou), /her groIn, her rʌbIn/ (hair — growing /rubbing; i.e., pomade) — are common, as are puns — as in the progression from *Ricinus communis* (castor-oil plant) to "communism" and its potential for baldness, or the transformation of "may we ever go" to "Mary had a goat."

On the other hand, there is a large body of literature which seeks to identify these elements of English in the Caribbean as instances of simplified or deficient linguistic repertoires, or else to define some of these elements as English and others as components of that peculiar set of languages-in-continuum which is seen to exist among non-European peoples along the Equator. Although the selections cited here span only a decade, extensive documentation of these types of language usage, and these attitudes toward them, can be cited from periods throughout the Caribbean's short history. The poor, uneducated, or rural people of the Caribbean are as capable of using Standard English linguistic forms interchangeably with coinages and borrowed forms as are people in other geographical locations.

The role of Caribbean English as a distinctive entity vis-à-vis other national types of English is perhaps best characterized by its literature and the lyrics of its *reggae* music. In *Guerrillas,* whose paperback cover carries such notices as "Gripping — Conradian . . . Naipaul draws the heart of darkness from a sun-struck land — *Time Magazine*," the Trinidadian V.S. Naipaul uses his English thus:

> The cafes would be closed when the film finished and he went outside; the rum shops would be closed; there would only be a coconut cart, more full of husks than coconuts, a few people sleeping below the shop eaves, drunks, disordered people, and an old woman in a straw hat selling peeled oranges by the light of a flambeau.
>
> Eventually a long-distance taxi came with two other passengers, and Bryant got in. He waited until they were on the highway before he said, "Thrushcross Grange."
>
> When they were out of the factory area the driver fumbled for something on the floor of the car, next to the accelerator; and Bryant, sitting at the back, heard the sound and understood the signal: the driver had a cutlass. Bryant was nervous. He said, "But like everybody is a bad-John these days"; and was surprised at the tough way the words came out. The driver didn't reply. He gave a little grunt; and he grunted again when some minutes later — Bryant saying, "Here! Here, nuh! Where you going?" — he set Bryant down and took his money. The headlights of the taxi swept on, the red taillights receded; and Bryant was left alone in the darkness. [Naipaul 1975]

Although Naipaul has criticized the Caribbean to such an extent that in the region he is thought of as an Englishman, Trinidad clearly taught him much of the language he uses. We enjoy, too, the confidence of a Forbes Burnham, who won oratorical prizes in his London undergraduate days, and of the worldwide adoption of *reggae* lyrics, even by English and American singers. The Trinidadian thinker C. L. R. James has frequently lamented the mass of ignorance and falsehood concerning the Caribbean, the existence of which causes obvious truths about the area to seem like revelations. Caribbean English exists in non-native contexts only in those Caribbean territories whose dominant languages are *not* English — i.e., places where French, Spanish, or Dutch is the official language. In the other territories — just as in the United Kingdom, India, or Australia — in its constantly changing forms, and with its particular functions, lives Caribbean English, the compliment which the Caribbean has paid its constructors.

REFERENCES

Bennett, Louise. 1966. Miss Lou's Views. *Listen to Louise,* side A, track 8. Jamaica: Federal Recording Company.
Bryant, Hawley. 1966. Song of Guiana's children. *Learning by radio: a children's booklet — broadcasts to schools.* Guyana: Ministry of Education.
Ebert, Alan. 1975. "God" is dead. *Essence* 7: 5.
Francisco, Slinger [The Mighty Sparrow]. 1968. *Sir Garfield Sobers.* Trinidad: National Recording Company.
Haynes, Lilith M. 1973. Language in Barbados and Guyana: attitudes, behaviours, and comparisons. Ph.D. dissertation, Stanford University.
James, C. L. R. 1966. Kanhai: a study in confidence. *New world: Guyana independence issue.* Guyana: New World Group Associates.
Lamming, George. 1974. *Natives of my person.* London: Pan Books.
Layne, Paul. 1972. Posthumous papers of Luap Enyal. *Music Man* (Barbados).
Mair, Lucille. 1969. The student and the university's civilizing role. *Caribbean Quarterly* 15: 2-3 (Trinidad).
Naipaul, V.S. 1975. *Guerrillas.* London: Ballantine Books.
Reisman, Karl. 1970. Cultural and linguistic ambiguity in a West Indian village. In *Afro-american anthropology,* ed. N. Whitten and J. Szwed. New York: Free Press.
———. 1972. Contrapuntal conversations in an Antiguan village. *Penn-Texas Working Papers in Sociolinguistics* 3.
Roberts, Peter. 1978. Personal communication. Barbados.

PART III

Contact and Change: Question of a Standard

14

American English: From a Colonial Substandard to a Prestige Language

HENRY KAHANE

For more than two millennia, there has been a chain of world languages, one after the other. Each of these phases is linked to a certain constellation of cultural features developed in a certain area; and the culture of that area carries the language abroad.

Thus Greek, in the period of Hellenism, carries the culture of intellectualism in science, philosophy, and art, and becomes a must for the educated from Rome to Asia Minor. Latin is resuscitated in the Carolingian period for the necessities of ecclesiastic and mundane administration, and for seven or eight centuries remains the vehicle of written communication in the Western world. The chivalric culture of medieval aristocracy, rising in Provence and France, carries these languages (often not clearly separable) over the Western world and beyond, from England to the Crusader states. Renaissance Italy brings us into the modern world, with the educated courtier who combines the two traditions of the humanist and the knight; Italian is part of his equipment. And French, again in the eighteenth and nineteenth centuries, spreads through the innumerable courts modeled after Versailles, and the language of the courts survives as the language of international diplomacy, sifting down into the bourgeoisie and remaining a distinctive mark of that bourgeoisie far beyond Europe, in Latin America, the Middle East, and Africa.

Ours is the day of American English. As early as 1780, John Adams made a remarkable statement (which, not by chance, is the starting point also for the paper by Shirley Heath in this volume). He proved to be prophetic when he said: "English [i.e., American English] is destined to be in the next and succeeding centuries more generally the language of the world than Latin was in the last, or French is in the present age. The reason is obvious, because the increasing population in America, and their universal connection and correspondence with all nations . . . force their language into general use." What is remarkable in Adams's statement is his percipience at such a pristine stage in the history of the country.

Indeed, in 1780 American English is still the underdog, still a colonial substandard. The colonial regime reaches its end, but the linguistic class system is still vigorous. "A gentleman," says Princeton's President Witherspoon in 1781, "will not imitate a peasant." In this diglossia, British English is the *H* language, the prestige language. Loyalty to the British tradition means, linguistically, purism. We are reminded of the language question in early modern Greece, around 1800: during the struggle for independence, the upper classes, who often were loyal to the Ottoman overlord, tried to resuscitate their *H* language, essentially learned Byzantine Greek, as the national standard, while rejecting the vernacular because of its democratic implications. America's *H* language, in the early period of the Republic, and far beyond, continued the British elitist tradition, building on three models: current standard English, the English classics, and the Greco-Latin strain in Western neo-humanism. To the conservative mind, the winds of change, the forces of linguistic emancipation, spell loss of the linguistic values: loss of the past, loss of norm, loss of standard. Three specific aspects evidence the deviation of the American language from the British standard: the prevalence of the vernacular in the evolving new standard; the growth of unorthodox lexemes and structures labeled innovations; and the openness toward adoption of foreign elements.

The decolonized society of the New World represents a most interesting linguistic experiment. It tries to be a society for Everyman, and its language develops into a language of Everyman. The new norms of life imply acceptance of the vernacular as the foundation of the standard. The social revolution is evident in the democratization, the informalization of its linguistic representation. The story of spoken American English, of the American koiné, is, indeed, one of linguistic democratization. It has been in existence from before 1700, and it survives, in principle, into our days, in the prestige accorded to our relatively integrated American vernacular. Dr. Benjamin Rush, signer of the Declaration of Independence, rejects the British paradigm: "The present is the age of simplicity of writing in America." Noah Webster, to whom language was as national as customs, habits, and government, sensed early, in 1789, a divergence of the "language in North America from the future language of England." Webster was, so to speak, the discoverer of the national language; but who was its speaker? The pioneer has been suggested; the average Ohio boatman of 1810, the plainsman of 1815, the cultural misfit, or simply the colonist. But the real activists in the koiné-forming process are the children who indoctrinate newcomers' children by imposing the norms of the koiné. Linguistic adaptation is achieved in just one generation.

The essential developments of American English, then, consist of a decline in Anglophilia, the standardization of informal speech, the leveling of social dialects, the integration of foreign elements. These developments are, from one standpoint, the symptoms of — or from another standpoint, the stimuli for — the upward mobility of American society. The pioneers of yesteryear have turned into middle-class citizens. In principle, the koiné-forming agents of the past are still at work in our time: pulpit, school, and publishing, vitalized, of course, by that macro-force, the electronic media. Webster's "standard of our vernacular tongue" is today's "Network Standard."

Nowhere, I am tempted to say, is Network Standard as faithfully codified as in that monumental dictionary known as WIII, Webster's Third. WIII appeared in 1961, and it immediately provoked a most interesting debate, essentially concerning the level of the American English inventorized. The controversy unfolds before the background of our own contemporary problems. There evolve three major grounds of objection to WIII: permissiveness, trust in usage, and loss of tradition. Yet, to the defenders of the work, the true promoter is not the teacher but the sociologist. The dictionary is a report on what is, not on what should or should not be, and WIII offers, as has been said, "a full account of the resources of the American language of the 'sixties." The preceding WII, in 1934, presented the formal style of the language then current but by now recessive. WIII records the informal style of the 'fifties which is developing into the new standard. The speech patterns of the middle class are replacing the habits of the so-called literary aristocracy; conversational style permeates written communication; the difference between the two forms of expression, written and spoken, which long marked Western civilization, has narrowed down in our age and culture. The inclination toward informality as well as the reduced distinction between the written and spoken levels are correlated with a noticeable position against purism. WIII, as an objective lexicological inventory, is at the same time a document evidencing the change in society. Informality of style, increased exposure to language, and lexical explosion reflect the forces of modern life as they have been evolving in the half-century since World War I: mass education, the growth of democracy, unprecedented movements of populations, the expansion of mass media, social and intellectual movements, urbanization, technological developments, increased magazine and newspaper reading, travel. Transformed into the medium of language, these innovations mean multiplication of technical jargon, gobbledygook, colloquial manufacture of neologisms, slang. In short, the rapid changes of life are mirrored in language, in our American English.

We come to the second phase of our story. With the events of the First World War, and increasingly since the Second, the former Cinderella has turned into the world language of our times. The development follows an old cycle. The internationally dominant position of a culture results in a forceful expansion of its language, with the reverse correlate: the expansion of the language contributes, by its very expansion, to the prestige of the culture behind it. A world language is the most typical case of an *H* language: the language of the upper classes in a diglossic environment. The concept of "world language" implies a two-pronged process of linguistic acquisition and integration.

As to acquisition: at a certain historical moment the prestige language, as the prime carrier of modern developments, social, intellectual, and technical, must be learned by the foreigner wanting or needing to be up-to-date. The forms of second-language acquisition have varied, of course, from culture to culture: the sons of the wealthy Roman families were taught Greek by Greek slaves (obviously the archetype of our profession); Latin for the Byzantine bureaucracy was provided in government schools; the instruction of Latin in the Middle Ages lay in the hands of the Church; French in eighteenth- and nineteenth-century Germany was transmitted by tutors and governesses, and in our century is taught by the government-sponsored schools of the Alliance Française. Today, an unprecedented demand has turned the teaching of American English into an American academic industry labeled ESL or TESL, aiming at maximum efficiency in teacher-training, textbooks, and testing.

The second impact, integration, is the linguistic correlate of a cultural model: the prestige language becomes the fountainhead of widespread and large-scale borrowing of, essentially, characteristic lexemes. The sum of these borrowings evidences the sundry linguistic fields which represent the impact emanating from the source culture and involving the man on the street.

The difference between these two kinds of diffusion, acquisition and borrowing, is of sociolinguistic interest. Whereas the acquisition of an international prestige language is widely a classbound process, the borrowings from the same language easily become everyone's possession. The *terminus technicus* of foreign origin has a general appeal. The Latinisms of imperial Rome borrowed by Hellenistic Greek, as evidenced in the Egyptian papyri, survived in the Byzantine demotic; the Gallicisms of the chivalric culture borrowed by

German survived in the rustic Middle-Low German dialects; the fashionable Italianisms spreading in the colonial empire of Venice on the Greek coasts and islands became a mark of fishermen and farmers. The lexical democratization of a world language is, perhaps, most evident in the case of the Greek of early Christianity: a large set of technical terms spread and became part and parcel of everyday speech — *angel/ devil/ bishop/ church.* The same happens now with American English.

The diffusion of Americanisms is, by itself, a process characteristic of these times. This unprecedented explosion of Americanisms is the effect of a concatenation of events. With the political preponderance of the United States after World War II, its technological advances, its supremacy in world economics, and the new forms of its way of life exerted their global influence. The visibility and audibility of these influences, supported by the developments of that second industrial revolution, the mass media, internationalized information. The mass media of the target countries — press, film, television, advertising, commercials — are the channels which spread the high prestige of Americanness, and the prestige of Americanness is linguistically transformed into Americanisms. These cover the linguistic fields of mass media/pop art/economics/business/the consumer society/ technology/the lifestyle of the young. The Americanisms abroad, interestingly, circumscribe essentially the same linguistic fields which we considered as the characteristic lexical features of Webster's Third.

One typical issue of the German weekly, *Der Spiegel* (April 29, 1974), contained more than 160 Americanisms, covering primarily American business organization, its cult of efficiency, and its hectic informal style of life, with a stress on both social relations and technology. Characteristic examples of business organization: *Team/Broker/ Promoter/Service.* Terminology of efficiency: *Know-how/Trend/ Test/Lobby.* Social psychology: *Image/Fan/Stress/Backlash.* Fads: */Jogger/Jeans/Rock/Afro-look.* Technology: *Hifi/Instant-on/Aftershave Lotion/Bulldozer.* Calques: *Gehirnwäsche* ∿ *brainwashing/ Speerspitze* ∿ *spearhead/Kletterer* ∿ *climber/umwickeln* ∿ *involve.* These borrowings clearly render the European image of America.

And finally, a glimpse of the third phase in the history of a world language — the attitudes displayed by those who are affected by it. This process has recently been investigated by a young scholar at the University of Illinois, Pierre Trescases. I shall try to outline some of his insights into the very illuminating case of France.

French has twice been a world language itself, in the twelfth century, and again from the seventeenth to the nineteenth; but twice

it has also been on the passive end of the process, in the sixteenth
century, when the giant of the Renaissance, Italy, covered the West
with Italianisms, and now in the twentieth century with the impact
of Americanisms. The Italian episode, although different in certain
ways from the American, is of considerable interest to us; since it has
concluded, it allows us to evaluate from a historical perspective those
facets which, in the present-day case of American English, are still
in the midst of evolution.

The impact of the Italian Renaissance hurt the French pride. It
hurt what Humanistic tradition labeled the *Hercule gaulois,* the Gal-
lic Hercules. In states where citizens feel a political-cultural inferiority, language turns into their foremost symbol of national defense.
Defense of the language means defense of the nation; in Yardeni's
recent phrasing, linguistic patriots consider borrowing anti-patriotic.
Du Bellay, the great sociolinguist of the times, wrote in 1549: "The
same natural law which requires everyone to defend his birthplace
likewise obliges us to watch over the dignity of our language." Similarly, the foreign language turns into a symbol of the foreigner —
since he is disliked, his language is disliked. The Italians are disliked
because of their courtly style, displayed, above all, at the court of
Henry III (1574-89); they are disliked because of their cultural
hegemony, their successful minority in France, their mores. The
effeminate Italians (mused a contemporary author, Estienne Pasquier) as represented by the courtiers, have an effeminate language . . . their language is corrupt, since they have dissolute mores.
The famous linguist Henri Estienne stated in 1578 that neologisms
go hand in hand with the new (that is, bad) mores. The words *charlatan* and *bouffon* are from Italian; but a Frenchman could not be
a *charlatan* or a *bouffon,* only an Italian could. The foreignisms
turn into a class symbol. The Italianisms are the mark of courtly
life, that is, of an aristocratic style; and the bourgeoisie of the time
rejected them as characteristic of that upper class.

The attitude of the French toward today's Americanisms presents, *mutatis mutandis,* the same picture. After World War I and
increasingly after World War II, the United States, replacing French
hegemony, becomes a menace to French pride. Out of the feeling
of military-political inferiority grows an intellectual superiority
complex, resulting in a cultural-ethical hostility toward the United
States. The language becomes the symbol against which the hostility is most strongly in evidence. Americanisms symbolize colonial-
ism; they are America's fifth column; they express submission; they
reveal a preference for dollars over francs. The defense of the *génie*

français is realized through a defense of the French language, and linguistic nationalism takes on a warlike character. Duhamel said in 1968: "Our first duty is to watch over the purity of our language. Importing vocabulary is a sign of weakness." The enemy is *franglais*. Americanisms are danger/invasion/cancer. Borrowing is treason. Foreignisms are compared to useless immigrants. Etiemble, the foremost fighter against *franglais,* has written an exposé with the slanted title, *From French Prose to Atlantic Sabir. Atlantic sabir* means Atlantic pidgin; in other words, he interprets American English as the base language of a new *lingua franca* which replaces French.

Let me phrase the battle of the French intelligentsia against Americanisms succinctly, as a set of conservative political and cultural attitudes. The anti-attitude symbolizes a belief in tradition and norm, in elitism, in the intellectual's skepticism toward technology; it symbolizes an anti-democratic reaction against the women, the young, and mass culture; it symbolizes anti-Americanism and a rejection of multilingualism and multiculturalism. The attitude against Americanisms, in short, reflects the struggle against the cultural and social revolution which marks the decline of the traditional French civilization.

To sum up my observations, by interpreting the example of American English as the prestige language of today's world, I have tried to isolate three facets involved in this process of ascent. First, the evolving of a new style of life, of modernism, of dynamics in the culture behind the source language, makes it dominant at a certain period of history. Second, the spread of the language obeys the principle that "the medium is the message." And third, a complex pattern of acceptance and rejection exists in the target cultures, with the forces of tradition battling the magnetism of change. Only all three phases together — growth, diffusion, and attitudes — tell us the story.

REFERENCES

Bellay, Joachim du. 1549. *La deffence et illustration de la langue françoise.* H. Chamard ed., 1948. Paris: M. Didier.

Dillard, Joey Lee. 1972. *Black English: its history and usage in the United States.* New York: Random House.

———. 1975. *All-American English.* New York: Random House.

Duhamel, Jean. 1968. O.R.T.F. et la langue française. *Revue des Deux Mondes* (April 1): 386-92.

Estienne, Henri. 1578. *Deux dialogues du nouveau langage françois italianizé et autrement desguizé, principalement entre les courtisans de ce temps.* P. Ristelhuber ed., 1885. Paris: Alphonse Lemerre. [The relevant passage is in I, 96.]

Etiemble, René. 1952. De la prose française au sabir atlantique. *Les Temps Modernes* (8): 291-303.

Jung, Marc-René. 1966. Hercule dans la littérature française du XVIe siècle: De l'Hercule courtois à l'Hercule baroque. *Travaux d'Humanisme et Renaissance* (79). Genève.

Kahane, Henry, and Kahane, Renée. 1976. Abendland und Byzanz: Sprache. *Reallexikon der Byzantinistik*, ed. P. Wirth. Amsterdam: Verlag Adolf M. Hakkert. I, 345-640.

———. 1977. Virtues and vices in the American language: a history of attitudes. *TESOL Quarterly* (11): 185-202.

———. 1979. Decline and survival of Western prestige languages. *Language* (51): 183-98.

———, and Roberta Ash. 1979. Linguistic evidence in historical reconstruction. In Rauch and Carr (1979): 67-121.

Mathews, Mitford M., ed. 1931. *The beginnings of American English: essays and comments.* Chicago: University of Chicago Press.

Pasquier, Estienne. ca. 1560. *Choix de lettres sur la littérature, la langue et la traduction.* D. Thickett ed., 1956. Textes Littéraires Français. Genève: E. Droz. [The relevant passage is on p. 88.]

———. 1560-1621. *Oeuvres choisies.* L. Feugère ed., Paris, 1849; reprinted Genève: Slatkine Reprints, 1968. [The relevant passage from the *Recherches de la France*, II, 91-92.]

Rauch, Irmengard, and Carr, Gerald E. 1979. *Linguistic method: essays in honor of Herbert Penzl.* The Hague: Mouton.

Read, Allen Walker. 1936. American projects for an academy to regulate speech. *Publications of the Modern Language Association of America* (51): 1141-79.

Sledd, James, and Ebbitt, Wilma R. 1962. *Dictionaries and that dictionary: a casebook on the aims of lexicographers and the targets of reviewers.* Chicago: Scott, Foresman.

Trescases, Pierre. 1978. Les attitudes françaises envers les grands courants d'emprunt: italianismes et americanismes. Ph.D. dissertation, University of Illinois at Urbana-Champaign.

Webster III. 1961. *Webster's third new international dictionary.* Springfield, Mass.: G. and C. Merriam Co.

Wells, Ronald A. 1973. *Dictionaries and the authoritarian tradition: a study in English usage and lexicography.* The Hague: Mouton.

Yardeni, Myriam. 1971. *La conscience nationale en France pendant les guerres de religion (1559-1598).* Publications de la Faculté des Lettres et Sciences Humaines de Paris-Sorbonne, sér. "Récherches," 59. Louvain and Paris.

15

American English: Quest for a Model

SHIRLEY BRICE HEATH

In the late eighteenth century, when successful completion of the American Revolution depended in large part on diplomacy which would insure a substantial loan from the French and the Dutch, there appeared in the mailbags of the Continental Congress a long and curious letter from John Adams. In the midst of his mission to gain money for continuing the Revolution, Adams had written a letter proposing that the United States consider seriously the social and linguistic consequences of spreading English around the world. In this and other letters, Adams proposed an institution to do what the British had never seriously done: to extend English around the world. This challenge, if taken up by the United States, should carry two responsibilities: to determine a model of American English, and to consider political and economic forces critical to the spread of American English (Heath 1976b).

Fifty years later Francis Lieber, a German immigrant to the United States, envisaged a rather different approach to establishing American English as an international language, and as the second language of many U.S. citizens. Lieber, the first editor of the *Encyclopaedia Americana* and a prominent political philosopher, corresponded with a great number of academic and political decision-makers in the United States. In this correspondence he periodically considered ways in which Americans should view their language, and the unique role in language history for which American English was destined. He urged scholars to study English in its non-native contexts, i.e., in those locations outside Great Britain to which English had been transplanted. American scholars, in particular, should focus attention on how varieties of American English developed within the United States. Numerous scholars of the period set up American English and British English as two subjects of synchronic inquiry. Lieber proposed instead to study American English diachronically, as it became first a variety of British English and then a language form which itself developed varieties.

Attention to English in its American non-native context

during the first century of nationhood is marked by two methods
of determination, exemplified by the approaches of Adams and
Lieber. The first, proposed by Adams, aimed to give a public institution the task of prescribing and promoting a language standard
as an ideal for individual speakers for international use, and for the
nation as a promoter of English as an international tongue. In this
case, the quest for a model depended on the elite's recommending
a standard, using it in their own writings and public speech, encouraging its use in American literature, and altering or possibly
eliminating societal influences contrary to maintenance of this
model (Read 1936, Heath 1976b). The second model, urged by
Lieber, was a process for studying language in use and language
change; the goal was to define and describe American English in
use. This approach was intended not to establish one language
form as a model, but to describe the existing structures of American English, to discover patterns of language change, and to report
attitudes toward language change. Lieber, a non-native speaker of
English, proposed a description of American English as it was
used in specific contexts, and a comparison of this description
with one of British English in similar contexts. Lieber wished
these descriptions to be available over time, so they might indicate patterns of change for the two language varieties. Specifically, these data might enable scholars to draw conclusions regarding the processes of change a language of wider communication might undergo in non-native contexts. In addition, Lieber
believed study of the acquisition of English by non-native speakers in America would indicate changes in English introduced by
speakers of different mother tongues. Furthermore, such studies
involving individual speakers would reveal some of the reasons
why English was chosen and maintained as a second language by
different groups in the United States. What functions did English
serve for citizens who also retained their mother tongue in the
United States? In other words, Lieber proposed that Americans
did not yet know enough about their language use and changes
to establish a single model. If they indeed decided to establish
a model, they would need to know much more than they then
knew.

Each of these methods of developing a model, that proposed
by Adams and that undertaken by Lieber, illustrates specific types
of linguistic awareness about American English and its spread to
contexts beyond the United States. Each suggests a different attitude toward language, processes of language change and language

evaluation, and different uses for knowledge gained from the study of language. Each then becomes a valuable source for the study of the history of linguistics, language change, and the attitudes and behaviors of speakers in the period prior to the development of the public school system, the demise of public oratory, and an increased dependence on printed materials in the United States. Before the mid-nineteenth century, there was a decided focus on studying spoken language and its effect on determining American English. An American literature had not yet developed to the point of worldwide acceptance judged necessary by many intellectuals to insure establishment of language forms used in that literature (see Matthews 1892). Thus oral interactions, including conversations, college debates, public oratory, and lecture series, as well as the political talk of congressional leaders, were the data on which any description of American English had to depend (Heath 1976a). For Francis Lieber, these data were most important for their contribution to understanding processes of language change, and interrelationships between evaluations of language forms by specific groups and changes occurring in the language.

Francis Lieber and Notes on "Americanisms"

Now to examine the views of Francis Lieber on approaches to defining and describing American English, during a period of American history when quests for a model usually took the prescriptive approach. Lieber, for whom the study and recording of language was an avocation, is almost completely unknown among today's linguists.[1] Historians who have examined his writings and interpreted his influence on American culture have either spurned or overlooked his work on language (e.g., Friedel 1947). Yet this German-American political philosopher recognized, recorded, and analyzed many aspects of language variation and standardization. Born and raised in Prussia during the time of Frederick William III, Lieber grew up during the Napoleonic era, participated in the Waterloo campaign, and was wounded at the Battle of Namur. Arrested in 1819 for his political views, he was forbidden to study at any university except Jena, where he received his degree in 1820. Disillusioned in efforts to aid in Greece's war of liberation, Lieber went to Italy in 1822, where he found employment as a library assistant for Barthold George Niebuhr. Lieber returned to Germany in 1823 and was given permission to study in Berlin, but was arrested with a group of young liberals in 1823 and jailed for six months. In 1826 he went to England, where he taught languages and wrote for German periodicals. Within a year the opportunity to manage a gymnasium and swimming school in Boston gave him his long-awaited chance to come to the United States. Shortly after his arrival, however, Lieber became bored with his job and decided to prepare the *Encyclopaedia Americana,* a translation and remolding of the German encyclopedia *Conversations-Lexikon.* He published the first edition in thirteen volumes between 1829 and 1833. In 1835 he was elected to the chair of history and political economy at the University of South Carolina, where he remained for twenty-one years. There he wrote his *Manual of Political Ethics and Civil Liberty and Self-Government,* as well as numerous pieces on language and politics, patriotism, and the nature and origin of human language. He kept up an active correspondence with others interested in various aspects of language: William von Humboldt, Henry Schoolcraft, Joseph Story, Edward Everett, Henry Wadsworth Longfellow, John Pickering, and Albert Gallatin. In this correspondence and in his copious notes on language Lieber was not consistently scientific, detached, and objective; value terms and harsh judgments of speech and speakers occur throughout his work. With sometimes extreme inconsistency, he denounced "corruptions" of language one day and praised dialect diversity and vocabulary expansion the next. Yet his writings contain the essence of notions such as *register, variation,* and *pidginization.* He adapted and developed several terms for describing language change processes: *amplification* referred to the adornments of language or hypercorrections used by insecure speakers (see below); *holophrastic* referred to languages which were not "analytical," but "expressed whole phenomena with condition, mortification, gender, relation, etc. in one word" (NLI. 33-34). Many of Lieber's explanations, though couched in the phrases available in his day, have much in common with today's descriptions of language use in context.

As the Civil War approached, Lieber decided he could not remain in the South, where his long-standing opposition to slavery had made him increasingly unpopular. He went to New York, where he was appointed to the chair of history and political economy at Columbia College. In 1865 he transferred to the law school, where he devoted the remainder of his life to archival research and scholarship on military and international law.

During the 1849-51 period Lieber kept notes on language in the United States; these are included in ten notebooks he prepared during this brief period. In these notes he advocated systematic study of American English which would focus not only on lexicon, but also on the sound system and grammar of the language. He abhorred what he viewed as the narrow-minded obsession with lexicon which most other scholars of Americanisms followed in this period. Etymological studies of particular words also held little attraction for him. Lieber preferred to focus on what he considered the critical factors of language change: interactions among speakers, interrelationships between written and spoken channels, and the political power accorded the language in the development of political unity and in nationalism as a unifying attitude toward the state.

In the entry for "Americanisms" in an early edition of his *Encyclopaedia Americana,* Lieber called attention to what he viewed as the unique situation for linguistic investigations which the development of American English in the United States provided:

> . . . England and the United States afford the first in-
> stance in history of two great independent and active
> nations daily developing new and characteristic fea-
> tures, situated at a great distance from each other, and
> having a common language and literature. These rela-
> tions must, sooner or later, exert a decisive influence
> upon the common dialect; for no language is so settled
> as not to undergo continual changes, if spoken by a
> nation in the full vigor of social and political life.
> Authority, in regard to language, will go far, but never
> can withstand for a long time the energies and wants
> of a free, industrious and thinking people (1831: 211).

Lieber believed that scholars should consider, as part of the context of language, the sociocultural and political forces which promoted language and its relation to cultural affairs such as literature, art, and science. Of particular interest to language planners today is his analysis of language change in varying political contexts. Lieber believed language developed in accordance with circumstances. The U.S. government's democratic efforts and attempts to establish new political forces led to the creation of new words. A political philosopher, perhaps best known today for his publications on this topic, Lieber claimed that he introduced the words *nationalism, internationalism, individualism, city-state, interdependence, commonwealth of nations,* and *Pan-American* to the vocabulary of American English.

Processes of Change for Language Varieties in Contact

A major assumption behind Lieber's work was the right of linguistic minorities in the United States to retain their own languages
while adding English as a second language. Nevertheless, Lieber
spoke out strongly for the right of the American political system
to choose one language for "nationalization." He recognized that
the use of a common language in government and aspects of "national culture" (such as literature, journalism, art, and political
philosophy) was necessary. In these spheres an ideal American
English, as distinct from British English, would develop. This standard, or variety, drew the greatest attention from lexicographers.
However, additional varieties of American English would emerge
among various groups and in different regions. It was important
to recognize the development of all these varieties; only through
collection of data on uses of language in various contexts could
such an understanding of these varieties emerge. Knowledge about
language structure and use could inform decision-makers who
might formulate language policies or programs for others.

Lieber's ten notebooks of observations on language show his
irritation with the inadequacies of language data and the narrow-
ness of definitions used by those who attempted to prescribe language use. He charged that individuals failed to define the term
Americanism; furthermore, in many cases those who collected lexical items for volumes of Americanisms were not familiar enough
with British English to know of the existence of these same items
outside the United States. Lieber defined American contributions
to the lexicon of English as: 1) new words, 2) words with meanings which differed from those used in England, 3) words whose
original meanings had been preserved by Americans while British
usage had changed, 4) provincialisms preserved in use and meaning
in the United States just as they had been upon their introduction
to the colonies, and 5) words obsolete in England but still in use
in the United States (1831: 210-11).

Beyond careful attention to specific linguistic contexts of
lexical items, Lieber focused on the setting, speakers, and contexts
of usage in the United States. It was not enough to know that
change had taken place; the conditions and results of change were
most important. Lieber identified two major processes of change:
simplification and *amplification.* By *simplification* Lieber referred
to changes through which one language variety became simpler
than another variety: sentences were shorter, the lexicon smaller,
inflections fewer, paraphrases and repetitions more numerous.

Amplification was a process through which a language variety became more complex: the lexicon was more dependent on Latin, sentences were longer and included greater subordination, and inflections were increased. For Lieber the relative social, political, and economic conditions of speakers were major determinants of these change processes for language varieties in contact.

Lieber identified four conditions or occasions when language became simplified. In the first, a language was being acquired by either a native speaker or a second-language learner. The second occurred when speakers tried to alter their speech for comprehension by listeners of presumed low intelligence. The third took place when two languages came in contact and a pidgin resulted. The fourth was the condition in which one or more languages in contact became more "analytic." In today's terms, these conditions could be termed acquisition, adaptation, pidginization, and analytization. Acquisition was a condition which fascinated Lieber; he studied the process in his own children, in the children of slaves he observed in the Southeast, and in Laura Bridgeman, a child of some notoriety in the early nineteenth century scientific world because she was both blind and deaf. Lieber also noted that simplification, though of different types, took place in both first and second language acquisition. Reduplication was the most obvious feature of children's language. Lieber's notebook entry for *Pimmeky-Mimmeky* illustrates his attention to these features: "In England, at least in and about London, used by children and in familiar talk for puny, little with contempt, as a pimmeky-mimmeky boy. This word is harmozophonic and, at the same time has the reduplication, which children, savages etc. so much delight in" (NLI: 58). Lieber also noted that fewer phonological categories, a smaller lexicon, less inflection, and loss of the verb *to be* occurred in the early stages of both first and second language acquisition. Individuals acquiring a second language had a reduced lexicon, shorter sentences, and, in the initial stages of learning, merged the phonological systems of the mother tongue and the second tongue into a single system. Separation of the two systems came at a particular point of fluency. For German and English, Lieber predicted the areas of interference or merging in order of their likelihood of occurrence. He also wrote a "brief and practical German Grammar" in which he attempted to compare the structure and lexicon of German with that of English. He recommended in the preface a contrasting analysis of the two languages and the need for "practical grammars," explaining, "There is no way of teaching . . . so

cheering to the scholar as the one I have persued [*sic*] namely to
make of the many points of affinity, starting points of instruction.
I have, in addition, strictly adhered to the principle of making my
grammar as practical as possible, though I might entirely deviate in
doing so, from long established order" (1838). In correspondence
with his son, who was away in school in Germany, Lieber frequently
provided contrastive grammar lessons in English and German. He
was keenly aware of the problems facing German speakers who
wanted to learn English for practical uses in the United States.

Adaptation was the second condition for simplification to
which Lieber gave attention. One language variety is made simpler
by the speaker for the use of people who are regarded as not fully
competent, either linguistically or intellectually. Adapted language is the talk used in addressing young children, foreigners, and
those of a lower class or station. Lieber suggested that within
every community of speakers there existed individuals who were
regarded as unable to understand readily the normal speech of the
community. Power groups adapted their language in accordance
with predetermined notions of the abilities of those individuals.
The result of adaptation was that "everything not absolutely necessary to point out the most material and, generally, physical objects
is left out . . . hence all subjunctive, all nicer conditions, relations,
all mutual dependence, all delicate discrimination, all continued
expression of a condition already once indicated is non existing . . .
just as it finds no place in the nursery grammar" (NLVI: 168).

Lieber was particularly disturbed that some commentators on
language equated simplicity of grammatical form with simplicity
of cognitive development and abilities. While professor of political
philosophy at the University of South Carolina, Lieber had collected
numerous examples of Negro speech. He sometimes used these to
argue for a rational analysis of the language of blacks and other
powerless groups. To those who said that blacks and others who
used simplified varieties of English were incapable of abstract
thought, Lieber pointed out that language input to these individuals
often did not include abstractions. The attributes of objects or
events were not explained to either children or servants. Furthermore, professionals did not offer these explanations to their clients.
Instead, these individuals were given examples or applications of
abstract theories or descriptions of attributes. "So difficult is it
for the human mind to understand abstract ideas that to make
clear to a child, the meaning of any quality, for instance *malicious,
mild,* we explain the word and immediately give an instance which

latter [*sic*] makes the thing clear. The same with servants, the same with all people, lawyers, students of politics etc. The instance makes clear" (NLI: n.p.). Lieber charged that those who denied that West Indian creole languages or the language of American blacks used abstractions confused effect with cause. Their simplified language would show the effects of the simplification of language initiated by the power figure, the ultimate cause of any simple language used by powerless groups.

Yet another condition of simplification noted by Lieber for the first stages of language contact was pidginization. In cases of pidginization, there were restrictions on the uses for power languages. Lieber collected data from travelers in South America, the Caribbean, and the United States to substantiate his views of pidginization. In particular, his comparisons of Chinook jargon and what little knowledge he could gather of the pidgins and creoles of the Caribbean made him highly suspicious of a single-source theory for the origin of pidgin languages. Lieber noted the tendency toward truncation and monosyllables, retention of the intonation patterns of the first language, and the adoption of lexical items from the language of power. Lieber saw processual similarities shared by all pidgins and creoles, in terms of changes in the original languages of contact.

Lieber's final condition for simplification was that of analytization. He believed that certain language varieties, by the very nature of their grammar and the density of their lexicon, could be seen as representing a specific stage of language contact. Some languages were highly inflected; others, more "analytic," had less inflection. Lieber noted that for some languages which remained in contact over a long period of time, loss of inflection and the redistribution of functions among the remaining elements in the language resulted. Though he realized the history of American English was too brief to draw conclusions of this sort, Lieber could not resist speculating on changes in its lexicon. Lieber regarded English as highly polysemantic with each word carrying numerous meanings. However, there were far more homonyms in American English than in British English, and Americans used periphrastic constructions much more frequently. Lieber expressed this by saying: "The clavichord on which the Englishman plays has a wider keyboard. The American is far more fluent, but the Englishman possesses a richer stock of words" (NLI: 29).

Amplification was the opposite process of change for English in its non-native context; it occurred when individuals acquiring a new language, or style of speaking for particular uses, attempted to overcorrect or exaggerate stylistic features used by their language models. Insecurity about language use contributed to many types of amplification. This malady was not restricted to children, blacks, and foreigners; it also afflicted American writers who were insecure about the worth of their productions as measured against British and European standards. For those in the first category (children, blacks, foreigners, or others of lower status) Lieber noted the use of verb phrases instead of single verbs and the incorrect formation of verbs from nouns. For example, he heard a young black girl say, when looking at a picture of man looking through a telescope, "he is sighting something" (NLI: 24-25). Lieber believed that individuals who dealt with language in workaday communication, such as mariners or others who received directions, tended to form verbs from nouns; for example, *assemblaged* for *assembled, flighted* for *fled, certificated* for *certified, pleasured* for *pleased.*

Lieber observed that, when writing, U.S. citizens used words of Latin origin more frequently than Anglo-Saxon or English words. For formal uses Americans seemed to choose overstatement: politicians were called "great men," "men of great intellect." For this exaggerated language use, Lieber blamed newspapers, often written by journalists who had had, in his view, deficient educations and did not know how to write simple prose.

Other aspects of linguistic insecurity characterized American English. To hold one's place in conversation and to reinforce conversational partners, an American often used *well.* Tag questions and other mechanisms used by the insecure to "hedge" on the certainty of their statements were noted by Lieber. Of the Southern expression "most generally sometimes," Lieber said: "if I am asked what is the meaning, I would answer just what it indicates. It is the expression of an unskilled person asserting and taking away again, as an unskillful draughtsman rubs out half he has drawn. It means more than sometimes, less than most generally, brief it means generally" (NLI: IV, 32; V, 136).

The place of the word *interesting* as a filler in conversation was noted by Lieber as used by "many lightly educated persons who nevertheless largely mingle in society. . . It is a word used when want of command does not suggest the proper and specific word." Lieber judged that women and ministers were especially fond of it (NLI I, 46-47).

Conclusion

In considering language in non-native contexts, Lieber proposed processes of change and stipulated specific conditions which would restrict or encourage them. In particular, he observed that English or any language being introduced as an international or national tongue would assume specific functions because of its particular uses in the public sphere. He urged non-native speakers of English not to attempt to maintain their own language for literature, but to accept the predominance of English-language literature, law, science, and art. Language shift in certain functions was, however, specifically not recommended by Lieber; these functions were in-group associations with family and friends. The existence of what are today recognized as registers and domains of usage was noted by Lieber in his analysis of code-switching. He himself used English and German in much of his personal correspondence; he wrote poetry in German, political philosophy in both English and German, and official letters in English. He suggested that the order in which English should be learned was 1) politeness formulae, 2) "common intercourse" for public occasions, and 3) for the special purposes of business and specific occupations. The question of other domains was much more difficult; in these, non-native speakers would "feel the leaden weight of a foreign language weighing heavily on their tongue," and when they spoke of those things "dearest to their hearts," they would choose their mother tongue (1835: 202). However, they would also shift from language to language according to topic, setting, and audience.

Linguists and sociolinguists must today judge Lieber as a man ahead of his time. He was concerned with processes of language change and language in social contexts. He collected and commented on the development of pidgins and creoles, language varieties within English, and the language of the powerful and the powerless. He attempted to describe and name processes of change which occurred as a result of dialect convergence and the interrelationships of specific registers of individuals in social or professional contexts. He noted that when two speech communities which share a minimum of linguistic competence and common cultural understanding come together, each must adopt special strategies for communication. These strategies in turn lead to processes of language change, either simplification (occurring in acquisition, adaptation, pidginization, or analytization) or amplification which lead to shifts in syntax and lexicon.

As linguists eager for a view of language and language use in
past social contexts, we can only regret that Lieber's wide-ranging
interests and his increasing distraction by the Civil War and the
abolitionist movement kept him from devoting himself entirely to
recording language attitudes, speech events, and social and psychological forces of language change. His writings represent one way of
approaching the question of a model of American English. As an
immigrant to the United States during a period of intense nationalistic development, Lieber reacted to problems of national and
individual language choice. He recommended a policy promoting
a national language and tolerating other languages for use in education. He advocated cooperation of philologists, missionaries,
and government personnel in formulating language decisions. He
practiced and promoted careful observation and recording of language in use. He formulated theories of language change based on
his understanding of register and channel, constraints in communication between individuals of different class and educational
backgrounds, and his view of simplification and amplification
processes for languages in contact and interpersonal communication.

The type of linguistic relativism recommended and practiced
by Lieber decreased markedly after the mid-nineteenth century. By
the 1890's those who were trying to provide a model of American
English turned again to the prescriptivism Adams had recommended. Reformers seeking a model of American English wished
to place the responsibility for language choice and change on public institutions — namely, public schools and literary societies.
Grammars for those learning English as a second language during
this period prescribe grammatical rules, proscribe other languages,
and recommend specific behaviors for rapid assimilation (Heath
1980).

Historical research, often invoked to show "how we got
where we are," can also provide a perspective from which to compare current interpretations of behavior with interpretations of
past societies. In addition, a historically informed sociolinguistics
may help keep us from reinventing the wheel when we write our
programmatic statements or observe specific communities. Lieber
said: "A living language does not only mean a language spoken by
a living people, but also a living thing itself with all the capacities,
rights and necessities of life, that is, of *change, expansion,* and
elimination." He further recommended study not only of languages
themselves, but also of their ideologies: "The ideology of languages

is yet in its infancy, and waits the hand of genius to methodize and elucidate it. If, however, it shall continue to advance, as it has done within the last thirty years, there is no doubt but that it will, in time, throw considerable light on the history of man" (NL: n.p.). Lieber's study of English in non-native contexts offers a challenge — an assessment of where we have traveled in the hundred and fifty years since his quest for a model, and suggestion of attention to the ideology behind that model.

NOTE

1. Research for this paper was supported by a grant from the National Endowment for the Humanities in 1975 and from Winthrop College. Lieber was first introduced to an audience of linguists in "Standard English in the United States: An Early National View from an Inside Outsider," a paper given by this author at a University of Chicago conference on Language Variety and Its Implications for American Cultural Pluralism in 1977. Special acknowledgment is here given to Martha Holder of Winthrop College for her work as research assistant on this project. The manuscripts upon which this paper is based are in the Lieber collections of the Library of Congress, Caroliniana Library (University of South Carolina), and the Henry E. Huntington Library (San Marino, California). Citations from the ten volumes of Lieber's Notes on Language at the Huntington Library appear as NL, plus volume number, and are used here with permission of the Huntington Library.

REFERENCES

Friedel, Frank. 1947. *Francis Lieber: nineteenth-century liberal.* Baton Rouge: Louisiana State University Press.

Heath, Shirley Brice. 1976a. Early American attitudes toward variation in speech: a view from social history and sociolinguistics. Forum lecture, LSA Institute.

———. 1976b. A national language academy? Debate in the new nation. *International Journal of Sociology of Language* 11: 9-43.

———. 1980. Standard English: biography of a symbol. Pp. 3-32 in *Standards and dialects in English*, ed. T. Shopen and J. M. Williams. Cambridge: Winthrop.

Lieber, Francis. 1831. Americanism. Pp. 210-11 in *Encyclopaedia Americana*, I. Philadelphia: Carey and Lea.

———. 1835. *The stranger in America.* Philadelphia: Carey, Lea and Blanchard.

———. 1838. A brief and practical German grammar on a new plan with particular reference to the grammatical affinities between the German and English idioms.

Matthews, Brander. 1892. *Americanisms and Briticisms.* New York: Harper and Brothers.

Read, Allen Walker. 1936. American projects for an academy to regulate speech. *PMLA* 51: 1141-79.

16

Pringlish: Still More Language Contact in Puerto Rico

ROSE NASH

American English and Puerto Rican Spanish have been in contact on the island since the turn of the century, when the reins of government passed from Spain to the United States as a result of the Spanish-American War. Today a number of hybrid varieties of the two languages coexist with unmixed Spanish and English of the more standard kind. In previous articles I have described two of these: Spanglish and Englañol.[1]

Spanglish is used by native-born Puerto Ricans as a first language. Its chief characteristic is lexical borrowing from English with adaptation to Spanish phonology and morphology. Englañol is used by native-born Puerto Ricans as a second language. Its chief characteristic is syntactic and semantic transfer from Spanish into English. Although functionally bilingual, Englañol users are Spanish-dominant. By definition they are well-educated members of the middle and upper classes.

The present article will deal with a third major variety, which I shall refer to as Pringlish.[2] It is used as a first language by some 100,000 non-Puerto Rican Americans who have come to the island from various parts of the United States to live as permanent residents. Pringlish is a less obvious manifestation of language contact than either Spanglish or Englañol. It takes a long time to develop fully, and much of it remains in the mind of the speaker, where it cannot be observed directly. Nonetheless, Pringlish is a linguistic reality that can be investigated and described.

First, I shall draw a composite picture of the non-Puerto Rican native-English-speaking permanent resident (E) and explain the pertinent features of the non-native setting. Next, I shall describe the external and internal characteristics of Pringlish, introducing the concept of *reconceptualization,* which is crucial to an understanding of this form of language contact. Finally, I shall present experimental evidence and discuss the significance of Pringlish for linguistic research in general.

The Speaker and the Setting

Continentals (the local designation for non-Puerto Rican Americans) on the island fall into three major categories: tourists, temporary visitors, and our E, the permanent resident. In order to define E more clearly, it will be helpful to contrast these three groups.

In sheer numbers, the tourists predominate.[3] They come by the planeload from Thanksgiving Day in November until Easter, seeking in the tropical sun a respite from winter. They hug the beaches for the first few days, then venture into the Old City to practice their high school Spanish (a frustrating experience, since they will be answered by shopkeepers in English, and by others with "No hablo inglés"). Many fall in love with Puerto Rico and return year after year. Some even buy apartments in the luxury condominiums that line the ocean shore. But when they leave the island, after a few days or a few weeks, their English is intact.

The second-largest group is made up of temporary visitors, loosely defined as continentals who 1) have been on the island less than three years, and 2) have definite plans to leave on a certain date. They are, for the most part, military personnel on active tours of duty or federal employees on special assignments.[4] They work and play with other continentals in their organizations and do not become involved in Puerto Rican life. As is the case with American enclaves in many foreign countries, these people do not, figuratively speaking, ever leave home. And although they may pick up a few Spanish words during their stay, they, too, will leave the island with their English intact.

We come now to E, the permanent resident. In contrast to the other continentals mentioned above, E has no plans to leave the island in the foreseeable future, though he or she intends to do so after retirement. For the time being, at least, Puerto Rico is home — which means a job, a place to live, friends, hobbies, and, last but not least, civic responsibilities. E was raised in the American traditions of good citizenship and tries to improve what needs improvement. E becomes involved in local political issues, writes letters to the editor, joins cultural organizations, and even picks up trash on the beaches. E has Puerto Rican friends and neighbors, and genuinely likes some of them. E may be married to a Puerto Rican; this writer knows of many such marriages. At work, most of the people with whom E must deal are Puerto Rican bilinguals, and there is rarely any problem in communication. All of this may apply even to an E who cannot speak Spanish well.

An important factor contributing to this positive attitude is the

ready availability of good spoken and written American English, so
that E does not feel culturally isolated from the United States. Even
though E may spend the whole day listening to Spanish-accented
English, at night there are excellent programs from the U.S. on educational TV, first-run movies, and English-language radio; many Es
make a Sunday ritual of reading the *New York Times,* and may even
consider it an advantage to be able to control the amount of (native)
English they wish to hear and see.

E's level of education is well above average, and may have included study of one or more foreign languages. However, E has always lived in an English-speaking environment, and our most typical E came to Puerto Rico with little or no knowledge of Spanish.
In fact, one motivation for making the move was probably a desire
to learn Spanish in its natural setting. The new life in Puerto Rico
was inaugurated with attendance at language classes and the pur-
chase of many teach-yourself textbooks and records. The ambition
to become a fluent speaker of Spanish gradually disappeared because
E's Puerto Rican friends and colleagues prefer to use English with E,
and there is little opportunity to practice Spanish. Attempts to learn
to read Spanish are much more successful. The tremendous number
of orthographically similar words (cognates and loanwords), the
highly regular correspondences in morphological patterns, and a
fairly transparent syntactic structure make it possible to acquire a
reading knowledge quickly. Every E knows enough Spanish to understand public signs, make sense out of the daily newspapers, and read
letters and announcements that come in the mail.

Three main factors with regard to the non-native setting of
Puerto Rico provide the backdrop for the emergence of Pringlish:
1) geographical separation from the mainstream speech community
of the continental United States; 2) large numbers of fluent bilinguals; and 3) relaxed standards of correctness for English. These
factors affect E's language behavior in the following ways: 1) E
does not participate in mainstream language change, with its rapid
dissemination of neologisms; the need for innovation in E's language
must be supplied from local linguistic sources. 2) E uses English
more often with non-native speakers than with native speakers. 3)
E's adherence (or non-adherence) to rigid textbook/dictionary standards is no longer a matter of prestige, but a personal preference.

The Nature of Pringlish

Pringlish operates on two distinct levels — the external and the

internal. In its external aspects (which I consider a borderline manifestation of this form of language contact) the chief formal characteristic is the use of Spanish vocabulary in otherwise English contexts.
Following are some typical examples. (Glosses are approximate.)

Lexical substitution without adaptation to English morphology or
phonology

1) Foods

Let's get some *arroz con pollo* [chicken-'n'-rice] for dinner tonight.

My mother used to save the *chicharrones* [roast pork fat] for the
next day.

The price of *chuletas* [chops] has gone up to $1.75 a pound.

They always make their *jugo de china* [orange juice] from fresh
oranges.

I'll have a *medianoche* [hero sandwich] and a *café con leche* [coffee
with milk].

Would you prefer *pan criollo* [French bread] or *pan especial* [white
sandwich bread]?

Papas fritas [French fries] should be crisp, not soggy.

We put hot Italian *salchichas* [sausages] in the spaghetti sauce.

Boil the rice first with a little *sofrito* [spicy seasoning].

This is the best *sopa de carne* [meat soup] I ever tasted.

2) Places

On the new *autopista* [superhighway] you can get to Caguas in
twenty minutes.

The *biblioteca* [library] doesn't have that reference work.

We go to the *cine* [movie house] early to escape the crowd.

The *colmado* [grocery store] near my house stays open on Sundays.

If you're going to the *correo* [post office] please get me some stamps.

There's a *farmacia* [drugstore] right down the street.

Obras Públicas [government offices] said I would have to apply in
person.

You can pick up your check at *pagos* [bursar's office].

They shouldn't allow dogs to run around the *playa* [beach].

I had this suit made at the Hong Kong *sastrería* [tailor shop].

3) Varia

Have you heard the latest *chisme* [piece of gossip]?

(It was nice meeting you) *¡Igualmente!* [same here].

Let's get this *mamotreto* [fat file of papers] ready for HEW.

Somebody stole my *marbete* [auto license plate sticker].

You need *mucho dinero* [a lot of money] to stay at that hotel.

I've looked for another job, but there's absolutely *nada* [nothing] in my field.

My daughter got herself a new *novio* [boyfriend].

It's dangerous to live in a second-floor apartment without *rejas* [iron grills].

Sorry to be late, but I got caught in a terrible *tapón* [traffic jam].

Baker's is having a sale on *zapatos* [shoes].

Lexical substitution with adaptation to English morphology and phonology

1) Noun formations with *-tion* /šən/
They bought a house in the new *urbanization*. *[urbanización* = housing development]

I have a meeting today at the *Plannification* Board. *[planificación* = planning]

2) Verb formations with *-ing* /iŋ/
I'm not finished *ganchoing* the laundry.
[*gancho* = clothespin]

The heroine of the play was *ay-benditoing* all through the first act.
[*¡ay bendito!* = alas, alas!]

Substitutions or insertions in written English for effect[5]

Yo deseo saber [I want to know] if the rumor is true that says the *telefónica* [telephone company] is frantically installing new lines at the expense of good service.

The traffic jam at 7 a.m. *"no tiene nombre"* [is indescribable].

. . . the President's accidental *atropello* [attack] went virtually unnoticed . . .

. . . this crude assault on our *dignidad* [dignity] . . .

How much more *engaño* [fraud, trickery] must we put up with?

In order to receive, we have to give, no matter how meager our contribution. *"Toma y daca"* [give and take] as the saying goes.

As I was *taponing* it to Levittown . . . [*tapón* 'traffic jam']

The practice of *colegiacion* is widespread in Puerto Rico and gives
signs of becoming even wider spread: the lawyers have a *colegio* [pro-
fessional association], the architects do, even the electricians do, and
there's talk now of creating a *colegio* for the public relations people.

Language play in limericks

There is a young girl from Aguada /agwáda/
Who sits in her house doing *nada* /náda/ [nothing]
Though her job is to teach
She hangs out at the beach
As at present she's *desempleada* /desempleáda/ [unemployed]

There is a young girl from Condado /kondádo/[hotel area]
That at night walks from *lado* to *lado* /ládo/ [one end of the street
             to the other]
Though she's not in a show
She makes pretty good dough
But her work is not quite so *honrado* /onrádo/ [honorable]
(by Edna E. Viada)

When sportsmen enter Politics
They claim a right to do so
But when the contrary is done
They shrill and cry *"Abuso!"* /abúso/ [unfair!]
(by J. Sotomayor)

  In all of these examples, language-mixing was done consciously,
whether for convenience or for effect. The Spanish words and phrases
give a distinctly bilingual flavor to English, but both speaker/writer
and hearer/reader know that they are not part of English proper.
They are used as gestures of identification with the local culture and
with other Es as an in-group language style. When the occasion calls
for unmixed English (a trip off the island, or a visitor not familiar
with the local scene) a switch is made immediately with no difficulty
whatsoever. External Pringlish is, at all times, under E's control.

That is not the case with internal Pringlish. The changes that take place in E's English are so gradual that, by the time E becomes aware of them, they have already reached an advanced stage. For want of a more economical but equally appropriate term, I shall call this process *reconceptualization,* which means that some aspects of E's native English change permanently as a result of prolonged contact with non-native English. Reconceptualization is a function of time and is not under E's control. It simply happens because time, place, and E's lifestyle make it inevitable.

Reconceptualization is a twofold process: visual and semantic. The visual aspect starts before the semantic, but then they operate in parallel tracks. Within each process there are several consecutive stages, each building on the previous one. The time specifications given for each stage are the roughest of estimates, and would no doubt be contradicted by individual Es. For the rest, what follows is an accurate account, based on the personal testimony of dozens of continentals living in Puerto Rico.

Process I: Visual Reconceptualization

Stage 1 begins within the first six months after E's arrival in Puerto Rico. Stage 2 surfaces after one to three years. Stage 3 is reached by the end of the tenth year.

Stage 1: E notices that spelling errors in public signs and advertisements remain uncorrected:

PARQUIN [parking]
HAMBERGERS [hamburgers]
RATE 40¢ PER HOUR OR FRACCION [fraction]
FRIED CHIKEN [chicken]
HAWAYAN PUNCH [Hawaiian]
DINNING ROOM [dining]
HAM AND EGGS SANWICH [sandwich]
CHRIST IS COMMING [coming]
TURIST OFFICE [tourist]
BREKFAST SPECIAL [breakfast]

The initial reaction to such public spelling errors is one of mild amusement. However, amusement changes to amazement as more errors are picked up in the newspapers, in correspondence, and in the written English of one's colleagues, some of whom may be teachers of English. Since it is considered a serious social faux pas to correct one's equals without an invitation to do so, amazement subsides into frustration.

Stage 2: E becomes aware of memory problems that did not previously exist, being unable to recall the correct spellings of many words that are in the basic vocabulary. Upon encountering a potential spelling error in the writing of others, E becomes annoyed when the correct form does not come immediately to mind or when he or she is not absolutely sure that it is, in fact, an error. If E's job entails editing and polishing documents such as progress reports and grant proposals to the federal government, E may take great pains, in repeated readings, to find all such errors.

In E's own writing, the doubt typically appears after the word has been committed to paper in its full phrasal context form, which, upon review, does not "look right" to E. The sequence of events is as follows. (T = time of occurrence.)

T1   T2   T3
It will not be posible to grant your request at the present time.
T4
(. . . possible? possible?)

If E is particularly alert, T3 may of course be moved up:

T1   T2   T3   T4
It will not be posible to gr. . . . (possible? possible?)

Since Process I is limited to written English, the style tends to be formal. In the following typical examples, the spellings in doubt are lined up at Time 2. The Spanish parallels given at the right do not necessarily have meanings identical to the English words:

1) *Confusion between CC and C:*

| | abreviated? | |
| We are preparing an abbreviated? version . . . | | [abreviado] |

| | eficient? | |
| The most efficient? way to do it is . . . | | [eficiente] |

| | comitee?
commitee? | |
| The comittee? is now considering . . .
committee? | | [comité] |

| | supose? | |
| Let us suppose? that . . . | | [suponer] |

| | asist? | |
| I will be happy to assist? you . . . | | [asistir] |

The memory problems may also affect non-cognate words:

    weding?
The wedding? is scheduled to take place . . .

2) *Confusion between* C_1 *and* C_2 :

    proyect?
The project? in mind is . . .   [proyecto]

      cuestion?
There is no question? but that . . .   [cuestión]

      mencion?
I did not mention? the fact that . . .   [mencionar]

        jierarchy?
        jerarchy?
As we move up in the hieraquiy?   [jerarquía]
        hierarchy?
        jerarchy?

3) *Confusion between* C_1 *and* $C_1 C_2$:

      telefone?
Please include your telephone? number.   [teléfono]

        rythm?
In order not to disturb the rhythm? of . . .   [ritmo]
        rithm?

      conexion?
I see no connexion? between . . .   [conexión]
      conection?
      connection?

4) *Confusion between* V_1 *and* V_2 :

      responsability?
As this is not my responsibility? . . .   [responsabilidad]

      tabacco?
      tobaco?
Imports of tobacco? products . . .   [tabaco]
      tobbaco?

      mistery?
It is hardly a mystery? that . . .   [misterio]

desarmament?
The disarmament? talks . . .   [desarme]

5) *Varia*

accion?
We need a better plan of action?   [acción]

inmediately?
Please send this order immediately?   [inmediato]
imediately?

falt?
This situation is the fault? of . . .   [falta]

pront?
promt?
Looking forward to your pronpt? reply. . .   [pronto]
prompt?

cheque?
As soon as we receive your check? for . . .   [cheque]

Aptitud?
Aptitude? tests will be given . . .   [aptitud]

Stage 2 is alarming to E, especially if E has always been proud of being a good speller. E vows increased vigilance and consults the dictionary for verification at the slightest tinge of doubt.

Stage 3: E decides that strict adherence to conventional English spelling practices at all times is both troublesome and unnecessary. It is troublesome first because of the time demands of verification, and second because E has lost confidence in his/her ability to recognize every un-English spelling. It is unnecessary because deviant spellings in Puerto Rican English so often go unnoticed and uncorrected, and it seems pointless to make an issue of orthographic conventions that in many cases are arbitrary or redundant anyway. Process I of reconceptualization has run its course when E adopts a double standard of correctness. In writing destined for places off the island, where misspellings might be taken as a sign of poor upbringing, vigilance is maintained insofar as possible; in writing for local consumption, however, E relaxes vigilance and loses anxiety over the possibility of missing or producing a spelling error (which may then occur).

The changes that take place during the process of visual reconceptualization of English are directly related to the intensity of E's exposure to written Spanish. The chief factors are: 1) Spanish spelling patterns that are absent in English (e.g., *-ción* as a noun formative); 2) spelling patterns that occur in both languages but are more (or less) frequent in Spanish (e.g., *cc* vs. *c*); 3) differing graphemic representations for the same phoneme(s) (e.g., /kw/ = *qu* in English, *cu* in Spanish); 4) the influence of cognate-word spellings, which are identical to their English counterparts much of the time (e.g., *legal, color, radio*) and tend to become superimposed upon the English form in memory whenever an association is established.

Process II: Semantic Reconceptualization

Stage 1 begins after one year of residence has elapsed, and reaches its peak of activity sometime between the third and fifth years. This marks the onset of Stage 2.

In describing this process, it will be helpful to first present a set of sentences typical of those heard and seen every day in Puerto Rico, and then to chart E's changing reactions to them:

(1) Please write your name and direction.
(2) The outfielder couldn't recuperate the ball.
(3) I try to keep up with actualities.
(4) We met on the street by casualty.
(5) The meeting will be celebrated at 10 a.m.
(6) Too much coffee is inconvenient for you.
(7) Class is dispatched.
(8) He considered my remark an injury.
(9) The final bill ascended to thirty dollars.
(10) Don't molest me now, I'm busy.

Those familiar with the writer's previous work on language contact will recognize that these sentences are Englañol — products of the Spanish mind interacting with English matter. In Process II, there is also an interaction, but it is not the counterpart of Englañol. That is, we are dealing here not with English mind and Spanish matter, but with *English mind and Spanish mind interacting through the medium of English matter.*

The distinction is crucial to an understanding of Pringlish. The primary motivating force is contact with non-native English, rather than direct influence from Spanish. In effect, E learns a new variety of English which contains a built-in reflecting mirror that helps E to learn Spanish as well. As this happens, E's established concepts and standards of acceptability are permanently modified, at least with respect to the non-native setting.

Presented with sentences like the above, individual judgments may be one of these:

A) It's not acceptable, and I don't understand it.
B) It's not acceptable, but I understand it.
C) It's acceptable, because I understand it.

If E's judgments are always A, then Stage 1 has not yet begun; English is still conceptualized in terms of a monolingual standard, and semantic deviations are rejected.

If E's judgments are sometimes A and sometimes B, then Stage 1 has begun.

If E's judgments are always B, then Stage 1 has run its course.

If E's judgments are sometimes B and sometimes C, then Stage 2 has begun.

If E's judgments are always C, then Stage 2 has run its course.

Semantic reconceptualization is the transition from the beginning of Stage 1 to the end of Stage 2. We can now deal with the characteristic features of each stage.

Stage 1: E learns techniques for coping with Englañol in those cases where there are no other more experienced Es in the vicinity to help out. The techniques follow.

First, E can look for clues to meaning in the situational context. For example, if sentence (1) is directed to E along with a piece of paper that is obviously an application for something E wants or needs, it would be reasonable to conclude that the intended meaning was "Write your name and street address." Should the transaction prove successful with this interpretation, E can then reconfirm the newly established synonymous relationship between *address* and *direction* by practical experimentation at the next opportunity, perhaps asking someone for the direction of the First National Bank. Care must be taken to approach a well-dressed Puerto Rican, who is likely to be bilingual, rather than an American tourist.

Second, E could scan the sentence word-by-word to locate words that suggest Spanish cognates previously seen or heard. After determining the meaning(s) of the Spanish word, E could test them to see if the transferred meaning disambiguates the sentence. Thus if E recognizes the formal similarity between English *direction* and Spanish *dirección,* it is a relatively straightforward procedure to clear up the mystery. Here, too, a new synonymous relationship is established — and, as a bonus for effort, E has learned a little more Spanish. This technique is more sophisticated than guessing from situational context, and it requires keeping a pocket bilingual dictionary at hand, but it presents an interesting challenge to the intellectually curious.

During Stage 1 E becomes more and more adept at using these

techniques, either singly or in combination, for coping with new everyday situations requiring an understanding of Englañol vocabulary and usage. Sentences that would formerly be judged unacceptable as English lose their strangeness and become comprehensible. By the end of Stage 1, E can translate Englañol on sight, and probably supply the source Spanish as well:

(1)   Please write your name and direction.
      ”   ”   ”   ”   ” address.   [=dirección]

(2)   The outfielder couldn't recuperate the ball.
      ”   ”   ”   recover   ”   ”   [=recuperar]

(3)   I try to keep up with actualities.
      ” ” ” ” ” ” ” current events.   [=actualidades]

(4)   We met on the street by casualty.
      ”   ”   ”   ”   ”   ” chance.   [=casualidad]

(5)   The meeting will be celebrated at 10 a.m.
      ”   ”   ”   ”   held   ”   ”   ”   [=celebrar]

(6)   Too much coffee is inconvenient for you.
      ”   ”   ”   ” ” bad   ”   ”   [=inconveniente]

(7)   Class is dispatched.
      ”   ” dismissed.   [=despachar]

(8)   He considered my remark an injury.
      ”   ”   ”   ”   ” insult.   [=injuria]

(9)   The final bill ascended to thirty dollars.
      ”   ”   ” came up ”   ”   ”   [=ascender]

(10) Don't molest me now, I'm busy.
      ”   bother ”   ”   ”   ”   [=molestar]

Stage 2: E produces sentences with Englañol characteristics.
      Throughout Stage 1, E has retained the ability to distinguish between native and non-native English by consistently applying a monolingual criterion based on past (pre-Puerto Rican) experience. As the process of reconceptualization continues, the distinction becomes blurred, and E can make sure judgments only where sentences contain grammatical errors. By the end of Stage 2, if a sentence is well formed, intelligible, and appropriate to the situational context, it will be accepted by E as normal English.
      The changed criterion of acceptability permits E to use the now-familiar variety of English in his/her own performance. The re-

conceptualized English appears in conversations not only with Englañol speakers, but with other Es as well.

Three types of performance have been observed. In the first, E repeats expressions heard from other Es:

> *Can I stay with this until tomorrow?*
> (" " keep " " ") [quedar con]
>
> *He's a real self-starter.*
> (" " " go-getter) [emprendedor]
>
> *I think you're pulling my hair.*
> (" " " " " leg) [tomar el pelo]

Although E may be aware of the Spanish origins of the replacements, the fact that they are copied from other native English speakers gives them an implied stamp of approval.

The second type of performance utilizes the knowledge gained in Stage 1 as a communication strategy. It is used with Spanish speakers whose command of Standard English vocabulary is limited (such as one's students, if E is a teacher of freshman English). Thus, if a student asks "What is my note on the exam?" and E has neither the time nor the inclination to launch into a lesson on English vocabulary, it is a labor-saving device to answer, "Your note on the exam is X" [*nota* = grade, mark]. E may also initiate the conversation this way, as insurance that the message will be understood:

> Did you *approve* that course [*aprobar* = pass]?
>
> I will now answer any *doubts* [*duda* = question on the subject material].
>
> Everyone must *assist to* class when there is a quiz [*asistir* = attend].
>
> You'll have to fill out a *solicitude* [*solicitud* = application].
>
> Now go to the *library* and buy your textbooks [*librería* = bookstore].

The third type of performance represents a much deeper change in E's English. E is not aware of the Spanish influence unless it is called to his/her surprised attention. In this ultimate stage of reconceptualization, E spontaneously produces sentences *that reflect Spanish rather than English logic.* Two examples will illustrate this. The first is a sentence uttered by the writer herself:

> *I bought the pieces for the boat.*

which, in pre-Pringlish days, would have been:

I bought the parts for the boat.

The boat referred to is a sailboat from which a rudder pin and bottom screw-in plate had been stolen.

At this point, a brief sojourn into bilingual lexicography is necessary. There are two Spanish-English cognate word pairs, *parte/part* and *pieza/piece.* All four words have high frequencies of occurrence. In each pair the words share many senses and are translational equivalents for each other. Thus, *parte* and *part* match up in

	un libro			a book
parte de	una hora	=	part of	an hour
	un país			a country

and in numerous other collocations. Similarly, *pieza* and *piece* match up in

	ajedrez		chess	
pieza de	música	=	musical	piece
	museo		museum	

and in numerous other collocations. Notice that *parte* and *part* signify inseparable portions of a larger whole, while *pieza* and *piece* signify independent entities not attached to anything else. Because of this fundamental difference in meaning between Spanish *parte* and *pieza,* cognates do not match up in

pieza de respuesta/recambio = spare *part*

Since rudder pins and bottom screw-in plates are replaceable items that fall into the category of independent entities and a boat without them is still a boat, and since *"part* of a boat" suggests something like the front, back, or bottom part, that word, after reconceptualization, would seem inappropriate and even misleading. Thus, the writer had unconsciously transferred Spanish logic to English performance in formulating the Pringlish sentence.

The second example, also uttered by an E after a relatively short period of residence in Puerto Rico, is:

I have to make the shopping.

In pre-Pringlish days, E would have said:

I have to do the shopping.

Involved here is the lexical split of Spanish *hacer* into its most frequent translational equivalents, *to make* and *to do*.[7] The usual rule of thumb given to students in English classes for choosing is something like "*do* means 'perform an action'; *make* means 'produce a result.'"

do the cooking	make a meal
do one's best	make a good showing
do homework	make a study
do your duty	make a sacrifice
do nothing	make a gesture

While such an explanation is too simplistic to account for all idioms, it is evident that, in monolingual English, *do* is process-oriented and *make* is goal-oriented. The Spanish expression *hacer compras* can be either, depending on whether the shopping is for fun or a chore to be completed in the shortest possible time. Pringlish allows E to make this choice linguistically as well: *I like to do the shopping* (=it's a pleasant way to pass time) vs. *I have to make the shopping* (=otherwise there won't be anything to eat in the house).

The more logical use of *make* to express goal/result-oriented activity wherever semantically appropriate is greatly strengthened by the dozens of idioms with *hacer* that E hears in their translated Englañol form:

to make someone a favor [*hacer favor a alguien* = do someone a favor]

to make errands [*hacer recados* = to run errands]

to make a shadow [*hacer sombra* = to cast a shadow]

to make wonders [*hacer maravillas* = to work wonders]

to make the suitcases [*hacer maletas* = to pack]

Discussion

English in a non-native setting can be investigated in two ways. One approach is to look from the outside in, which involves seeing English as a foreign element imposed upon the local language and culture, interacting with it, and producing highly observable manifestations of language contact. The second approach, from the inside out, takes the native English speaker as a starting point and charts the changes that take place in the speaker's mind as a result of language contact. To the extent that language exists in the speaker as well as in society, both approaches are valid.

In describing Pringlish, I have focused on the inside-out approach with the notion of reconceptualization. In addition to anecdotal evidence from speakers themselves, we now have experimental evidence as well. A brief summary of the project follows.[8]

A set of twenty Englañol sentences interspersed with five monolingual English sentences was presented to 117 subjects for evaluation of acceptability. Of this group, 56 were either Spanish-dominant or fully bilingual; the remaining 61 subjects were continentals ranging in age from 13 to 66 years and ranging in length of stay in Puerto Rico from under one month (tourists) to over ten years (permanent residents). From the background questionnaire the subjects were asked to fill out, we know that the continental English-speaking group had an average of 13.4 years of formal education, or approximately one and one-half years of college. The sentences were presented orally to the subjects via tape recordings; the reader was a native speaker of English. (This may have affected the results.) The response form gave the subjects only boxes to check; the subjects did not see the sentences in written form. (This may also have affected the results.) Half of the subjects were asked to check acceptable sentences, the other half to indicate unacceptable sentences. The sentences heard by the subjects were:

1. Puerto Rico is an island in the Caribbean Sea.
2. Smoking is not convenient for your health.
3. The robbers took all my values and left me nothing.
4. His note on the exam was very poor and he failed the course.
5. Some type was acting silly in the bar.
6. Education is a good thing to have these days.
7. The material of today's discussion is conservation.
8. Our politics is to hire more women.
9. Can you manage a car well enough to pass the driver's test?
10. The weather is fresh today.
11. He rented a house next to the ocean.
12. The heat made me transpire.
13. Some women like to use pants because they are more comfortable.
14. A Columbian and a Peruvian come from distinct countries.
15. People in air-conditioned buildings maintain their doors closed.
16. Give me your name and direction.
17. On world affairs, he is an extremely illustrated man.
18. The price of coffee has decreased this year.
19. Bilingual people dominate two languages.
20. People who want to swim take swimming instructions.

21. St. Thomas is a short trip by plane from San Juan.
22. If you pass by my office, we'll discuss the matter.
23. English vocals are difficult for Spanish speakers.
24. Second languages should be more stimulated around the world.
25. People usually don't talk about their familiar problems with strangers.

Here are the clues for the Englañol sentences (others are blank):

1.
2. [*conveniente* = good, beneficial]
3. [*valores* = valuables]
4. [*note* = mark, grade]
5. [*tipo* = guy, fellow]
6.
7. [*materia* = subject]
8. [*política* = policy]
9. [*manejar* = drive (a car)]
10. [*fresca* = cool]
11.
12. [*transpirar* = perspire]
13. [*usar* = wear]
14. [*distinto* = different]
15. [*mantener* = keep]
16. [*dirección* = (street) address]
17. [*ilustrado* = well informed]
18.
19. [*dominar* = command, know]
20. [*instrucciones* = lessons]
21.
22. [*pasar por* = drop in]
23. [*vocal* = vowel]
24. [*estimular* = promote, encourage]
25. [*familiar* = family (attr)]

The under-one-month group accepted 39 percent of these sentences, and the over-ten-year group accepted 54 percent. The in-between curve fluctuated back and forth, reaching its highest point of 56 percent at three years, then leveling off to about the same percentage of acceptance found among the fully bilingual group. While the many uncontrolled variables in this preliminary experiment do not allow us to call the results definitive, there is no doubt that the overall rise in acceptability among continentals is directly proportionate to their length of stay.

There are surely other speech communities in the world similar to Puerto Rico where the process of reconceptualization can and should be investigated by linguists interested in language contact. At issue is not only the influence of one language upon another, or the influence of one variety of a language upon another variety of the same language, but some very basic questions about the nature of language in general. It may be that what we have called "native language intuition" is something like a self-adjusting monitoring device that responds to environment. If this proves to be true, as Pringlish indicates, then we must redefine the notions of native speaker and native language.[9]

NOTES

1. See Nash (1970, 1971, 1976). For a survey of the political, social, and historical background of the language situation, see Nash (1977a).

2. A fourth variety, to be called "Espanglés," will describe the second-language Spanish of native English speakers. The hybrid labels were suggested by the writer's graduate students in linguistics.

3. According to the Office of Tourism of Fomento, the Puerto Rican agency for economic development, 70 percent of 1,376,466 registered hotel visitors in 1977 came from the United States. This would not include Americans who stayed with friends or relatives.

4. Most of the military establishments have been disbanded and the land and buildings given to Puerto Rico. Only two large bases remain at the present time, Fort Buchanan Army Base and Roosevelt Roads Naval Base. There is also a Coast Guard unit and a small R.O.T.C. contingent. Of the some 50,000 troops on active duty, 80 percent are continentals. The Army Reserve and National Guard are made up of Puerto Rican resident bilinguals. The largest federal agencies are the Customs Service, Postal Service, District Court for Puerto Rico, Department of Health, Education and Welfare, and the Department of Agriculture. Listings in the San Juan telephone book occupy almost seven columns.

5. Examples are from letters to the editor of the *San Juan Star,* Puerto Rico's English-language daily newspaper.

6. Comprehensive lists of formal correspondences in cognate word pairs are given in Nash (1977b). A large-scale computerized study of parallel Spanish-English vocabulary now in progress will also produce semantic and syntactic correspondences.

7. For an in-depth study of this problem, see Hagerty and Bowen (1973).

8. The experiment was conducted by Ken Nelson. A more complete analysis of the results than that given here appears in Nash (1978).

9. I wish to acknowledge many helpful discussions with Dr. Leo Korchin and Ms. Mary Wander.

REFERENCES

Anderson, Roger W., ed. 1978. *Proceedings of the colloquium on the acquisition and use of Spanish and English as first and second languages.* Twelfth Annual TESOL Convention, Mexico City, April 4-9, 1978.

Hagerty, Timothy W., and Bowen, J. Donald. 1973. A contrastive analysis of a lexical split: Spanish *hacer* to English *do/make/*etc. Pp. 1-71 in Nash (1973).

Makkai, V. B., and Heilman, L., eds. 1977. *Linguistics at the crossroads.* Lake Bluff, Ill.: Jupiter Press.

Nash, Rose. 1970. Spanglish: language contact in Puerto Rico. *American Speech* 45: 223-33.

———. 1971. Englañol: more language contact in Puerto Rico. *American Speech* 46: 106-22.

———. 1973. *Readings in Spanish-English contrastive linguistics* I. San Juan: Inter-American University Press.

———. 1976. Phantom cognates and other curiosities in Puerto Rican Englañol. *La Mondo Lingvo-Problema [Language Problems & Language Planning]* 5: 157-67.

———. 1977a. Aspects of Spanish-English bilingualism and language mixture in Puerto Rico. In Makkai (1977).

———. 1977b. *Comparing Spanish and English: patterns in phonology and orthography.* San Juan: Regents.

———. 1978. Semantic transfer in Puerto Rican English. In Anderson (1978).

17

The Life Cycle of Non-Native Englishes: A Case Study

RODNEY F. MOAG

The non-native varieties of English furnish fertile, and relatively untapped, ground for study of the processes of sociolinguistic change. These varieties have grown up in recent times as second languages in multilingual former colonies of Great Britain; hence the alternative terms "new Englishes" and "Third World Englishes." The three terms, as used by Kachru (1977) and others, are synonymous, save in the case of Caribbean English (where "non-native" does not apply, since the vernacular variety, Creole, is also English [LePage 1968: 440]).

The last areas to come under colonization, whether as British colonies or as protectorates of Australia or New Zealand, were the South Pacific Islands. Tonga, Samoa, Nauru, Fiji, Papua New Guinea, Tuvalu (Ellice Islands), the Gilberts, and the Solomon Islands were colonized in the late nineteenth and early twentieth centuries; all are independent now, while the Cook Islands, American Samoa, Niue, and the Tokelaus are not yet free. English plays a part as either a foreign language (FL) or a second language (SL) in all of the above. Since the emerging variety here has not been reported in the linguistically oriented literature, the first goal here will be to set South Pacific English in its rightful place alongside the other recognized non-native varieties of English. The second goal will be to set forth a tentative "life cycle of non-native Englishes" following the model of Hall's (1962) "Life Cycle of Pidgin Languages," including the constituent processes by which the variety begins as a FL, becomes a SL, and reverts to FL status again. I shall draw primarily on the case of Fiji, owing to my three years' research and university teaching in that country; but I shall also draw secondarily on data from other islands in the region, and from beyond.

Constituent Processes of the Life Cycle

Four processes are posited as significant constituents of the life cycle: transportation, indigenization, expansion in use and function, and institutionalization. A fifth, restriction of use and function, does not apply in all cases.

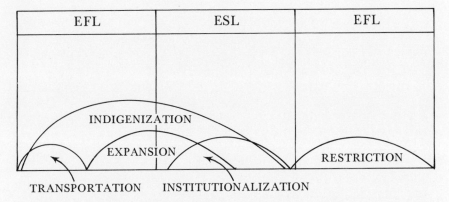

Figure 1. The Life Cycle of Non-Native Englishes

It is not possible to regard these as stages in the strict sense, since they are not fully consecutive. Each process begins in the order stated, but once under way, it overlaps with succeeding processes. Indigenization, for example, precedes, but runs concurrently with, expansion of use and function, and well into institutionalization.

Transportation

Little need be said about this first process, save that it involves bringing English into a new environment for purposes of a more or less permanent nature, such as colonial administration. Contact between English-speaking aliens and some segment of the local population, usually a very limited one, will be frequent and recurrent enough, and the dominance of the visitors will be clear enough, to require that the locals learn English. The most common case is that of a class of clerks trained and retained to assist a colonial administration, but other relationships are also possible. The first ESL group in the Belgian Congo consisted of house servants of English-speaking missionaries.

Indigenization

Indigenization, a term used in Moag and Moag (1977: 3), is a process of language change by which the new variety of English becomes distinct from the parent imported variety, and from other indigenized varieties elsewhere. Kachru (1977) has used "nativization" in much the same sense. The first step occurs when English-speaking newcomers come into contact with items of the local material and nonmaterial culture for which there are no equivalents in their home environment or language. In Fijian English, there can be no other word for *daruka* (a local vegetable) or for *vesi* (a local hardwood), since they are not known or named elsewhere. Similarly, institutions such as *kerekere* (a system of gaining things by begging for them from members of one's own group — a recognized system in Fijian society [Capell 1973: 95]) and *mataqali* ("the primary social division in Fiji" [Capell 1973: 142]) have no precise or succinct English translations. Hence, only local terms for them will serve.

A multilingual, multicultural setting such as Fiji's leads to multiple borrowing. *Bhājī* (a class of greens), *dāl* (a class of lentils), *pūjā* (a Hindu devotional ceremony), and *divālī* (the Hindu festival of lights) are items and concepts drawn from Hindi.

Weinreich's (1951: 85) hierarchy of the likelihood of borrowing lists "sentence words without syntactic function," such as interjections, as having "very great" likelihood of borrowing, whereas "free morphemes with syntactic functions," such as nouns and verbs, have only "considerable" likelihood. Samples of indigenized varieties of English from around the world would seem to call for free lexical items being in first (rather than second) position, in terms of either degree of borrowing or order of occurrence.

Bright (1973: 213) identifies two types of initial contact between colonials and natives in the New World, one focusing on the indigenous culture, the second focusing on the conqueror's or invader's culture; both resulted in the borrowing of such free morphemes. Bright does not rank these chronologically or in any other way, but the former seems typical of situations relating to exploration or trading, while the latter would be typical of established conquest and colonization. In the South Pacific, an extended period of sandalwood trading, whaling, exploration, and later mission activity preceded actual colonial rule, but these all involved the use of the vernaculars (see Geraghty 1978 and Schütz 1972: 29-35).

At least some early linguists recognized that language contact situations could result in structural as well as lexical borrowing (Boas 1929: 6). This later led to the recognition of linguistic areas in South Asia (Emeneau 1956), the Balkans, and with Indian languages in California (Gumperz 1968: 466). More recently the transfer of discourse features, including communicative norms (Richards 1982), have been noted. In this initial phase of the indigenization process, however, there are conditions which effectively block borrowing above the lexical level from native languages into English, and probably vice versa. Local learners of English are subjected to an extremely high degree of exposure to native speaker models, whether in the classroom or on the job, and they use English primarily for communication with native-speaking aliens. Under these conditions there is full reinforcement of native-like features of the language. Non-native features which second-language speakers might introduce would not only find no reinforcement, but would be very likely to receive explicit correction. The situation is completely reversed later, but at this point the sociolinguistic climate will tolerate only the importation of specific items for which there is no direct equivalent in the imported native speaker model of English.

The second phase of the indigenization process comes when members of the local colonial elite (and/or the cadre of menial servants) begin to use English for communication among themselves. This happens in two distinct though not necessarily disconnected ways. First, English may begin to be used as a lingua franca, in addition to or instead of local link languages, enabling those of different language backgrounds who may work or live together, due to the new colonial system, to communicate with each other in a more intensive way than was customary in the pre-colonial situation.

Second, English often tends to become the preferred medium for discussing topics associated with the alien, but now in most senses dominant, culture. Both of these tendencies can occur, and will reinforce each other, in a multilingual setting where they are the harbingers of the more generalized expansion of use and function to come. The topical conditioning of the use of English can operate in a monolingual setting as well, when the new items and institutions brought by the new rulers are alien and have no ready equivalents in local language or culture. This phase sees the transfer of more native features into English, as locals bring familiar items and conventions in their own languages and cultures into play in the new situation. These include additional lexemes, grammatical features through direct transfer or overgeneralization, and communicative norms.

This particular phase tends to have considerable longevity, persisting as long as English education remains an elitist phenomenon. In Fiji, the government assumed responsibility for education in 1916; it began promoting English by insisting that schools teach it in order to receive government grants-in-aid, and by requiring that only certified teachers teach it. A full generation later, in an anthropological study of the second-most-important island, Quain wrote that "all but the highest education is accomplished in the language of Bau (Standard Fijian). I did not see more than half a dozen Fijians on Vanua Levu with a working knowledge of English, and most of these had been imported from more sophisticated regions to perform official duties" (1948: 68). Through the colonial period three separate commissions urged giving greater prominence to English, but not until the 1960s were enough school-agers actually enrolled in secondary schools to make this possible (Fiji *Report* 1970). The New Hebrides are still in this stage, with the government having taken over education from the churches (who used the vernaculars) in the late 1950s.

Subsequent phases of the indigenization process run concurrently with later processes in the life cycle. They will, therefore, be subsumed under the following two sections.

Expansion in Use and Function

This process begins with the extension of English (or the degree of its use) to new domains, particularly education, the media, and government services. English may have been used in these domains previously, but only by an elite group of locals; witness the quote from Quain, cited above.

Obviously, expansion must first take place in the domain of education, since the requisite skills of literacy and aural comprehension must be acquired before the populace can use English for paperwork and face-to-face contact with clerks and government officials. That English-medium education is a necessary but not a sufficient condition for the diffusion of the language through the society is exemplified in the South Pacific by the island kingdom of Tonga. This monolingual nation has English-medium education from the upper primary grades onward, but English is still a foreign (not a second) language in the society. A Tongan can do everything he needs to do, save complete his high school matriculation, in his own language. Radio broadcasting is almost exclusively in Tongan, the weekly newspaper is bilingual, and all government communications are either bilingual or, at the lower level, solely in Tongan. The English versions are principally for the benefit of the expatriates who work at higher administrative levels in the government, or as secondary school teachers. This example indicates that the concept "home-school bilingualism" (Kloss 1966: 10; Christopherson 1973: 74) is inadequate, since it does not tell us anything about the role of the home language and the school language in other domains of societal activity.

The expansion process, if fully run, sees the role of English shift from that of a foreign to a second language. This process seems to be blocked in monolingual societies, whatever the stage of development of the local vernacular. In a number of multilingual settings it is clearly influenced, and even potentially precluded, by the pres-

ence of a contending local "mid language" (Abdulaziz 1972) already
operating as a lingua franca, such as Swahili in East Africa and Pidgin
in three Pacific nations. The degree of expansion possible for English
will be governed by several factors, including the prestige of the mid
language, its degree of "language modernization" (Kloss 1966: 15) or
"state of development" (Ferguson 1977: 44), and its functions and
degree of use within the critical domains.

In the New Hebrides, for example, a condominium government
is jointly administered by Great Britain and France; some children attend English-medium schools, and others French-medium schools.
Pidgin, locally called Bichelamar (Guy 1964), is the only language
which can unite all the people. It is already used widely by all the
churches, in the bilingual newsletters published by both governments
(one English and Bichelamar, the other French and Bichelamar), and
in the speeches and tracts of major political parties; furthermore, it
has more radio air time than either colonial language. English seems
destined to play a fairly limited role in the New Hebrides, particularly if Pidgin should undergo two final steps in its growing legitimati-
zation, i.e., becoming the medium of instruction in primary school,
and being made the official language of government (as now seems
likely).

Pidgin is also expanding in use and function in Papua New Guinea (Wurm 1977: 334). Its official promotion for use in education and
as the official language of the country has been thwarted as much by
the presence of a competing local lingua franca, Hiri Motu, as by the
expansion of English. Both local languages enjoy sufficient use in
both formal and informal domains to limit the advance of English.
This is less true in the Solomon Islands. There, though Pidgin is the
sole national lingua franca, it is still basically an oral language occupying only domains of informal social contact, oral political activity, and more indigenous types of radio programs. English, for the
time being at least, has full sway in written domains, though this
could change quite rapidly if the current efforts to standardize
Pidgin orthography are successful.

Multilingual nations such as Fiji, which lack a contending national lingua franca, give English a clearer path to second-language
status. The neutral role of English in such situations has been acknowledged by several writers, including Kloss (1966: 8) and Pride
(1978). This neutrality is political in character, i.e., giving no group
the advantage of having its own language singled out for official status. Also important is the social neutrality of English which functions
as follows within monolingual societies or groups. Many vernaculars

have special registers, or systems of address, for persons of distinct
social standing. Fijian has a chiefly subcode; Tongan has distinct
forms for addressing commoners, nobility, and royalty; a septimodal
system exists in Samoa (Malia 1976). Under the impact of modernization, young people growing up in these societies today do not gain
active control over these special subcodes. Tongans and Fijians have
told me that they find English the only safe medium in which to address those of higher status (Moag 1978c: 74). English not only hides
their inability in the specialized vernacular registers, but also allows
them to meet traditional superiors on a more or less equal footing.
This is aided by the fact that English in the second-language context
has a more limited repertoire of social variants.

The birth of an informal variety. On the one hand, lack of internal variation makes the non-native variety of English a social as
well as political leveler. On the other hand, a major feature of the
indigenization and expansion processes is an increase in internal variation through the creation of a separate stylistic variant used for informal purposes. Such varieties are well reported for West Africa,
India, Singapore and Malaysia, and the Philippines. Because of the
special situation in the Caribbean, the informal variety came first
and became mother tongue for imported plantation workers. The
catalytic agent for these informal varieties is often the "all-English
rule" in government or mission-operated schools. Teachers and ad-
ministrators institute the rules as a means of providing maximal practice in the target language. The pupils, showing far more sociolinguistic awareness than their pedagogues, immediately realize that the
English they have been taught in the classroom is entirely inappropriate to their activities on the playground. In the absence of any
precise model, they are forced to draw upon their own resources —
with the result that this variety shows a much higher proportion of
local and interlanguage (Selinker 1972) features. Two investigators
have documented the influence of local languages in Fiji, though
using different names for the new variety of English: " 'the dialect'
seems to share certain grammatical features with Fijian" (Kelley
1975: 36-37). "Fiji Pidgin seems to have an identical vowel system
and shared politeness markers and gestures to Fijian" (Geraghty
1977: 4-5).

The first name employed for the informal variety of English
in Fiji was "playground English." I have elsewhere coined the term
"Colloquial Fiji English (CFE)" (Moag and Moag 1977: 3) and have
cited a few characteristic borrowed lexical items. *Paisa* (money),
choro (to steal), and *paidar* (on foot) are taken from Fiji Hindi.

Fijian examples such as *kasou* (drunk), *lamu* (afraid), and *talasi* (to steal) are in this category. None of these items would be found in Standard Fiji English.

The results of languages in contact are, of course, two-way, involving mutual borrowing. This does not mean, however, that the degree of borrowing will be equal in each direction. At the most superficial level (that of lexemes) the number of items borrowed into local languages from English, which serves as "a global carrier wave for news, information, entertainment, and administration and as the language in which has taken place the genesis of the second industrial and scientific revolution" (Strevens 1977: 115), will be far higher than that which even the most indigenized variety of local English takes on from the vernaculars. Moag (1979) mentions the extensive English borrowings in Fiji Hindi and Fijian, and lists of English loans in Fijian appear in a phonological treatment by Schütz (1978). Mutual borrowing has been documented in all other major ESL areas as well. The following extreme (but not an atypical) example was overheard from a young female Fiji Indian sales clerk: "*Shīlā* account book use *karā,* I think." ('Shila used the account book, I think.') The italics show that the female name, *Shīlā,* and the verb *karā*, needed to make the borrowed verb "use" syntactically acceptable, are the only native items in the sentence. The order of major constituents (subject-object-verb) in the kernel sentence clearly marks it as Hindi, not English.

In a language contact situation such as in Fiji, on the discourse level, casual observations seem to indicate that more features are borrowed into English from vernaculars than vice versa. The balance of borrowing tips in the opposite direction on the semantic-syntactic level. This suggests two complementary clines of borrowing which, together, illustrate an approximate representation of the effects of long-term contact. It is given here in the hope of sparking the detailed studies needed to test its validity.

Institutionalization of the New Varieties

This is a gradual process, and it is not easy to pinpoint precisely when it begins. Several factors play an important role in the process, however; these are dealt with in turn below.

The role of local creative writers. The publication in Australia of the Papuan Vincent Eri's novel, *The Crocodile,* in 1970 and the publication in New Zealand of *Sons for the Return Home* by the Samoan Albert Wendt in 1973 were hallmarks in the evolution of the newly emerging South Pacific literature. These were, however, directed as much at audiences in native English-speaking countries as at island audiences. Though no novels have yet been published by writers in Fiji, their poems and short stories are clearly directed mainly to a home audience. The founding of the South Pacific Creative Arts Society and the publication of the *Mana Annuals,* beginning in 1973, expressly "to influence islanders to write, and . . . to submit what they write," and the appearance of *Mana Review* since 1976, containing literary criticism as well as creative writing, are symptomatic of both the regional character and the ongoing nature of South Pacific literature. The motivation for these writers was aptly expressed by one of their number, Subramani: "At the moment there is a great deal of interest in creative writing in Fiji, and it is clear from recent developments that local writers will employ English to examine themselves and communicate their identities to the rest of the world" (1978: 142). There is, to date, a certain amount of literary activity in the vernaculars in Fiji (Moag 1978a: 135-37), and writers from the New Hebrides sometimes translate their works into Pidgin.

The first generation of creative writers in the region have, for the most part, received their secondary or tertiary training abroad, in native English-speaking countries. The crop of younger writers now coming up are largely students at the University of the South Pacific in Fiji; they have received all of their education in an ESL environment. A distinctly regional character is found in the works of both groups, in terms of both themes and linguistic norms. Hindi words and phrases are liberally sprinkled throughout the works of Nandan, Pillai, and Subramani; Fijian terms appear in the writing of Seru and others. Nacola's plays liberally employ Colloquial Fiji English (1976).

Local literary activity becomes institutionalized when it becomes regenerative. Works from all of the above-mentioned authors play a large part in the English curriculum of the University of the South Pacific, and are now finding their way into the secondary school curricula. This new literature serves dual functions, motivating students to take up the pen themselves, and providing a model for accepted norms when they do so. The local importance of English writers in India, West Africa, and the Caribbean is well reported elsewhere in the literature.

The role of localization of teachers. LePage (1968: 439-40) provides a very clear description of the linguistic consequences of the extension of secondary education to the general populace, and of the subsequent localization of the teaching staff in the Caribbean. In the colonial period a local elite, taught and trained by expatriate English-speaking teachers, usually finished their educations abroad, in native

English-speaking countries such as the United States, Canada, or Britain. The bulk of the population acquired no meaningful competence in standard English during their few years of primary education. Nowadays more secondary schools have been built, and teacher training institutions are opened locally; a generation of students arises which has been taught completely by West Indian teachers, and which has received all of its training in the home country. I would agree with LePage that this produces "speakers of a more divergent dialect" (1968: 439), but not with his proposed remedial program to correct the steadily widening gap between "what is supposed to be happening in the schools and what is actually happening" (1968: 440). Increasing divergence from the imported native model during the institutionalization period is as inevitable as it is abhorrent to most expatriate (and even local elite) observers and educators (Kachru 1977: 33).

The opening of the University of the South Pacific in 1968 meant that, by 1972, locally trained diploma- and degree-holders were being supplied to the education systems of the eleven South Pacific nations which that institution serves. In Fiji, secondary teachers, and all tertiary ones save at the university itself, are localized. A growing proportion of them are locally trained, largely by ESL speakers. Secondary schools in the other South Pacific nations are still predominantly staffed by expatriate teachers, but localization is under way and should be complete within the foreseeable future.

The end result of localization of teachers is a stable situation in which the young people of the society learn the formal variety of English from second-language-speaking locals, who also learned it from second-language speakers. There is negligible input from native-speaker models, particularly aural ones.

The role of the media. The press and radio also play a part in the legitimization of the new non-native English. In terms of a spoken model, all locally originated programs in Fiji, both scripted and ad-libbed, are now handled by local personnel. As was the case with secondary education, the Fiji Broadcasting Commission was staffed and run by expatriates up to the 1970s in all its English-medium activities. English-language staffs are still expatriate in the New Hebrides and in American Samoa, but are fully localized elsewhere, though the amount of English versus vernacular programming varies markedly along at least two dimensions throughout the South Pacific. The multilingual (ESL) countries have a substantial amount of English-language programming, while the independent monolingual (EFL) nations, Tonga and Samoa, have little save the international news

relayed from Radio Australia. Colonial versus independent status is
also a significant dimension, as evidenced by the higher proportion
of English programming in the monolingual Cook Islands and American Samoa. Local English program personnel have generally not received their language training overseas. Native models still comprise
a small part of the radio service, however, both through relayed news
broadcasts and through a few transcribed programs furnished from
the BBC and the Voice of America. There is no television in the region outside the French territories, save in American Samoa, which
airs both locally originated educational programs and commercial
programs from the United States on film.

The print media in Fiji and the rest of the South Pacific are at
a less advanced stage of localization. Most writers and subeditors for
Fiji's two daily English newspapers are locals, but the chief editor and
one or two writers on each are still expatriates. Conditions vary from
country to country, according to language situation and political
status. The New Hebrides has no commercial press. The English text
for the biweekly newsletter put out by the colonial government is,
not surprisingly, written by expatriates. The bilingual weekly papers
in Tonga and Samoa have already been mentioned above.

Even with full localization of the media, there will inevitably
be a higher proportion of native-speaker-model material in the written domain than in the aural one. Papers use numerous items from
the international news services, and popular books and magazines
abound in the bookstores. The English-language movies are all imported from native-speaking countries, but their clear lack of relevance to the local context, and their only occasional attendance
(compared to daily newspaper reading) gives them less influence as
a model. It seems clear that local news items will be read or listened
to with greatest attention, and that the local themes, cultural assumptions, and language style will have the greatest real impact. Several
observers, including LePage (1968: 441), have pointed out that
speakers of the "new Englishes" often believe themselves to be speaking one of the older, more accepted, models, usually British English.
The distinction between idealized and real behavior is all important
here. If the kind of conditioned switching between different varieties
within the new English outlined by Kachru (1977: 32) exists, then
we must conclude that, on the subconscious level at least, speakers
are aware of the differences that distinguish their own indigenized
English from that of other native-speaking and second-language-speaking countries, and that they can select, albeit intuitively, a model
to follow. Within this context the localization of media staff becomes

clearly significant, both as a creative force and as a reinforcing one. Movies, broadcasts, and printed matter produced outside the region become peripheral. The role of the media has been little acknowledged (hence their situation has not been reported) in treatments of the other new Englishes. Observations during travel and casual reports by others seem to substantiate a similar pattern of the change from expatriate to local staff, and performance model, in the English media of most Third World countries.

The role of vernacular use and policy. The place of the vernacular languages in the overall language use pattern has a direct bearing on the role which English can assume. A brief "sketch of language use patterns in Fiji" appears in Moag and Moag (1977: 9-10), and a more detailed "sociolinguistic sketch of Fiji" can be found in Moag (1978c: 69-77). Basically, Fiji society is moving away from the linguistic diversity which Gumperz (1968: 469-70) cites as typical of "intermediate" societies, though this is happening at different rates in different communities. For the Indians, the first stage involved the disappearance of the regional Indian languages and the adoption of Fiji Hindi as home language by all of the present generation (Moag 1977, 1979). Fijian dialects are still spoken in their home regions, but are increasingly influenced by the standard dialect (Schütz 1972: 107). Geraghty's (1977) research shows instances of whole villages adopting standard dialect.

The second stage involves the decreasing participation in religious and other cultural rituals where formal or ritual varieties of Hindi or Fijian are used. Rituals which are retained are altered to curtail the use of these varieties. The very different Indian and Fijian firewalking ceremonies are now run mainly as fund-raising events for temples, or as attractions at tourist hotels, respectively; English is used, in deference to the new type of audience. The third stage involves enlarging the functions of the new informal variety of English, Colloquial Fiji English (CFE), with two results. First, more specialized local lingua francas are forced out — Pidgin Fijian and Pidgin Hindi are still used, but less so. Second, use of the inter-communal contact code is extended into contexts involving only members of one community. Geraghty (1977: 4) reports the use of CFE between Fijians, and attributes this to the carryover of English's high prestige even to the homegrown informal variety.

As urbanization and development proceed, more and more locals aspire to white-collar jobs, and to the English competence needed to obtain them. Two studies of Indian parents in Fiji in the 1950s showed a clear preference for English rather than vernaculars in the schools

(Adam 1958). A fourth stage in the ascendancy of English involves
the modification of official policies so as to advance English and down-
grade vernaculars. Through the 1950s, secondary school pupils prepared for and took the Hindi and Fijian language exams in both the
junior and senior Cambridge examinations, thereby achieving enough
proficiency in the standard formal variety to be able to read and take
part in cultural events, etc. Now that vernaculars are optional, non-
examinable subjects, they receive little attention, if indeed they are
taught at all (Moag 1978a: 135). Thus the educational system has
passed from a biliterate to a transitional one (Fishman 1978: 409),
where the vernaculars are used as media of instruction, with accompanying ESL classes, only for the first three years, and solely for the
purpose of preparing pupils to function in the succeeding seven or
more years of English medium ahead. The products of this system exhibit what I have termed "skewed bilingualism" (Moag 1978b: 3).
Students have functional competence in only one formal language
variety, Standard Fiji English. Whenever they wish to participate in
formal activities, then, whether inter- or intra-communal, people
will naturally use English. Siegel (1973: 2) found a shift from Standard Hindi to English in formal domains. Moag (1979) reports most
Fiji Indians having only passive aural competence in Standard Hindi.
Fijian is in a somewhat better situation than Hindi, owing both to
the use of the same alphabet as English and to the slower pace of
modernization within that community (Moag 1978a: 136), but Geraghty (1977) does report that urban Fijians tend to avoid traditional
activities in which formal Fijian is used. The relative position of vernaculars versus English in other South Pacific countries has already
been mentioned.

Restriction of the Use and Function of English

This final stage in the life cycle is not evident in any South Pacific nation. It does appear imminent in the Philippines, and is clearly
under way in other multilingual nations of Asia and Africa. It involves
the displacement of English by a local official language, usually through
the processes of language planning as described by Rubin and Jernudd
(1971) and others, in those very domains of government activities,
education, and the media which had permitted English to rise to a
position of dominance during the pre-independence period. Fishman
has rightly pointed out that a society cannot tolerate the luxury of
two languages occupying the same functional territory (1978: 411).
Thus when newly independent governments of the Philippines, Malaysia, and India (among others) mount vigorous campaigns promoting

the national language, English is bound, in time, to revert to the status of a foreign language studied and used by a small elite — the status which it held much earlier in the life cycle. In Malaysia, for instance, Malay has become the language of instruction not only through secondary schooling, but in many university subjects as well. Anyone obtaining a government job must know it, whatever his mother tongue.

This new EFL stage contrasts with the EFL stage at the beginning of the life cycle, in that use of English is more limited. The elites in the new independent nations use English only in technical and scientific subjects at the university level, and for some professional activities, whereas formerly the local colonial elite used the language in all activities relating to school and work.

The concept of life cycle implies that there is both a beginning and an end to the process and organism under study. Once the local national language is firmly established, the creative writing, media activities, and other support mechanisms in English will fade. There could then be a reorientation away from the indigenized non-native model and toward an external native model of English. This potential death of the new English variety has not yet happened in any country, but may be in the cards for Malaysia, the Philippines, and perhaps even India.

Some Implications of the Proposed Life Cycle

The above life cycle for non-native varieties of English is tentative at this point. It is presented here as a theoretical construct, but one formulated after considerable research and observation in ESL societies in the South Pacific and elsewhere. Detailed studies of English-using societies around the world could further test its validity. The remainder of this article will briefly cover some questions arising from the life-cycle construct, and from the linguistic results of English becoming an institutionalized second language.

Salient Questions Arising from the Life Cycle

Does the language situation truly stabilize after institutionalization of the indigenized variety? One basic tenet of linguistics is that language is always changing. Is it possible that language situations, too, are forever in a state of flux? The East Indians, who form roughly half the population of Guyana, have recently lost their native Hindi; the present generation has Creole (English) as its native tongue (Bickerton 1977). However, the remainder of the populace has had Creole as L1 since the country was settled, and there are no significant indigenous

languages. In Fiji, an ESL society, the present generation of Chinese
have already switched to English (Yee 1974: 16). A similar trend may
be under way in Singapore (Platt 1977: 364). Is it possible that the
tendency to use Colloquial Fijian English with communal mates could
eventually cause the larger vernaculars to succumb? Might second-language status for English prove to be only a passing phase, with English
inexorably becoming a native language in some societies and a foreign language in others? This would not be inconsonant with "the
spread of English" as described by Fishman et al. (1977).

What becomes of the informal variety when English reverts to
FL status? The most informal and indigenized varieties are the code-
mixed ones found in the Philippines and India (Kachru 1977: 33).
Will Mixmix in the Philippines (Sibayan 1977), colloquial Malaysian
English (Tongue 1974; Paauw 1977), and others gradually fade from
use under the ascendancy of Tagalog, Malay, etc.? If so, what will
take their place? Will they, on the other hand, undergo further change,
probably in the form of relexification from the national language,
thereby becoming an informal variety of the vernacular? These varieties will bear careful watching in the next decade or two.

Is restriction of use and function the final stage in the process?
Or will further changes be in store? It seems difficult to imagine Third
World nations becoming so isolated from the currents of world events
that they would revert to sole use of the vernaculars. It even seems
improbable today that another language might displace English as the
international language of science and technology. The one certainty
in studying anything, however, is that the currently prevailing innovations will seem grossly outmoded to the next generation.

The Linguistic Effects of ESL Status

Skewed bilingualism. For English to be a second language, its use
must not be restricted to a small elite, but must be fairly generalized
in the society. It is difficult to set a minimum percentage, but in a
modernizing society Kloss's suggestions of "all literate adults" and
"all secondary school graduates" (1966: 15) seem to adequately define the segment of the population which will be bilingual. It is important to recognize that monolingual EFL groups will persist in
outlying geographic areas and in lower social classes.

Localized performance model. The inevitable localization of the
performance model of English was discussed earlier. Bickerton (1977:
55) refers to the absence of a native model in the English of Fiji,
stating that this places it "intermediate between Pidgin and 'good
foreigner version.' " The indigenized model is both conditioned and
supported by the internal function of the new variety cited next.

Internal function of English. In the ESL society, English is used primarily for internal purposes. A small elite continues to use it for external (international) purposes, but it is not a linguistically significant group in the society.

A more native-like language acquisition. With a foreign language, only the formal variety is acquired; learning takes place largely through formal study, mainly in adolescence or adulthood. During the colonial period, the study of English may well begin in the earliest primary classes, and a good deal of informal learning goes on when other subjects are taught in the English medium. With English occupying a broad range of domains in the ESL, post-colonial society, many children acquire some active competence in the informal variety of English before entering school. Further learning of this variety continues in school, through playground activities, and in informal socialization, shopping, and other activities outside of school.

Informal learning here also plays a larger role in the acquisition of the formal variety. Besides English-medium classes — where formal correction of errors may still go on — less formal learning takes place when one attends public functions, reads newspapers, notices, and the like, or listens to the radio. Strevens (1977: 115) states the new functional role of the formal variety thus: "There came a demand in the wake of independence . . . for English to be taught for practical communicative use. The assumption was that English would continue as part of a general education for citizenship, but would be separated from the literary, social, and cultural values of Britain or the United States." According to Kachru (1977: 32), English (a second language) "imbedded in the native sociocultural matrix of the area" comes to have a pattern of acquisition much like that of native languages.

Vernaculars endangered. Expansion of the use and function of English brings about a corresponding decrease in use and function of the vernaculars. I have already raised the question of whether the vernaculars can long survive in this limited role. Informal English is already making inroads into their remaining domains. The experience with Gaelic in Ireland teaches that a vernacular cannot be reclaimed, even by a massive program, once it has been abandoned by the vast majority (97%) of the population.

In ESL nations like Fiji it is still not too late. Governments must engage in language planning to determine the balance of roles for English and the vernaculars which is in keeping with the long-term goals of the society; then they must devise and implement plans to bring them into being. All potential plans must, of course, be cost effective, but the initial research need not be prohibitively expensive. In 1973 the Maori Education Unit of the New Zealand Council for Educational Research launched a five-year study of language use and attitudes in areas of Maori settlement, at a cost of $70,000 (Benton 1975: 3). The resulting plans will serve only 8 percent of New Zealand's population. Other countries are engaged in even more ambitious programs to benefit small linguistic minorities. Since the total population is involved in issues of language choice and policy in ESL societies, the highest priority should be given to conserving and effectively using the nation's language resources, including its vernaculars.

REFERENCES

Abdulaziz, M. H. 1972. Triglossia and Swahili-English bilingualism in Tanzania. *Language in Society* 1: 197-213.

Adam, R. S. 1958. Social factors in second language learning. Ph.D. dissertation, University of London.

Benton, Richard A. 1975. Sociolinguistic survey of Maori language use. *Language Planning Newsletter,* East-West Culture Learning Institute 1(2): 3-4.

Bickerton, Derek. 1977. Pidginization and creolization: language acquisition and language universals. Pp. 49-69 in Valdman, ed. (1977).

Boas, F. 1929. Classification of American Indian languages. *Language* 5: 6.

Bright, William. 1973. North American Indian language contact. Pp. 210-27 in Dil, ed. (1976). Also in Sebeok (1973).

Capell, A. 1973. *A new Fijian dictionary.* 4th ed. Suva: Government Printer.

Christopherson, Paul. 1973. *Second language learning: myth and reality.* Harmondsworth: Penguin.

Dil, Anwar, ed. 1976. *Variation and change in language: essays by William Bright.* Stanford University Press.

Emeneau, M. B. 1956. India as a linguistic area. *Language* 32: 3-16.

Eri, Vincent. 1970. *The Crocodile.* Ringwood, Victoria, Australia: Penguin.

Ferguson, Charles A. 1977. Linguistic theory. In *Bilingual education: current perspectives.* Vol. II: Linguistics. Washington, D.C.: Center for Applied Linguistics.

Fiji. 1970. *Report for the Year, 1970.* London: Her Majesty's Stationery Office.

Fishman, Joshua A., et al. 1977. *The spread of English.* Rowley, Mass.: Newbury House.

——— . 1978. Bilingual education: what and why? In Lourie and Conklin, eds. (1978).

Geraghty, Paul. 1977. Fiji Pidgin and bilingual education. *Fiji English Teachers' Journal* 12: 2-8.

——— . 1978. Fijian dialect diversity and foreigner talk: the evidence of pre-missionary manuscript. In Schütz, ed. (1974).

Gumperz, John J. 1968. Types of linguistic communities. In Joshua Fishman, ed., *Readings in the sociology of language.* The Hague: Mouton.

Guy, J. B. M. 1964. *Handbook of Bichelamar.* Canberra, Australia: Australian National University. Pacific Linguistics, series C, no. 34.

Hall, Robert A., Jr. 1962. The life cycle of Pidgin languages. *Lingua* 11: 151-56.

Kachru, Braj B. 1977. The new Englishes and old models. *English Teaching Forum* 15(3): 29-35.

Kelley, Sister Francis. 1975. The English spoken colloquially by a group of adolescents in Suva. *Fiji English Teachers' Journal* 11: 19-43.

Kloss, Heinz. 1966. Types of multilingual communities: a discussion of ten variables. Pp. 7-17 in Lieberson, ed. (1966).

LePage, Robert B. 1968. Problems to be faced in the use of English as the medium of education in four West Indian territories. Pp. 431-42 in Joshua Fishman et al., *Language problems of developing nations.* London: John Wiley and Sons.

Lourie, Margaret A., and Conklin, Nancy Faires, eds. 1978. *A pluralistic nation: the language issue in the United States.* Rowley, Mass.: Newbury House.

Lieberson, Stanley, ed. 1966. *Explorations in sociolinguistics.* Bloomington: Indiana University Press.

Malia, Sister Mulipoya-Lui. 1976. Review of *Pidgin and Creole languages* by Robert A.Hall, Jr. *Journal of African Languages* 6: 83-86.

Mana Annual of Creative Writing. 1973. Suva, Fiji: South Pacific Creative Arts Society.

Mishra, Vijay, ed. forthcoming. *Rama's banishment: a centenary volume of the Fiji Indians.* Australia: Heinemann.

Moag, Rodney F. 1977. *Fiji Hindi: a basic course and reference grammar.* Canberra, Australia: Australian National University Press.

———. 1978a. Vernacular education in Fiji. *South Pacific Journal of Teacher Education* 6(2): 134-40.

———. 1978b. Bilingualism-biculturalism: where is it going in the Pacific? *Directions* 1: 3-7.

———. 1978c. Standardization in Pidgin Fijian: implications for the theory of Pidginization. Pp. 4: 68-90 in Schütz, ed. (1978b).

———. 1979. The linguistic adaptions of the Fiji Indians. In Mishra, ed. (forthcoming).

———, and Moag, Louisa B. 1977. English in Fiji: some perspective and the need for language planning. *Fiji English Teachers' Journal* 13: 2-26.

Nacola, J. 1976. *I native no more.* Suva, Fiji: Mana Publications.

Nandan, Satendra. 1974. My father's son. Pp. 12-16 in Wendt (1974).

Paauw, Scott H. 1977. Malaysian English: a descriptive study. Unpublished Research Paper, Universiti Sains Malaysia.

Pillai, Raymond. 1975. Preliminary inspection. *Mana Annual of Creative Writing 1974.* Suva, Fiji: South Pacific Creative Arts Society.

Platt, John. 1977. A model for polyglossia and multilingualism (with special reference to Singapore and Malaysia). *Language in Society* 6: 361-78.

Pride, John. 1978. Communicative needs in the learning and use of English. Paper presented at the East-West Center Conference on English as an International Auxiliary Language. Honolulu, Hawaii, April 1-15, 1978.

Quain, Buell Halvor. 1948. *Fijian village.* Chicago: University of Chicago Press.

Richards, Jack. 1972. *Error analysis: perspectives on second language acquisition.* London: Longman.

———. 1982. Singapore English: rhetorical and communicative styles. In this volume.

Rubin, Joan, and Jernudd, Bjorn H., eds. 1971. *Can language be planned?* Honolulu: University Press of Hawaii.

Schütz, Albert J. 1972. *The languages of Fiji.* Oxford: Clarendon Press.

———. 1978a. English loanwords in Fijian. In Schütz, ed. (1978b).

———. 1978b. *Fijian language studies: borrowing and pidginization. Bulletin of the Fiji Museum.*

Sebeok, Thomas A., ed. 1973. *Current trends in linguistics.* Vol. 10: *Linguistics in North America.* The Hague: Mouton.

Selinker, L. 1972. Interlanguage. *International Review of Applied Linguistics* 10(3): 209-31.

Seri. 1974. Fiji. Pp. 4-6 in Wendt, ed. (1974).

Sibayan, B. P. 1977. Language and identity. Paper presented at SEAMEO Regional Language Centre, Twelfth Regional Seminar, Singapore.

Siegel, Jeff. 1973. A survey of language use in the Indian speech community in Fiji. Unpublished field study for the Culture Learning Institute, East-West Center, Honolulu.

Strevens, Peter. 1977. English for special purposes: an analysis and survey. *Studies in Language Learning* 2(1): 111-35.

Subramani. 1975. Sautu. *Mana Annual of Creative Writing 1974.* Suva, Fiji: South Pacific Creative Arts Society.

———. 1977. Tell me where the train goes. *Third Mana Annual of Creative Writing.* Suva, Fiji: South Pacific Creative Arts Society.

———. 1978. English for Fiji? *South Pacific Journal of Teacher Education* 6(2): 140-43.

Tongue, R. 1974. *The English of Singapore and Malaysia.* Singapore: Eastern Universities Press.

Valdman, Albert, ed. 1977. *Pidgin and creole linguistics.* Bloomington: Indiana University Press.

Vatoko, Kali, and Leomala, Albert. 1975. "Nomo Stap Long Taon" and "Mi Stap Sori Nomo." *Mana Annual of Creative Writing 1974.* Suva, Fiji: South Pacific Creative Arts Society.

Weinreich, Uriel. 1951. Research problems in bilingualism, with special reference to Switzerland. Ph.D. dissertation, Columbia University.

Wendt, Albert. 1973. *Sons for the return home.* Auckland, New Zealand: Longman Paul.

———. 1974. *Some modern poetry from Fiji.* Suva, Fiji: South Pacific Creative Arts Society.

Wurm, Stephen A. 1977. Pidgins, Creoles, lingue franche, and national development. Pp. 333-57 in Valdman, ed. (1977).

Yee, Sin Joan. 1974. *The Chinese in the Pacific.* Suva, Fiji: South Pacific Social Sciences Association.

PART IV

New English Literatures: Themes and Styles

18

Non-Native English Literatures: Context and Relevance

S. N. SRIDHAR

The emergence of a large body of creative writing in English by its non-native users demands that we develop critical perspectives for understanding, evaluating, and appreciating such writing.[1] This body of writing comes primarily from former British colonies, such as the countries in the Indian subcontinent, in East and West Africa, and in the Caribbean.

Although the history of non-native creative writing in English goes back almost two centuries, quantitative — and, more important, qualitative — strides in such non-native English literatures (NNELs, hereafter) are a phenomenon of the last four or five decades. In India, literature in English by Indians may be said to have come of age in the late 1930s, with the publication of novels by Mulk Raj Anand (*Untouchable*, 1935), Raja Rao (*Kanthapura*, 1938), and R. K. Narayan (*The Bachelor of Arts*, 1937). In West Africa, similar development has been even more recent, a product of the late 1950s and 1960s (Chinua Achebe, *Things Fall Apart*, 1958; Cyprian Ekwensi, *Jagua Nana*, 1961; Gabriel Okara, *The Voice*, 1964; Wole Soyinka, *The Interpreters*, 1965, and *A Dance of the Forests*, 1960). The same is true of East Africa as well (Wa Thiong'o Ngugi, *Weep Not Child*, 1964).

The biggest spurt in English writing has come in the years immediately surrounding the demise of the British Empire — an irony that has not been lost on the critics.[2] A creative impetus was provided by the nationalist movements, and by the revival of native traditions and reaffirmation of national dignity that came in their wake. In addition, two other factors were at play whose roles in this literary renaissance have not been sufficiently noted. One is the growth in bilingualism in English, creating sizeable numbers of English-knowing *indigenous* people who could be counted on as a potential audience for the new literature (see, e.g., Fishman et al. 1978; Reddy 1979). The second factor is related to the first but is more specific. It may be referred to as the (relative) "de-bureaucratization of English," i.e., the increasing confidence with which non-

native writers came to handle the language in registers other than the
legal and administrative. This point is brought home when we compare the stilted and cliché-ridden style of the conversations used in
Indian fiction around the turn of the century with those found in
more contemporary writings. Here is an English translation of a passage from a Sanskrit purāṇa (Iyer 1905: 623; quoted in Holstrom 1973;
22): "O best of Brahmins, grieve not; I shall enquire into the case, and
with Sundareshwara's grace find out the truth and do the needful."
Note the use of bureaucratic clichés such as "enquire into the case,"
"do the needful." Non-native creative writing in English has come a
long way from that teething stage, developing a diversity of themes,
a variety of forms and techniques, and, not the least, an authenticity
and idiomatic expressiveness.[3]

   However, literary critics, language teachers, and (to a lesser extent) linguists have yet to realize the significance of this literature's
existence. The spread of English around the world is an unparalleled
phenomenon, as is the widespread creation of literature by non-native
writers. Perhaps the only similar situations have involved the use of
Latin in medieval and Renaissance Europe and the use of Sanskrit in
South Asia throughout the subcontinent's history. Other smaller-
scale parallels are the use of French by writers from francophone
Africa, Spanish in Latin America, and, in a restricted sense, the use
of Arabic in the Muslim world. The need for new critical perspectives has just begun to be realized in literary circles; see, e.g., Wright
(1976), Larson (1972), Griffiths (1978), Walsh (1970), Mohan
(1978), as well as the references in Narasimhaiah (1976) and Sridhar
(1980). Comparative studies are still needed.

   My aim is to point out why NNEL should be of interest to linguists and to teachers of English as a second language. The rest of this
article deals with the following topics: the glottopolitics of NNEL;
analyses of some linguistic and literary processes employed to extend
the potential of the English language to express alien meanings; the
"difficulty" of NNEL and its "relevance" to native and non-native
speakers of English. My observations below should apply, by and
large, to writings from South Asia, Southeast Asia, and East and West
Africa — but not to the Caribbean, where English is not non-native
in the same sense.

The Choice of English for Creativity

   The emergence of non-native English literatures should be viewed
as an aspect of the worldwide spread of English documented by Fish-

man et al. (1978) and others. In many parts of the former British Empire, English came to serve as the link language between linguistically separated native populations, and as the language of the "intellectual makeup" (Rao 1943) of the emerging intelligentsia.[4] Although English came to play other roles, including serving as the language of administration and of law, it is the first two roles, together with its international spread, that are responsible for the development of English literature by indigenous writers. In India and West Africa, English is the primary mode of inter-regional communication among the educated. In West Africa, English is the only language in which a fair number of people are literate. (Contrast Swahili in East Africa in this respect, and the "national" languages in India.) Furthermore, for sizeable sections of the population — though still, admittedly, a minority — English is the primary language of expression. Because of their educational training, some people feel more at home in English than in their mother tongue. Although some are bilingual writers (A. K. Ramanujan writes in both English and Kannada, and Chinua Achebe writes in English and Igbo), the majority write only in English.

These writers have been criticized for "whoring after foreign gods" by ultranationalist critics who believe that one can only express oneself in one's mother tongue. Obiajunwa Wali in Nigeria and Buddhadeva Bose and Sacchidanand Vatsyayan in India[5] are among those who consider writing in English "a dead end." Implicit in this criticism are the following claims: that it is somehow "unpatriotic" to write in a language that is not native to the land; that one cannot express oneself as well in a foreign language as in one's own; and that no non-native writer can write as well as a native writer. Therefore the former is doomed to second class status, if not to outright oblivion.

These assumptions have been challenged by the writers and defenders of NNEL. The charge of treason is countered by pointing out that English was the language of national unification and the vehicle for the expression of nationalist sentiment during the freedom struggle. National leaders whose patriotism is beyond reproach, such as Mahatma Gandhi and Jawaharlal Nehru, wrote in English. Measuring patriotism by one's choice of language betrays a naïve and unthinking approach to such questions. A language belongs to whoever uses it, and is not the sole property of its native speakers.

In his celebrated essay, "English and the African Writer," Chinua Achebe (1965) rejects the claim that it is impossible for anyone to use a second language as effectively as his first. For some non-native writers, English is the sole language of literary expression; hence the question of whether they would have written better in their mother tongue does not arise. For others, the choice of English seems to be determined by the theme. For example, Achebe, who writes poetry in Igbo and English but fiction only in English, says, "I think certain ideas and certain things seem better done in Igbo and other things seem better in English " (1975: 33).

The third assumption, that no non-native writer can write as well as a native writer, is contradicted by the examples of Joseph Conrad, Samuel Beckett, Vladimir Nabokov, and others. However, the writers themselves take a different tack in responding to this criticism. Most claim that they are not competing with native writers. Raja Rao, in his well-known and often-quoted preface to *Kanthapura,* says: "We cannot write like the English. We should not. We cannot write only as Indians. We have grown to look at the large world around us as part of us. Our method of expression therefore has to be a dialect which will some day prove to be as distinctive and colorful as the Irish and the American. Time alone will justify it" (Rao 1943: viii). Chinua Achebe (1965: 29-30) expresses a similar conviction:

> So my answer to the question, Can an African ever learn English well enough to be able to use it effectively in creative writing? is certainly yes. If on the other hand you ask: Can he ever learn to use it like a native speaker? I should say, I hope not. It is neither necessary nor desirable for him to be able to do so. The price a world language must be prepared to pay is submission to many different kinds of use. The African writer should aim to use English in a way that brings out his message best without altering the language to the extent that its value as a medium of international exchange will be lost. He should aim at fashioning out an English which is at once universal and able to carry his peculiar experience. . . . It will have to be a new English, still in full communion with its ancestral home, but altered to suit its new African surroundings.

Although most non-native writers feel that they can express themselves best in English, they need to "nativize" the language to suit their particular purposes. This nativization involves experimenting with the expressive resources of the language on various levels: vocabulary, collocation, idiomaticization, syntax, and rhetorical patterning. It also involves adaptations of English (Western) literary forms such as the lyric, the novel, the short story, and the poetic drama to express the writers' individual sensibilities.

Nativization of English in NNELs

While using English to express shades of thought and feeling that are not indigenous to that language's native speech community, non-native writers have found it necessary to introduce various innovations. These innovations — referred to as processes of nativization — have been studied from a linguistic point of view by Kachru (1969), Bokamba (1982), Angogo and Hancock (1980), and others. Here I shall only briefly allude to the literary-aesthetic motivation or justification for these innovations.

The most obvious problem, of course, is that of nomenclature: finding words for culturally bound everyday objects. Most authors simply resort to borrowing: *dhobi* (washerman), *kumkum* (vermillion mark), *obi* (receiving hut), and so on, with explanatory glosses either embedded in the text itself or appearing in an appendix. However, this process impedes the flow of the narrative and constitutes a conscious attempt to bridge the cultural gap. A more subtle and certainly more effective device involves "contextualizing" the new item by embedding it in a passage that makes the meaning of the term self-explanatory. This process is referred to as "cushioning" in Young (1976). Consider an example from Amadi's *Concubine:* "The *okwos* tore the air, the drums vibrated under expert hands and the *igele* beat out the tempo meticulously" (1965: 35). As Young says, it is obvious from the context that *okwos* and *igele* are musical instruments, with the *okwo* possibly being a wind instrument and the *igele* some sort of a percussion instrument whose primary function is to keep the beat. Although this device leads to inclusion of some extra detail, the greater integration of the new items into the context, and the unobtrusiveness of the introduction, make it worthwhile. This subtle weaving of native and non-native elements makes R. K. Narayan's prose read smoothly, while Mulk Raj Anand's style remains self-consciously experimental.

A more difficult problem is that of conveying modes of feeling and thinking peculiar to the writer's cultural milieu. To quote Raja Rao again, "one has to convey the various shades and omissions of a certain thought-movement that looks maltreated in a foreign language" (1943: ix). In this area we find the widest variety of experimental devices, all of them drawing on the author's mother tongue. The most common device is *calquing* or loan translation (see Bokamba 1982; Kachru 1981; Zuengler 1982). Successful loan translations may be said to have the property of *transparency*, despite their being literal translations of words and collocations from a foreign language. For example, consider expressions such as *dining*

leaf, receiving hut, and *bell-metal voice,* as well as idiomatic expressions such as Raja Rao's *a crow-and-sparrow story* (for cock-and-bull
story), *a palm-width of land, to beat one's mouth and shout,* and *to
stitch up one's mouth,* or Narayan's *If I hear your voice, I'll peel the
skin off your back.* Not all *calques* are successful, however, especially
when the translations lack the affective associations of the original. A
case in point is Anand's literal translation of a Hindi swearword as
"brother-in-law." Yet, by successfully resorting to the native language, the author is able to avoid hackneyed expressions (e.g., "fresh
as a flower") and to create the cultural atmosphere of his work. As
the Nigerian poet and dramatist John Pepper Clark points out, such
translations come about because the author finds that "a thought you
have has been very well expressed already in your mother tongue; you
like that manner of expression so much you want to transplant it into
English" (Clark 1972: 68).

Let us discuss two examples from Raja Rao's *Kanthapura.* In the
first, an old woman asks a favor of a young man. In the Kannada sociocultural context it is customary for the favor-giver to make light of his
generosity, so as to minimize the asymmetry of the situation created
by the role reversal. Raja Rao conveys this subtle convention by literally translating the Kannada idiom into English: "Is it greater for you
to ask, or for me to say yea?" (1943: 11). The effect would not have
been the same had the author used an expression such as "Your wish
is my command." A second example involves a host-guest interaction
which calls for repeated coaxing on the part of the host and considerable coyness on the part of the guest. Raja Rao re-creates this Indian
convention by having his hosts use translated Kannada expressions
such as "Take only this much milk, aunt, just this much" and "Take
it, Bhatré, only one cup more, just once." As C. D. Narasimhaiah
aptly observes, "With people like us [Indians], used to being coaxed,
the English forms, 'Won't you have a second helping?' or mere 'Sure
you don't care for more?' will be ineffective and even considered dis-
courteous" (1968: 13).

In these two examples, it is not "cognitive meaning" or "illocutionary force" that differentiates the native and non-native versions.
Rather, it is the choice of language considered appropriate to a given
speech situation. These differences in linguistic conventions may lie
at the heart of the differences between native and non-native varieties
of languages; they seem to be best studied by contrasting "contextual
units" of the sort that Kachru (1966) has described.

In addition to the lexical, phrasal, and idiomatic transplants from
the mother tongue, many authors' styles are also marked by the infu-

sion of native-language syntactic patterns. For example, the Indian poet Nissim Ezekiel deliberately parodies "Indianisms" in the poem "Goodbye Party for Miss Pushpa" (Ezekiel 1976).

Most writers, however, intend not to parody but to re-create the tempo and the feel of the native form in the English work. To convey the "breathless" quality of the native Kannada narrative, Raja Rao resorts to endless coordination, the closest possible approximation of the chain of participial clauses that mark the Kannada narrative. The following passage from *Kanthapura* (Rao 1943: 137) is illustrative:

> Then the police inspector saunters up to the Skefflington gate, and he opens it and one coolie and two coolies and three coolies come out, their faces dark as mops and their blue skin black under the clouded heavens, and perspiration flows down their bodies and their eyes seem fixed to the earth — one coolie and two coolies and three coolies and four and five come out, their eyes fixed to the earth, their stomachs black and clammy and bulging, and they march toward the toddy booth; and then suddenly more coolies come out, more and more and more like clogged bullocks. . . .

A syntactic device favored by R. K. Narayan is the verbless sentence fragment (equivalent of Kannada and Tamil discourse patterns): "Don't touch, not completely dry yet," "We must be serious about it, no time to joke, no joking matter" (Narayan 1976: 135, 69). He also uses sentences without subjects, especially in narratives:

> When a man says "I love you" . . . it sounds mechanical. . . . Perhaps credible in Western society, but sounds silly in ours.

> He wondered how it was. . . . Speculated why he should not move to Daisy's flat, a neutral area. . . .

> [There is] Still a lot of space — why don't you buy a few things that you may need on the way?

More obvious characteristics include questions without inversions: "And you'll allow me to speak?" "Brother, you are with me?" "But I can hold meetings for you, Moorthy?" (Rao 1943: 126, 125). Such questions in standard English request confirmation, while in this text they are direct translations of Kannada questions which do not involve inversion. Raja Rao also uses left and right dislocation to re-create the effect of the oral narrative, as in "My heart — it beat like a drum" and "And he can sing too, can Jayaramachar" (Rao 1943: 163, 14).

Such transference of mother-tongue patterns into English also serves to overcome the problem of "linguistic alienation" which plagues all non-native writers (Ogundipe-Leslie 1969). It bridges the cultural gap and makes the use of the alien medium more acceptable to the non-native speakers themselves. When carried to extremes, however, it poses serious problems of intelligibility and exposes the writer to the charge of preciosity. The more bizarre specimens from the Onitsha market literature illustrate this danger. Consider this passage from Frank Odili's *What Is Life?* "Why not to your spiritual interest in God keep the good rule of your main created life? Are you actually redundant in fetching up your needs when you are physically looking fit to that? If you are not, then, what is your most greatest need of the life? Do you want to be greedy . . ." (quoted in Collins 1968: 16).

Clearly there is a need to separate deviations from native English that result from inadequate learning of English from those deviations that result from deliberate experimentation by writers proficient in English. Gabriel Okara experiments with the subject-object-verb word order, attempting to reproduce his native Ijaw structures. In the following passage from *The Voice* (1964: 13) one is hard put to divine the aesthetic function of the inversion, except in the vicinity of the second sentence:

> It was the day's ending and Okolo by a window stood.
> Okolo stood looking at the sun behind the tree tops
> falling. The river was flowing, reflecting the finishing
> sun, like a dying away memory. It was like an idol's
> face, no one knowing what is behind. Okolo at palm
> trees looked. They were like women with their hair
> hanging down, dancing, possessed. . . .

Proverbs abound in non-native English novels. As Achebe says, "Proverbs are the palm-oil with which words are eaten," and Nigerians seem to be as rich in this oil as in petroleum crude. Proverbs are also frequently used by the better writers of Indian fiction in English. They provide shorthand character sketches, or quintessential statements of motifs and conflicts; they mediate between authorial comment and objective description; and they serve as objective correlatives of crucial, sensitive developments in action (see Lindfors [1968] for a detailed study). For instance, Okonkwo in Achebe's *Things Fall Apart* (1959: 6) is characterized with a single proverb: "If a child washes his hands, he could eat with kings." This statement refers to Ikonkwo's qualities as a self-made man whose industry and discipline led to his achievement of high status in his community. Okonkwo's fate as a tragic hero is summed up (1959: 117) in a choral comment on a proverb: "The saying of the elders was not true: that if a man said yes his *chi* (or personal god) also affirmed. Here was a man whose *chi* said nay despite his own affirmation." As distillations of traditional wisdom, proverbs provide the author with a convenient shorthand for depicting implied value systems.

The use, abuse, or non-use of proverbs can itself differentiate characters. Wole Soyinka's *Interpreters* and Amos Armah's *The Beautiful Ones Are Not Yet Born* contain few proverbs, reflecting the dissociation of urban and rural sensibilities. On the other hand, the abuse of proverbs by a character through distortion of meaning is an effective device to convey his flouting of traditional values.

The expressive potential of proverbs and other culture-bound speech patterns is brought out by Achebe in the following passage (1965: 29):

> Allow me to quote a small example from *Arrow of God* which may give some idea of how I approach the use of English. The Chief Priest is telling one of his sons why it is necessary to send him to church:

> "I want one of my sons to join these people and be my eyes there. If there is nothing in it you will come back. But if there is something then you will bring back my share. The world is like a Mask, dancing. If you want to see it well, you do not stand in one place. My spirit tells me that those who do not befriend the white man today will be saying 'had we known' tomorrow."

> Now supposing I had put it another way. Like this for instance:

> "I am sending you as my representative among these people — just to be on the safe side in case the new religion develops. One has to move with the times or one is left behind. I have a hunch that those who fail to come to terms with the white man may well regret their lack of foresight."

> The material is the same. But the form of the one is in character, and the other is not. It is largely a matter of instinct but judgment comes into it too.

These authors' experimentation with English involves another dimension of particular interest to sociolinguists, especially to those involved with ethnography of communication. This is the artistic use of speech stratification and conversational conventions. Wole Soyinka's brilliant use of language is marked by the assured facility with which he moves from one speech style to another in the complex linguistic

environment of his characters. In *The Interpreters* and *The Road* he
freely moves from Standard English to pidgin to Yoruba, and through
different mixtures of all three, as the situations — or the sociolinguistic
variables — demand. (For a discussion of the use of pidgin in literature,
see Todd 1974: ch. 5.) In Achebe's *No Longer at Ease,* Joseph talks to
his foreign-educated brother Obi in Standard English on the telephone.
Soon afterward, turning to his friends, he comments in pidgin, "'E like
dat. Him na gentleman. No fit take bribe" (Achebe 1961: 77). A similar creative use of speech variation in Singapore and Malaysian English
writing is discussed in Platt (1980).

Before we leave the topic of experimentation with language, we
must note that not all non-native English writers use "nativized" English. Raja Rao's *Kanthapura* and Okara's *Voice* are, no doubt, instances of sustained experimentation, but with other authors and in
other works the extent of innovation varies widely. This seems especially true of poetry.

Non-native writers of English have experimented with literary
forms, as well as with the language itself. Raja Rao's *Kanthapura*
breaks the bounds of the novel as we know it in the West, taking on
the form of a *sthaḷa purāṇa* (local legend). It embodies such traditional devices of oral literature as the tale within a tale, frequent autobiographical asides, injections of direct address to the listener, and
rhetorical questions concerning the right or wrong of individual actions. Its structural principle is dictated not by the Aristotelian unities
but by the centrality of the community which undergoes upheaval
during the freedom struggle. The author has not attempted to write
a realistic novel. Like every traditional Indian story, his involves my-
thologizing characters and events, giving them added meaning and stat-
ure. The same quality that would make *Kanthapura* a failure as a realistic novel also makes it a doubly realistic narrative: while we are aware
that the events have been transformed in the narrator's mythopoeic
imagination, we also recognize that this makes the Indian narrator
authentic and credible.

To take an African example, let us consider Wole Soyinka's
Dance of the Forests (1963), written in celebration of Nigeria's independence. This play successfully integrates traditional performance
skills with the structure of Western drama. (See Griffiths 1978 and
Larson 1972 for detailed analyses.) Emphasizing the continuity of
past, present, and future, and fulfilling the traditional injunction to
invoke one's ancestors in any contemporary celebration, *A Dance of
the Forests* embodies a continuous interplay between the lands of
the living and the dead. The climax involves the descent of the half-

child (the unborn child of a woman who died pregnant ages ago), symbolizing the past in the making of the present. Soyinka resorts to traditional Yoruba dramatic practice at this point. During the concluding "dance of the child acrobats," the half-child is tossed into the air and apparently caught on the points of two knife-blades. The play's brilliant poetic dialogue is interlarded with song, mime, and dance.

The Question of Relevance

The non-native English writer's experimentation with language and form raises several questions. First is the issue of intelligibility (see also Nelson 1982). Does these authors' introduction of native language make their works obscure? Can native speakers of English be expected to acquire the cultural and literary background needed to fully comprehend this literature?

As was pointed out earlier, there are good and bad ways of introducing culture-specific materials. A mature artist such as Achebe or Narayan usually takes care to embed the strange material in a self-explanatory context. Such embedding, in fact, may be proposed as a measure of success in the evaluation of non-native literatures. This criterion derives from the principle of the autonomy of the work of art as well as from a sense of responsibility to the reader. On the other hand, as T. S. Eliot says, one need not understand every word in order to enjoy and appreciate a creative work: "Good poetry communicates before it is understood." Moreover, the alleged difficulty in understanding non-native literature in English seems to be no greater than that involved in understanding any important work, be it *The Waste Land* or *Paradise Lost* or *Ulysses.*[6] Different readers react to these writers and their works on different planes of understanding; to paraphrase Eliot again, "You get from poetry what you bring to it." Generations of non-native students have enjoyed and profited from their study of English literature without ever having seen a daffodil or a snowflake. On the other hand, if one is doing serious literary criticism, one should equip oneself with a knowledge of the author's cultural and literary traditions.

Should non-native literatures in English be judged in terms of the canons of English literature, or with reference to other native literatures? Because they are written in English, these literatures demand to be considered in the company of other works in English. To twist Achebe's phrase: If one writes in a world language, one should be prepared to be judged by world standards. (In this respect, the protests of some African critics that "Western standards cannot be applied to their literature" seem hypocritical. By the same token, I consider the poetry of Sri Aurobindo and the novel *The Serpent and the Rope* by Raja Rao to be failures, no matter how "uniquely Indian" the sensibility they express.[7]) At the same time, non-native English literatures also belong to the canon of native literatures, if only because English is one of the many languages in the usually multilingual countries where such literature is written. In short, the approach to these literatures must be no different from that used in comparative literature in general.

What is the relevance of this literature to professional linguists and to teachers of English as a second language? For linguists, the growth of non-native English literatures provides a unique opportunity to study the nativization of English in different mother tongue groups, and to compare the similarities and differences in the processes of indigenization. The linguist might even arrive at a grammar for breaking the rules of grammar (see, e.g., Sridhar forthcoming). He might also investigate the relationship between the creative writer's deviations from the norm and the deviations current among speakers of that non-native variety of English. And then, of course, there is that sociolinguist's paradise — the question of attitudes toward nativization held by non-native speakers themselves.

Linguists also have an opportunity here to study the empirical basis of the oft-made distinction between productive and unproductive innovations in the language. The bold linguistic innovations found in the works of Amos Tutuola and G. V. Desani are often characterized as stylistic cul-de-sacs, whereas those in books by Raja Rao or Wole Soyinka are hailed as breakthroughs. What linguistic factors contribute to such differences in response?

In order to bring out the relevance of this literature to the teaching of English as a second language, I must backtrack a little. As Kachru (1981) rightly observes, the TESL profession has proceeded far too long on the assumption that non-native speakers' major motivation for learning English is the so-called integrative one; i.e., to culturally identify oneself with the native English speech community. Most learners of English today are in the so-called Third World countries, and they learn English primarily as a tool for acquiring scientific and technological skills. In many of these countries English is learned primarily for *internal* use, to communicate with speakers of other languages *within* the country. In these contexts English will have to serve as a vehicle for conveying various native cultures, traditions, customs, thought patterns, and social concerns. The English teacher must teach the kind of English that can serve this function. Creative writers (who represent the most acute and sensitive observers of a culture) have been struggling to fashion English into a suitable medium for the expression of their immediate social and cultural reality. If English teachers are to "deliver the goods" to speakers of these "other" languages, they must teach the kind of English best suited for these speakers' needs. What better resource do we have, in this attempt to identify the possibilities and limitations of nativization, than writings which succeed or fail precisely on this count?

The use of non-native literatures for teaching the English language also helps overcome another major pedagogical problem, that of developing culturally suited teaching materials. Instead of trying to teach English to students from Malaysia or Ghana through "April is the cruellest month breeding/Lilacs out of the dead land mixing/Memory and desire . . ." when for them April is "no more or less cruel than any other month and summer cannot surprise one if it is summer all year round" (as Anthony Burgess [1970] wrote, describing his frustration in trying to translate the poem into Malay), why not use literature that deals with the life that is familiar to them, that they can identify with?

Finally, non-native English literatures can and should form a part of the ESL teacher's training because no language teaching is complete unless it introduces the learner to the richness and beauty of the language's literature. And no teacher is adequately trained who fails to understand and appreciate the language and culture of his students. Non-native English literatures offer a unique shortcut by which the teacher can acquire this essential knowledge and understanding.

NOTES

1. I am grateful to Braj B. Kachru, Manfred Görlach, Ann Lowry Weir, and Narayan Hegde for their thoughtful comments on an earlier version of this article.

2. "There is a sense in which English [in India] never had it so good. The obituary notices written for the language, written and postponed over the last seventeen years [since India's independence in 1947], have now been reluctantly withdrawn" (Rajan 1965: 80). This seems to be true of non-native writing in French as well. See, for example, Jean-Paul Sartre's preface to Frantz Fanon's *Les damnes de la terre* (1961).

3. The jargon-ridden style illustrated here should be distinguished from the style marked by *register confusion*, or rather *register neutralization*, that marks much of non-native writing in English even today. The latter is perhaps an inevi-

table outcome of the development of institutionalized non-native varieties removed from active contact with native varieties in their original sociolinguistic
settings. The earlier style was stiff and severely cramped in its ability to express
the full range of emotions and thought patterns; the contemporary styles are
not so limited. For further discussion, see Kachru (1969), Young (1971), and
Sridhar (1975).

4. As Rajan puts it, "a large slice of Indian life, and particularly of its decision-
making strata, continues to reason and act in English" (1965: 81). For a detailed
discussion of the continued use of English in India, see K. Sridhar (1977).

5. Cf., e.g., Sacchidanand Vatsyayan ("Agyeya")'s remark at the 5th All-India
Writers' Conference, December, 1965: "To be an Indian as a writer is first and
foremost to write Indian, to write in an Indian language." For a detailed account
of the controversy generated by Buddhadeva Bose's criticism, see Lal and Raghavendra Rao (1960).

6. "If intelligibility were the only difficulty, then no user of English would
tolerate the insult to his intelligence of all the lengthy commentaries to, say,
Eliot's *Waste Land*" (Gunasinghe 1966: 148).

7. "The uniqueness of these emerging literatures is to be found in their
'exotic' local color, 'quaint' speech patterns and rhythms, neologisms, and
(more significantly) the protest quality of their writing. To accept them simply
for these largely sociological characteristics is to apply more generous critical
standards than are evoked in assessing the work of white writers in English"
(Wignesan 1966: 113).

REFERENCES

Achebe, Chinua. 1959. *Things fall apart.* Greenwich, Conn.: Fawcett.
———. 1961. *No longer at ease.* New York: Astor-Honor.
———. 1965. English and the African writer. *Transition* 18: 27-30.
———. 1975. Interview in *In person: Achebe, Awoonor, and Soyinka.* Ed.
     Karen Morrell. Seattle: African Studies Program, University of Washington.
Amadi, Elechi. 1965. *The Concubine.* London: Heineman.
Angogo, Rachel, and Hancock, Ian. 1980. English in Africa: emerging standards
     or diverging regionalisms? *English World-Wide* 1 (1): 67-96.
Bokamba, Eyamba. 1982. The Africanization of English. In this volume.
Burgess, Anthony. 1970. Bless thee, Bottom. *Times Literary Supplement,* Sep-
     tember 18, 1970, p. 1024.
Clark, John P. 1972. Interview in *African writers talking.* Ed. Cosmo Pieterse
     and Dennis Duerden. New York: Africana.
Collins, Harold R. 1968. *The new English of the Onitsha chapbooks.* Athens:
     Ohio University Center for International Studies.
Ezekiel, Nissim. 1976. *Hymns of darkness.* New Delhi: Oxford.
Fishman, Joshua, et al. 1978. *The spread of English.* Rowley, Mass.: Newbury
     House.
Griffiths, Garrett. 1978. *A double exile: African and West Indian creative writ-
     ing between two cultures.* London: Marion Boyars.
Gunasinghe, Siri. 1966. Commonwealth poetry conference, Cardiff: a com-
     mentary. *Journal of Commonwealth Literature* 2: 148.

Holstrom, Lakshmi. 1973. *The novels of R. K. Narayan.* Calcutta: Writers' Workshop.

Iyer, B. R. Rajam. 1905. *Rambles in the Vedanta.* Madras: Thompson.

Kachru, Braj B. 1966. Indian English: a study in contextualization. In *In memory of J. R. Firth.* Ed. C. E. Bazell et al. London: Longman.

―――. 1969. English in South Asia. In *Current trends in linguistics,* vol. 5: *Linguistics in South Asia.* Ed. Thomas E. Sebeok. The Hague: Mouton.

―――. 1976. Models of English for the Third World: white man's linguistic burden or language pragmatics? *TESOL Quarterly* 10 (2): 221-39.

―――. 1981. The pragmatics of non-native varieties of English. In *English for cross-cultural communication.* Ed. Larry Smith. London: Macmillan.

Lal, P., and Raghavendra Rao, K., eds. 1960. *Modern Indo-Anglian poetry: an anthology and a credo:* Calcutta: Writers' Workshop.

Larson, Charles R. 1972. *The emergence of African fiction.* Bloomington: Indiana University Press.

Lindfors, Bernth. 1968. The palm oil with which Achebe's words are eaten. *African Literature Today* 1: 2-18.

Mohan, Ramesh, ed. 1978. *Indian writing in English.* New Delhi: Orient Longman.

Narayan, R. K. 1976. *The painter of signs.* New York: Viking.

Narasimhaiah, C. D. 1968. Indian writing in English: an introduction. *Journal of Commonwealth Literature* 5: 3-15.

―――, ed. 1976. *Commonwealth literature: a handbook of select reading lists.* Delhi: Oxford University Press.

Nelson, Cecil. 1982. Intelligibility and non-native varieties of English. In this volume.

Ogundipe-Leslie, Omalara. 1969. *The palm-wine drinkard:* a reassessment of Amos Tutuola. *Présence Africaine* 71: 99-108.

Okara, Gabriel. 1964. *The Voice.* London: Andre Deutsch.

Platt, John T. 1980. Varieties and functions of English in Singapore and Malaysia. *English World-Wide* 1 (1): 97-121.

Rajan, B. 1965. The Indian virtue. *Journal of Commonwealth Literature* 1: 79-85.

Rao, Raja. 1943. *Kanthapura.* London: Oxford University Press. (First published, 1938, Allen and Unwin.)

Reddy, G. A. 1979. *Indian writing in English and its audience.* Bareilly, India: Prakash Book Depot.

Sridhar, Kamal K. 1977. The development of English as an elite language in the multilingual context of India: its educational implications. Ph.D. dissertation, University of Illinois at Urbana-Champaign.

Sridhar, S. N. 1975. A note on Gopal Honnalgere's *Zen Tree and the Wild Innocents. Journal of Indian Writing in English* 1 (2): 31-34.

―――. 1980. A bibliography of non-native English literatures. Program in Linguistics, State University of New York at Stony Brook. Mimeographed.

―――. Forthcoming. The anatomy of deviation: toward a syntactic typology of non-native Englishes.

Todd, Loretto. 1974. *Pidgins and Creoles.* London: Routledge and Kegan Paul.

Walsh, William. 1970. *A manifold voice.* London: Chatto and Windus.

Wignesan, T. 1966. Literature in Malaysia. *Journal of Commonwealth Literature* 2: 113-23.

Wright, Edgar, ed. 1976. *The critical evaluation of African literature.* Washington, D.C.: Inscape.

Young, Peter. 1971. The language of West African literature in English. In *The English language in West Africa*, ed. John Spencer. London: Longman.
———. 1976. Tradition, language, and reintegration of identity in West African literature. In Wright (1976).
Zuengler, Jane. 1982. Kenyan English. In this volume.

19

Style Range in New English Literatures

ANN LOWRY WEIR

The new English literatures are essentially a linguistic legacy of the British colonial period. The body of scholarship discussing the development of such literatures in various genres and specific regions (see, e.g., Aggarwal 1981; King 1979; Narasimhaiah 1976) or providing an overview of such literatures in a world context (see Jones 1965 and King 1980) has been slowly increasing in recent years. Students of English or comparative literature have traditionally studied the uses, changes, and stylistic innovations in English within the confines of its native areas.

Research on new English literatures remains on the periphery of the traditional boundaries of English studies. During the last two decades, however, scholars of literature and linguistics have recognized — and partly described — this new dimension of English literature and its linguistic, cultural, and literary implications. Here I shall focus on selected aspects of stylistic devices used in two such new English literatures, Indian English and Caribbean English, with special reference to fiction by R. K. Narayan, Mulk Raj Anand, and V. S. Naipaul.

The Novel in New Contexts

The novel, after developing in Europe, later became a significant literary genre in areas of colonial influence. The United States was one of the first and most significant places where a new literary tradition developed, based on European (primarily British) models. Mark Twain's *Huckleberry Finn* (1885) has been cited as "a major turning point in American writing, the point at which American style came into its own as distinct from British style." Telling his story in the words of the young, uneducated Huck, Twain used nonstandard English "not for local color, but for character" (Traugott and Pratt 1980: 338). Since then, American writers of widely varying backgrounds have made their protagonists tell their own stories in language just as authentic as it may be nonstandard. The novels of Jewish writers such as Saul Bellow and Philip Roth, southern writers including William

Faulkner and Eudora Welty, and black writers, among them Zora
Neale Hurston and Ralph Ellison, indicate the kaleidoscope of voices
rising from the pages of twentieth-century American fiction.

The English language and the novel as a genre were transplanted
to other colonial regions as well. As significant numbers of Indians,
Africans, and others became educated in English, a few were attracted to the novel, the sonnet, and other non-indigenous literary forms.
The changes in English vocabulary and syntax were more rapid and
obvious among these writers and speakers than among those for
whom standard English is the sole or primary tongue. A dazzling and
highly unusual Indian writer, G. V. Desani, has described his own
stylistic experimentation as follows: "I have chosen the craft of
writing. And my entire linguistic creed . . . is simply to find a suitable medium. I find the English language is that kind of medium. It
needs to be modified to suit my purpose" (Narasimhaiah 1978: 406).

Though Indian, African, and Caribbean literatures in English
are small and new when compared to their British or American counterparts, they have, after some hesitation on the part of both local
and international critical establishments, been received into the family of world literatures in English. Third World writers in English
must tread a fine line between the perils of incomprehensibility on
one hand and nondescriptness on the other. Their works must appeal
to large and potentially lucrative American and British markets; yet
each novel must contain "exotic elements" of character, theme, and
setting, as well as language, if it is to succeed financially. A contemporary American writer can earn a living by writing books which characterize (or caricature) one of the nation's numerous ethnic groups
(e.g., John Updike on American WASPs); whether his books appeal
to readers in London or Lagos or Lahore makes no difference. Not
so for the Indian, African, or Caribbean writer.

The Indian and Caribbean Situations

Indians have been writing English-language fiction for the last
half-century. Of the first generation, three writers are generally
viewed as outstanding: Mulk Raj Anand, R. K. Narayan, and Raja
Rao. All three published their first fictional works in the 1930s;
while Raja Rao has since divided his intellectual efforts between fiction and philosophy (or combined them, as in his novel *The Serpent
and the Rope*), Anand and Narayan have continued to devote themselves to fiction, occasionally writing essays and autobiographical
works as well. Though born only a year apart, the two are in most

other respects quite unalike. Mulk Raj Anand, born in 1905, spent his early years in the Punjab; he traveled to Britain for his higher education and became involved with leftist political thinkers during the 1930's. His progressive political orientation combined with his Indian background to result in *Untouchable* (1935), his first published novel and still his most famous work. During the subsequent decades Anand has continued to wield his literary pen in the interests of sociopolitical causes.

R. K. Narayan was born in 1906, at the opposite end of the subcontinent. He speaks Tamil as well as English, and knows some Kannada; his life has been spent mainly in Madras and Mysore, and he has traveled abroad only in his later adulthood. Whereas Anand is known for his political commitment, Narayan is equally noted for his philosophical detachment and irony. His first novel, *Swami and Friends,* was published (as was Anand's) in 1935. Among the score of novels, stories, and essay collections to appear since that time, *The Financial Expert* (1952) is one of his most praised works; the protagonist, Margayya, has been hailed as "probably Narayan's greatest single comic creation" (Walsh 1971: 19).

Whereas English is a second language in India, it is the primary language in much of the Caribbean. As the literary scholar Ramchand (1970: 82) has noted, for the Caribbean writer there is "no possibility of choice between English and another language" — one writes in English if one writes at all. The indigenous Carib population was erased long ago, and was replaced by African, European, and East Indian immigrants, all with different languages. While the British were able to assert the supremacy of English in the administrative and educational systems, this did not entail the demise of African and Indian languages and speech patterns in the Caribbean.

White authors have been publishing their fictional works since the early years of this century, but novels by non-white Caribbean authors are a more recent development. Whereas Indian English fiction was developing in the 1930s, non-white Caribbean authors did not begin receiving widespread notice until the 1950s. The independence of the former British West Indies is likewise more recent than India's. One wonders whether political independence must be in the offing for literary figures of a different race to be "taken seriously" by the Western/white critical establishment. No doubt those who have studied African literatures in English have asked themselves this same question.

Among Caribbean writers there are several important black novelists, including George Lamming and Wilson Harris. V. S. Naipaul is at least their equal. Most critics agree that Naipaul's longest novel, *A House for Mr. Biswas* (1961), is one of the very best Caribbean English novels to date. He is a generation younger than Anand and Narayan; at about the time when the two elder authors were born, Naipaul's grandfather moved from Uttar Pradesh to Trinidad. The grandson lived on that island from his birth in 1932 until leaving for Oxford in 1950. He has remained in Britain since that time, although taking numerous trips abroad, including journeys to India and back to Trinidad, and he has married a British woman. His first published novel, *The Mystic Masseur,* appeared in 1957.

Naipaul himself has written (1973: 12) of the predicament of the Indian (or Indian-descent) writer in English: "It is an odd, suspicious situation: an Indian writer writing in English for an English audience about non-English characters who talk their own sort of English. . . . I cannot help feeling that it might have been more profitable for me to appear in translation." The Indian critic Mukherjee (1971: 23) has also alluded to this situation in her discussion of the problems of trying to establish a distinct literature in a language in which a great literature (in this case, British) already exists. Much has been written on the use of English by Indian novelists; critics have analyzed sentence structures, the uses (or avoidance) of Indian words, and other elements. Two important second-language problems mentioned by Ramchand (1970: 78) with regard to Caribbean authors also have application in the Indian context. First, "there may be difficulties of expression arising from an inadequate grasp of basic features of the language"; second, "an author who thinks in one language instinctively and writes in another is liable to modify the adopted language," perhaps even unconsciously. These adaptations and variations from British Standard English have been noted, often in tones ranging from lament to ridicule, by Western scholars and critics.

New Styles in New Settings

Rather than looking at the language of the narrator, or the themes and structure, or exotic elements of plot and setting — as most critics of Indian English and Caribbean English fiction have done so far — I shall here focus on the language of the fictional characters themselves, and the methods and contexts in which that language is conveyed. Dialogue is of primary importance; I shall examine the spoken language of the characters, rather than the written language of the authors. All three authors considered here are quite capable of writing and speaking standard English, but this is not true of their fictional creations, Bakha, Margayya, Ganesh, and Mr. Biswas. Indeed, the difference between the style of the narrative and the voice of the fictional character can be developed with the intent of heightening incongruity (Ramchand 1970: 102). While such incongruity is often emphasized for its comic effect, Ramchand asserts that "dialect is [now] used in so many different human contexts by West Indian writers that it has been freed of the stereotype" of the comic Negro or other minority figure (1970: 88). Of the many possible ways to use English in dialogue of non-native speakers (or simply non-speakers) of English, the novels of Anand, Narayan, and Naipaul demonstrate some of the most creative and diverse options. Following a discussion of the three authors' techniques, I shall briefly assess their similarities, differences, and implications for future work by these and other authors.

R. K. Narayan: *The Financial Expert*

The Financial Expert, like Narayan's other novels, contains few Indian words, and those that do appear are carefully italicized: *ghee, dhoti, puja, karma,* and *sanyasi,* for example. The goddess Saraswathi, mentioned in passing at one point, is carefully described in a footnote for the reader unfamiliar with Hindu mythology. Despite the care he obviously feels obliged to take to insure that a Western reader will understand his work, Narayan apparently feels that the advantages of English outweigh the disadvantages. In an interview he once observed: "Until you mentioned another tongue I never had any idea that I was writing in another tongue. My whole education has been in English. . . . I am particularly fond of the language . . . it is . . . very adaptable . . . and it's so transparent it can take on the tint of any country" (Walsh 1971: 7). The word "transparent" is interesting in this context — implying a sort of clarity on one hand, but reminding us of a barrier, something that must be looked through, on the other.

All of the characters in *The Financial Expert* speak grammatically correct English, sometimes surprisingly so. Margayya, the financier of the title, is the main speaker, but subordinate figures also provide examples of proper — verging on ornate — dialogue. A peasant observes, "We should not talk about others unnecessarily" (Narayan 1953: 13); a police inspector announces that Margayya "has come after his son, Balu, about whom a card has emanated from here" (p. 138). The correct uses of "unnecessarily," "emanated," "about whom," and a passive verb construction in these sentences are typical of Narayan but unlike the dialogue of most other non-native English novelists. One is led to consider two possibilities: either the people in the small South Indian village of Malgudi speak grammatically, albeit not in English, and Narayan is simply conveying their speech patterns to an English-speaking readership; or else he is concerned with portraying the foibles of his characters through means other than grammar or accent. The former prospect, of universal correct speech, seems less likely when one looks at an early episode involving Margayya's son, Balu, while he is still a small boy: " 'Don't say so,' screamed the boy in his own childish slang. 'I'm hurt. I want a peppermint' " (p. 10). If this is "his own childish slang," it is difficult to see how an adult could have conveyed the message much differently.

Only on one occasion does Narayan mention that his characters are actually speaking a language other than English. When Margayya goes to see a priest, hoping for advice on how to win the Goddess of Wealth to his cause, the priest "recited a short verse and commanded Margayya to copy it down in Sanskrit, and side by side take down its meaning in Tamil" (p. 45). The obvious implication is that Margayya is a native speaker of Tamil. Indeed, there is no occasion on which he or other Malgudi residents would need to speak a language other than Tamil, for theirs is an out-of-the-way spot, visited rarely by people from other parts of India, and even less often by those from other parts of the world. Narayan's main fictional intent seems to be to portray — some might say, expose — universal human dreams and foibles such as greed, pride, humility, and compassion by dealing with everyday people in an unimportant village. Though the reader is constantly aware that *The Financial Expert* is set in India, one is not so likely to think about the characters' speech patterns. In Narayan's case, the style of the narrator is not substantially different from the styles of the speakers.

Mulk Raj Anand: *Untouchable*

What a contrast when one examines Mulk Raj Anand's *Untouchable*! While Narayan's English may be "transparent," Anand's is spattered with so many Hindustani words that the Western reader may feel he is looking through frosted glass. Sentence structure remains nondeviant in both narration and dialogue, but within a sentence it is not unusual to find one or more non-English words. What is the average Western reader to make of dialogue such as this: " 'So proud of his izzat! He just goes about getting salaams from everybody' " (Anand 1935/6: 13). The Westerner might be familiar with *salaam*, but it is less likely that he will know the meaning of *izzat* (honor) — a word which is, in itself, somewhat difficult to define, since it has deep cultural and often caste connotations. The problem is further heightened by a failure to italicize Hindustani words when there is an English word that would be written the same way: "Angrez log" (English people) may look like a kind of firewood to one who is not aware of the proper pronunciation, much less the accurate meaning of the term. The Western reader can understand statements such as "He walked like a Laften Gornor!" (p. 53) and "The santry inspictor that day abused my father" (p. 56), but he will probably assume that these are merely mispronunciations of English words, rather than terms which have been borrowed from English and which now have been nativized with their own roles in other Indian languages.

A wide range of styles can be found in this one small book. Bakha, the eighteen-year-old illiterate sweeper who is the title character, often seems quite childlike in thought as well as speech. However, occasionally the reader encounters dialogue such as this: " 'My father is ill,' replied Bakha, 'so I am going to sweep the roads in town and the temple courtyard in his stead' " (p. 39). Here the uses of "ill" and "in his stead" seem a bit odd. And while the reader is expected to know the meanings of words like *izzat* (honor), *bania* (merchant caste), *gulabjamun* (Indian sweet), *vilayat* (England, abroad), and *swadeshi* (native, indigenous) from a context which is sometimes nonexistent, one is occasionally provided with a bit of over-information. For example: "Bakha felt weak. He realized that an Untouchable going into a temple polluted it past purification" (p. 64).

The most contextually significant phrases in *Untouchable* are not the untranslated non-English words, but the phrases which have been translated from Hindustani into English. These consist primarily of swear words, "Ohe, lover of your mother" (p. 10), "you illegally begotten" (p. 15), "cock-eyed son of a bowlegged scorpion" (p. 51), and many others. All of these terms appear only in dialogue, of course, whereas the direct borrowings described above occur in both dialogue and narrative. These epithets, so numerous and so literally translated, can affect the reader in either of two ways: they can seem jarring, or they can soon come to be viewed as routine and meaningless. With Anand, it is important to remember that style is not insignificant, but it remains always the handmaiden of the ideological message. In *Untouchable,* which perhaps seems best when read as it was written — that is, at a whirlwind pace — Anand intends to show the unjustifiable and seemingly eternal oppression of the sweeper.

Bakha cleans latrines and gutters; he eats food which others fling
from their second-story windows, even though it may first land in
the street; he can't even brush past a brahmin, whereas a man from
the same high caste has license to molest Bakha's sister, who should
be equally untouchable. Though several solutions to the problem of
untouchability are presented near the end of the novel — involving
Christ, Gandhi, and the prospective arrival of the flush toilet — Anand
stresses not the solution, but the shocking and depressing problem itself. With that intent in mind, his frequent use of abusive dialogue is
both appropriate and meaningful, and therefore stylistically important.

  Untouchable is unusual in that one of its characters is a British
missionary who speaks Hindustani. We know that none of the Indian
characters speaks his language (i.e., our language), and we are constantly reminded of that fact when we hear utterances such as *are;
hai, hai; han; nahin;* and so on. But Colonel Hutchinson, a Salvation
Army man, must be able to deal with these people on their own
terms if he is to spread the Gospel among them, and thus he must
speak (or try to speak) Hindustani. Anand notes that, although the
Colonel's "tongue was like a pair of scissors which cut the pattern of
Hindustani into smithereens," Bakha nevertheless "felt honored that
the sahib had deigned to talk Hindustani to him, even though it was
broken Hindustani" (p. 135). The author then elaborates on swear
words, the only Hindustani phrases known by most sahibs, giving
both the originals and the English translations. The Colonel's wife is
not happy to see the sweeper boy approaching her house: "Bakha
had not known the exact reasons for her frowns, but when he heard
the words bhangi and chamar, he at once associated her anger with
the sight of himself" (p. 145). It is abundantly clear that while
Bakha's speech appears in English on the printed page, the author
has translated that speech from another language.

V. S. Naipaul: *The Mystic Masseur* and *A House for Mr. Biswas*

  In *The Mystic Masseur* and *A House for Mr. Biswas,* all of V. S.
Naipaul's important characters are of Indian descent. In the former,
Ganesh, the mystic masseur, and his wife, Leela, are able to speak
Hindi, though they do not do so as a matter of course. This short
novel focuses primarily on them; on Leela's father, Ramlogan; and on
a couple of other adults. The narrative covers a number of years, but
since Ganesh and Leela have no children the characters and their linguistic abilities remain much the same throughout.

A House for Mr. Biswas covers the entire life span of Mr. Biswas, from the day of his birth to his death forty-six years later. Mr. Biswas (like his creator, V. S. Naipaul) is a third-generation East Indian in the West Indies. He speaks Hindi in his youth, and his mother, Bipti, never learns any other language, even though she lives all her life on an island where only one-third of the population is of Indian descent and fewer still know Hindi. Mr. Biswas first uses English dialect to talk with his friend Alec, a schoolboy of Portuguese descent who does not know Hindi. Later, after Mr. Biswas has married Shama and moved in with the Tulsi family (his in-laws), the narrator notes that "there was as yet little friendliness between them [Shama and Mr. Biswas]. They spoke in English" (Naipaul 1961: 104). This lack of friendliness is likewise manifest in Mr. Biswas's relations with other residents of the Tulsi compound: "Mr. Biswas nearly always spoke English at Hanuman House; it had become one of his principles" (pp. 118-19). Later, after all four of his children have been born and the older ones are attending school, Mr. Biswas's elderly mother comes to live with them for a time; by then, "though the children understood Hindi they could no longer speak it, and this limited communication between them and Bipti" (p. 426). Thus Mr. Biswas's initial lack of "friendliness" with his bride will result, a generation later, in adult offspring who speak only one language (English), just as Mr. Biswas's mother spoke only one language (Hindi).

One can trace the ascent of English dialect throughout the novel, even though the whole work is written in English. Naipaul uses a three-part system: 1) standard (educated) English dialogue stands for Hindi speech, unless otherwise noted; 2) English dialect is conveyed as spoken; 3) in a few rare cases English dialogue is spoken by one of the characters, but the hesitation and care with which he/she speaks is always noted by the narrator. Until the time of his marriage, Mr. Biswas and his own family speak Hindi (i.e., standard English); then he and his wife speak English dialect, but she and her relatives speak Hindi. When the couple move out of the Tulsi house, they and their children speak only English dialect, except on a few occasions where "Hindi" speech is again used.

Naipaul's use of standard English for Hindi dialogue may seem odd at first glance, but his method is "surprisingly effective" (White 1975: 39). The characters are native speakers of Hindi, and hence would be acquainted with Hindi grammar and vocabulary through daily use, if not through schooling. Pronouns, verb forms, and articles — some of the most noticeable "problems" in dialect — are all used correctly in the "Hindi" dialogue. One brief example may serve

to note this shift. Here his older daughter begins by accusing Mr.
Biswas:

> "Ma said you beat her," Savi said.
> Mr. Biswas laughed. "She was only joking," he said in
> English.
> "She upstairs, rubbing down Myna," Savi said, in En-
> glish as well. [p. 194]

The first sentence, " 'Ma said you beat her,' " is in Hindi because of
the proper verb form, the past tense "said." Naipaul says the father
is answering in English, because the correct sentence structure ("She
was only joking," *not* "She only joking") would otherwise have implied Hindi. And Savi's final statement, "She upstairs," could stand
without the narrator's explanation that it is in English — for it to have
been in Hindi, the girl would have had to say, "She *is* upstairs." Perhaps Naipaul notes the use of English because Savi's last previous
statement was in Hindi. As soon as her father speaks English, however, she replies in kind. Here we see an example of "a tendency in
West Indian dialects . . . to dispense with tense markers in the verb
where context or where another grammatical feature is adequate"
(Ramchand 1970: 95).

Linguists have noted various features in the English speech of
Indians, and in Indian English fiction. One such feature is the reduplicated item, "used for emphasis and to indicate continuation of
a process" (Kachru 1976). While Kachru has observed such items in
the novels of Anand and Raja Rao, they also occur in Naipaul's work.
With regard to Ganesh, the mystic masseur, people "said, 'He full
with worries, but still he thinking thinking all the time' " (p. 32);
Ramlogan, Ganesh's prospective father-in-law, later queries, " 'Ain't
you was learning learning all all the time at the town college?' " (p.
35). A second such feature mentioned by Kachru is "the formation
of an interrogative construct in which Indian English speakers do not
necessarily change the position of the subject and the auxiliary items."
Leela's first question for Ganesh, her husband-to-be, is " 'You could
write too, sahib?' " (p. 45). Often the tag "not so?" at the end of a
statement also gives interrogative force. Finally, some word forms
which appear in Hindi have been portrayed in the "Hindi" (i.e.,
standard English) speech of Mr. Biswas's relatives. When he is a small
child, his mother once "cried, 'Stop this bickering-ickering and let us
go to look for the boy' " (p. 28). Also appearing are "paddling-add-
ling," "apologize-ologize," and his sister-in-law's impatient disparage-
ment of Mr. Biswas's reading tastes in her reference to "Marcus Au-

relius Aurelius." These constructs do not normally appear in the English dialect speech of the characters, but the potential for generating new word forms in English dialect seems to lie in this type of reduplication. (See also Kachru 1981 and in press.)

Several kinds of situations best lend themselves to the use of the vernacular language — bargaining, joking, lying, swearing (Fishman 1982) — and the non-native speaker usually avoids English in such situations. Naipaul points out the uniqueness of the following episode:

> "This insuranburning," Mr. Biswas said, and his tone was light, "who going to see about it? Me?" He was putting himself back in the role of the licensed buffoon. . . .
> Mrs. Tulsi began to splutter. "He want," she said in English, choking with laughter, "to jump — from — the fryingpan — into — into"
> They all roared.
> "— into — the fire!"
> The witty mood spread. [p. 204]

Much later in this dialogue, the narrator notes that Mrs. Tulsi is "still chuckling over her own joke, the first she had managed in English."

While many other features of English dialect could be mentioned, with examples from the speech of Naipaul's characters, it is more profitable to move now to an analysis of the uses of Hindi in Trinidad. Naipaul makes observations on several such uses, either in his own narrative or through the mouths of his fictional characters. When Ganesh's father takes the youngster to a school in town for the first time, their appearance and dress are noted by the local residents:

> "Let them laugh," the old man replied in Hindi. . . .
> "Jackasses bray at anything."
> "Jackass" was his favorite word of abuse; perhaps because the Hindi word was so rich and expressive: *gaddaha.*
> [p. 20]

Here it is not only the sound of the Hindi word, but the fact that he doesn't want the bystanders to understand his comment, that causes the father to choose Hindi.

Ganesh, as a masseur, later uses Hindi as part of his "mystical process" when dealing with those who come to him for treatment.

Leela acts as his translator when he deals with his black clientele. When she says she wants to end her involvement in translating, Ganesh acquiesces, saying, " 'I only wanted to make sure this time. It make them feel good, you know, hearing me talk a language they can't understand. But it not really necessary' " (p. 136). In *A House for Mr. Biswas,* Shama fails to give a black customer in the Tulsi shop the treatment the woman feels she deserves; the woman demands to see the manager. Then "Mrs. Tulsi spoke some abuse to Shama in Hindi, the obscenity of which startled Mr. Biswas. The woman looked pacified" (p. 85). Here it is not the *content* of the speech, but the mere *existence* of it, that has mollified the non-Hindi-speaking customer. On another occasion, however, a black man who wants to prepare a "buth suttificate" for Shama's children is said to have "disliked the way Indian women had of using Hindi as a secret language in public places" (p. 43).

Lest it be thought that the Hindi-speaking population of Trinidad is linguistically omniscient, Naipaul satirizes the Indians' own fascination with words they do not know or understand. When the Tulsis set Mr. Biswas up in business, his shop is named "Bonne Esperance." And when Ramlogan and Ganesh have agreed that the latter should marry Leela, the following discussion of the wedding invitations occurs. Ganesh protests at first:

> "But you can't have nice wording on a thing like a invitation."
> "You is the educated man, sahib. You could think of some."
> "R.S.V.P.?"
> "What that mean?"
> "It don't mean nothing, but it nice to have it."
> "Let we have it then sahib! You is a modern man, and too besides, it sound as pretty wordings." [p. 49]

"Modernity," especially with regard to marriage customs, is also treated in *A House for Mr. Biswas* (pp. 99-100), with a similar satirical intent.

From the quotations of Naipaul's characters, it should now be clear that the author attempts to convey a certain type of West Indian speech almost solely by modifying English syntax. Naipaul does not change spellings or anything of that nature; as a result, his dialogue is extremely readable but also very Caribbean. As one critic put it, "The main features of the native language he preserves are the simplified grammar, limited vocabulary (very few completely foreign words of African and Indian origin), and slightly unique but plain syntactical structures, with normal spelling." His dialogue is "not far removed" from West Indian Standard English (Hamner 1973: 77). In Naipaul's novels, even those without much education know how to spell when they write; Leela is a bit flamboyant with her punctuation, but otherwise her two early written statements are quite clear:

> NOTICE, IS. HEREBY; PROVIDED: THAT, SEATS!
> ARE, PROVIDED. FOR; FEMALE: SHOP, ASSISTANTS!
> [p. 44]

> *I, cannot; live: here. and, put; up: with. the, insult; of:*
> *my. Family*! [p. 89]

Later, when Ganesh is on his way to wealth and fame, Leela modifies her spoken English. ("She used a private accent which softened all harsh vowel sounds; her grammar owed nothing to anybody, and included a highly personal conjugation of the verb to be" [p. 155].) She becomes involved in social welfare work and writes a report for a newspaper. By now her punctuation has dwindled to an acceptable level.

Leela writes only one article, but Mr. Biswas is a full-time journalist for a number of years, and Naipaul's Ganesh and Narayan's Margayya both publish books. Those books are on quite different subjects, but the fictional creations of both authors show almost a greater fascination with printing than with language itself. When Mr. Biswas seeks his first job as a reporter, he is "thrilled to see the proof of an article, headlined and displayed. It was a glimpse of a secret" (p. 320). When Ganesh shows his published book to a neighbor, they marvel over the status the words have assumed on the printed page — " 'They look so *powerful*,' Beharry said" (p. 97). Both Ganesh and Margayya have encounters with printers, and both try to avoid betraying their ignorance. First, Naipaul's masseur:

> "Look, how much you know about this thing?". . . .
> Ganesh smiled. "I study it a little bit."
> "What point you want it to be in?"
> Ganesh didn't know what to say.
> "Eight, ten, eleven, twelve, or what?" Basdeo sounded impatient.
> Ganesh was thinking rapidly about the cost. He said firmly, "Eight go do me."
> Basdeo shook his head and hummed. . . . [p. 96]

And then Narayan's Margayya:

> Lal asked: "Shall we print in demy or octavo?"
> . . . Margayya frankly blinked. . . . He said grandly:
> "Each has its own advantage; it's for you to decide. . . ."
> . . . .
> But Lal turned up with a new poser for him: "Shall
> we use ordinary ten-point Roman or another series which
> I use only for special works? It's also ten-point but on an
> eleven-point body."
> Body? Points? Ten and eleven? What was it all about?
> Margayya said: "Ah, that is interesting. . . . I should like
> to see your eleven-point body." He had a grotesque vision
> of a torso being brought in by four men on a stretcher.
> [pp. 83-85]

There is one great difference between Naipaul's character and Narayan's, however. Whereas Ganesh, the mystic masseur, is interested in writing as a creative process, Margayya, the financial expert, is publishing a book written by someone else, purely in hopes of making money in the bargain. His motive is not self-expression, but self-advancement.

Conclusion

Enough of the fictional characters; let us return now to the authors themselves for a final assessment. Narayan, who writes both narrative and dialogue in standard English, is an author directly concerned with South India, though his works have universal human implications and themes. Anand, whose dialogue constantly reminds us that the characters are *not* speaking English, is the writer of India at large; whether set in a Punjab village or an Assam tea plantation, a peasant hut or a rajah's palace, his works have a pervasive (some might say, overwhelming) ideological intent. Naipaul is largely a man without a country. Unlike some black Caribbean writers who have sought to return to their African roots, he has repudiated both the India of his ancestry and the Trinidad of his youth.

Coulthard has asserted that the expatriate experience may have important effects on Caribbean writers, delivering them "from temptations of local color [and] general folksiness" while also making them aware of "greater complexities of human relationships in the world outside the West Indies" (Coulthard 1962: 71ff.). Though our Caribbean writer, Naipaul, is the only expatriate of the three, Narayan and Anand have also demonstrated their abilities to avoid the pitfalls of folksiness and provincialism. Were this not so, their novels would appeal only to linguists interested in non-native Englishes. But, fortunately, these three writers have also captured the attention of literary scholars, as well as captivating the general reading public. Their positions in world English literature are assured. Furthermore, they have helped to establish the legitimacy of Indian English and Caribbean English literatures, thus paving the way for other writers in these areas.

REFERENCES

Aggarwal, Narindar K. 1981. *English in South Asia: a bibliographical survey of resources.* Gurgaon and New Delhi: Indian Documentation Service.

Anand, Mulk Raj. 1935/6. *Untouchable.* Delhi: Orient, 1970.

Bailey, Beryl. 1966. *Jamaican creole syntax.* Cambridge: Cambridge University Press.

Coulthard, G. R. 1962. *Race and colour in Caribbean literature.* London: Oxford University Press.

Fishman, Joshua A. 1982. Sociology of English as an additional language. In this volume.

Hamner, Robert D. 1973. *V. S. Naipaul.* New York: Twayne.

Jones, Joseph. 1965. *Terranglia: the case for English as world literature.* New York: Twayne.

Kachru, Braj B. 1976. Indian English: a sociolinguistic profile of a transplanted language. In *Dimensions of bilingualism*, special issue of *Studies in Language Learning* (Unit for Foreign Language Study, University of Illinois).

———. 1981. The pragmatics of non-native varieties of English. In L. Smith, ed., *English for cross-cultural communication.* London: Macmillan.

———. In press. *The Indianization of English: the English language in India.* New Delhi: Oxford University Press.

King, Bruce. 1979. *West Indian literature.* London: Macmillan.

———. 1980. *The new English literatures: cultural nationalism in a changing world.* New York: St. Martin's Press.

Mukherjee, Meenakshi. 1971. *The twice-born fiction: themes and techniques of the Indian novel in English.* New Delhi: Arnold-Heineman.

Naipaul, V. S. 1961. *A house for Mr. Biswas.* Harmondsworth: Penguin, 1969.

———. 1957. *The mystic masseur.* Harmondsworth: Penguin, 1964.

———. 1973. *The overcrowded barracoon.* New York: Alfred A. Knopf.

Narasimhaiah, C. D. 1976. *Commonwealth literature: a handbook of selected reading lists.* Delhi: Oxford University Press.

———. 1978. *Awakened conscience: studies in commonwealth literature.* New Delhi: Sterling.

Narayan, R. K. 1953. *The financial expert.* New York: Farrar, Straus and Giroux/ Noonday Press, 1959.

Ramchand, Kenneth. 1970. *The West Indian novel and its background.* New York: Barnes and Noble.

Theroux, Paul. 1972. *V. S. Naipaul: an introduction to his work.* New York: Africana Publishing.

Thorpe, Michael. 1976. *V. S. Naipaul.* Writers and Their Work #242. London: Published for the British Council by Longman Group.

Traugott, Elizabeth Closs, and Pratt, Mary Louise. 1980. *Linguistics for students of literature.* New York: Harcourt Brace Jovanovich.

Walsh, William. 1970. *A manifold voice: studies in commonwealth literature.* London: Chatto and Windus.

——. 1971. *R. K. Narayan.* Writers and Their Work #224. London: Published for the British Council by Longman Group.

——. 1973. *V. S. Naipaul.* Edinburgh: Oliver and Boyd.

White, Landeg. 1975. *V. S. Naipaul: a critical introduction.* New York: Barnes and Noble.

PART V

Contextualization:
Text in Context

20

Meaning in Deviation: Toward Understanding Non-Native English Texts

BRAJ B. KACHRU

In order to avoid explanatory digressions, I shall assume that we agree on some basic concepts and terms.[1] First, in describing the non-native varieties of English worldwide (whose users constitute roughly 30-40 percent of English speakers), a distinction has to be made between the institutionalized and the performance varieties (see, e.g., Smith 1981). Second, in terms of language use in such non-native contexts, we must separate what we have labeled as a "deviation" from a "mistake." As explained in the chapter on "Models for Non-Native Englishes," a deviation can be contextualized in the new "unEnglish" sociolinguistic context in which English actually functions; its "meaning" must, therefore, be derived with reference to the *use* and *usage* appropriate to that cultural context. Such use results in a number of productive processes which are variety specific and context specific. Because such innovations have gone through various processes of nativization, both linguistically and culturally, a description of such formations must consider the context of the situation (Kachru 1980b) as relevant for the analysis. A mistake, on the other hand, does not necessarily have an underlying sociolinguistic explanation: it may be essentially a marker of acquisitional inadequacy, or it may indicate a stage in language acquisition. A discerning native or non-native speaker will not consider a mistake to be within the linguistic code of English. Through such an approach we will gain better understanding of the functional identity of these varieties of English, varieties which are used in an entirely different network of personal interactions, media needs, and register ranges as compared to their native counterparts. The fast-increasing body of the non-native English literature (a subject to which I will return later) thus acquires a defining context, as we have seen in the preceding chapters by Weir and Sridhar. If that context is not appropriately understood, the significance of this literature is diminished.

Two Perspectives: Theoretical and Applied

I shall first provide both a theoretical and an applied context
within which to discuss the topic. In recent years, two central issues
have been brought to the forefront. One is what I consider the applied concern: in applied linguistics, for example, Kaplan (1966
[1980]; see also Clyne [1981]) has raised a set of questions concerning the "cultural thought patterns" in intercultural education.[2]
Kaplan's concerns are essentially pedagogical and are specifically related to the teaching of English as L_2. He claims that "the English
language and its related thought patterns have evolved out of the
Anglo-European cultural pattern. The expected sequence of thought
in English is essentially a Platonic-Aristotelian sequence, descended
from the philosophers of ancient Greece and shaped subsequently
by Roman, Medieval European, and later Western thinkers" (400-
401). He continues, "learning of a particular language is the master-
ing of its logical system" (409). In keeping with his pedagogical focus,
Kaplan argues that "the foreign student is out of focus because the
foreign student is employing a rhetoric and sequence of thought
which violates the expectations of the native reader" (401). The
teacher's reaction, therefore, is likely to be that the student's paper
"lacks cohesion, organization or focus."

Kaplan also makes two other points. One is that "applied linguistics teaches the student to deal with the sentence, but it is necessary to bring the student beyond that to the comprehension of the
whole context" (410). Second, "it is necessary to recognize that a
paragraph is an artificial thought unit employed in the written language to suggest a cohesion which commonly may not exist in oral
language" (411). Fourteen years later, in a 1980 addendum, Kaplan
confesses that "the kind of discourse study recommended in this
paper has never caught on" (416). He then identifies points on which
he has changed his view during the intervening fourteen years. However, one point which still remains valid is the culturally or linguistically determined "preferred order in discourse bloc" (416).

Now let us turn from the pedagogical concern to the theoretical
issue. Ferguson (1978, 1982) raises an important question which directly relates to research on any aspect of multilingualism. Referring
to not-so-uncommon language situations of "diglossia, standard language with dialects, decreolization continuum, and so on. . . . Most
linguists are getting reconciled to the fact that they must include an
account of variation in writing the grammar of a language" (1978:
99). Recognizing such situations, linguists must ask, "What goes on
in a speech community that uses let us say four languages?" (1978:

101). That situation is typical of, for example, parts of Africa or South Asia. Such questions cannot be of merely marginal interest to linguists — for the fact is that monolingualism, a linguist's dream for descriptive convenience, is not the general rule, but the exception in language situations.

Ferguson is correct in observing that theoretical generalizations and "universal explanatory principles" (Ferguson 1982) cannot be formulated without accounting for such situations. He recognizes the "natural status" of "the notion 'a language,'" but at the same time he believes that "such an assumption does not exclude the study of partial, restricted and marginal language behavior" (1978: 98). The criteria for determining the unit for such a description are *autonomy, stability,* and *functional range* (1978: 98). Clearly, Ferguson is here thinking of a special type of linguistic behavior, while at the same time he is raising a more general issue: "if variation turns out to include varieties so different that we would want to call them different languages, we might still have to put them in grammar." Taking the linguistic bull by its horns, he asserts: "I am saying multilingualism may be a legitimate object of linguistic description" (1978: 104).

Any investigation of non-native Englishes is a study in bi- or multilingualism, and it warrants a fresh theoretical and descriptive perspective. In presenting the above views of Kaplan and Ferguson, I do not claim that their positions have not been espoused by others before or since. I am merely using their claims as typical of two positions, and as a convenient point of departure.

How, then, has linguistic research proceeded toward understanding and describing the non-native Englishes? The insights gained through earlier research on such varieties parallel those which linguists gained at various stages in the development of linguistic theory. There is a parallel between the dominant linguistic paradigms and the attitudes, descriptive techniques, and methods used to describe these varieties.

Such research had roughly three phases. The first emphasized the acquisitional characteristics within the framework of specific language acquisitional models. Almost identical models and hypotheses were applied to language learning situations in, for example, Africa, South Asia, and Japan. These situations clearly differ in terms of motivations for learning, traditions of teaching, and the functional uses of English (see, e.g., Kachru 1980a; Smith 1981; Strevens 1980). However, since it was claimed that "integrative" motivation is better than "instrumental" motivation, that dictum was applied to all L$_2$ situations. One earlier exception to such studies, though not a peda-

gogically oriented one, is Schuchardt's (1891 [1980]) paper on
"Indo-English." Schuchardt could serve as a model for many who
followed him, but unfortunately this paper was not available in English until Gilbert translated and published it in 1980. The field essentially remained with prescriptivists, who isolated language study
from language use, whether in acquisitional or in functional terms.

The structural approach to language dominated until the early
1960s. The inadequacies of this phase for the study of non-native
Englishes were essentially four. (1) There was no recognition of the
functional displacement of language and its implications for linguistic
innovations. (2) Emphasis fell on L_2 acquisition with "native-like"
control, with no distinction between institutional and performance
varieties. (3) "Interference" came to be viewed as a "violation" of
the code of L_1. (4) Units of language were segmented for easy taxo-
nomic classification, with the sentence being the highest unit of description. As far as I know, the concept of "interference varieties"
as legitimate varieties of English did not emerge from the side of the
native speakers of English until Quirk et al. (1972) recognized such
varieties among the varieties of contemporary English in their monumental grammar.

The structuralist paradigm, as we already know (and I will not
beat the dead horse), was inadequate not only to account for language description, but also to account for the underlying differences
in the institutionalized varieties of English. This point, in another
context, has been discussed for almost two decades by, among others,
Firth, Halliday, Labov, and Pike.

In American linguistics it was not until what has been called the
"Chomskyan revolution" that new insights were gained in language
description, especially about the interrelationship of sentences. Such
analyses were a natural step toward our understanding of the cohesion and interrelation of syntactic networks. But again, the paradigm
was not related to the functional aspects of non-native Englishes.
Then came an era of acute cynicism in the 1970s, with new explorations in various branches of linguistics and essentially a rethinking of
the goals of the discipline. A vital contribution of this period is the
analysis and descriptions of units larger than the sentence, and understanding concerning the choices which users of a language make as
members of a society. As a result of such theoretical concerns, the
empirical focus has rapidly come to rest on several "socially realistic"
paradigms of linguistic research.[3] In the 1970s some paradigms were
more influential than others, but only a few affected the research on
and understanding of the complex phenomenon of second-language

study: for instance, Labov's work, and that of Halliday (especially 1973 and later), Hymes (1962 and later; see also Saville-Troike 1982), Gumperz (1964 and later), and Ervin-Tripp (for a discussion see, e.g., 1978).[4] The concept of "contrastive discourse" or "contrastive stylistics" never gained any serious adherents, though some studies have been attempted in this direction using various models (e.g., Dehghanpisheh 1972; Larsen-Freeman 1980; Maftoon-Semnani 1979; Sajavaara and Lehtoneh, in press; Trimble and Trimble 1978; see also, for references, Houghton 1980). On the whole, very little insightful research has been done on multilinguals' linguistic behavior, especially in traditionally multilingual societies. Perhaps the earlier attitude toward multilingualism in the West is partly responsible for this situation.[5]

Nativized Englishes: Directions in Research

The nativized Englishes have still not been given the attention they deserve in variational or literary studies, or in work on contrastive discourse or language acculturation. This is unfortunate, since the history of non-native Englishes is a long one, going back almost two hundred years in some parts of the world, and covering such culturally and linguistically dissimilar contexts as Africa, South Asia, the Far East, the Philippines, and the West Indies. With such a deep-rooted tradition in linguistically and culturally pluralistic societies, we have a priceless repository of material for research on the study of language acquisition, acculturation, and change.

In terms of acculturation, two processes seem to be at work. One results in the *deculturation* of English, and another in its *acculturation* in the new context. The latter gives it an appropriate identity in its newly acquired functions. The Indians have captured the two-faceted process by using the typical Sanskrit compound *dvija* ("twice-born") for Indian English. (The term was originally used for the Brahmins who, after their natural birth, are considered reborn at the time of caste initiation.) Firth (1968: 96) therefore is correct in saying that "an Englishman must de-Anglicize himself"; as must, one could add, an American "de-Americanize" himself, in their attitudes toward such varieties, and for a proper appreciation of such acculturation of Englishes (see Kachru, in press).

This initiation of English into new culturally and linguistically dependent communicative norms forces a redefinition of our linguistic and contextual parameters for understanding the new language types and discourse types. Those who are outside these cul-

tures must go through a *variety shift* in order to understand both
the written and the spoken modes of such varieties. One cannot,
realistically speaking, apply the norms of one variety to another variety. I am not using the term "norm" to refer only to formal deviations
(see Kachru 1980a); rather, I intend to refer to the underlying universe of discourse which makes linguistic interaction a pleasure and
provides it with "meaning." It is the whole process of, as Halliday
says, learning "how to *mean*" (1974). It is a very culture-bound concept. To understand a bilingual's mind and use of language, one
would have, ideally, to be ambilingual and ambicultural. One would
have to share responses to events, and cultural norms, and interpret
the use of L_2 within that context. One would have to see how the
context of culture is manifest in linguistic form, in the new style
range, and in the assumptions one makes about the speech acts in
which L_2 is used. A tall order, indeed!

This redefined cultural identity of the non-native varieties has
not usually been taken into consideration.[6] There have been primarily three types of studies in this area. The first type forms the main
body — understandably so, since these are devoted to pedagogical
concerns. In such studies, any deviation has been interpreted as vio-
lating a prescriptive norm, and thus resulting in a "mistake." The
urge for prescriptivism has been so strong that any innovation which
is not according to the native speaker's linguistic code is considered
a linguistic aberration. If one makes too many such "mistakes," it is
treated as an indication of a language user's linguistic deprivation or
deficiency. Second, some linguistic studies focus on formal characteristics without attempting to relate them to function, or to delve into
the contextual needs for such innovations. This separation between
use and *usage* has masked several sociolinguistically important factors about these varieties. The third group of studies deals with the
"contact literature" in English, perhaps used on the analogy of "contact languages." Such literature is a product of multicultural and
multilingual speech communities, and it extends the scope of English
literature to "literatures in English." Most such studies are concerned
with the themes, rather than with style. (For further discussion, see,
e.g., Sridhar 1982 and Weir 1982).

Strategies, Styles, and Domains

In relating the strategies, styles, and domains of language use, a
configuration of factors must be considered, the most important being the underlying cultural assumptions. The verbal strategies and cul-

turally determined innovations are, therefore, not necessarily "linguistic flights" (Whitworth 1907: 5) to be avoided, since these are not part of *native* speakers' linguistic repertoires. These strategies and devices are meaningful to the "insider" who actually uses the variety of English, though in an "outsider's" judgment such innovations might "jar upon the ear of the native Englishman" (Whitworth: 1907: 5).[7] The question then is: Who is to judge? This point has been demonstrated with reference to black English by Labov (1969), and with reference to the non-native Englishes by, among others, Bokamba (1982), Chishimba (1980a and 1980b), Kachru (1965 and later), Kandiah (1981), Llamzon (1969), Platt (1980), Richards (1982), and Stanlaw (1982).[8]

The concept of *cohesion* has both formal and functional prerequisites which ideally must be seen from an "insider's" point of view. In culturally and linguistically pluralistic contexts, language *shift* and *mix* may be part of the repertoire. (For a detailed discussion and bibliography, see Kachru, in press.) In many situations where the *domain* seems to be identical between varieties, we might find that the language type which is considered *appropriate* is not necessarily identical. Even in the varieties of English, there is a mutual expectancy between the culturally determined domain and the appropriate language for it. It is not merely a question of finding a one-to-one relationship between the domains and language types in different varieties. In addition to style range, one must consider the more complex, and to some extent more elusive, proficiency range within each variety.

Cohesion and Coherence in Text

Considerable confusion is involved in the use of terms such as *text, discourse,* and *narrative* (see Rauch and Carr 1980). Following Halliday (1978: 108-9), I will use *text* to refer to "the instances of linguistic interaction in which people actually engage: whatever is said, or written, in an operational context, as distinct from a citational context like that of words listed in a dictionary. . . . In other words, a text is a semantic unit; it is the basic unit of the semantic process." Functionally, "text can be defined as actualized meaning potential." (See also Halliday and Hasan 1976.)

There is no paucity of anthropological, sociological, and linguistic frameworks available for such analysis.[9] My concern is neither to evaluate such studies nor to select any particular one for its methodology. I will simply mention two concepts used by Widdowson which have methodological bearings on "the area of enquiry that goes under the general name of discourse analysis" (1979: 61). Widdowson is particularly appropriate here because he has had an impact on general studies and pedagogical materials related to "communicative competence," especially in English as L_2. In his 1979 study, he proposes the concepts of *rules of usage* and *rules of use*. Rules of usage "represent the language user's knowledge of the formal system of his language" (64). This is, as he says, language competence in the Chomskyan sense. Rules of use "account for the language user's knowledge of speech acts . . . and constitute the basic communicative source of reference." The first type is termed *cohesion procedure,* and the second type, *coherence procedure.* If put in an alternate framework, the first refers to the *formal* appropriateness, and the second to *functional* appropriateness. (See also Kachru, in press, and earlier.) Widdowson agrees that both are "subject to variation." He is also aware that problems arise when we attempt to transfer rules of use from one universe of discourse to another. The question for us then is, What *norms* apply to the institutional varieties with reference to *cohesion* and *coherence* procedures? The appropriateness of these procedures is with reference to what may be termed the communicative unit (Sinclair and Coulthard 1975), the contextual unit (Kachru 1965 and later, esp. 1980c), or the context of situation (Firth 1957). These units essentially constitute participants in "interactive acts" (Widdowson 1979: 68), and are determined by the "context of culture" and "context of situation." What is "contextual deviation" from the native speaker's point of view is appropriate in terms of "procedures," outlined by Widdowson, for the non-native contexts.[10]

A *variety shift* may, then, entail knowledge about the "procedures" specific to a *localized* variety of English. It seems, furthermore, to be very significant for understanding the "contact literatures" in English.

Contextualizing Text Types

I shall consider a number of text types, ranging from newspaper headlines to a number of sentences, in order to bring out the variety-specific "meaning" in deviation. First, let me illustrate my point by using selected examples from English-language newspapers in Asia, essentially from South Asia. These newspapers have the largest reading public and are the primary link across the region. English is the only language in which practically every political division in (for example) India has a newspaper. The long journalistic tradition and continuing intranational needs for communication have gradually fostered the development of specific South Asian newspaper language types in headlines, announcements, advertising, etc. Below I shall consider, among others, some headlines, reviews, and announcements of events such as marriages and deaths.

A native speaker of English, not familiar with the cultural and linguistic pluralism in South Asia, considers these language types lexically, collocationally, and semantically deviant. Such a reaction is understandable. Nevertheless, in South Asian or African English, it is through such formal deviation — including that of mixing — that language acquires contextual appropriateness. True, native speakers' cohesive and coherence procedures have been "violated." But how else can a "transplanted" language acquire functional appropriateness? A language pays a linguistic price for acculturation — for not remaining just a "guest or friend," but, to use Raja Rao's words (1978: 421), for becoming "one of our own, of our own caste, our creed, our sect and of our tradition." This family identity cannot be given to a guest without initiating him into the tradition. The price for acquiring such membership is nativization. It is with reference to such nativization that the following examples should be understood.

Panchayat system upholds ideals of human rights[11]
(*The Rising Nepal*, Kathmandu, December 17, 1978; one
   column)

More subsidy for gobar gas plants
(*The Hindustan Times*, New Delhi, May 7, 1977; one column)

Krishibank branch needed
(*The Bangladesh Observer*, Dacca, June 21, 1979; one column)

Shariat courts for attack
(*Dawn*, Lahore, December 3, 1979; one column)

Indian Muslims are bumiputras
(*The Sunday Times*, Singapore, April 26, 1981; one column)

JNU karamcharis begin dharna
(*The Statesman*, New Delhi; May 12, 1981; one column)

Marathwada band over pandal fire
(*The Indian Express*, New Delhi; May 9, 1981; one column)

DESU workers gherao staff
(*The Indian Express*, New Delhi, May 9, 1981; one column)

Paan masala "causes rare disease"
(*The Hindustan Times,* New Delhi, May 5, 1981; one column)

"Lakhpati" swindler held
(*The Hindustan Times,* New Delhi, May 9, 1981; three columns)

55 Jhuggis gutted
(*The Hindustan Times,* New Delhi, May 3, 1981; one column)

"Shaleenta" drive ends
(*The Statesman,* May 3, 1981; one column)

This type of mixing is not restricted to headlines. Consider the following randomly selected reports:

Urad and moong fell sharply in the grain market here today on stockists offerings. Rice, jowar and arhar also followed suit, but barely forged ahead. [*The Times of India,*
New Delhi, July 23, 1977]

Fish stalls in many small markets have nothing for sale.
Rohu costs Rs 16 a Kg. while bekti, parshe and tangra
are priced between. . . . Hilsa, which is the most popular
among the Bengalis in the rainy season. . . . [*The Statesman,* Calcutta, May 12, 1979]

This type of nativized lexicalization raises several points. For instance, when an appropriate English lexical item is available, why do
papers like *The Times of India* or *The Statesman* prefer a native
item, for example, *jowar* (sorghum), *arhar* (pigeon peas), or the various types of fish?

Reviews

It is difficult to say whether the following review of a performance by the well-known classical musician M. S. Subbulakshmi
could have been presented without profuse lexicalization from register-specific items from Sanskrit:

"Chandrasekhara" (Dr. V. Raghavan's composition) was
rendered with a clear intonation as to set off the structural
beauty. Together with the alapana it was a grand essay of
Kirvani. . . . Dharmavati was chosen for Ragam, Tanam and
Pallavi. Singing with an abandon, M. S. set off the distinct
character of the mode and followed with a methodically
improvised Pallavi. The swaraprastara was full of tightly
knit figures. [*Deccan Herald,* Hyderabad, July 26, 1977]

The same is true of the following illustration:

> The note dhaivat, komal and suddha seemed to be eluding
> the singer at times. The other thing which Gaekwad would
> have done well was to avoid billing ragas in succession with
> most notes in common. (The first three ragas had gandhar,
> madhyam, dhaivat, and nishadh, all suddha.) [*The States-
> man,* New Delhi, May 8, 1981]

There is no attempt in such writing to explain the terms or concepts. Bilingual and bicultural competence is taken for granted. The
native speaker of English, if unfamiliar with such contextually appropriate mixing, is naturally marked an "outsider."

In a sense, such illustrations represent development of a typical
register of music, for example, in Indian English which may be unintelligible even to an uninitiated Indian English speaker.

Matrimonial Advertisements

The matrimonial advertisements listed below are from prestigious
national English newspapers. All involve mixing, mainly with borrowed
Sanskrit lexical items. Mixing of the type illustrated here is restricted
to the Hindu community, and to what are called the "caste Hindus."
The advertisements (from *The Hindu,* Madras, July 1, 1979) are obviously from educated families who have traditional views on social
stratification and color consciousness, and who place complete re-
liance on the horoscope for finalizing the alliance.

> Wanted well-settled bridegroom for a Kerala fair graduate
> Baradwaja gotram, Astasastram girl . . . subset no bar. Send
> horoscope and details.

> Correspondence invited, preferably for mutual alliance, by
> Smartha family of Karnataka. Write with full family details.

> Non-Koundanya well qualified prospective bridegroom below
> 30 for graduate Iyangar girl, daughter of engineer. Miruga-
> servsham. No dosham. Average complexion. Reply with
> horoscope.

The term *mutual alliance* in the second example is a culturally
significant collocation; it refers to an arrangement by which X's daughter marries Y's son and Y's daughter marries X's son. Whatever the
other advantages of such an alliance, one obvious advantage is that it
restricts the giving or receiving of the dowry.

In Asian varieties of English we notice mixing or lexical innovations of other types, too. Consider the following:

> Tanku Abdul Rahman blessed newly-weds . . . with "tepung
> tawar". . . . The "akad nikah" took place last Thursday.
> [*New Straits Times,* Kuala Lumpur, April 27, 1981]

> Matrimonial correspondence invited from respected Punjabi
> families for my son . . . clean shaven. [*Times of India,* New
> Delhi, May 10, 1981]

In the above Malaysian example, the mixing is determined by
the religion. In the second case, *clean shaven* has a serious religious
connotation: it is indicative of non-conformism with traditional
Sikhism in India.

In the matrimonial context another collocation, *minor wife,*
common in Thai English, is worth mentioning here. It refers to a
"mistress"[12] who is socially accepted as next to (major) wife, e.g.,

> Police said yesterday they could find no motive for the
> killing but said that Mr. Prapruet had a minor wife who
> lived in the same soi as his family. [*Bangkok Post,* April
> 29, 1981]

Obituaries

The non-native users of English have their own way of dealing
with death, just as with getting married. The announcement about
death, the metaphor of death, and the outward manifestations at
funerals are very culture and religion specific. If the medium in which
one is to talk of death or to write about it is a non-native language,
it certainly must first be acculturated. In South Asia, for example, a
person leaves "for heavenly abode" (*The Hindustan Times,* New Delhi,
May 8, 1981) due to "the sad demise." In North India, among Hindus
and Sikhs, there will be "kirtan and ardasa for the peace of the de-
parted soul" (*The Hindustan Times,* June 30, 1979). An alternate
form of announcement is that "the untimely tragic death . . . of . . .
happened . . . on . . . uthaoni ceremony will take place on . . ." or
the "chautha-uthala" will be performed. In Pakistan, an announcement may state that a person's "soyam Fateha will be solemnized
on" and "all the friends and relatives are requested to attend the
Fateha ceremony" (*Dawn,* March 14, 1979). The ethnic plurality of,

for example, Singapore reflects in the mixing such as "karumakiriye puniathanam pooja will be held on . . ." (*New Straits Times,* Singapore, April 29, 1981).

In many of these announcements the underlying metaphor is of the native language. Once it is re-created into English (even if it is "deviant" from a native speaker's point of view), it immediately establishes a cultural and emotional bond with the local reader. For such a reader it is neither sentimental nor over-ornamented; it is contextually proper, and any other way of expressing it would be culturally inappropriate.

Invitations

Wedding invitations, for example, reveal another cultural aspect. The unit of interaction is the family, not the individual. The invitation is written in such a way that a native speaker of English finds it impersonal and vague. A typical printed invitation in North India might read:

> You will be glad to know that the marriage ceremony of dear ——— will be celebrated at ———. Mehndirat and devgoan will be performed on ———. You are requested to make it convenient to reach here with family well in time to participate in all the connected ceremonies. In case you would like me to invite anyone else from your side, kindly intimate the name and address.

Why is English chosen for such personal, culture-specific contexts? That brings in the question of language attitudes, which I will not address here.

Letters

Letters, either personal, or not so personal, are an excellent medium through which to study the transferred cultural norms in personal interactions. Such correspondence is essentially treated as a mere change of the mode of communication, from spoken to written. What one would say normally in L_1 in face-to-face interaction is expressed in written English. In English the written mode, even in personal interaction, has several rhetorical prerequisites; these include directness in presenting the point, very little stylistic ornamentation, and emphasis on the information content. On the other hand, a typical letter from South Asia, the Far East, or Africa will have the following characteristics: an extremely deferential lexical spread based on the politeness hierarchy of the L_1, and abundant use of blessings in the opening and concluding paragraphs. If the writer is senior in age, the use of blessings seems excessive to a person who is not part of the culture. One might find mentioned names of gods who will bless the receiver of the letter. Perhaps this characteristic of Indian letters made Goffin (1934) remark that Indian English has a moralistic tone, and the Indians cannot keep God out of their English. Consider, for example, the following:

> I always send my love and prayers to you all everyday: unseen unheard. May Lord Shiva always protect you all and look after you.

> I am quite well here hoping the same for you by the virtue of mighty god. I always pray to god for your good health, wealth and prosperity. [*The Tribune,* Chandigarh, November 22, 1978]

Consider also the following from Africa (quoted in Chishimba 1980b):

> I have exhorted you then to exorcise the spectre which has been hovering over us like the sword of Damocles.

> Your deportment of late has been so unruly that you are now deemed a misfit in this academic institution. With effect from the issue of this letter of admonishment, I expect you to shrink your tentacles within the boundaries of learning.

The two pieces are written by a headmaster, the first in the school magazine, and the second as a letter of warning to a student.

Excessive ornamentation in construction of sentences may result from more than one underlying cause: for instance, deferential style used for one's teacher, register-mixing, culturally different notions of what is "grand" style, or a different concept of what it means to sound learned. Consider the excerpts from a letter received by my colleague Charles Osgood:

> I beg to invite your kind attention to the insatiable thirst for knowledge of an obscure bibliophil [*sic*] that compels him to be a suppliant for your munificence. To get down to brass tacks, I have a good mind to be enlightened by your [all the volumes], but my chronic financial stringency obfuscates the lofty idea. I am on my uppers. In my frowzy den I can only sigh and weep for your latest work (book or research paper).

Would you mind enlightening the thirsty palmer languishing in the icy quagmire of despondency on the names and addresses of the professors adorning the Department of Linguistic Science, University of Illinois?

Acknowledgments

The ornateness and transfer of the deferential style from L_1 to L_2 can be illustrated from another source of educated non-native English, namely, acknowledgments in published books. What might appear unnecessarily docile or servile to a Western reader is again dependent on how an Asian or an African views a teacher or a superior in his culture, and on how the L_1 provides formal choices to structure such a cultural attitude. In English, these factors must be presented in a complex way, and native speakers are left to draw their own conclusions.

> For me, this work has been a labour of love, without any financial and secretarial assistance whatsoever. My great Guru passed away before the work could be completed. I can now only console myself by dedicating it to his revered memory. [J. Singh, *Siva Sūtras;* Delhi, 1979]

> The author takes this opportunity to express his indebtedness to . . . for his stately kindness, expansive sympathy and charitable guidance without which the work would not have taken the shape. [S. P. Singh, *English in India;* Patna, 1978]

> I owe a deep debt of gratitude to our beloved . . . who corrected me when I was wrong, encouraged me when I was right; supported me when I was in need and shared my responsibilities in the fulfilment of the tasks before me. I must thank, further though in an un-Indian manner, my own younger brother. [K. P. S. Choudhary, *Modern Indian Mysticism;* Delhi, 1981]

That such a style is important for cultural identity can be shown from an interesting example. When an acculturated (nativized) native speaker of English wants to acquire an Indian identity, and claims the prerogative of being a *śiṣya* ("disciple"), he or she will use the same Indianized English style. In his introduction to the *Vaiṣṇava Āchāryas,* Chuck,[13] who became Acyutānanda Svāmī and "is preaching in India" (ix), adopted the same style for expressing gratitude to his guru.[14]

I offer my prostrate obeisances first unto all the devotees
that have surrendered unto his divine lotus feet and next
unto the devotees who will in the future take shelter of
his lotus feet, and I then offer my humble obeisances unto
his lotus feet again and again. May he bless this first translation attempt so that it may be accepted by the Lord Sri
Kṛṣṇa, and may he engage me in the service of the six Go-
svāmīs of Vṛndāvana, Lord Caitanya, and Rādhārāṇī.
[*Songs of the Vaiṣṇava Ācāryas;* Los Angeles, 1974: xviii]

Let me now provide an example of a different text type from
West Asia (Israel and Iraq). Israeli and Iraqi statements on a raid on
a nuclear plant appeared in "unofficial translations" issued by the
two governments, as given in *The New York Times* (June 9, 1981).
The first paragraphs of the Israeli text read:

The Israeli Air Force yesterday attacked and destroyed
completely the Osirak nuclear reactor, which is near Baghdad. All our planes returned home safely.
    The Government finds itself obligated to explain to en-
lighten public opinion why it decided on this special oper-
ation.

The last sentence says, "We shall defend the citizens of Israel in good
time and with all the means at our disposal." Let us contrast this with
the Iraqi statement:

In the name of God, the merciful, the compassionate.
    Great Iraqi people, sons of the glorious Arab nation,
it has been known to us from the beginning that many
parties local and international, were and still are behind
the eagerness of the backward and suspect Iranian regime
to stir up the dispute with, conduct aggression against and
begin the war against Iraq.

After almost five short paragraphs, the statement then adds, "Compatriots, today we declare that the Zionist enemy planes yesterday
carried out an air raid on Baghdad." The concluding paragraphs say,

The road Iraq has taken in its victorious revolution —
the road of freedom, independence and progress, the
road of cohesion between the leadership and the masses —
will not be abandoned. This road will remain wide open.
    God willing, victory to our heroic people and glory to
our Arab nation.

It is evident that the rhetorical devices used in these two statements are distinctly different. One might ask: Does this variation provide clues for "cultural variation" which manifests itself in certain type of discourse, and which reveals a "preferred order in discourse blocs" (Kaplan: 1966 [1980] : 416)?

What do the other examples from various text-types given above show? Several theoretically and pedagogically important points may be made here. We see at work a number of formal devices used to create the "deference hierarchy" or the "politeness phenomenon" which is an essential part of being a member of these speech communities. This politeness hierarchy is thus formally created in the communicative repertoire of L_2. By this device a text that is, for example, deviant at the collocational level acquires appropriateness at the "communicative level." It is therefore not mere lexical (or collocational) interference, but transfer (or re-creation) of a "communicative act" or "interactive act."[15] In order to capture the "meaning" of such texts, the *native* speaker has to see the other (non-native) varieties of English as an integral part of the other culture, and he must view such texts as a crucial part of culturally determined interaction.

"Contact Literature" in English: Another Look

Let me now return to a substantial body of non-native writing in English, termed "contact literature." The critic Narasimhaiah (1978)has made a plea for broadening the appeal of English studies from that of "English literature" to "literature in English." The concept of "contact literature," as stated earlier, is an extension of "contact language." A language in contact is two-faced; it has its own face, and the face it acquires from the language with which it has contact. The degree of contact varies from lexical borrowing to intensive mixing of units. Contact literatures (for example, non-native English literatures of India, Nigeria, or Ghana, or the francophone literatures, or the Indian Persian) have certain formal and thematic characteristics which make this use of the term "contact" appropriate.

Using a *non-native* language in native contexts to portray new themes, characters, and situations is like redefining the semantic and semiotic potential of a language, making language mean something which is not part of its traditional "meaning." It is an attempt to give a new African or Asian identity, and thus an extra dimension of meaning. A part of that dimension perhaps remains obscure or mysterious to the Western reader. In purely linguistic terms, it entails developing a meaning system appropriate to the new situations and

contexts. One has to make various choices to make the linguistic resources of L_2 function in situations where formal equivalence is not
always possible.

   In understanding the texts, one therefore must remember several
points. First, in such literature all the characters use English; the same
is not true in real life, since English is only one code in a multi-coded
society. Second, English is used in all the situations for all interactions —
which, again, is not how English actually functions. Third, each character is assigned a style or a style range appropriate to his or her function. The writer Mulk Raj Anand, for example, is forced to make difficult choices in *Coolie* and *Untouchable:* no real-life coolie speaks English, and no untouchable uses English for interaction within the family. If we use Bernstein's terms, in real life, most of these characters
will be using a "restricted code" of their regional language. In a number of areas such codes may even be stigmatized, since they will have
speech markers to identify each subgroup on the caste hierarchy. How
does one re-create all this relevant linguistic and cultural information
in another language? Whatever the device a writer chooses, it is a *deviation* for an outsider.

   This predicament of a non-native creative writer in English, for
example in India, began as early as 1874, when a Bengali, Lal Behari
Day,[16] "translated Indian terms instead of their pure English equivalents to maintain the Indian local colour as well as to add a distinct
Indian flavour" (Sarma 1978: 329). Day was Indianizing English for
stylistic effect, consciously attempting to re-create a style repertoire
in L_2 which would be contextually appropriate to India. The following excerpt is stylistically perhaps one of the first attempts toward
nativizing English in "contact literature" in India. (Later, in the
works of Mulk Raj Anand, Khushwant Singh, Raja Rao, and others,
such devices became a characteristic of an Indian identity of English.)

   "Come in," said Badan, and jumped out of the verandah
   towards the door. "Come in, Acharya Mahasaya; this is
   an auspicious day when the door of my house has been
   blessed with the dust of your honour's feet. Gayaram
   fetch an *asan* [a small carpet] for the Acharya Mahasaya
   to sit on." [Day 1874: 48; quoted in Sarma 1978: 330]

   Note that Day is conscious of making his Bengali peasant speak
"better English than most uneducated English peasants." He apolo-
getically explains to his "Gentle reader":

Gentle reader, allow me here to make one remark. You perceive that Badan and Alanga speak better English than most uneducated English peasants; they speak almost like educated ladies and gentlemen, without any provincialisms. But how could I have avoided this defect in my history? If I had translated their talk into the Somerset or the Yorkshire dialect, I should have turned them into English, and not Bengali peasants. You will, therefore, please overlook this grave though unavoidable fault in this authentic narrative. [Day 1874: 61]

The technique and motivation for such stylistic effect have not changed since Day wrote these words. And the need for innovating such stylistic devices has not changed since Day articulated non-native creative writers' concerns (in 1874), and Schuchardt (1891 [1980]) analyzed such innovations from a linguistic point of view.

In contact literature, then, we see that deviation acquires a meaning at each level and reveals itself like a spectrum. The lexical deviation acquires meaning at the sentential level, and a deviant sentence is meaningful in relation to other sentences. But the appropriate functional meaning is part of the text type, within the context of situation. I have provided a number of such illustrations at various levels in other studies. (For further references, see, e.g., Aggarwal 1981, Kachru 1965 and later, and Chishimba 1980a, b.)

Implications

The perspective presented here may confuse a prescriptive, norm-oriented English specialist. I am not making particular pedagogical claims. My concern is to point out that, as an object of serious linguistic and literary research, the non-native Englishes have many facets. A number of these are still untouched, and several others have been under-researched. I shall enumerate some of them here.

First, the bilingual's discourse — both "mixed" and "unmixed" — is itself an object of study for what Ferguson terms "bilingual's grammar" (1978). Through such studies we might gain deeper understanding about the communicative strategies of multilingual societies.

Second, our understanding of variational study is still restricted to bidialectalism and some code-mixing. We have only begun research in stable multilingual societies in terms of areal features (e.g., Emeneau 1956; Masica 1976).

Third, English is unique in its distribution over culturally and linguistically distinct situations. On the basis of the types of nativi-

zation, it might be possible to develop universals of bilinguals' behavior. English provides one constant linguistic variable which can
be used for such generalizations.

Fourth, contrastive studies seem to have stopped where they
should actually have begun. In the long tradition of such studies, no
attempt has been made to arrive at a serious understanding of contrastive discourse, and to analyze the cultural and linguistic transfers
which change cohesive and other characteristics of texts. The "interference" phenomenon which received so much attention at the phonological and lexical levels, and some attention at the grammatical level,
has yet to be fully explored in its all manifestations, especially in
discourse.

Fifth — and here I return to contact literatures in English — the
thematic studies of non-native English literatures have yet to study
how culture-bound styles are "transcreated" in L_2 with close approximation to the style range available to a writer in his L_1. The "transcreated" style undoubtedly has an underlying model, be it from the
native oral tradition, the L_1 style range, or the concept of style based
on Sanskritic or Perso-Arabic traditions (in South Asia). *Kanthapura*
of Raja Rao is a case in point.

Sixth, research during the last decade has provided many insights
into the structure and function of code-switching and code-mixing.
The implications of these phenomena on language change are significant. At first the change may be gradual or register-specific, but slowly it spreads — as happened, for example, in several Indian and African
languages. (For a detailed discussion and references, see Kachru 1978,
1980c, 1981, and Paradis 1978.)

All these aspects are interrelated. If we are to understand the
workings of the bilingual's code repertoire and the use of such repertoires, it is essential that we understand all of them, in order to understand the ecology of language function.

Conclusion

There is now clearly a need for an attitudinal change toward the
institutionalized non-native Englishes. Equally important, there is a
need to redefine research areas and priorities, both in theoretical
terms and for applied research. It may also be useful to consider
whether the generalizations made for the formal and functional characteristics of non-native Englishes apply to other institutionalized
non-native languages across cultures and language areas; for example,
French, Arabic, Persian, or Sanskrit.

Are there any universals of nativization or linguistic acculturation? If so, what implication do they have for language acquisition, for language use, and for our understanding of the mystique of bilingualism or multilingualism?

In applied linguistics, too, we need new perspectives for research on communicative competence, and specifically on English for cross-cultural communication. It is through such research that we can gain insight about the pragmatics of English in non-native contexts. And, finally, given the status and spread of English around the world and its variation, we might agree with Ferguson (1982: vii) that "the whole mystique of native speaker and mother tongue should probably be quietly dropped from the linguists' set of professional myths about language."

NOTES

1. An earlier version of this chapter was presented as an invited paper at the Seminar on Varieties of English, SEAMEO Regional Language Center, Singapore, April 20-24, 1981.

2. For a discussion and references to later publications of Kaplan and others on this topic, see Clyne 1981, and particularly Houghton 1980.

3. See, e.g., Labov 1970, 1972a, b; for the Firthian contribution and other relevant references, see Kachru 1980b; for a historical perspective, see, e.g., Newmeyer 1980.

4. Other theoretical and applied studies are: Alston 1980, Christensen 1965; Cicourel 1969; Cole 1978; Dressler 1977; Gray 1977; Grimes 1975; Lakoff 1972; Monaghan 1979; Morgan 1977; Myers 1979; Posner 1980; Rauch and Carr 1980; Sankoff 1980; and Van Dijk 1977.

5. For relevant references see, e.g., Kachru 1981 and Paradis 1978.

6. By and large, the insights of such models and research have not been applied to non-native Englishes. An exception is the application of the Firthian framework of contextualization to some South Asian English texts. (See Kachru 1965 and later; see also Kandiah 1981, which raises several interesting questions.)

7. I cannot resist the temptation of quoting below the complete paragraph of Whitworth so that these words are not interpreted out of context: "I hope no one will take up this little book expecting to find an amusing collection of those linguistic flights to which imaginative Indians occasionally commit themselves. I am myself too painfully conscious of the immense superiority of Indians to Englishmen in the way of acquiring foreign languages, for the preparation of any such work to be a congenial task to me. No; my purpose is entirely different, and is perfectly serious. For many years past, both in hearing arguments from the Bar and in reading Indian books and newspapers, I have been struck with the wonderful command which Indians — and not only those who have been to England — have obtained over the English language for all practical purposes. At the same time, I have often felt what a pity it is that men exhibiting this splendid facility should now and then mar their compositions by little errors of idiom

which jar upon the ear of the native Englishman. Considering, in conjunction with this great natural ability, that the Indians are the inheritors of the most elaborate language that the world has known, and that their forefathers regarded grammar (vyákaran) as a vedánga or limb of their sacred veda, it seems well worth while to try and render them a small service by showing them how their admirable knowledge of our language may be made still more complete" (Whitworth 1907: 5-6).

8. See also, e.g., studies in Bailey and Görlach, in press; Kachru 1981; Smith 1981.

9. For references to some such selected works see note 4, above.

10. For discussion on the need for *local* (non-native) contextual parameters for description of non-native Englishes, among others, see Bokamba 1982; Chishimba 1980a, b; Kachru 1965 and later, particularly in press.

11. The glosses of native words used in these examples are as follows: *panchayat,* council of five, village council; *gobar,* cow dung; *krishi,* agriculture; *shariat,* canon law of Islam; *bumiputra,* native son — in India the expression *son of the soil* is used in this context; *karamchari,* employee; *dharna,* sit in; *band,* stoppage of work, strike; *pandal,* podium, marquee; *gherao,* surrounding and detaining a person to extract a concession; *paan masala,* a mixture of areca nut, lime, tobacco, etc., used for chewing with a betel leaf; *lakhpati,* a millionnaire — *lakh* is one hundred thousand (usually of rupees); *jhuggi,* an improvised hovel in a slum colony; *shaleenta,* courtesy. Note that all the native lexical items have more or less appropriate equivalents in English, but the native words are preferred for their contextual appropriateness.

12. "Minor wife" seems to be the translation of Thai *miā noí* "little wife"; *soi* refers to "a lane." I am grateful to Lyle F. Bachman for providing these equivalents.

13. Only the first name is given in the text.

14. The style used here is typical of acknowledgments in South Asian languages and is clearly indicative of a culturally determined hierarchy of politeness which is transferred to English. Consider, for example, the following English "rendering" of a passage from a book in Hindi (Krishna Kumar Goswami: *Shaikshik vyākaraṇ aur vyāvhārik hindī;* Delhi: Alekh Prakāshan, 1981): "The main inspiration for writing this book came from respected teacher Professor Ravindranath Srivastava. He not only inspired me but also read the manuscript carefully and suggested many corrections which enabled the book to come in its present form. I can never repay him for his guidance [teacher's debt], therefore without any formality, I bow my head to him with respect and dedicate this book to his lotus feet." [pp. viv-vv].

15. For an excellent cross-cultural and cross-linguistic study, see "Universals in Language Usage: Politeness Phenomena," by P. Brown and S. Levinson (in Goody 1978).

16. Perhaps before Day there were other Indian creative writers. For example, as Sarma (1978: 329-30) says, Sochee Chunder Dutt had also "used Indian words liberally," but "the credit for practising Indian English as a distinct form goes to Lal Behari Day. He made use of the devices of Sochee Chunder Dutt with better discrimination and a more serious purpose."

REFERENCES

Aggarwal, Narindar K. 1981. *English in South Asia: a bibliographical survey of resources.* Gurgaon and New Delhi: Indian Documentation Service.

Alston, William P. 1980. The bridge between semantics and pragmatics. Pp. 123-34 in Rauch and Carr (1980).

Bailey, Richard W., and Görlach, Manfred, eds. In press. *English as a world language.* Ann Arbor: University of Michigan Press.

Bokamba, Eyamba G. 1982. The Africanization of English. In this volume.

Brown, P. and Lavinston, S. 1978. Universals in language usage: politeness phenomena. In Goody, ed., 1978.

Chishimba, Maurice M. 1980a. The English language in the sociolinguistic profile of Zambia: the educational aspects. Manuscript.

———. 1980b. Some bilingual and bicultural aspects of African creative writing. Manuscript.

Christensen, F. 1965. A generative rhetoric of the paragraph. *College Composition and Communication* 16: 144-56.

Cicourel, A. V. 1969. Generative semantics and the structure of social interaction. *International Days of Sociolinguistics.* Rome.

Clyne, Michael. 1979. Communicative competences in contact. *ITL* 43: 17-37.

———. 1981. Culture and discourse structure. *Journal of Pragmatics* 5(1): 61-66.

Cole, Peter. 1978. *Syntax and semantics: pragmatics.* Vol. 9. New York: Academic Press.

Day, Lal Behari. 1874. *Govinda Samanta or History of a Bengal raiyat.* London: Macmillan. 2 vols. [Reprinted 1878 under the title *Bengal peasant life.*]

Dehghanpisheh, E. 1972. Contrastive analysis of the rhetoric of Persian and English paragraphs. In *Proceedings of the second annual seminar of the Association of Professors of English in Iran.* Tehran. Department of University Relations and Cooperation/Association of University Professors of Iran.

Dressler, Wolfgang U. 1977. *Current trends in text linguistics.* New York: Walter de Gruyter.

Emeneau, Murray B. 1956. India as a linguistic area. *Language* 32: 3-16.

Ervin-Tripp, Susan. 1978. Whatever happened to communicative competence? Pp. 237-58 in Kachru, ed. (1978).

Ferguson, Charles A. 1978. Multilingualism as object of linguistic description. Pp. 97-105 in Kachru, ed. (1978).

———. 1982. Foreword. In this volume.

Firth, J. R. 1957. *Papers in linguistics: 1934-1951.* London: Oxford University Press.

———. 1968. Descriptive linguistics and the study of English. In F. R. Palmer ed., *Selected papers of J. R. Firth 1952-59.* Bloomington: Indiana University Press.

Goffin, R. C. 1934. *Some notes on Indian English.* S.P.E. Tract no. 41. Oxford: Clarendon Press.

Goody, E. N., ed. 1978. *Questions and politeness: strategies in social interaction.* Cambridge: Cambridge University Press.

Gray, B. 1977. *The grammatical foundations of rhetoric: discourse analysis.* The Hague: Mouton.

Grimes, J. E. 1975. *The thread of discourse.* The Hague: Mouton.

Gumperz, John J. 1964. Linguistic and social interaction in two communities. In Gumperz and Hymes, eds., *The ethnography of communication*, special issue of *American Anthropologist* 66(6), part 2.

Halliday, M. A. K. 1973. *Explorations in the functions of language*. London: Edward Arnold.

———. 1974. *Learning how to mean: explorations in the development of language*. London: Edward Arnold.

———. 1978. *Language as social semiotic: the social interpretation of language and meaning*. Baltimore: University Park Press.

———, and Hasan, R. 1976. *Cohesion in English*. London: Longman.

Hartmann, R. In press. *Contrastive textology*. Heidelberg: Gross.

Houghton, Diane. 1980. Contrastive rhetoric. *English Language Research Journal* 1: 79-91. Birmingham, England: Department of English, University of Birmingham.

Hymes, Dell. 1962. The ethnography of speaking. Pp. 13-53 in T. Gladwin and W. Sturtevant, eds., *Anthropology and human behavior*. Washington, D.C.: Anthropological Society of Washington.

Kachru, Braj B. 1965. The *Indianness* in Indian English. *Word* 21: 291-410.

———, ed. 1978. *Linguistics in the Seventies: directions and prospects*. Forum Lectures presented at the 1978 Linguistic Institute of the Linguistic Society of America. Special issue of *Studies in the Linguistic Sciences* 8, 2 (Fall).

———. 1978. *Code-mixing as a verbal strategy in India*. In James Alatis, ed., *International dimensions of bilingual education*. GURT. Washington, D.C.: Georgetown University Press.

———. 1980a. Models for new Englishes. *TESL Studies* 3: 117-50. Division of English as a Second Language, University of Illinois. (Also in this volume.)

———. 1980b. "Socially realistic linguistics": the Firthian tradition. *Studies in the Linguistic Sciences* 10,1 (Spring): 85-111. Also in *International Journal of the Sociology of Language* 31: 65-89.

———. 1980c. The bilingual's linguistic repertoire. To appear in B. Hartford and A.Valdman, eds., *Issues in international bilingual education: the role of the vernacular*. New York: Plenum.

———. 1981. Bilingualism. Pp. 2-18 in *Annual Review of Applied Linguistics: 1980*. Rowley, Mass.: Newbury House.

———. In press. *The Indianization of English: the English language in India*. New Delhi: Oxford University Press.

Kandiah, Thiru. 1981. Lankan English schizoglossia. *English World-Wide: A Journal of Varieties of English* 2 (1): 63-81.

Kaplan, Robert B. 1966. Cultural thought patterns in inter-cultural education. *Language Learning* 16: 1-20. Also in K. Croft, ed., *Readings on English as a second language: for teachers and teacher trainees*. 2nd ed. Cambridge: Winthrop, 1980.

Labov, William, 1969. The logic of nonstandard English. *Georgetown Monographs in Languages and Linguistics* 22. (Also in Lavov 1972b.)

———. 1970. The study of language in its social context. *Studium Generale* 23 (1): 30-87. (Also in Labov 1972b.)

———. 1972a. *Sociolinguistic patterns*. Philadelphia: University of Pennsylvania Press.

———. 1972b. *Language in the inner city: studies in the black English vernacular*. Philadelphia: University of Pennsylvania Press.

Lakoff, R. 1972. Language in context. *Language* 48(4): 907-38.

Larsen-Freeman, Diane, ed. 1980. *Discourse analysis in second language research.* Rowley, Mass.: Newbury House.

Llamzon, Teodoro A. 1969. *Standard Filipino English.* Manila: Ateno University Press.

Maftoon-Semnani, P. 1979. A contrastive study of the rhetorical organization of American-English and Persian expository paragraphs. Ph.D. dissertation, New York University.

Masica, Colin P. 1976. *Defining a linguistic area: South Asia.* Chicago: University of Chicago Press.

Monaghan, J. 1979. *The neo-Firthian tradition and its contribution to general linguistics.* Linguistiche Arbeitern, 73. Tübingen: Niemeyer.

Morgan, J. L. 1977. Linguistics: the relation of pragmatics to semantics and syntax. Pp. 57-67 in *Annual Review of Anthropology.* Palo Alto, Calif.: Annual Reviews.

Myers, Terry, ed. 1979. *The development of conversation and discourse.* Edinburgh: Edinburgh University Press.

Narasimhaiah, C. D. 1978. *Awakened conscience: studies in commonwealth literature.* New Delhi: Sterling.

Newmeyer, Frederick J. 1980. *Linguistic theory in America: the first quarter-century of transformational generative grammar.* New York: Academic Press.

Paradis, Michel. 1978. *Aspects of bilingualism.* Columbia, N.C.: Hornbeam Press.

Platt, John, and Weber, H. 1980. *English in Singapore and Malaysia: status, features, functions.* Kuala Lumpur: Oxford University Press.

Posner, Roland. 1980. Semantics and pragmatics of sentence connectives in natural language. Pp. 87-122 in Rauch and Carr, ed. (1980).

Quirk, Randolph; Greenbaum, S.; Leech, G.; and Svartvik, J. 1972. *A grammar of contemporary English.* London: Longman.

Rao, Raja. 1978. The caste of English. Pp. 420-22 in Narasimhaiah (1978).

Rauch, Irmengard, and Carr, Gerald F. 1980. *The signifying animal: the grammar of language and experience.* Bloomington: Indiana University Press.

Richards, Jack C. 1982. Singapore English: rhetorical and communicative styles. In this volume.

Sajavaara, K., and Lehtoneh, J., eds. In press. *Jyvaskyla contrastive studies 5: papers in contrastive discourse analysis.* Jyvaskyla: University of Jyvaskyla.

Sankoff, Gillian. 1980. *The social life of language.* Philadelphia: University of Pennsylvania Press.

Sarma, Gobinda Prasad. 1978. *Nationalism in Indo-Anglian fiction.* New Delhi: Sterling.

Saville-Troike, Muriel. 1982. *The ethnography of communication: an introduction.* Oxford: Basil Blackwell.

Schuchardt, Hugo. 1891. Das Indo-Englische. *Englische Studien* 15: 286-305. [English translation in *Pidgin and creole languages: selected essays by Hugo Schuchardt,* ed. and trans. Glenn G. Gilbert. London and New York: Cambridge University Press.]

Sinclair, J. M., and Coulthard, R. M. 1975. *Towards an analysis of discourse.* London: Oxford University Press.

Smith, Larry E., ed. 1981. *English for cross-cultural communication.* London: Macmillan.

Sridhar, S. N. 1982. Non-native English literatures: context and relevance. In this volume.

Stanlaw, J. 1982. English in Japanese communicative strategies. In this volume.

Strevens, Peter. 1980. *Teaching English as an international language.* Oxford: Pergamon Press.

Sugimoto, E. 1978. Contrastive analysis of English and Japanese technical rhetoric. Pp. 177-97 in Trimble et al. (1978).

Trimble, M. T.; Trimble, L.; and Drobnic, K. 1978. *English for specific purposes: science and technology.* English Language Institute, Oregon State University.

Van Dijk, T. A. 1977. *Text and context: explorations in the semantics and pragmatics of discourse.* London: Longman.

Weir, Ann Lowry. 1982. Style range in new English literatures. In this volume.

Whitworth, George C. 1907. *Indian English: an examination of the errors of idioms made by Indians in writing English.* Letchworth, Herts: Garden City Press. (Later edition, 1932, Lahore.)

Widdowson, Henry. 1979. Rules and procedures in discourse analysis. Pp. 61-71 in Terry Myers, ed., 1979.

Contributors

AYO BAMGBOSE is Professor of Linguistics in the Department of Linguistics and Nigerian Languages, University of Ibadan.

EYAMBA G. BOKAMBA is Assistant Professor of Linguistics in the Department of Linguistics, University of Illinois, Urbana.

CHIN-CHUAN CHENG is Professor of Linguistics and of Chinese in the Department of Linguistics, University of Illinois, Urbana.

DENNIS R. CRAIG is Professor of Linguistics in the Department of Education, University of West Indies, Kingston, Jamaica.

CHARLES A. FERGUSON is Professor of Linguistics in the Department of Linguistics, Stanford University.

JOSHUA A. FISHMAN is Distinguished University Research Professor in Social Sciences in Ferkauf Graduate School, Yeshiva University, New York.

LILITH M. HAYNES is former Benedict Distinguished Visiting Professor in the Department of English, Carleton College, Northfield, Minnesota. Currently she is associated with the Department of Literature and Linguistics, Universität Essen-Gesamthochschule, West Germany.

SHIRLEY BRICE HEATH is Associate Professor of Anthropology and of Education, College of Education, Stanford University.

BRAJ B. KACHRU is Professor of Linguistics and of Education in the Department of Linguistics, University of Illinois, Urbana.

HENRY KAHANE is Emeritus Professor of Linguistics and Professor in the Center for Advanced Study, University of Illinois, Urbana.

RODNEY F. MOAG is Director of Language Communication Specialists, Ann Arbor, Michigan.

ROSE NASH is Professor of Linguistics and of English in the Department of Humanities, Inter-American University of Puerto Rico, Hato Rey.

CECIL NELSON is Assistant Professor of English in the Department of English, Indiana State University, Terre Haute.

JACK C. RICHARDS is Professor in the Department of English as a Second Language, University of Hawaii at Manoa.

KAMAL K. SRIDHAR is Assistant Professor of Linguistics in the Department of Linguistics, Queens College, Flushing, New York.

S. N. SRIDHAR is Assistant Professor of Linguistics in the Program in Linguistics, State University of New York, Stony Brook.

JAMES STANLAW is a doctoral student in anthropological linguistics in the Department of Anthropology, University of Illinois, Urbana.

PETER STREVENS is Director of the Bell Educational Trust, Cambridge, England, and Fellow of Wolfson College, Cambridge University.

ANN LOWRY WEIR is Senior Editor at the University of Illinois Press, Urbana.

JANE E. ZUENGLER is a doctoral student in applied linguistics at Teachers College, Columbia University, New York.

Index